Regional Trade Agreements in the GATT / WTO: Article XXIV and the Internal Trade Requirement

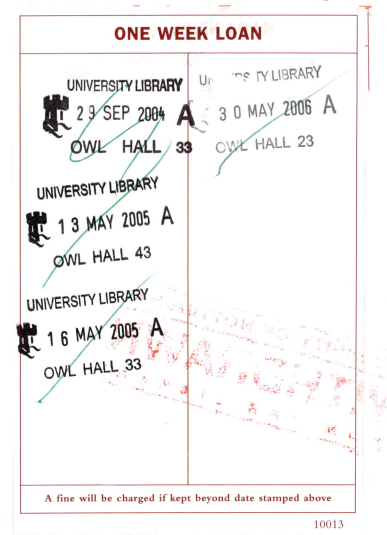

Regional Trade Agreements in the GATT / WTO

Article XXIV and the Internal Trade Requirement

James H. Mathis

With a Foreword by
Jagdish Bhagwati

T · M · C · ASSER PRESS

The Hague

Published by T·M·C·ASSER PRESS
P.O.Box 16163, 2500 BD The Hague, The Netherlands

Sold and distributed in North, Central and South America
by Kluwer Law International,
101, Philip Drive, Norwell MA 02061

In all other countries, sold and distributed
by Kluwer Law International, Distribution Centre,
P.O.Box 322, 3300 AH Dordrecht, The Netherlands

100281937⁴

ISBN 90-6704-139-4

FOREWORD.

The *economic* theory of Preferential Trade Agreements (PTAs), or discriminatory trade liberalization for and among a subset of nations, was first analyzed with fundamental and startling insight by Jacob Viner (1950). He destroyed the intuition that any move towards free trade was welfare-enhancing, for the country itself or for the world, or for both. He introduced us memorably to the notion of trade diverting –- and here, he meant not diversion in the old and approving sense of entertainment but in the modern and castigating sense of distorting – Free Trade Areas (FTAs) and Customs Unions (CUs). In other words, in the economists' jargon, discriminatory *approaches* to freeing trade were not monotonically welfare-improving.

The *legal* scholars of GATT and trade law, chiefly the giants Robert Hudec, John Jackson and Kenneth Dam in the United States, were quick to follow suit. Their classic writings on Article XXIV of the GATT, which provides an exception to the MFN obligation for contracting parties provided they go all the way and create FTAs and CUs which are supposed to reduce internal trade barriers fully rather than settle for a lesser preferential arrangement, are still a pleasure to read. They are in the best tradition of a creative interaction between the economic and the legal disciplines. Indeed, today, as my own work with Robert Hudec, resulting in a major two-volume publication by MIT Press underlines, that interaction has become yet more profound.[1]

Today, however, the Vinerian *caveat* is no longer the Prince in *Hamlet*. True, the issue of trade diversion is still important; and Professor Panagariya and I have taken strong issue with the claims made even by a greatly sophisticated economist such as Lawrence Summers that trade diversion is a concern to be dismissed summarily from a serious policy discussion.[2] In fact, the issue of trade diversion should be more of a concern than the politicians and the supportive economists recognize.

But the real concerns nonetheless are quite different today from when Viner wrote about PTAs in 1950 in his celebrated work. They arise from the fact that what I have called the Second Regionalism today – to distinguish it from the First Re-

---

[1]   Cf. Jagdish Bhagwati and Robert Hudec (eds), *Fair Trade and Harmonization: Prerequisites for Free Trade?* MIT Press: Cambridge, Mass., Volumes 1 and 2, 1996.

[2]   Cf. Jagdish Bhagwati and Arvind Panagariya, "Preferential Trading Areas and Multilateralism – Strangers, Friends or Foes?", reprinted as Chapter 2 in Bhagwati, Pravin Krishna and Panagariya (eds), *Trading Blocs: Alternative Approaches to Analyzing Preferential Trade Agreements*, MIT Press; Cambridge, Mass., 1999.

gionalism after the Treaty of Rome almost forty years ago – has succeeded wildly in taking root and proliferating than the earlier one which failed.[3]

There are in fact two overriding concerns that have attended the success as measured only by survival and spread rather than by whether it is good in a normative sense:

- The systemic but "static" issue, raised by this immense proliferation, that I have called the "spaghetti bowl" problem in identifying and christening it; and
- The "dynamic" or "time-path" issue, for those of us who want nondiscriminatory multilateral free trade, as to whether such PTAs are going to be "building blocks" towards such a goal or whether they will act as "stumbling blocks", again a problem sharply defined by me and explored in several writings, both my own and those of many others such as Professors Panagariya, T.N. Srinivasan, Andre Sapir, Christopher Bliss, Alan Winters, Pravin Krishna, Philip Levy, David Greenaway, Robert Staiger, Kyle Bagwell, Robert Lawrence and Caroline Freund since the early 1990s and now generally known as the stumbling *versus* building blocks problem.

This book by Dr. Mathis is, I believe, a first important legal contribution to the subject since the period of the Second Regionalism. Its value lies in revisiting the earlier legal scholars in light of the GATT years' experience and the new proliferation of PTAs in the WTO. It asks whether "go all the way" rules are really being respected in the current practices of the proliferating PTAs and draws attention forcefully to the need to have the PTAs conform to these important restrictions on the kinds of PTAs being formed and approved under Article XXIV. I found it particularly interesting because it provides in one single place, and with mastery of the subject matter, a historical record of the thinking and policy on PTAs (Part I), the evolution of ideas and practices on PTAs at the GATT after the Second World War (Part II), then an excellent analysis of the legal aspects of the working of Article XXIV in particular at the GATT, and then the experience with PTAs after the WTO replaced GATT (which became one leg of three in a tripod) in 1995.

The "building blocks" question is also presented in its legal dimension. If there is an emerging "multipolar" trading system, then one important issue is whether the members of PTAs tend to apply within the PTA the rules obtaining in the WTO. Mathis reads recent cases to conclude that this is so. But there is also the question: do the WTO rules themselves get adjusted to reflect what the "hegemon"-centered PTAs have enacted. The latter has been the case, in my view, with intellectual property protection; and it is being asked for when the United States, for example, ne-

---

[3]   Cf. Jagdish Bhagwati, *The World Trading System at Risk*, Princeton University Press: Princeton, 1991. Some later writers have called the Second Regionalism the "new" regionalism. The different economic and political reasons for the spread of the Second Regionalism have been the subject of several speculations.

gotiates a Free Trade Agreement with Jordan, builds linkage to labour standards into it, and then declares that this is a "template" for others to follow! The "normative" question then is: should we approve of this role of PTAs? In terms of international relations theory, this amounts to "divide and get your way": changes which are not negotiable with, say, developing countries on IPP and on labour standards in multilateral negotiations, are accepted by weak or small developing countries such as Jordan and Singapore in one-on-one bilateral PTAs by a hyperpower like the United States, and the coalition of the developing countries at Geneva in multilateral negotiations begins to break down.

No scholar, or student or policymaker who wants to be fully informed about the legal aspects of PTAs and their long evolution and current status at the WTO can afford to ignore this book. Dr. Mathis deserves our gratitude.

October 2001   JAGDISH BHAGWATI
                                      University Professor, Columbia University
                                      & External Adviser to the Director General, WTO

ACKNOWLEDGEMENTS

Associates and superiors from the Department of International Law at the University of Amsterdam and the Amsterdam Law School have all been helpful through my many inquiries regarding the research. For this, thanks to Friedl Weiss, Ed Völker, and Jan Jans. I have also benefitted from the challenging comments by the other members of the review committee, Peter Jan Kuijper, Petros Mavroidis, André Nollkaemper, and Nico Schrijver. I also thank Henk Houweling for bringing A.O. Hirschman's inter-war perspective into the picture.

A special thanks is due to Carmen Pont-Vieira at the WTO Secretariat. While respecting the de-restriction rules, she has also been able to provide some insight into the nature of the review process, and has suggested possible directions for me. From the U.S. Congress, I would also like to thank Frank Record and the other staff for allowing me to visit the House Committee on Foreign Relations and for his guidance during my times there.

A number of guest speakers in the European Union International Trade Law Programme have assisted my themes, albeit unknowingly. Although too many have passed by to list all here, I would like to thank by name Ivo van Bael, Jacques Steenbergen, Eric Stein, John Usher, and Ed Vermulst. I especially thank Brian Hindley for his critical remarks on an earlier draft of the law and economics chapter.

My other economist friends have also indulged me on various lecture tours as I have tried their patience in resolving the relationship between trade creation and GATT Article XXIV. Whether or not the results appear heretical to them, I heartily thank Aad van Mourik, Phedon Nicolaides, Hassan Qaqaya and Teun Schmidt. I also thank Ronald Wonnacott for sharing his thoughts with me on NAFTA cumulation. Although not on the lecture circuit, Louis Kuhnen has also made the extra effort to enlighten me on many technical aspects.

Many missions on behalf of the European Institute in Maastricht were made for civil servants from Central and Eastern Europe and South America. Comments from those participants broadened my perspective about regionalism. In many ways this research was motivated by some of their questions. Likewise, gratitude to the authors with whom I have not had have discussions, but who raised the issues upon which I have tried to expand, Jagdish Bhagwati, F.A. Haight, Frieder Roessler, Richard Snape. It goes without saying for all the above-mentioned, that opinions and errors found within remain solely the product of the author.

It may be a cliché to end by noting the sacrifices made by family, but in my case this is the evident reality. I only hope to make good on my promise to my beloved wife to make up for all of those lost weekends. Similarly, my brother Mike's steadfast support of my choices in the larger endeavours of life has made all of this possible.

Finally, this book is dedicated to my parents, who believed that education was the only thing that could never be taken away.

Amsterdam, December 2001   JM

SUMMARY TABLE OF CONTENTS

DETAILED TABLE OF CONTENTS

PART FOUR:
THE WTO RESPONSE   191

NOTE ON TERMINOLOGY

There are a variety of terms and acronyms being used to describe preferential trade agreements, and this text is going to attempt some consistency according to the following conventions. Use of the term *preferential trade agreement* is intended to encompass all possible types of preference exchanges, those falling both within and without the scope of GATT Article XXIV. It is hoped that the surrounding text makes clear what is being described. In addition, there is an effort made in Part One to distinguish between the various types of preferential agreements employed prior to the GATT.

The term *regional trade agreement* or *regional agreement* is used here to refer to all the possible arrangements that may fall within the power of review of the WTO Committee on Regional Trade Agreements (CRTA). This includes those agreements contemplated by GATT Article XXIV and GATS Article V as well as certain trade agreements notified according to the GATT Enabling Clause Decision.

Customs unions, free-trade areas, interim agreements leading to either, and regional integration agreements are all distinct legal entities and will be identified accordingly. The various abbreviations for regional agreements, including PTAs, RTAs, FTAs, CUs, etc., are generally avoided in the primary text, but necessarily preserved in quotations as drawn from others.

The use of the term "member" should also be clarified. A number of passages necessarily discuss members of regional agreements and Members of the WTO. To permit the distinction to remain clear, the term is capitalised when it refers to WTO Members and not capitalised when it refers to members of a regional agreement. Likewise, the term "non-members" refers to parties who are not members of a regional trade agreement even while they may be WTO Members.

As for European Community terminology, in this text the conventions applied to the EEC, EC, and EU refer to the historical period in which the reference is framed as according to the appropriate Treaty. However, contemporary legal acts dealing with the external commercial relations of the European Community are designated as acts of the EC or the European Community rather than as of the European Union.

ABBREVIATIONS

AB	Appellate Body (WTO)
ABR	Appellate Body report (WTO)
ACP	African, Caribbean and Pacific territories
AD	antidumping
ANDEAN	Andean Common Market
APEC	Asia-Pacific Economic Cooperation
ASEAN	Association of South-East Asian Nations
BOP	balance of payments
BTA	border tax adjustment
CEFTA	Central European Free Trade Agreement
CET	Common External Tariff
CIS	Commonwealth of Independent States
CP	Contracting Party (Parties)
CRTA	(WTO) Committee on Regional Trade Agreements
CU	Customs union
CUSTA	Canada-US Free Trade Agreement
CVD	countervailing duty
DC	developing country
DSB	(WTO) Dispute Settlement Body
DSU	(WTO) Dispute Settlement Understanding
EA	Europe (Association) Agreement
EC	European Community (or Communities)
EEA	European Economic Area
EEC	European Economic Community
EFTA	European Free Trade Association
EPA	Economic Partnership Agreements (EC-ACP)
EU	European Union
FDI	foreign direct investment
FTA	free-trade area
FTAA	Free Trade Area of the Americas
GATS	General Agreement on Trade in Services
GATT	General Agreement on Tariffs and Trade
GSP	Generalised System of Preferences
H&S	hub and spoke systems
ITO	International Trade Organisation
LDC	less developed country
MERCOSUR	Mercosur Mercado Común del Sur (Southern Common Market)

MFA	Multi-fibre Arrangement
MFN	most-favoured nation
NAFTA	North American Free Trade Agreement
NGO	non-governmental organization
OECD	Organisation for Economic Cooperation and Development
OEEC	Organisation for European Economic Cooperation
ORC	other regulations of commerce
ORRC	other restrictive regulations of commerce
PA	Partnership Agreement, EC-ACP Cotonou Agreement
PR	panel report (GATT/WTO)
PTA	preferential trade agreement
QR	quantitative restriction
RA	regional agreement
ROO	Rule(s) of Origin
RTA	regional trade agreement
SAT	substantially-all trade
TBT	technical barriers to trade
TRIMS	trade related investment measures
TRIPS	Agreement on Trade-Related Aspects of Intellectual Property Rights
UK	United Kingdom
UN	United Nations
UNCTAD	United Nations Conference on Trade and Development
USC	United States Code
USTR	United States Trade Representative
VCLT	Vienna Convention on the Law of Treaties
VER	voluntary export restraint
WG	Working Group
WTO	World Trade Organisation

INTRODUCTION

This book is about one of the oldest "trade and..." problems -- that being the question of trade and discrimination within the context of regional trade agreements. As we tell our students, the legal principle of non-discrimination is fundamental to the multilateral trading system. Discrimination is "bad" and non-discrimination is "good". Some tend to think of discrimination only in its negative form, as discrimination *against*, and then have to resolve that with *preference,* which is also discrimination, even though it is a favour.[1] In GATT law the granting of a favour is not a good thing if it is discriminatory. One could better say in the first place that preference and discrimination are interchangeable as they can both come in two flavours, positive and negative. Both abridge the non-discrimination principle. A positive preference that is offered to one party is an effective act of negative discrimination as to another, and visa versa.

However, when it comes to permitting regional trade agreements in the WTO, the non-discrimination rule appears to be turned on its head. GATT Article XXIV is supposed to grant an exception from the rule for free-trade areas or customs unions when the regional members exchange a most extensive set of positive preferences. This infers lots of positive discrimination for them and lots of potentially negative discrimination for everyone else. Thus we ask, why does GATT require positive preferences to such a degree in order to permit a regional exception from the non-discrimination rule?

There seems to be little question that the economic considerations don't validate this exception rule, especially if one takes the view that the Article should be interpreted to require a nearly 100% preference exchange between members. Shortly after the ink was dry on the ITO Havana Charter (1948), Jacob Viner in the Customs Union Issue (1950) was able to break through the logic of this construction in regard to the possible negative economic consequences of requiring complete (positive) discrimination in a regional agreement. As far as economic welfare of the world as a whole was concerned, there was nothing in particular to recommend a complete preferential exchange on a regional level. In point, since such an exchange could substitute less efficient regional producers in place of more efficient world producers, world welfare could be worse off as result. In 1963, Kenneth Dam in his Chicago law article titled, "The Legacy of a Misconception" gave Article XXIV a serious working over in the context of Viner's trade creation and

---

[1]   The Concise Oxford Dictionary defines *preference* as, "(L)iking of one thing better than another ... favouring of a country by admitting its products at lower import duty". *Discriminate* is to, "(B)e set up, or observe, a difference between...".

diversion. Dam concluded that the Article XXIV rules could not distinguish between good customs unions and bad ones unless an amendment was made to the provisions, or that the Article be functionally re-interpreted. This would encourage only those positive preferences between members that would not result in undue trade diversion for non-members. This would result in less positive discrimination occurring for members but also less negative discrimination against the non-members.

Since the trading system is made up of rules, there is yet an idea that some notion or concept of compatibility should be applied to determine which regional trade agreements ought to be permitted and which ones ought to be avoided. The theme pursued here is that the rules as written require a nearly complete set of preferences to be exchanged between members, and accordingly, this is the way regional members should be compelled to proceed. In other words, Article XXIV has it quite right overall as originally drafted in 1948, and as it has been supplemented by the GATT 1994 Understanding on the interpretation of the Article. Thus, whether or not the world may be made worse off in a welfare sense by requiring complete exchanges, the trading system, including the WTO and its non-discrimination provisions, would be the better off.

How one has come to such a contrary position deserves a bit of explanation. A solely economic criterion for compatibility might suggest that regional members be permitted to choose their preferences so that they only select those positive ones that will not cause trade-diverting effects for non-members. This assumes however that there is only one flavour of preference (positive), or that this is the only variety regional members can have on their menu. Historically, meaning pre GATT, this did not seem to be the case. Even while Jacob Viner was disclosing his insight on the possibility of trade-diverting customs unions, he also added this practical caveat.

> "Customs union, if it is complete, involves across-the-board removal of the duties between the members of the union; since the removal is non-selective by its very nature, the beneficial preferences are established along with the injurious ones, the trade-creating ones along with the trade-diverting ones. Preferential arrangements, on the other hand, can be, and usually are, selective, and it is possible, and in practice probable, that the preferences selected will be predominantly of the trade-diverting or injurious kind."[2]

There is sufficient evidence in the drafting record to demonstrate that the "all or nothing" approach to regional trade agreements adopted by the drafters was intended to avoid this probability in several possible aspects. The first as Viner mentions, was to prevent regional members from only selecting the diverting preferences that

---

[2]   J. Viner, **The Customs Union Issue**, Carnegie Endowment, 1950, p. 51.

would act to harm non-members. A second but closely related objective would be to require the members to actually install positive preferences that would create internal trade. These could hurt non-members, but the purpose of the exception contemplates that.[3] A third possibility orients the theme of this book, that regional members could also install negative preferences. These would not hurt the trade of any non-members directly and could actually benefit their trade. However, regional negative discrimination could do a lot of damage to one member relative to another.

The literature on regional trade agreements seems to be primarily dedicated to exploring the possibilities presented by the first and second aspects noted above.[4] Not much is said about the third, although even from a traditional welfare perspective the gains and losses to each member were also indicated by Viner to be a component of the larger calculation. This aside, even if a welfare-oriented analysis captured all three elements, this would still not be the end of the matter. As far as the WTO compatibility of regional trade agreements is concerned, the crux of the criteria should not be directed to overall welfare as it may or may not result. Rather, the idea is to limit the exception for non-discrimination to the two particular types of regional agreements that are to fulfil identical internal (positive preference) requirements. Not surprisingly given the drafting history, the free-trade area is to resemble the same internally trade-creating characteristics as the completed customs union. As simply drafted, this requires the elimination of duties and quantitative restrictions on all but a small share of the trade between the members, and the elimination of other protectionist commercial instruments, also as between them. As we know from history, not all customs unions have made the grade on this rather imposing test, and most free-trade areas probably have not.

This is where the problem of negative preferences between regional members comes into play, even though the possibility of both *positive* and *negative* preferences operating within any regional trade agreement is often dismissed as unlikely. Ironically enough, the question of negative discrimination as it may occur in the larger trading system is a nearly ubiquitous concern. Any commercial policy instrument that permits a range of selectivity raises it. Examples include contingent trade instruments such as anti-dumping and countervailing duties, those permitting emergency action for safeguards or balance of payments, and remedies against oth-

---

3   Recalling Article XXIV:4, that the purpose of a customs union or free-trade area, "should be to facilitate trade between the constituent territories and not to raise barriers to the trade of other contracting parties ...".

4   Not suggesting disapproval of the literature more confined to these aspects. However, see for the broader picture, for early GATT, Gardner Patterson, **Discrimination in International Trade, The Policy Issues, 1945-1965**, Princeton University Press, Princeton, 1966. More in the WTO context, Thomas Cottier, *The challenge of Regionalization and Preferential Relations in World Trade Law and Policy*, European Foreign Affairs Review, V. 2, 1996, pp. 149-167.

er "unfair" public and private practices affecting trade.[5] GATT/WTO rules are full
of mini-MFN statements surrounding these instruments. From the 1970's and 80's,
we also know that the trade system was highly concerned with the problem of grey-
area measures. These bilateral agreements suspended MFN treatment (and other
GATT rules) in order to enact selective quantitative restrictions or some other
measure. Outside the regional context, the frequency and legality of negative discrimination is clearly a preoccupation of WTO Members.

However, in examining the applicability of GATT rules to regional systems, the
assumption seems to persist that all preferences exchanged by regional members
are positive, a view tending to find some resonance among the most active regional territories. Rather than contest that point by isolated examples, which do not offer proof, one instead proceeds from the position of a hypothetical. Assuming that
regional members were applying negative preferences in their agreements, then
what could or should GATT law say about it, if anything? On this question certain
defences tend to rise. They include the idea that the rules are so unclear on the required conduct of regional members that there is no resolution possible within the
framework of the GATT, as it emerged in 1947 or even now in the WTO.[6] Failing
the "we just don't know" argument, one can also experience a more venomous defence stating that regional members, by invoking Article XXIV, have wholly immu-
nised themselves from the GATT rules that would otherwise apply if only they
weren't in a regional trade agreement. A third argument indicates that special parties require a special application of the Article's rules. Particularly for developed-
developing country arrangements, the substantially-all trade requirement is too severe and should be modified to accommodate the developmental levels of the parties. There is an attempt made to rebut all of these positions in the succeeding chapters.

On the topic of how regional members treat each other, it is also unavoidable to
approach some delicate terrain. While regional parties have clearly had the functional legal capacity through the GATT years to eliminate certain trade flows from
their own arrangements, it is also apparent that some of these deletions can reflect
the relative territory size and market power of the various participants.[7] Certainly
the most difficult working group reviews in the GATT were encountered in
large/small and developed/developing country arrangements. Large regional members do not want to be characterised as hegemonic, friendly or otherwise, and certainly do not want to be reminded of anything relating to the colonial or imperial

---

5   Referring to U.S. Section 301, see for examples, *"Case Studies of Aggressive Unilateralism"*,
in Thomas Bayard and Kimberly Elliott, **Reciprocity and Retaliation in U.S. Trade Policy**, Institute
for International Economics, Washington D.C., 1994, pp. 101-300.

6   For just one example, through the GATT-47 years, there was never a clear determination made
of whether regional members should be allowed, not be allowed, or be required, to impose safeguards
upon each other.

7   This was Hirschman's thesis, as explored within. It is also suggested more contemporaneous-
ly by some of the "hub and spoke" literature.

past. However, once the possibility of negative preference within a regional setting is placed in issue, a certain amount of historical recollection is inevitable. Here, the treatment recalls some of the early discourse, with the caveat made that the author is not asserting that all the inter-war evils are preparing for reoccurrence in the era of the WTO.

The above considerations regarding preference suggested a possible thesis. While Viner and Dam were correct that Article XXIV requirements were economically irrational, perhaps the intent of the drafters for Article XXIV was not to provide solely for an economic result. Maybe the objective was also legal and political in nature by attempting to affect the course of economic diplomacy by the new obligations contained in the GATT Agreement. Drawing from its preamble, perhaps the purpose of Article XXIV together with Article I was not only to provide for the expansion of world trade, but to also attempt to eliminate discrimination in international commerce. Perhaps this stated objective is not necessarily synonymous in all cases with the concept of trade expansion, and maybe it deserved a bit more attention on its own merits.

This led to a more precise expression. In spite of the economic irrationality of Article XXIV requirements, the alternative to requiring regional members to exchange a nearly complete set of preferences could be even worse. Therefore, the question was joined: is MFN (and perhaps other GATT rules) suspended by the operation of Article XXIV only as to the non-members? To express positively, to what extent do GATT rules apply to the trade of members within a regional trade agreement?

The early inquiry focused on the nature of preferences in the pre-GATT era and the relationship between negative discrimination in commerce and the impending resuscitation of the MFN principle. If it were found that the advocates of the multilateral most-favoured nation clause were cognisant of the dangers of both positive and negative discrimination within preferential systems, then perhaps the drafters also contemplated some prospects along these lines. This would justify a high and mutual exchange of preferences between members regardless of certain external economic effects. However, this historical strand, while present, was not easily distilled from the larger history nor are the provisions easily capable of being separated for their legal effects. Paragraph 8 requirements can be understood to reduce internal discrimination and at the same time reduce the incidence of regional systems overall. Thus, both internal and external purposes could be served by the substantially-all trade requirement. At the same instance however, there was also nothing evident in GATT's pre-history surveyed that excluded outright the possibility that the drafters were also attempting to control the conduct of regional members within their arrangements.

Since the free-trade area form has been seen to grant a greater flexibility for regional members than the customs union, the origins of this exception were also of interest. The future use of preferential systems was of clear concern for the developing countries going on record during the Havana negotiations in 1948. For them, the negotiated standstill at Geneva was an unfairness, as they had not yet had opportunity to establish their own regional systems and so could not avail themselves of the standstill provisions found in the MFN Article. The customs union exception was claimed impractical for them given its administrative complexities; and the specialised development exceptions accorded in the Havana draft required a voting endorsement, as in the manner of a waiver. The introduction of a free-trade area exception to accompany the customs union provision was most likely the result of these concerns. However, this insight also did not illuminate the question of MFN control over intra-regional trade, as the context for the new free-trade area exception also appeared to be nearly wholly developmental in nature. This would provide an avenue for developing countries to establish larger regional markets in order to obtain the possibilities of more competitive scales of production, albeit by more comprehensive exchanges of preferences than those likely considered in pre-war arrangements.

It was not until the GATT practice emerged that there was an apparent appreciation of the possibilities of flexibility offered by the free-trade area exception as between developed and developing countries. Starting with the Overseas Association review in 1958, working party members commenced the process of attempting to determine what "substantially all trade" should require. This and later reviews revealed a pattern that the issue of trade coverage was most intractable in agreements between developed and developing countries. Many commentators and review parties saw the mutuality requirement as mandating the re-establishment of colonial structures. The EEC legal argument on the point was consistent with this view, that Part IV of the GATT could also be "read in" to the list of articles permitted as exceptions to the trade coverage requirements of paragraph 8 of Article XXIV. However, while the issue was often focused upon the "right" or necessity of developing countries to re-impose trade measures as to their more developed partner, not so much attention was paid to what degree the EEC was also reserving options of contingency in regard to its own trade opening commitments.[8] This and later reviews indicated that flexibility in the form of free-trade areas was being sought by developed and developing members, although the coverage requirements for both customs unions and free-trade areas were identical in the coverage provisions.

Once free-trade areas are identified as the leading vehicle for possibly exercising internal discrimination, some attention should be paid to the particular mechanisms that grant such flexibility in these agreements. Here, chapters have been provided to concentrate on rules of origin and on regional safeguards. For origin rules, there is a long history of non-member complaints regarding their external diversionary possibilities. There is however the similar possibility to use the rules to affect the trade between members. There is also a long history in the use of rules in

---

[8]   The EEC and its regional partners dominated the GATT-47 practice regarding free-trade areas, and it is unavoidable that any review of the era would be mainly concerned with EEC regional agreements.

the design of regional systems to reflect the concept of hub and spoke as contrasted to area treatment. This background is traced to the original EEC plan and the relationship to the (later) EFTA states. Safeguards within regional systems can be shown to diverge from the GATT, and now WTO, rules and examples are drawn here from both the CUSTA (now NAFTA) and the Europe Agreements between the EC and countries of Central and Eastern Europe.

For both the GATT-1947 and the WTO practice, there is also a contrast made between the developments occurring in the dispute resolution process and the positions maintained by the regional proponents in the working group reviews. While evolutionary, GATT panels, and now the WTO Appellate Body, have gradually come to reject the view that Article XXIV has granted regional members a right to establish self-autonomous regimes outside the framework of the GATT. However, the context for raising this central question has also developed over time. In GATT-1947, the right of a panel to even commence an inquiry as to the characteristics of a particular regional agreement was firmly opposed by regional respondents. They argued that mere notification of the existence of a regional agreement to the proper GATT authorities acted to secure the most-favoured nation exception outright, in the absence of a negative or amending recommendation from the Council. Although unreported, the impact of Bananas I and II (1993 and 1994) had certain legal reverberations in establishing that a panel could not avoid at least some prima facie examination of a regional agreement when a member had chosen to invoke it as a defence to a GATT Article violation.

To date, The WTO Appellate Body has reversed (in part) dispute settlement panels in two cases raised concerning Article XXIV.[9] The reversals on certain points appear to affirm the trend from GATT-1947 favouring the imposition of legal criteria for the qualification of regional agreements. Thus, the first AB case rejected the panel's attempts to reconcile the provisions of paragraph 4 and 8 of the Article. Paragraph 4 was found by the AB to be "purposeful" but not expressing a legal obligation. This holding may suggest that paragraph 8 requirements, even though unsettled, do express criteria which must be met according to the provisions, and not through the lens of economic effects such as trade diversion. The second panel found expressly that intra-regional safeguards were permitted according to paragraph 8, although Article XIX was not listed as an article exception. This view was rejected by the Appellate Body (but without ruling the opposite, i.e., that the listing of Articles was exhaustive). Both AB reports established the notion of Article XXIV as a *conditional* exception. Parties asserting its defence must affirmatively demonstrate that the conditions of the Article's provisions in paragraphs 5 and 8 have been met, and that a measure violating a GATT article must be shown

---

[9] *Turkey – Restrictions on Imports of Textile and Clothing Products*, Report of the Panel, WT/DS34/R, Report of the Appellate Body, AB-1995-5, WT/DS34/AB/R, adopted 19 November 1999. *Argentina – Safeguard Measures on Imports of Footwear*, Report of the Appellate Body, WT/DS121/AB/R, 14 December, 1999.

as necessary between members in order to excuse the violation. Thus, there appears to have been a clear rejection of any so-called "autonomous regime" theory for regional trade agreements under WTO law.

Since the WTO Committee on Regional Trade Agreements is charged with making recommendations on the compatibility of agreements, the bearing these cases could have on that process is also examined. This is done by comparing the holdings of the cases to the systemic discussion in the CRTA as reported by the WTO Secretariat. Although it would be easy if all regional proponents' arguments made in the CRTA had been overturned by the Appellate Body, this is certainly not the case. Rather, a number of regional opponents have dedicated their position thoroughly to a trade-diversion approach for the Article. This is understandable given the lack of an historical criteria applicable to paragraph 8 requirements. However, even while the cases have not set out the ultimate criteria, the direction has been pointed toward a meeting of paragraph 8 as a condition in order to invoke the exception. This means that the burden of qualifying a regional trade agreement has fallen toward the proponents. However, the emphasis in the examination is not on the basis of welfare effects, but on the coverage requirements of the paragraph itself.

The question remains whether the rejection of an autonomous regime theory might also apply to the trade between regional members. For this question, the WTO is an international organisation and the question is treated here as one of treaty interpretation with reference to the Vienna Convention on the Law of Treaties (VCLT 1969). VCLT Article 41 1(a) has the bearing on the question of whether two parties to the WTO treaty may vary their GATT rights and obligations as between themselves. The argument made here is that GATT Article XXIV is itself a negotiated and permissive expression for bilateral modification for customs unions and free-trade areas and controls which GATT rules may be suspended by its own terms. Article XXIV terms would therefore control even where regional members can argue that their particular modifications do not otherwise affect the WTO rights of non-members to the regional agreement.[10]

This should have implications for multilateralism more generally. If GATT's non-discrimination objective encompasses now the necessity to discipline an emerging *multipolar* trading system, comprised of leading territories and their respective free-trade partners, then a higher bar to regional formations must also be considered in the service of this task. Likewise, to the extent that GATT/WTO rules can be encouraged to be operative within regional agreements, then the risk of di-

---

[10] Overall, one understands that the issue of negative discrimination between regional members must centre on the interpretation to be given to GATT Article XXIV:8, and in respect to the internal trade requirements of sub-paragraphs (a)(i) for customs unions and (b) for free-trade areas. The two provisions found in both sub-paragraphs that relate directly to the problem, are the *substantially-all trade* requirement for the elimination of duties and other restrictive regulations of commerce, and the listing of GATT articles permitted to be applied as exceptions between regional members.

vergence between regional systems and the multilateral trading system should also be diminished.

As stated at the outset, non-discrimination is the fundamental principle underlying the multilateral trading system. As such, the role and purpose attributed for MFN will also tend to define the purpose of the WTO itself. Thus, where MFN's function is viewed narrowly as only a trade-expansion instrument, then it may well deserve to succumb to a host of other "trade and ..." considerations that raise some fundamental questions between internationally accepted norms of behaviour and trade in the process of economic integration. On the other hand, if the importance of eliminating discrimination in international trade can also be recognised for its own merits, then there remains the possibility that a deeper notion of legitimacy for the WTO and its rules may also emerge.

Part One:
PRE-GATT PREFERENCE AND THE MFN RESPONSE

Part One provides background on the use of trade preferences prior to the General Agreement on Tariffs and Trade (GATT-1947), and the efforts made to counter preference by entry into force of the general most-favoured nation treatment obligation (MFN, or the MFN clause). The history of legal developments commences in the inter-war years and is taken through the Havana Charter ITO sessions in 1948 and up through the final text settled for GATT Article XXIV, the Article providing for the primary regional exceptions.[1]

In modern times we view the use of preference between territories as an initial violation of the general rule of most-favoured nation treatment. However, for much of the last century discriminatory preferences between states were the norm for international economic diplomacy. While MFN clauses existed in various bilateral trade agreements, there was no multilateral framework for its application and the clause, when in effect, was applied by some only conditionally. The GATT MFN clause incorporated drafting aspects of prior bilateral treaties, but due to its multilateral and unconditional nature, it did not express the prior customary practice between trading nations.[2] Rather, GATT MFN was a decidedly dramatic departure from the previous practice.

The focus of the historical review here is to extract from the record the elements that tie the re-emergence of MFN to the GATT provisions also made for regional preferential exceptions. Several themes are emphasised by this, including the point

---

[1]   General Agreement on Tariffs and Trade, opened for signature, 30 October 1947, 61 Stat A3, T.I.A.S. No. 1700, 55 United Nations Treaty Series 187; Protocol of Provisional Application of the General Agreement on Tariffs and Trade (1947), 55 U.N.T.S. 308. GATT Article I, paragraph 1 providing for most-favoured nation reads: "With respect to customs duties and charges of any kind imposed on or in connection with importation or exportation or imposed on the international transfer of payments for imports or exports, and with respect to the method of levying such duties and charges, and with respect to all rules and formalities in connection with importation and exportation, and with respect to all matters referred to in paragraphs 2 and 4 of Article III, any advantage, favour, privilege or immunity granted by any contracting party to any product originating in or destined for any other country shall be accorded immediately and unconditionally to the like product originating in or destined for the territories of all other contracting parties".

[2]   MFN or similar obligations are found in a number of other GATT Articles, including Article III:7, IV, V:2,5,6, IX:1, XIII:1, XVII:1, and XX:j. John H. Jackson, *World Trade Law and the Law of GATT*, the Mitchie Company, Charlottesville, Virginia, 1969, p. 255. Jackson has characterised MFN and National Treatment (GATT Article III) as "two types of 'economic-equality' norms ...". Besides economic arguments for MFN, he describes the "political" policies justifying the clause as, "Without MFN, governments could form trade cliques and groupings more readily. These special groupings can cause rancour, misunderstanding and disputes, as those countries 'left out' of favours resent their inferior status." John H. Jackson, *Equality and Discrimination in International Economic Law*, The Year Book of World Affairs, 1983, pp. 225 and 232.

of validating GATT MFN for its intended role to close out the interwar preferential systems. This was accomplished by imposing a high internal trade requirement for customs unions, as settled in Geneva (1947) and for free-trade areas as added in Havana (1948), what we now refer to as the GATT Article XXIV:8 requirements. Decidedly, the interpretations given to that paragraph's terms act in the practice to define the legal scope of the GATT MFN obligation. Since the two Articles together could significantly limit the sovereign commercial policies of the Contracting Parties, how the drafters viewed the provisions is relevant, particularly in light of the ambiguity surrounding the paragraph 8 provisions.

In this review there is an emphasis on elements of the history that were directed to intra-regional behaviour, both as to the positive preferences which would affect third parties, like the U.S. in respect to the Commonwealth preference issue, but also as to the possibility of negative preference as employed between regional partners. As to third parties, the allegations of injury are replete in the commentary as to the loss of access to resources and to markets. As between partners, the hazards of negative preference are also not absent from the historical record. This could permit the suggestion that the GATT rules as finalised provided more than a mechanism to secure the expansion of world trade by way of mutually reciprocal exchanges based upon MFN. In addition, the Articles taken together could have impact on the conduct of the regional members themselves. At the core of this consideration is the degree of trade coverage intended to be required between the regional members, the substantially-all trade requirement, and the question of which restrictive measures could be continued between such partners. Overall, the issue is fully centred on the paragraph 8 requirements contained within GATT Article XXIV.

It remains a ubiquitous feature in the literature to recount the various weaknesses and loopholes of Article XXIV regarding its interpretation in actual GATT practice. To the contrary, the drafting record indicates an intention to establish a "narrowest of all possible avenues" for future preferential systems. That the free-trade area provisions contributed in Havana so closely mimicked those already established for customs unions indicates that the new MFN clause was not sought to be diluted by the inclusion of this new possibility. Since the Geneva provisions reflected proposals advanced by the most stalwart MFN proponents, including the United States, the final Havana provisions as extended to free-trade areas were not perceived to diminish the new MFN obligation.

Chapter 1
INTERWAR PREFERENCE AND THE CASE FOR MFN

"I said that if the British and the United States governments could not agree to do everything within their power to further … a restoration of free and liberal trade policies, they might as well throw in the sponge and realize that one of the greatest factors in creating the present tragic situation in the world was going to be permitted to continue unchecked in the postwar world …". Sumner Welles, *(1947)*.

1.1 Introduction

This chapter will lay the historical groundwork for the re-establishment of the multilateral most-favoured nation principle following the Second World War. The purpose of the investigation is to identify the legal objectives underlying the later regional provisions in the GATT as they provided for exceptions from MFN. Thus, the chapter outlines certain events regarding the use of preferences in international trade during the inter-war period, and especially as these practices would eventually be either permitted or proscribed by the emerging MFN provisions. In this, the notion of "economic nationalism" was at the forefront throughout the decade prior to the outbreak of World War II. A primary device for executing this strategy was the employment of regional preferences, both positive and negative.

As a general most-favoured nation treatment was not applied during the period, the tension between existing patterns of preference and the re-establishment of MFN emerged as a first distinct issue in the discussions of the post-war planners. The motive of terminating preference by the use of MFN was attributable to a mix of economic, political and legal concerns. Economically, much of the debate could be characterised in rather mercantilist terms as the external exclusionary effects of the British Imperial Preference came to the centre of the issue as far as the United States was concerned. However, both countries also underpinned their Atlantic Charter discussions by the objective to not repeat the Versailles Treaty and the resulting inter-war experiences. The objective was to establish the credibility of MFN at the outset and to arrange a set of rules to lend support for its coherent application over time.

1.2   The Paris Convention (1916) and inter-war preferences

The period of planning at the conclusion of the First World War did not find allies
in any way united on the question of installing an MFN principle. Rather, the tone
at Versailles, and the conduct of the conference itself, has been described more as
an exercise in the repudiation of MFN.[3] Hirschman cited the 1916 Paris Economic
Conference preamble as evidence of the mood between the allies, as

> "(T)he representatives of the Allied governments ... declare that, after forcing upon
> them the military contest in spite of all the efforts to avoid the conflict, the Empires
> of Central Europe are today preparing, in concert with their allies, for a contest on the
> economic plane, which will not only survive the reestablishment of peace, but will at
> that moment attain its full scope and intensity."[4]

1.2.1   *Provisions regarding MFN at Versailles*

The recognition that an economic war would continue after suspension of the military conflict led the allies to adopt many of the techniques allegedly employed by
the German government. Hirschman concluded that,

> "(O)ne after another we find enumerated all the fundamental policies of refined eco-
> nomic nationalism with which we have become so well acquainted in the period be-
> tween the two wars--restricted access to raw materials and resources, *preferential
> treatments and discriminations*, restrictions on the activities of aliens, antidumping
> legislation, differential transport rates, autarky, not only with respect to key indus-
> tries, but on a practically universal scale by means of subsidies, tariffs, prohibitions,
> etc. Even a cursory view of this amazing Pandora's box raises doubts whether these
> measures were devised for defense only."[5]

---

3   The practices at issue included, the rapid and targeted expansion of exports relative to other
countries, the use of unfair competition in trade, notably predatory dumping of exports, the intent to
destroy competitive industries in other countries to prevent them from industrialising, and the export
of capital and personnel to obtain financial control or dominance over key foreign enterprises. According to Hirschman, Germany was already arming for the next round of economic and commercial warfare, or was at least perceived to be so acting. Albert O. Hirschman, **National Power and the Structure of Foreign Trade**, University of California Press, Berkeley, 1945, (expanded edition 1980), p. 54.

4   A.O. Hirschman, Ibid., at pp. 60-61, quoting from H.W.V. Termperly, **A History of the Peace
Conference of Paris**, Vol. V, London, 1921, p. 367. Jacob Viner suggested that while the agreement
in Paris was mainly directed to the Central Powers, there was also a growing disillusion with the MFN
principle. This was demonstrated by the retention of preferential relations for a time between the European powers as to the Central and neutral powers and to the United States. Jacob Viner, **The Customs Union Issue**, Carnegie Endowment, 1950, p. 24.

5   A.O. Hirschman, Ibid., at pp. 6-61 (italics added) , making reference to "Resolutions of the
Paris Economic Conference of the Allies, June, 1916, Transitory and Permanent Measures of the Allied Countries". The resolution text is reprinted in full in Hirschman, Ibid., at pp. 163-165.

This allied approach at Versailles conflicted with that envisioned by the United States as enunciated by the third of President Wilson's Fourteen Points for a post-war system based on non-discrimination. According to Young, the two views became conflicting fountainheads of the economic sections of the final Treaty of Versailles. This was exhibited by the compromise demonstrated in Articles 264 and 265, according to Hirschman, whereby Germany was required to grant MFN to the allies, but, "without stipulating anything with respect to the commercial policy of the Allies." The worst possible compromise was said to have evolved, "combining as it did the principle of full economic sovereignty and the practices of restriction and discrimination".[6] John Maynard Keynes also established this point as central in the context of the economic provisions.

> "The miscellaneous Economic Clauses commence with a number of provisions which would be in accordance with the spirit of the third of the Fourteen Points, if they were reciprocal. Both for imports and exports, and as regards tariffs, regulations, and prohibition, Germany binds herself for five years to accord most-favoured-nation treatment to the Allied and Associated States. But she is not entitled herself to receive such treatment."[7]

1.2.2   The effect of Versailles provisions on German diplomacy

The effect of this resulting imbalance is imprecise, but it has been claimed to have led Germany, also relieved of its colonies, to evolve a diplomatic strategy of turning upon its smaller neighbours for the implementation of a bilateral and preferential policy.[8] Condliffe provided a reflective description of the strategy describing what we might now refer to as a "hub and spoke" regional system. It also employs the terminology familiar to monopoly abuse.

> "They were, in fact, building a new trading system, the centre of which was the German military economy - a bilateral system in which all the traffic should flow to and from the centre. This system was not designed to broaden into multilateral inter-

---

[6]   A.O. Hirschman, Ibid., at p. 66. Point three of the Fourteen Points provided for, "The removal, so far as possible, of all economic barriers and the establishment of an equality of trade conditions among all the nations consenting to the Peace and associating themselves for its maintenance".

[7]   J.M. Keynes, **The Economic Consequences of the Peace**, Harper and Row, New York, 1920, (1971 Edition), pp. 62 and 102. However, Keynes did not assign the difficulties of the peace to the economic provisions, but to those concerned with reparations. Also contrary, Jacob Viner indicated a dual motive in the economic provisions, to effect discrimination against the Central powers as well as to form a system of protection against the neutral parties, particularly the perceived competitive position of the United States. J. Viner, Supra note 4 at pp. 24-27. As such, inter war European preferences were also attempted to avoid U.S. commercial pressure and its conditional MFN clause.

[8]   As quoted in Asher Isaacs, *More Recent Commercial Policies in Europe*, from **International Trade**, R.D. Irwin, Inc., Chicago, 1948, in Andrew J. Kress, (Ed.), **The Economics of Diplomacy**, School of Foreign Service, Georgetown University, Washington, D.C., 1949, pp. 360-407 at p. 377.

change in which there would be room for all the great trading countries to cooperate. It was designed to supplant and destroy the world trading system that Great Britain had built up and that the United States was trying to revive. Its methods are best understood when compared with those by which great monopolistic corporations have attempted, by horizontal and vertical integration to destroy the trade of their competitors."[9]

Hirschman made some effort to document why the allied parties failed to constrain this development of economic nationalism between the wars, placing some significant share of the responsibility on the United States for its unwillingness to reduce its own trade barriers. This was said to have placed the allies in the difficult position of waging America's "free trade war" but without access to American markets. Additionally, he cited the premature break-up of the war-time agencies; a failure by the Americans to appreciate the degree of fear which had evolved among the allies concerning the threat of economic domination; and finally, the dismissal by free traders in England and the U.S. of the idea that any state, "could use commercial relations for ends of national power."[10]

Michael Heilperin also provided reflective accounts of the responses of various countries confronted with German bilateral policies. He quoted Howard Ellis who provided a description of the linkage between "bilateralism" and "preferentialism" whereby,

> "It should be sharply emphasized that this power of the current-account debtor in a given bilateral relation cannot be brought to bear upon a particular country *unless* the bilateral trade of the two is separated from the rest of its trade."[11]

1.2.3   The rise of "economic nationalism"

Within twenty years after the conclusion of the Versailles peace, the effect of the inter-war policies had risen to the level of alarm as the same set of policies were also being blamed for the cause of the great economic depression. As William Culbertson wrote,

> "(W)e have witnessed since the (first) World War an unprecedented revival of mercantilism. Fear stimulated by economic losses, social disorders, the destruction of

---

9   A. Isaacs, Ibid., at p. 378, quoting Condliffe from a non-identified source.

10   A.O. Hirschman, Supra note 3 at p. 68. This is not to suggest that a similar lack of awareness governed policy at the closing of the Second World War.

11   Howard S. Ellis, *Bilateralism and the Future of International trade, Essays in International Finance*, No. 5, Princeton University, 1945, p. 10, quoted in, M.A. Heilperin, **The Trade of Nations**, Longmans, London and New York, 1946, p. 114. "The tactics of 'isolate and rule' are very applicable in this context". Heilperin, Ibid., at p. 115.

classes, war, and rumors of war has revived mercantilistic policies as drastic as those of the age of Colbert, Frederick the Great, and Cromwell ...".[12]

Nationalism was a sufficient danger in any period, but it was rendered even more dangerous by its capacity to capture commercial policy instruments for its service. It was this linkage between the two which raised the term "economic nationalism" to a common usage in the later inter-war period, and that period of time immediately proceeding World War II.

An appreciation of the risks of connecting commercial instruments to the policies of greater national diplomacy may not have been well appreciated at the conclusion of the First World War. By the commencement of the Second World War, the unabated effects of the policies and their contribution to tensions between the powers could not have likely escaped notice by even the United States in its relatively isolated position. What was seen to emerge in the comparable period of post-war planning for Second World War was a stronger proposition relying upon the original non-discrimination provisions of the Fourteen Points. If economic nationalism required an environment tolerant of commercial discrimination, the corrective policy was to change this environment so as to eliminate the conditions for discriminatory practices.

1.3   MFN issues prior to Geneva Negotiations (1947)

The challenge confronting the so-called post-war planners in the early 1940's was understood to be similar to that which confronted the Allies in 1916, as "the fear of economic aggression and the prevention of its recurrence will be a major preoccupation of our future peacemakers."[13] However, the ultimate direction in which arrangements proceeded were markedly different from the outset of the process, as the United States and Great Britain assumed a more activist role in framing the final conditions even while the military conflict was in process. As such, much of the documentation available to identify the revival of multilateral conditions for trade is contributed from the American and British commentary, most notably, Richard Gardner's **Sterling Dollar Diplomacy**.[14] The purpose of this section is to only

---

[12] "My concern here is to emphasize that the problem of commercial policy today is, in a broad approach to our life, a part of the problem of nationalism ..." William S. Culbertson, **Reciprocity**, McGraw-Hill Co., New York, 1937, reprinted in A.J. Kress, Supra note 8 at pp. 18-19.

[13] A.O. Hirschman, Supra note 3 at p. 71.

[14] Richard N. Gardner, **Sterling-Dollar Diplomacy in Current Perspective**, Columbia University Press, New York, 1980 edition. Since these countries were in a leadership position during the war, events focus on their negotiations for the revival of normal trade relations, including the application of nondiscrimination. Gardner recounted events leading through the Savannah and Bretton Woods conferences for both monetary and trade aspects.

draw from this work, and others, those aspects of the negotiations and contemplated arrangements which were sought to address preferential systems in light of the emerging principle of non-discrimination.

1.3.1   Non-discrimination as the central objective

Gardner's account demonstrates without difficulty that the American planners placed the revival of the non-discrimination principle at the centre of their policy regarding post-war economic arrangements.[15] Moreover, he attributed this motivation, at least in the earlier phases, to a desire to curb the practices of economic nationalism and the use of certain commercial instruments. As he concluded, "The U.S. post-war planners were united in their determination to break completely with the legacy of economic nationalism and economic isolationalism ...".[16]

The advocates of the policy could summon a long train of precedent for a U.S. position supporting non-discrimination. This commenced as early as Washington's famous farewell speech "to hold an equal and impartial hand, neither seeking nor granting exclusive favours or preferences". It was re-stated by John Hay's declaration of the open door in regard to China at the beginning of the 20th century; and finally, to Wilson's third of Fourteen Points declaring, "the removal so far as is possible, all economic barriers and the establishment of an equality of trade conditions ..."[17]

While the revival of a non-discrimination principle was pre-eminent and ascendant in U.S. policy, the desire to return to a liberal trading system was also rising in the United Kingdom.[18] There was however a critical difference between the two, as the British considered that the first priority should be placed upon the reduction of trade barriers between the major partners, and particularly upon a reduc-

---

[15]   Gardner quoted a number of commentators to establish this theme. "Pasvolsky warned that unwillingness to abandon policies of economic warfare would constitute 'the greatest danger that can confront us after the war ... Likewise, White argued that, '(J)ust as the failure to develop an effective League of nations has made possible two devastating wars within one generation, so the absence of a high degree of economic collaboration among the leading nations will, during the coming decade, inevitably result in economic warfare that will be but the prelude and instigator of military warfare on an even vaster scale.' " R. Gardner, Ibid., at p. 8.

[16]   Gardner indicated that the goal of implementing nondiscrimination was not the only component of multilateralism in U.S. planning, but among the other components, the reduction of trade barriers and economic (lending) reconstruction, non-discrimination was pre-eminent. R. Gardner, Ibid., at p. 12. It would follow that the policy would therefore tend to support a strong non-discrimination clause and seek to narrowly prescribe any exceptions to it.

[17]   R. Gardner, Ibid., at pp. 16-17.

[18]   "In the early years of the war-time Government the reconstruction of such a regime became a major objective of British no less than of American planning ..." R. Gardner, Ibid., at p. 27.

tion of U.S. barriers.[19] As this division became more attenuated through the negotiations, it is suggested that the U.S. justification for asserting a non-discrimination appeared to become more mercantilist. A contributing cause of this shift was the later tendency to view its major ally's colonial preference as the central object to be affected by the revival of non discrimination, particularly as this position became increasingly defensive on the question of U.S. trade barriers.

1.3.2 The rise of the colonial preference issue

In earlier times Britain's Imperial preference had been cited by Americans as a best indicator of an open door policy. However, the Commonwealth system became a point of contention as preferences were expanded by the Ottawa Agreements of 1932 in response to the economic depression. As Cordell Hull has been singly identified with the American position on the resurrection of the MFN principle, his well-cited positions on the evils of the Commonwealth forged the linkage between the MFN principle and the termination of this particular preference system. According to Gardner,

> "(T)he climax of this campaign against Imperial Preference came with Hull's appointment as Secretary of State. American producers, beset by the Great Depression, were looking anxiously to foreign markets. In the midst of their difficulties they were met with the Ottawa Agreements, which not only increased the preferences granted to Britain by the Empire but inaugurated a comprehensive system of preferences in favour of the Empire by the United Kingdom."[20]

That the Commonwealth became the central issue is clear if one examines the amendments introduced by the Ottawa Agreements with which Hull was so intensely concerned. H. P. Whidden described the main changes implemented.

> "(I)n return for new or increased preferences in the Dominions on British products, mostly manufactured goods, Britain bound itself to levy duties on foreign (non-empire) imports ... to control by quotas the purchase of meats ...; not to reduce below

---

[19]   The rationale was twofold, first, the preservation of special economic ties between the members of the British Commonwealth, and second, the practical need to obtain an increase in British exports after the war to make up for the loss of foreign exchange receipts caused by war time losses. R. Gardner, Ibid.

[20]   To Hull, these agreements, constituted, "the greatest injury, in a commercial way, that has been inflicted on this country since I have been in public life". R. Gardner, Ibid., at p. 19, citing Congressional House Ways and Means testimony, Hearings on H.J. Res. 407, 76th Congress., 1st session, 1940, Vol. i, p. 38. "The campaign against discrimination concentrated with particular intensity on preferential practices in the British Empire". R. Gardner, Ibid., at p. 18.

10 percent the recently imposed British duties on foreign commodities; and to continue the duty-free admission of many products from the Dominions."[21]

Accordingly, the changes,

"...have constituted a substantial addition to the network of trade barriers restricting the free movement of international commerce, and, if maintained in the postwar period, would provide a serious obstacle to the restoration of multilateral trade based on equality of treatment ..." Ottawa therefore, "... marked the passing of the open door in virtually all of the world dependencies ..."[22]

1.3.3   *The distinction between protectionism and preference*

Although the main change implemented at Ottawa was to raise protection against third-country goods, detrimental enough from the U.S. view, there was perceived to be a difference between its own prohibitive levels of protection and the use of preferences in international trade as exhibited by the Commonwealth after Ottawa. Culbertson offered an explanation in 1925 of the difference between preference and protection.

"Protection of the home market for the benefit of national industries is an expression of nationalism. Its object is to diversify a nation's economic life and to afford varied opportunities for the application of the genius of a people (citing Alexander Hamilton's *Report on Manufacturers*, 1791). It is in no sense aggressive ... Preference, on the other hand, is an expression of modern imperialism. In contrast with the policy of protection it is aggressive. In its extreme form as found in the French policy of assimilation, it seeks to extend to new areas (e.g., Indo-China) the control of the eco-

---

[21]   Howard P. Whidden, *Preferences and Discriminations in International Trade*, Committee on International Policy, Carnegie Endowment for International Peace, New York, 1945, pp. 5-30, reprinted in A.J. Kress, Supra note 8 at pp. 21-22. "In most cases the United Kingdom was one of the parties to the arrangement, and not all Commonwealth countries granted all other Commonwealth countries preferences". Kenneth W. Dam, **The GATT: Law and International Economic Organization**, The University of Chicago Press, 1970, (Midway Reprint, 1977), p. 42.

[22]   H.P Whidden, Ibid., at p. 19. The effect of Ottawa on U.S. trade during the thirties, and therefore its direct domestic impact upon economic interests in the post war plan was also noted by him, "That the bilateral trend of trade during the thirties was aggravated by the Ottawa Agreements is suggested, however, by the fact that British imports from the United States continued to decline throughout the decade while imports from the dominions and colonies continued to increase". Culbertson categorized the system previous to Ottawa as "open door". William S. Culbertson, **International Economic Policies**, D. Appleton, New York, 1925, p. 303, reprinted in Kress, Supra note 8 at pp. 270-275.

nomic system of the country which happens to have the political power to impose the preferential conditions ..."[23]

While Culbertson demonstrated a certain premonition for the later U.S.-British dispute, he also appeared to recognise the political purpose for preferences where they might serve to extend the control of one state's economic system over that of another. The later dispute, at least from the U.S. view, would emphasise more the resulting exclusionary effects of such an extension.[24]

1.3.4   *The Atlantic Charter debate (1941)*

The question of reintroducing nondiscrimination to international trade came to the centre of the U.S.-British relationship in what Gardner cited as "the first definition of multilateralism", as found in the August 1941 Atlantic Charter, the joint declaration of principles enunciated by President Roosevelt and Prime Minister Churchill.[25]

The issue over the economic portion of the text for the proposed declaration concerned the use of the phrase, "access without discrimination on equal terms". This provision was drafted by Sumner Welles who represented Cordell Hull and the Department of State in the negotiations. While his text was a response to Churchill's initial draft proposal, the Welles formulation was viewed with outright concern by the British for its implications for the 1932 Ottawa convention and the Commonwealth preference system. Churchill's counter-proposal was to drop the explicit reference to discrimination and to tie the obligation subject to the phrase, "with due respect for their existing obligations". Cordell Hull's recorded reaction to the Atlantic Charter provision indicates the importance he attached to this question on behalf of the State Department,

---

[23]   "(U)nfortunately, these two policies are often treated by some British writers and publicists as inseparable and equally entitled to praise or blame". W.S. Culbertson, Ibid., at pp. 185-186, also quoted in Gardner, Supra note 14 at p. 18.

[24]   "An exclusive reciprocity agreement between South Africa and Australia, for example, is open to the same objection as an exclusive reciprocity agreement between the United States and France. Excluded nations cannot be expected to accept the fiction of empire in justification of their exclusion from extensive areas of the earth's surface. British control of large areas has been tolerated because of a liberal commercial policy, and careful students of international relations have watched with much concern the growth of imperial preference". W.S. Culbertson, Ibid., at p. 192. Thus, for Culbertson, there was no distinction where exclusionary effects were present.

[25]   Gardner referred to the "second" expression of MFN as that provided in Article VII of the Mutual Aid Agreements of 1942 negotiated between the United States and Great Britain, as "directed ... to the elimination of all forms of discriminatory treatment in international commerce, and to the reduction of tariffs and other trade barriers". See generally, Gardner, Supra note 14 at pp. 54-68.

"... since it meant that Britain would continue to retain her Empire tariff preferences against which I had been fighting for eight years. Mr. Churchill had insisted on this qualification; Welles had argued for a stronger declaration ... the President gave in."[26]

However, Welles recollected a somewhat different view in that he made his case on a common theme intended to appeal to both the parties. This took aim at the predatory and political aspects of commercial policy practices from the inter-war years.

"I said ... that it seemed to be imperative that we try to agree now upon the policy of constructive sanity in world economics as a fundamental factor in the creation of a new and better world and that except through an agreement upon such a policy by our two governments there would be no hindrance whatsoever to the continuation later of the present German policies of utilizing trade and financial policies in order to achieve political ends."[27]

This recollection may be the last documented notation from an American policy maker connecting non-discrimination to inter war economic nationalism. As the MFN clause evolved through preparations of the Mutual Aid Agreements and onto the stage of the ITO preparatory work through Geneva in 1947, U.S. policy appears from all documentation available to have became solely oriented upon extinguishing the British Commonwealth preference.

1.3.5   The U.S. policy context

If there was a change in policy orientation, it could have been attributable to the domestic political situation in the United States. As the U.S. came out of the war, the Truman Administration confronted a new protectionist Republican Congress. Non-discrimination continued at the centre of the policy, but the Administration's

---

26   Cordell Hull, **The Memoirs of Cordell Hull,** Macmillan, New York, 1948, pp. 975-976.

27   "I said that it was not a question of phraseology, but that it was a vital principle which was involved. I said that if the British and the United States governments could not agree to do everything within their power to further after the termination of the present war, a restoration of free and liberal trade policies, they might as well throw in the sponge and realize that one of the greatest factors in creating the present tragic situation in the world was going to be permitted to continue unchecked in the postwar world ..." R. Gardner, Supra note 14 at p. 45, quoting from Sumner Welles, **Where are we Heading?,** London, 1947, pp. 13-14. The final agreed upon clause read as follows: "with due respect for their existing obligations, to further the enjoyment by all States, great or small, victor or vanquished, of access, on equal terms, to the trade and to the raw materials of the world which are needed for their economic prosperity ..." R. Gardner, Ibid., at p. 46. To contrast, the earlier Welles draft read, "Fourth, they will strive to promote mutually advantageous economic relations between them through the elimination of any discrimination in either the United States of America or in the United Kingdom against the importation of any product originating in the other country; and they will endeavour to further the enjoyment by all peoples of access on equal terms to the markets and to the raw materials which are needed for their economic prosperity." Ibid., at pp. 43-44.

argument for it in the Congress necessarily shifted to reflect the demands of American economic interests, particularly as they were seen to be excluded from British markets. As far as trade flows were concerned, the British system certainly presented greater barriers for the Americans than the far-away markets of middle Europe. Whatever injuries had been promulgated by the Axis policies were rendered less important over time as these countries were militarily defeated in any event. Likewise, the new threat of state socialism, the "new economic nationalism" as Heilperin called it, was only beginning to emerge as a concern in the formulation of the multilateral policy.

Therefore, while non-discrimination remained at the centre of U.S. policy, its only possible basis for retaining post-war domestic support was for the administration to link the policy to the trading gains derivable by its acceptance and implementation. This appeal would have to be based on the exclusionary effects of the British Commonwealth system, as the new provisions would ultimately challenge this system.

Near the end of the process of seeking legislative endorsement for the MFN principle, the emphasis on dismantling the Commonwealth system became a conditional requirement for Congressional support of the ITO process itself. Not so ironically, linkage between MFN and the Commonwealth also was a significant factor in the loss of support in the Congress for the process in Geneva. This was demonstrated by the Administration's literal guarantee to Congress that U.S. negotiators would deal a fatal blow to the Commonwealth preference at the negotiations in Geneva. If this blow could not be delivered, the Administration admitted in open Congressional testimony that there would be little point in supporting the (resulting) ITO Charter. Since ultimately the British did not yield their position, there was no retreat position for the Administration to stand upon other than to admit that the Charter negotiations had failed in their expressed purpose.[28]

1.3.6   Conclusion on the Commonwealth Preference

As a U.S. and British agreement was essential to forming a post-war multilateral trading institution, the rift between them over the status of the Commonwealth preference increasingly undermined their common interest in support of it. The shift of emphasis as the debate moved into the ITO negotiation phase was however unfortunate in another respect, as the justification for an MFN provision tended over time to only reflect the circumstances of this well-documented debate. It is not

---

[28]   R. Gardner, Ibid., pp. 349-350. Although Gardner was not attempting to treat the same issue on point. For his account, there is absent any indication from the domestic political debate a suggestion that the purpose of the clause would be to serve a larger political goal of re-instituting fair play in the trading system or an attempt to constrain the political use of commercial policy. While such an opinion might have well been retained by the planners, the public domestic argument for the principle appears to have been purely a matter of what we would now refer to as the "market access" issue.

so difficult to understand why commentators since have tended to equate the purpose of the principle only with the trade objectives of GATT parties in seeking the expansion of world trade. A conception of GATT MFN as it evolved can be drawn from the latter stages of this history in isolation to suggest that the principle was intended to serve GATT parties as a market-access guarantee. The result is that the MFN principle is more often than not attributed with mercantilist intent.

This is in contrast with a more expansive role for the principle as it would function to underpin a multilateral trade system. Since such a system was intended to eliminate bilateral and preferential sub-systems, this conception of the principle becomes relevant when the attempt is made to isolate the relationship between the final MFN clause and the exceptions that would eventually be settled for certain preferential exchanges. Thus, depending upon one's view of the purpose of MFN, the regional exceptions provided in the later GATT Article XXIV provisions could have served to permit a great number of preferential systems, as long as they did not result in producing exclusionary effects as to the trade of other parties. Alternatively, the provisions could have been dedicated to curtailing the number of such exchanges outright so that the MFN principle itself would retain its greatest scope of application to the trade of all the members.

1.4   Categorising inter-war preferential systems

The Commonwealth preference was not the only inter-war system to be affected by an emerging non- discrimination clause, as certain other preferential exceptions to MFN were also a part of common practice. A determination on how to treat these other systems was also at issue in resolving which preference practices would be either discouraged or endorsed by the MFN clause.[29]

1.4.1   *Whidden's preferential categories*

In attempting to reconcile an emerging multilateral MFN principle with existing regional systems, Whidden made a 1945 survey of preferential systems in use during the inter-war period and then added an assessment as to which systems should be tolerated to derogate from MFN.[30] He designated these following categories.

---

[29] Since MFN was contained as a provision in a large number of bilateral trade agreements, legal analysis would relate to describing those conditions by which MFN could, or could not, be required to be exacted when a trade agreement party extended a preference to a third territory.

[30] The question being, for which types of arrangements should outsiders be willing to forego a claim for equitable treatment in regard to their trade? H.P. Whidden, *Preferences and Discriminations in International Trade*, Committee on International Policy, Carnegie Endowment for International Peace, New York, 1945, pp. 5-30, reprinted in A.J. Kress, Supra note 8.

Frontier traffic. The U.S. and most other trading countries commonly recognised a 10 mile zone of exception along a border area, where to deny the exception would cause hardship for border commerce. A simple example would be where a customs frontier passes through a city.[31]

Customs unions, recognising the standard U.S. practice in its bilateral trade agreements to acknowledge exceptions in respect to advantages accorded in a customs union to which either signatory was (or would thereafter) be a party. MFN would then be accorded to the new formed territory.

Tariff assimilations in which the metropolitan area and its colonies are to be treated as a single unit. Whidden's example was the French system of incorporating its colonies, particularly Madagascar, Guadaloupe, Martinique and Indochina.[32]

Colonial Preference.[33]

Regional preferences and low tariff clubs. Whidden distinguished this group from the category of colonial preferences by surveying in detail a number of inter-war declarations made in Europe and various arrangements formed in Latin America.

In attempting to isolate the British and U.S. attitude toward such arrangements, he concluded that no consistent practice appeared to evolve in either recognising or refusing to recognise the granted preferences as exceptions to the MFN clauses. However, he did determine that there was a tendency to endorse arrangements when the countries concerned had some former historical relationship which was more close in the past then during the present.[34] In the inter-war period, three other examples were noted by Whidden wherein a number of countries attempted to

---

[31] H.P. Whidden, Ibid., p. 9.

[32] Whidden noted the criticism of Haight who described such systems as essentially preferential in diverting the regular flow of international trade to the colonies in favour of the metropolitan area. H.P. Whidden, Ibid., citing, F.A. Haight, *A History of French Commercial Policies*, Macmillan, New York, 1941, p. 248. The cornerstone of the criticism is in the isolation of the colony from the general flow of international commerce which would otherwise be competitive with the metropolitan area producers.

[33] As discussed in the previous section.

[34] H.P. Whidden, Supra note 30, at pp. 14-15. For European arrangements, he concentrated on the 1930 Oslo convention and the 1934 Baltic arrangement. A best example recognised by both powers was the Baltic group which exchanged preferential tariff concessions between 1924 and 1932. "In this case the great powers were willing to accept the exemption from most-favoured-nation treatment in commercial treaties signed by members of a group of countries which had been long associated historically through ethnic, economic or political ties". Along similar lines the U.S. recognised exchanged preferences as exceptions to MFN in its 1937 Agreement with Czechoslovakia in regard to the Danubian area clause for preferential arrangements in agriculture products.

create a conventional formula for reducing trade barriers and where other parties would recognise these preferences without invoking MFN. As also recounted by Jacob Viner, these efforts generally grew out of the Geneva Economic Conference of 1927 and attempted to adhere to the principle contained in the 1929 report of the Economic Committee of the League of Nations. This, "recommended the granting of exceptions to the most-favoured-nation clause in the case of multilateral conventions of a general character".[35]

1.4.2 Viner's preferential categories

As an aspect of his study of customs unions published in 1950, Jacob Viner also reviewed the types of preferential systems employed by territories in the inter-war years. He provided detailed discussion of the relation between these preferences and the MFN principle as it was then applied in pre-existing bilateral agreements and as later included in the draft Havana Charter for the ITO. Viner was primarily concerned with customs unions and his thesis remains widely cited for the proposition that economic considerations do not support a blanket exception from MFN for customs unions. We do not treat this aspect of his work here at this time. Rather, Viner's work also has value for its description of the origins of certain preferential systems and particularly how the traditional treatment of customs unions, by receiving an exemption from MFN, should also be treated by the later exception provided for free-trade areas.

As he explained, since a customs union by definition provides for the elimination of tariffs between its members, the question of compatibility with the MFN clause must always arise.[36]

> "It came to be widely accepted, however, that the most-favored nation obligation did not cover the commercial relations inter se of members of a customs union, since by virtue of such union they had become for tariff purposes, even if for no other purpose, a single entity in the relations with outside states."[37]

Although he cited several cases where the *completeness* of a formation was challenged or challengeable as it was portrayed as a customs union, it was generally ac-

---

[35] H.P. Whidden, Ibid., at pp. 13-14, also indicating that the Oslo format was eventually doomed by the disagreement resulting from the Ottawa Conference of 1932 amending the Commonwealth system preferences and the 1931 protective British Tariff.

[36] Jacob Viner employed a definition of customs unions that included the following: 1) the complete elimination of tariffs as between the member territories; 2) the establishment of a uniform tariff on imports from outside the union; and 3) an apportionment of customs revenue between the members. J. Viner, Supra note 4, p. 5, and citations therein.

[37] J. Viner, Ibid., at p. 6.

cepted in the practice between nations that territory formations would not invoke the MFN clause. From this practice,

> "(T)he fact that customs union was generally regarded as compatible with most-fa-vored-nation had the result that customs union was promoted whereas otherwise some other form of preferential arrangement would have been chosen."[38]

This would of course lead to a discussion of these other forms of preferential agreements and the manner in which they were treated according to MFN clauses. Viner indicated that a desire to escape the rigours of MFN, together with an unwill-ingness to complete full customs unions, led parties to, "establish the propriety of other types of relaxations of, or exceptions from, the most-favored-nation rule."[39]

He determined that there were three categories of preferences applicable to the inter-war period. These included the Imperial Preference characterised by *political* ties; regional agreements as characterised by *propinquity*; and plurilateral agree-ments characterised by the number of participants.[40] As to each, Imperial Prefer-ence developed as an MFN exception to the extent that territories were subject to common sovereignty. In this, he noted that some authors included the concept of tariff assimilation, whereby, "the rates of duty of the tariff of the mother country are enforced also in the colony, the trade between these two units being free ...".[41] Viner did not fully equate the two categories, noting that,

> "(F)or the most part, however, imperial preferences takes other forms than tariff as-similation. They are in some cases the gradual product of several centuries of evolu-tion, and even within an empire the forms and degrees of preferences vary from col-ony to colony".[42]

Viner separately categorised "regional agreements", whereby a trade agreement would provide for MFN exemptions for specified countries. However, as such pref-erences would relate to MFN,

---

[38]   J. Viner, Ibid., at p. 14.

[39]   A point later applied in the principle text to the role of free-trade areas. J. Viner, Ibid., at p. 15.

[40]   J. Viner, Ibid, at p. 15. A thesaurus provides the following substitutes for "propinquity": near-ness, closeness, contiguity. Thus, this category appears to be most closely associated with a modern characterisation of "regional" trade agreements.

[41]   Citing as examples, the case of France and some of its colonies, the United States and Puerto Rico, and of Japan and Formosa. "From the economic point of view there is little or no difference be-tween tariff assimilation and a customs union, the chief difference being that when tariff assimilation is introduced within an empire, it is invariably imposed by the mother country without having to be 'ne-gotiated', and the tariff is framed to suit the needs and wishes of the mother country's economy with-out much, if any, reference to the interests or wishes of the colonies". J. Viner, Ibid., at pp. 16-17.

[42]   His final comment on the relationship between the two indicated that tariff assimilation can be seen as a most severe form of colonial preference, a point he believes was lost on American legislation which permitted sanctions against colonial preferences, but not tariff assimilation. He attributes this to the U.S. bias in favour of customs unions. J. Viner, Ibid., p. 17.

"(T)he inclusion of such clauses frequently reflected little more than a sentimental contemplation of the desirability in the abstract of closer economic relations with countries with which there were - or it was pleasant to think that there were, or could be developed - specially close ties of sentiment and interest arising out of ethnological, or cultural, or historical political affiliations."[43]

A final category of plurilateral agreements related to the League of Nations Economic Committee report of 1929, as mentioned above, which recommended the use of plurilateral tariff cutting conventions in order to improve the world economic situation. In their final form, such conferences would be open in principle to the adhesion of other interested states on the basis of reciprocal exchanges.[44]

1.5   Chapter Conclusion

In calling for the Atlantic joint declaration in 1941, Gardner reported that President Roosevelt declared that the pronouncement was necessary to send a signal to both potential victors and the vanquished that post-war principles would not be a replay of the Versailles Treaty, that there was hope that the cycle could be broken. In this sense, the decision to seek a joint statement in the first instance related closely to a reflection of the parallel period of 1916-1917.[45] The leading press in England was also cited in viewing the Charter's declaration in this broader context. Thus, the Charter was said to forecast, "an integrated world economy and not a series of independent and mutually exclusive systems".[46]

Within the larger frame of international economic relations, these statements appear to consistently reflect a larger goal sought to be achieved. Perhaps Richard Gardner also sensed the loss of the identity of this greater objective in concluding that it was rather unfortunate that an issue like Imperial preference was raised in

---

[43] J. Viner, Ibid., p. 19, citing for example the "Balkan", "Nordic" or "Central American" arrangements.

[44] League of Nations, Monetary and Economic Conference, Draft Agenda, Geneva, 1933, cited in J. Viner, Ibid., note 30 at p. 34. "In the plurilateral clause, on the other hand, the emphasis, express or implied, is always on the nonexclusiveness of the arrangement and on the substantial number of countries contemplated as members of a prospective arrangement. J. Viner, Ibid., at p. 22. Whidden varies from this as he bundled both the plurilateral and regional categories together. Viner's treatment presents greater legal accuracy if one considers that a plurilateral low tariff club would be open to nonmembers on the basis of reciprocity, while a regional agreement would not. A modern term "open regionalism" appears to be a contemporary application of the concept of a low tariff club.

[45] "No doubt he remembered the unfortunate experience of Woodrow Wilson, who had drafted a unilateral statement of American war aims during the first world war in ignorance of the secret treaties already concluded between America's allies." R. Gardner, Supra note 14 at p. 41.

[46] "The considerable number of people in this country who are already planning our post-war trade in terms of barter, bilateralism, trade zones, clearings, exchange control, and by the concepts of the 'between wars' era must begin at once to recast their ideas". R. Gardner, Ibid., at p. 50, citing the Banker and News Chronicle respectively.

direct form, and that "the controversy about it became such a celebrated part of the history of the Atlantic Conference".[47] For the purposes of understanding MFN's later application to preferential systems, it may also have been unfortunate that the imperial preference debate may have narrowed an appreciation of what the non-discrimination clause sought to achieve.

---

[47] R. Gardner, Ibid., at p. 53.

Chapter 2
ITO NEGOTIATIONS FOR A REGIONAL EXCEPTION

"... the principal objective in the drafting of the customs union and free-trade area provisions became to tie down, in the most precise legal language possible, the conditions that such regional groupings would have to fulfil in order to escape prohibition under the most-favoured nation clause as preferential arrangements ..." *Kenneth Dam, (1970).*

2.1   Introduction

This chapter relates the GATT MFN obligation to the GATT Article XXIV exception provided for free-trade areas. As such, it is not intended to be a discussion of all of the legal elements presented by the exception Article.

As Viner noted, complete regional formations in the form of customs unions territories had long received exemption from the MFN principle in bilateral arrangements. This treaty practice was carried forward before Geneva and was retained through the Havana Conference and the final ITO Charter. Partially preferential systems, whether they be Imperial/colonial structures or otherwise, were sought to be challenged by the emerging MFN principle. We will see that Havana parties also sought to retain certain prerogatives for future preferential agreements between developing countries. Here it is documented that this was a significant commercial policy issue in Havana, and one that certainly gave rise to a consideration for the inclusion of a free-trade area exception, and in the context of complementing the provisions that were also settled for other economic development and reconstruction preferences. Thus, the debate over which preference systems would be permitted to continue after MFN came into force, and which new systems would be permitted to be established, was essentially a negotiation over the scope of application of the new MFN provision itself. The result in Havana evidenced a legal and institutional hierarchy for Members to engage future preferences, with differing levels of organisational oversight to be exercised, depending upon the degree of preferences exchanged and the purposes for which they were to be enacted. The chapter and Part concludes with an overview of the Article XXIV provisions as finally incorporated into the GATT.

Neither Whidden nor Viner referred to any system under the terminology of a "free-trade area", and one is left to determine which systems described by them, if any, might have been contemplated by later drafters in providing a GATT MFN exception for free-trade areas. To this, the viewpoint of each author should be taken into account. Whidden's purpose was to outline the pre-existing arrangements and then to argue that most of them should not be granted an MFN exemption. Viner's purpose was to build an economic argument that customs unions were not *per se* positive for world welfare as a whole and therefore should not receive a *de jure* MFN exception on definitional criteria alone. As such, he did not pass any explicit judgement on the qualifications of lower-order systems as to the emerging require- ments. However, he did maintain an overall conclusion that the draft Havana Char- ter had accorded too many exceptions from MFN for regional agreements on too many counts. He accepted as only partially valid the claim that the Charter would have serious impact on the future course of preferential systems.[1] Whidden's more strict conclusions were similar to what was later identified as the U.S. State depart- ment proposals for exceptions to MFN in the Geneva negotiations as,

"It seems clear that the principle of equality of treatment would involve the elimina- tion of trade preferences between neighbouring countries where they do not automat- ically lead to complete customs unions."[2]

While Whidden contemplated a possible role for preferential systems in a post-war Western European Union, he favoured only complete customs union formations, which he described as advancing a more sound economic justification. In this, Whidden anticipated the economic objections to any completed preference system in addressing a London Economist editorial of March of 1944. This claimed that damage to outsiders was higher in a customs union than in a regional arrangement, since "discrimination against outsiders reaches its limit in the former". From

---

[1]   Jacob Viner, **The Customs Union Issue**, Carnegie Endowment, 1950, p. 120. He referred to MFN exceptions for partial customs unions (absent a requirement for revenue allocations and treatment of non-origin products), free trade areas, and regional agreements in the interest of economic develop- ment, as per Article 15 of the Charter, titled "Preferential Agreements for Economic Development and Reconstruction". In the absence of this Article, the regional possibilities would include only customs unions, free-trade areas, interim agreements leading to them, and the 2/3 waiver provisions of the Gen- eral Agreement.

[2]   H.P. Whidden, *Preferences and Discriminations in International Trade*, Committee on Interna- tional Policy, Carnegie Endowment for International Peace, New York, 1945, pp. 5-30, reprinted in the **Economics of Diplomacy**, Ed. A.J. Kress, Georgetown University, Washington, 1949, at p. 18; and cit- ing, Haberler, G., **The Political Economy of Regional or Continental Blocks** (Ed. Seymour E. Har- ris), McGraw Hill, New York, 1943. He thereby proposed that, aside from customs unions, that an in- ternational commercial policy organisation would apply the following minimum criteria where neces- sary to permit preferential arrangements on a temporary basis and in exceptional cases: to be effected by duty reductions and not by increases in duties to outsiders; that margins of preference not to be bound (no prejudice to reduction of duties to outsiders); that preferences be confined to important sup- ply commodities; that preferences be designed to achieve more efficient production and better balanced economies.

Whidden's view, a customs union was seen to benefit outsiders in regard to its increasing purchasing power obtained through more efficient production.[3]

2.2   Havana provisions for future preference systems

The U.S. and British proposals for the most-favoured nation clause followed the lines of agreement that had been settled between them in preparation for the UN Conference on Trade and Employment (1946).[4] This compromise provided for a standstill for listed annexed preferences, including the Commonwealth preferences, as provided and finally incorporated into GATT Article I:2.[5] All future preferences within the annexed systems would be subject to MFN. In addition, the U.S. submitted draft proposals for what would later become GATT Article XXIV. These clauses followed the pattern established according to its own bilateral MFN agreements formed according to the U.S. Reciprocal Trade Agreements Act. As such, the U.S. opening position recognised a granted exception from MFN for customs union territory formations.[6]

Both Dam and Jackson stated that a primary goal which the United States sought to accomplish in the ITO Charter and the GATT was the dismantling of trading preferences and preferential systems, particularly the Commonwealth system established by the 1932 Ottawa arrangement.[7] Viner suggested that the American goals were multiple: to obtain rehabilitation of the MFN principle, to promote the reduction of tariffs, to eliminate intra-imperial preferences via a multilateral framework, and to renounce official trade barriers other than duties.[8] He suggested that these goals were well reflected in the initial drafts. While certain existing preferences were listed and acknowledged as permitted exceptions to the general MFN rule

---

3   H.P. Whidden, Ibid., p. 18, a point challenged on an economic basis by Viner in his 1950 contribution. However, Viner did not argue a broader MFN exception for partial regional preferences, indicating generally throughout his treatise that the Havana Charter had already accorded too many loopholes for MFN. An open membership concept for preferential systems, such as contained in the Montevideo agreement, was also not considered by Whidden as possibly consistent with MFN, and later U.S. proposals did not include any exception for open-reciprocity agreements.

4   The following four documents may be cited in this chapter: 1) the original American draft (September 1946) "Suggested Charter for an International Trade Organization of the United Nations"; 2) draft charter revised at the London meeting of the preparatory committee of the International Conference on Trade and Employment, October-November, 1946, "London Draft, 1946"; 3) further revised by the Committee to the Conference, April-August 1947 in Geneva, "Geneva Draft, 1947"; and 4) Charter as revised in Havana, November 1947 - March 1948, "Havana Charter".

5   Karin Kock, **International Trade Policy and the GATT, 1947-1967**, Almqvist & Wiksell, Stockholm, 1969, p. 114. In the Havana Charter, The MFN clause was titled under chapter IV as Article 16.

6   Kenneth W. Dam, **The GATT: Law and International Economic Organization**, The University of Chicago Press, 1970, (Midway Reprint, 1977), p. 274.

7   K. Dam, Ibid., at p. 42; John H. Jackson, **World Trade Law and the Law of GATT**, the Mitchie Company, Charlottesville, Virginia, 1969, p. 577.

8   J. Viner, Supra note 1 at p. 110.

of Article I of the GATT, the original Geneva Final Act did not acknowledge the possible exception from MFN for any regional arrangements other than those to facilitate frontier traffic or for customs unions. As according to Dam, the U.S. proposals constituted only a short paragraph permitting a customs union exception.[9] Jackson likely caught the appropriate flavour of the exception overall as intended by the U.S. drafters. As he put it, "... *even* the United States recognized the legitimacy of an exception for customs unions".[10]

A significant exception to this viewpoint at this point in time in the drafting would have been the paragraph included in the London Draft Charter (1946), providing for a 2/3 majority vote, whereby, "(T)he members recognize that there may in exceptional circumstances be justification for new preferential arrangements requiring an exception to the provisions of (the chapter dealing with customs unions)". According to Viner, as the Geneva Draft (1947) introduced the concept of interim agreements leading to customs unions, a sufficient degree of flexibility was obtained by those added provisions (presumably), and the paragraph as quoted was dropped from the customs union chapter. It did however later emerge in a modified and far more comprehensive form in a new Havana Charter chapter dealing with "Economic Development".[11] This chapter Article should also be considered for any light it can shed on developments in the customs union chapter, especially for its later provisions regarding free-trade areas. The Development Article also permitted preferences and was a subject of debate in regard to the overall compromise formed regarding the role of future preferences and the MFN obligation.

2.2.1   *Havana Charter, Chapter III, Article 15: Economic Development and Reconstruction*

The proposal for the Geneva Draft (1947) was the first to provide a chapter on Economic Development. This retained the requirement of a majority 2/3 vote for approval of,

> "preferential arrangements between two or more countries, not contemplating a customs union, in the interest of the programmes of economic development or reconstruction of one or more such countries".[12]

---

[9]   K. Dam, Supra note 6 at p. 274.
[10] J. Jackson, Supra note 7 at p. 577, italics added.
[11] J. Viner, Supra note 1 at p. 115, his note 21.
[12] J. Viner, Ibid., at p. 116. Free-trade areas were not yet introduced to the customs union chapter until the later Havana Draft. Thus, the paragraph quoted refers only to customs unions.

This Article was expanded in the Havana Draft, Article 15, titled "Preferential Agreements for Economic Development and Reconstruction".[13] While retaining the concept of pre-approval by a 2/3's voting procedure as above, a new section was added that provided the possibility for self-declaratory preference. This was to be available to contiguous territories or those belonging to the same "economic region"; and as necessary,

> "to ensure a sound and adequate market for a particular industry or branch of agriculture which is being, or is to be, created or reconstructed or substantially developed or substantially modernized".[14]

Neither reciprocity nor reduction to zero-duty levels was required. However, a provision was made for the adherence of other members that would also be able to qualify as parties to the preference agreement and the preferences permitted were not intended to exceed ten years. Article 15 did not specify that the parties to such preferences were required to be least or lesser developed countries, although the conditions of the preference activities permitted can be said to resemble an infant industry type of justification and the title of the Article refers to development. Although the two-thirds voting provisions did not apply, organisational control was not abandoned for the contiguous-party exception in Article 15:4, as the exception continued to be subject to the provisions of paragraphs 5 and 6 of the Article. Paragraph 5 indicated that the Organisation may,

> "as a condition of its approval, require a reduction in an unbound most-favoured-nation rate of duty proposed by the Member in respect of any product so covered, if in the light of the representations of any affected Member it considers that rate excessive".[15]

---

[13] "The Members recognize that special circumstances, including the need for economic development or reconstruction, may justify new preferential agreements between two or more countries in the interest of the programmes of economic development or reconstruction of one or more of them". Proposed redraft, Article 15:1, E/CONF.2/C.8/26, 17 March 1948. According to the interpretive note, "The Organization need not interpret the term 'economic region' to require close geographical proximity if it is satisfied that a sufficient degree of economic integration exists between the countries concerned". Ibid., Ad Article 15. According to Hudec, Article 15 was "unacceptable" to the United States when later attempt was made to include it in the GATT. Robert Hudec, **The GATT Legal system and World Trade Diplomacy** (2d. ed.), Butterworth, 1990, at p. 56, note 20.

[14] Havana Charter (1948), Article 15:4, (a)-(f). Other conditions are stated in the Article which are not mentioned here.

[15] E/CONF.2/C.8/26, Supra note 13 at p. 2.

2.2.2   *Havana's resulting hierarchy of preferences*

The apparent intended effect of the self-declaratory provisions of the Article was
to permit an industry or agriculture sector to be expanded between contiguous parties or economically integrated parties, assumedly in order to provide for an expanded market within some larger regional context. It does not appear that this portion of the Article contemplated granting authority for preferential systems in the
larger sense of regional integration, but rather to accommodate the special items
for a limited period of time as beneficial between developing countries, or at least
economically or geographically related parties. Thus, Article 15 would not be seen
as an overlapping provision with the later free-trade area exception, at least where
the latter would contemplate a more complete and permanent system of exchanges
by the parties.

What is also observed is that both sections dealt with preferences and both were
intended to become provisions of the Charter in its final form. One should therefore consider that the provisions of the two Articles were intended to be complementary in that they would not overlap in coverage but would be used to address
distinct situations. Therefore, it may be concluded that Article 15 was viewed as a
means of providing limited preferences between developing countries while the inclusion of a free-trade area exception was intended to service the notion of more
complete regional entities. As developed in some detail below, an important distinction between the two Articles as they emerged from Havana was that Article 15
retained the requirement of a waiver from MFN to be approved by a 2/3 vote of the
Charter Members, except for these contiguous sector preferences as noted. For regional groupings meeting the substantially-all trade definition in the customs union chapter, a less rigorous approval process was established, but with the consideration that a consensus of the Members could always impose modifications upon
an agreement. Thus, there appeared to emerge overall a type of hierarchy of institutional oversight and control for the preferential systems. The most complete systems to be contemplated provided for the lowest degree of voting control as prior
authorisation was not required, but these formations imposed the strictest conditions upon coverage. The Economic Development and Reconstruction partial preferences required pre-approval by two-thirds of the Members present. The least
complete exchanges also required no voting authorisation, but these exchanges
could not be closed to other qualifying Members and preferences exchanged were
to be temporary in nature.

2.2.3   *The Havana debate regarding future preferences*

As further recounted by Jackson, the provisions for free-trade areas and the other
provisions of what we now understand as Article XXIV were included in the Havana (1948) ITO Charter as Article 44 of Part IV, titled Commercial Policy. These

provisions replaced the earlier Geneva Charter (1947) text by a special protocol.[16] According to Haight, the new text, including for the first time the provisions for the free-trade area exception, was recommended by the subcommittee and was approved without any substantive debate.[17]

However, prior to the referral of the full committee to the subcommittee, an extensive discussion concerning the role of future preferential systems in relation to the MFN clause was held in Havana. These reported discussions by the Commercial Policy Committee (Committee III) extended over four meetings held in early December of 1947. Provided under the title of a "General Discussion" of Chapter IV (Commercial Policy), most of this commentary was dedicated to recording the positions of the parties regarding the unconditional MFN clause (Article 16) together with its negotiated standstill provisions for annexed (pre-existing) preferential systems. The issue raised was the manner in which these Geneva provisions had provided for a standstill for the existing preferential arrangements, but subjected future regional arrangements to a voting approval. Thus, at the centre of discussion was the relationship between the MFN Article on the one hand, and the development preferences provided by Article 15 and the customs union Article (Article 42) on the other.[18]

In reviewing the country-representative comments made during these meetings, it is apparent that many Havana parties were unsettled by the MFN compromise that had been reached at Geneva. Particularly controversial for the members was whether future preferences should be encouraged or discouraged, and if permitted, whether they should be subject to voting pre-approval by the organisation. This difficulty applied to both preferences that could be characterised as either "development" or "regional" in orientation. Thus, from the first meeting, the Syrian representative indicated the country's support for most-favoured nation treatment,

> "...but pointed out that exceptions had been admitted which would permit the continuation of existing preferential arrangements representing vested interests. However, there were certain countries within the same economic area, having traditional relationships which should not be overlooked even though these had not been formalized. His delegation had submitted amendments, both in Geneva and here,

---

16 J. Jackson, Supra note 7 at p. 578, citing at note 14, "Special Protocol Relating to Article XXIV of the GATT", 1948 (Agreement No. 7 in App. C). However, during the Havana process, the Article was referred to as Article 42, "Territorial Application of Chapter IV, Frontier Traffic and Customs Unions", rather than Article 44, its numbered Article in the final Havana Charter. This reflected the Charter's division of Article 42 into three separate Articles.

17 F.A. Haight, *Customs Unions and Free Trade Areas Under GATT: A Reappraisal*, Journal of World Trade Law, V. 6, No. 4, 1972, pp. 391-404, at p. 393, citing E/CONF.2/C.3/SR.44 and 47. This point is often cited to support the proposition that the free-trade area exception was not particularly well considered in the drafting, and occasionally to reflect upon the quality of the drafting itself.

18 Summary Record of the Commercial Policy Committee (Committee III). These meetings were reported at Havana between 3 and 11 December 1947 as meetings Four through Eight. E/CONF.2/C.3/SR.4 through SR.8.

which would permit the conclusion of new preferential tariff agreements for such economic areas."[19]

Likewise, the representative of Iraq noted that,

"He believed that preferential arrangements between small producing areas having complementary trade would not cause the dislocation which Article 16 was designed to prevent. Customs unions, although permitted under Article 42, required a long time to establish and involved administrative difficulties. Therefore preferential arrangements should be permitted as well as customs unions and supported the Syrian, Lebanese and Turkish proposals in this respect".[20]

The representative of Lebanon referred his comments directly to a proposal for the inclusion of provisions for preferential arrangements other than customs unions as he,

"... felt that one solution for the handicap (sic) of small countries with limited markets was regional co-operation through customs unions, free trade agreements, or preferential tariff agreements. His country knew the difficulties of customs unions and it was doubtful if many would be formed. He would present amendments to Articles 16 and 42 to allow free trade and preferential agreements for economic regions. He saw no reason why the smaller countries should not exchange preferences in order to compete with highly developed countries which did not need them or which might not be ready to reciprocate".[21]

It is evident that the development preferences provided in Article 15 were not considered by these parties to be sufficient, either because of the voting waiver required, or because of a desire to create larger regional markets, or as necessary to take into account more comprehensive development approaches. It is likely that many objecting parties blended all of these aspects in their orientation to seek a broader avenue for future regional systems.

The argument to include provisions for regional preferential systems other than customs unions appeared also to turn in part on the view that the negotiated standstill for certain pre-existing preferences, as provided in Article 16, was simply unfair to territories that were contemplating future systems. Thus, while the representative from Australia indicated that development preferences were already possible by Article 15 of the Charter (upon prior approval), the Venezuela representa-

---

[19] E/CONF.2/C.3.SR.4.

[20] Ibid., at pp. 1-2.

[21] Ibid., at p. 3. This comment contains the first reported reference from this debate to "free-trade agreements". Not only were these three middle-eastern countries supportive of the concept. A later note by Haiti indicates that the twelve countries in the Central America trade zone also sought a preferential system, although the term free-trade area is not used in that reference. Ibid., at p. 4.

tive indicated that, "he could not understand why the prior approval of the Organization was required for some and not for others".[22] Likewise, from the following meeting, Argentina expressed the concern that the MFN clause, "included exceptions for the benefit of certain countries and perpetuated discriminatory practices condemned elsewhere. Those exceptions should be made more equitable by the inclusions of complementary economic regions".[23] These comments suggest that the necessity of the MFN compromise reached in Geneva had its ramifications for the issue of future preferences in Havana.

It is helpful to note at this juncture that there was no reason to believe that Article 15 would not survive and be finally incorporated in an adopted and ratified Havana Charter. The inference to draw from this fact is that the later drafting of a free-trade area provision was not then contemplated to be a replacement for the Development Article's provisions. Since there was opposition to the pre-approval requirements contained in Article 15, it is at least likely that members, seeking an expanded possibility for future preferences without pre-approval, also found common ground with those who sought a regional grouping exception with lesser administrative severity than posed by the customs union requirement. A comment from the Chilean representative during the third meeting suggests as much as he,

"... stated that his delegation would advocate general provisions for preferential arrangements on a regional basis rather than the specific provisions of paragraph 2, Article 16, for the reason that, within the purposes of the Charter, provisions should be made for all, and the present preferential arrangements including those of his own country, were too limited to attain the expansion of trade envisioned by the Charter. It was possible to use the same arguments for establishing preference for economic regions as for customs unions".[24]

The conference record indicates generally that a large number of countries were committed to Charter additions which would permit less strict criteria for the creation of future preference systems, notwithstanding the unconditional MFN clause as incorporated in Article 16. As the representative of Ecuador noted, "It was significant that forty of the countries represented at the conference considered the system of preferential treatment indispensable to profitable world trade".[25]

---

22   Ibid., at p. 6. Furthermore, "he strongly supported the need for preferential arrangements for such groups of countries as the near East, Central America, other Latin-American countries and other geographic regions".

23   E/CONF.2/C.3/SR.5, at p. 2.

24   E/CONF.2/C.3/SR.6 at p. 3. Paragraph 2 of Article 16 provided for specific permitted preferences. In response, the France representative indicated concurrence with the notion of regional organisations, "but with the prior approval of the Organization, as a means of protecting third parties". Interestingly, this was opposed by the representative of Syria, which stated that it was unable to agree with France on the question of prior approval. Ibid at. p. 4.

25   E/CONF.2/C.3/SR.7, p. 1.

The argument against new preference systems was not however neglected on the record, as indicated by the comments of Australia, the United Kingdom and the United States. Thus, the Australian representative indicated opposition to regional arrangements (other than customs unions), but saw a need for small countries seeking to develop industries in inadequate markets to have access to certain preferences, but rather upon an individual article or commodity basis and with prior approval. From his view, the provisions already made in Articles 15 and 42 were quite adequate for this purpose.[26] The UK representative indicated that while existing preference systems were granted a standstill, "new preferences were not to be established and the existing ones were subject to a progressive reduction or elimination ... If the creation of new preferences were not subject to examination by the Organization, the position would have to be examined".[27]

Although comments by the United States are not prominent in these reports, the representative (Mr. Leddy) did express the position that,

"(E)conomic regional preference arrangements were not a promising device for economic development. Special circumstances justifying such an arrangement should be submitted to the Organization for its decision as to the net gain to world trade, otherwise the whole object of eliminating preferences would be undermined".[28]

From these reports, one can begin to see the outline of how a free-trade area exception could have provided an avenue for compromise to meet the various positions. First, the waiver for complete preference systems would not be required, but waiver would remain necessary for partial or individual sector preferences. The desire for regional formations to create larger markets could be respected where the proponents intended to exchange a sufficiently high number of preferences so as to emulate the regional trade characteristics that were already acknowledged for customs unions. With this higher bar in place, MFN might have a chance to establish itself, first through the standstill provisions for existing systems, and second, by requiring a more rigorous exchange for new systems. By providing the developing parties a means of bypassing the 2/3's voting requirement for more complete future regional systems, the perceived unfairness of the standstill permitted for pre-existing systems was less at issue. For partial or sectoral exchanges, the existing Development chapter would continue to apply.

Given the extensive debate and differences of opinion recorded prior to the referral, it is possible that the subcommittee report granting the new free-trade area exception reconciled the various objections that were already on record. Thus, to only add to Haight's comment above, the record may well disclose that there was a

---

[26] Ibid., at p. 3.
[27] Ibid., and apparently suggesting that the price paid for a standstill which would restrict the Commonwealth preference in the future was a system of pre-approval for new preferences.
[28] Ibid., at p. 4.

good reason why the new free-trade area provisions were passed without any need for significant further debate.

2.2.4 The introduction of a free-trade area exception

The debate recounted above also indicates that the question of future preferences was central to the consideration of the MFN obligation in the Havana forum. This was reflected by the terms of reference made in the referral to the drafting sub-committee, which was charged,

> "To consider and submit recommendations to both Committees regarding Articles 15, 16 (2) and (3) and 42...with a view to finding a solution of the question of new preferential arrangements".

The Report of the Joint Sub-Committee of Committees II and III on Articles 15,16 and 42 was reported on March 7, 1948 as E/CONF.2/C.3/78. A working party of this subcommittee held 29 meetings, the results of which formed the basis of the report.[29] Since the subcommittee was charged with viewing three Articles, changes to the proposed Article 15 were also forwarded to the Co-ordinating Committee of the Congress, and described in a separate report for which no citation is available. For the Article 42 provisions, according to the subcommittee report,

> "The text of Article 42 has been redrafted on the basis of proposals by the French delegation, the main change being to extend to free-trade areas the provisions relating to customs union, as requested by the delegations of Lebanon and Syria".[30]

As far as the inclusion of free-trade areas, an explanation of Article 42B stated that,

> "The second paragraph, providing for the establishment of customs unions, is based upon paragraph 2 (b) of the Geneva draft, but there has been added to it a new provision covering the establishment of free-trade areas. An amendment proposed by the United Kingdom (C.3/11, Item 10) has been incorporated, and it is felt that the new text of the Article largely covers an amendment proposed by Chile (C.3/11, item 11)".[31]

---

[29] The working group's report is contained in E/CONF.2/C.2&3/A/134, unavailable.

[30] C.3/11, Item 13." E/CONF.2/C.3/78, p. 5, italics added. Following on, "(T)his subject was considered to be of sufficient importance to require its separation from the other matters dealt with in Article 42, and accordingly the Sub-Committee recommends a separate article devoted exclusively to customs unions and free-trade areas". Ibid.

[31] Ibid., at p. 6, para. 23.

Finally, the report indicates that,

> "(I)n paragraph 4 the definition of a customs union, which was contained in the second sentence of paragraph 4 of the Geneva draft, has been amended and a definition of a free-trade area has been added. This describes a free-trade area as a group of two or more customs territories within which tariffs, etc. (except where necessary, those permitted under section B of Chapter IV and under Article 43) are eliminated on substantially all the trade between the constituent territories or at least on substantially all the trade in products originating in such territories".[32]

2.2.5   *Havana conclusion*

The Havana Article 15 provisions, as referred from the subcommittee, retained its pre-approval conditions. These were already opposed on record by a fair number of participants. It must be considered therefore that the inclusion of a free-trade exception in Article 42 was posed as an alternative solution which would permit regional preferences within wholly formed systems rather than partial systems, but absent customs union administrative formalities and the requirement of a 2/3 approval.[33] As such, the inclusion of the free-trade area exception may well have reflected a compromise whereby pre-approval for sectoral preferences was retained, but then also granting a simplified construction to those parties seeking to form complete regional entities but without the customs union requirements to establish territory treatment. Overall, such an inclusion might have served to rebalance the Geneva arrangements in light of the larger group of developing participants who were not parties to the earlier round and flowed in part as a consequence of the compromise reached in Geneva.

If this is correct, this conclusion at Havana reflected a substantial departure from the position of the drafters during the process in Geneva. The Geneva Charter itself was modified from the U.S. State Department proposals for customs union and frontier traffic exceptions only by the inclusion of permitted interim agreements. Since the commentators cited agreed that the purpose of the entire ITO exercise from the U.S. view was to terminate the use of preferences in international trade, then one would conclude that the U.S. either acquiesced in the compromise, did not become aware of it, or had already determined that the ITO process was doomed. The first suggestion seems the most likely.

While this author has not been successful in locating the subcommittee reports, one point remains persistent. The Havana provision for free-trade areas in Article 42 introduced this term for the first time into the commercial policy lexicon. As drawn from both Whidden and Viner regarding inter-war systems, the various

---

[32]   Ibid., at p. 7, para. 27.
[33]   See Central Drafting Committee, "Proposed redraft of the Final Text of Chapter III - Article 15", E/CONF.2/C.8/26, 17 March 1948.

terms for preferential systems in the period did not employ any formation known as a free-trade area. Since such a regional instrument was simply unknown in the pre-GATT practice, Viner drew the conclusion, which retains a certain relevance now, that

> "This term is introduced, as a technical term, into the language of this field by the Charter, and its meaning for the purposes of the Charter must therefore be sought wholly within the text of the Charter".[34]

Three ramifications are considered. First, the GATT Articles themselves must form the primary source as to what would constitute the nature of the requirements. Second, to the extent that the free-trade area provisions mimic those for customs unions, any previous practice developed to customs unions does have an informative role in determining the meaning of terms applied to free-trade area requirements when ambiguity occurs. Third, in the absence of experience with a free-trade area exception, where the functioning of such an area could not be compared to customs unions practice, then the implications of including the exception were not likely to be able to be appreciated at the time of the drafting. What is developed below is that within a short time after the Article became effective, that the inclusion of the free-trade area exception necessarily compelled an attempt to make a new legal distinction in practice between such an "area" and the previously condemned notion of partially preferential arrangements. This problem may have been exacerbated by the loss of the Development Article, which arguably would have served as a text providing demarcation. Whether or not that is the case, drawing any consistent line across this terrain would prove to be a most troublesome endeavour for GATT Parties, and one which even continues to trouble the review process of regional agreements in the contemporary practice.

2.3   The resulting intent of the Havana provisions

As indicated, pre-existing margins of preference between particular countries were negotiated to be subjected to identification and a standstill obligation according to Article I:2 of the GATT (Havana Charter Article 16:2). Preferential systems introduced thereafter were not to have been easily installed and qualified for MFN exceptions. Dam emphasised the restrictive nature of the new Article XXIV gateway and the structural link between the provisions of Article I and Article XXIV as,

---

[34] J. Viner, Supra note 1 at p. 124.

"... the principal objective in the drafting of the customs union and free-trade area provisions became to tie down, in the most precise legal language possible, the conditions that such regional groupings would have to fulfil in order to escape prohibition under the most-favoured nation clause as preferential arrangements ...".[35]

Jackson's view of the relationship between the two provisions was similar in part as,

"... the fear of some countries that the regional exception could be abused to allow the introduction of detrimental preference systems otherwise inconsistent with MFN was the motive power behind the elaborate draftsmanship that went into the other clauses of the regional exception".[36]

In point, both comments present a revealing view of the intent of the drafters as it reflected two compromises reached, the first being the standstill arranged in Geneva and the second being the inclusion of the free-trade area exception in Havana. However, the elaborate draftsmanship suggested by Jackson was mainly settled at Geneva, since customs union provisions were essentially extended to free-trade areas at Havana. When that first compromise had been reached, the criteria that would either secure it or permit it to be degraded by future commercial practices would likely have received a fair degree of attention by the drafters in regard to any language to be employed for other exceptions. Whatever exceptions are made possible by Article XXIV would serve as the primary gateway to offer or accept a preference outside the parameter of Article I MFN. Therefore, in the absence of the "the most precise legal language possible", the value of the negotiated standstill for existing systems would have provided for little additional meaningful restraint on the introduction of new preferential systems. This could not have been the intent of the drafters, even in consideration of the compromise reached in Havana for free-trade areas.

---

[35] Italics added. K. Dam, Supra note 6 at p. 275. Considering that Kenneth Dam adhered to the view that Article XXIV:4 should be re-interpreted to accommodate a more Vinerian approach in qualifying regional systems, that he would also identify the strict linkage between the Article I compromise and the provisions for Article XXIV, as contemplated by the drafters, is noteworthy. See also, J. Jackson, Supra note 7 at p. 602, and citing therein K. Dam, (1963), at p. 663.

[36] Although, several paragraphs later, he states that, "... the conclusion can be drawn that the compromise of the GATT draftsmen was intended to retain for GATT parties a considerable amount of the existing latitude to enter into regional arrangements of various types". J. Jackson, Supra note 7 at pp. 600 and 602.

2.3.1 *Extending customs union requirements to free-trade areas*

Such a view of the restrictive interpretation for Article XXIV finds support from an often- quoted summary of the American justification for advancing the customs union exception. From Wilcox,

"(A) customs union creates a wider trading area, removes obstacles to competition, makes possible a more economic allocation of resources, and thus operates to increase production and raise planes of living. A preferential system, on the other hand, retains internal barriers, obstructs economy in production, and restrains the growth of income and demand ... A customs union is conducive to the expansion of trade on a basis of multilateralism and nondiscrimination; a preferential system is not".[37]

The Wilcox statement is most often cited now for its failure to appreciate the possibility of Viner's trade diverting customs unions. However, the quotation also retains validity on its own merits by disclosing how parties may have viewed a free-trade area requirement in contrast to other types of preferential systems. This is to view the phrase not from its economic implications, but how it might inform a legal view of the hierarchy established for preferential systems, and how free-trade areas should be placed within such a hierarchy. Thus, one notes the difference above between the two types of preferential systems. This appears to turn upon the quality of internal free trade to be attained by the parties, as a preferential system "retains internal barriers" between the members. A customs union admittedly would have the legal capacity to eliminate such internal barriers.

Although the Wilcox statement does not mention the free-trade area provisions introduced at Havana, query how U.S. policy makers would have treated the exception as extended if they applied these criteria. If one assumes that the final result was compatible with the U.S. position, then a conclusion can be formed that free-trade areas were permitted upon the understanding that they would also eliminate internal barriers to trade in a manner similar to a customs union. Otherwise, and in light of Dam's notation above, there would be an absence of a legal basis to make any distinction between free-trade areas and disfavoured partially preferential systems. The intent of the drafters as to MFN would be overall undermined in the absence of such a distinction. Regional formations eliminating internal barriers to trade would therefore be supported as an MFN exception.[38]

---

[37] Clair Wilcox, **A Charter for World Trade**, Macmillan, New York, 1949, pp. 70-71, quoted in Dam, Supra note 6 at pp. 274-275, italics added.

[38] One can only speculate into which category Wilcox would have placed free-trade areas, as the term appeared later. Given the elements supplied in the statement, one could suggest that free trade areas eliminating all internal barriers to trade would have been favourably viewed as similar to customs unions.

Perhaps the strongest evidence in support of this view is the parallel textual identity of the requirements for the removal of barriers to trade for both legal forms, as both require that "duties and other restrictive regulations of commerce... are eliminated on substantially all the trade."[39] In the absence of documentation to the contrary, it follows that the simple correlation of the provisions indicates an expressed intent to equate the internal trade requirements for both forms. Since customs unions already benefited from a practice of receiving exceptions from the various bilateral treaties employing MFN clauses, a regional free-trade area agreement that met the same conditions *internally* could also be exempted, even in the absence of a common external tariff.

In support for this view, the requirement for the removal of barriers to trade remained somewhat consistent from Geneva through Havana, even as the free-trade exception was brought forward. The Geneva text provided that,

"A customs union shall be understood to mean the substitution of a single customs territory for two or more customs territories, so that *all tariffs and other restrictive regulations of members of the union are substantially eliminated* and substantially the same tariffs and other regulations of commerce are applied by each of the members of the union to the trade of territories not included in the union".[40]

To compare, the final Havana text portion of Article 44 provided as follows:

"A custom union shall be understood to mean the substitution of a single customs territory for two or more customs territories, so that *duties and other restrictive regulations of commerce* (except where necessary, those permitted under Section B of chapter IV and under Article 45) *are eliminated with respect to substantially all the trade* between the constituent territories of the union (or at least with respect to substantially all the trade in products originating in such territories)".[41]

There are two differences between the versions. One is a change in placement of the term "substantially" from the first draft's reference to tariffs and regulations (i.e., substantially all tariffs eliminated on the trade), to the second draft's position in reference to trade (i.e., duties eliminated on substantially all the trade). The other change is the addition in the second version of a listing of specific Articles designated as exceptions from the primary stated requirement. In the larger context, we know that the free-trade area provisions were also added. The question to raise is whether the change in placement of the term "substantially" might have had any

---

[39] Article XXIV 8(a)(1) for customs unions, Article XXIV(8)(b) for free-trade areas.
[40] Article XXIV:4, Final Act adopted at the Conclusion of the second session of the preparatory committee of the United Nations conference on Trade and Employment, Geneva, 1947, italics added.
[41] Italics added, subparagraph indicators omitted.

relation to the inclusion of a free-trade area provision, and if so, what? Hudec and Southwick have suggested the connection of the change in the placement of the term to the addition of the exception Articles listing. This would allow the second version to contemplate with more ease the notion that not all sectors need be covered to meet the requirement. The exceptions themselves as listed point to the possibility that some traded sectors may not be covered under the obligation.[42]

This is plausible even while the change might have also accommodated the free-trade area exception. On this point, one would consider the position of the drafter in attempting to delineate the new category of free-trade areas from other partially preferential arrangements. To draw a line for which non-customs unions arrangements would pass under Article XXIV, it may also have been the case that the placement was shifted to emphasise that partial rollbacks in duties and quantitative restrictions across a broad range of trade would not suffice for the requirements. Even while the second version more easily contemplates the elimination of coverage for sectors, at least according to the listed Articles, the requirement is arguably overall strengthened in designating that the *elimination* of duties and other restrictive regulations of commerce is a requirement. In this sense, the change in placement could also have reflected the introduction of free-trade area provisions as necessary to reflect a demarcation that was being intended between free-trade areas and lesser forms of partial preference systems.

Viner noted an additional change. This is shown for customs unions whereby the elimination is to be effected for "all trade in products originating in such territories", rather than all the trade between such territories. According to him this change reflected the circumstance that arose by an absence of a traditional definitional requirement that would have provided for allocations of customs revenues among members.[43] However, this change also can reflect an intent to make more parallel the requirements between free-trade areas and customs unions, since in the former arrangement the non-harmonisation of external commercial policy would necessitate a requirement that only goods of origin to each free-trade area member would be covered. While this is a softened requirement as compared to the Geneva Draft, it also indicates a closer alignment between the two situations that were under contemplation for the exception.[44]

---

[42] R. Hudec and J. Southwick, *Regionalism and WTO Rules*, in M. Rodríguez, P. Low, B. Kotschwar (Eds.), **Trade Rules in the Making**, Organization of American States and the Brookings Institution, Washington D.C., 1999, pp. 47-80 at p. 62, note 34.

[43] "(A) customs union set up without provisions for such allocation would need the benefit of this relaxation unless it was prepared to accept assignment of revenues according to place of collection". J. Viner, Supra note 1 at p. 114, his note 15. Viner considered this to be a meaningful diminution of the traditionally accepted requirements.

[44] This also suggesting that the elimination of "other restrictive regulations" was not intended to reach to the elimination of internal administrative checks for either customs unions or free-trade areas as would be necessary to determine the origin of the goods.

2.3.2   *Conclusion on the Havana provisions*

Whether the changes made as discussed above were consciously enacted in order to align the existing provisions with those of the new free-trade area is a matter of speculation in the absence of subcommittee drafting reports. However, what can be disclosed from the face of the provisions resulting in Havana is that there is no difference between the two forms for any of the requirements to be met for the coverage of internal trade. The only difference identified in the text is that relating to the external policies required to be adopted, since a customs union is required to substitute a common external tariff and a free-trade area may retain its individual member tariffs.

The intent of the drafters is therefore apparent from the provisions viewed overall. While an exception was being recognised for a new "regional" formation which did not create a customs territory, this free-trade area would nevertheless be required to meet the same test as a customs union, whatever that test might be, in regard to the elimination of its internal barriers to trade.

Although subcommittee documentation is scant, this conclusion is well supported from the identity of the provisions themselves, and not least, from the referral comment made by the subcommittee itself. As quoted above, the main change was, "...to extend to free-trade areas the provisions relating to customs union..." Such an *extension* would have reasonably served to retain the legal hierarchy that was being established. This allowed for a distinction between formations which fell under the customs union and free-trade area Article, those which fell under the Development chapter, and those that would not be permitted to be entertained by Organisation Members in deference to the new MFN obligation.

The final section will review Article XXIV requirements imposed upon regional parties in regard to the quality and degree of their internal trade to be liberalised and make an examination of the sequence of the Article's paragraphs to be applied.

2.4   **Part One Conclusion: the final GATT Article XXIV requirements**

GATT Article XXIV imposes two primary sets of requirements for the formation of a regional trade arrangement to operate as an exception from its Article I Most-favoured Nation obligation. One set is definitional in nature as it outlines the categories of arrangements that fall within the provisions of the Article. The other set of requirements establishes certain implementation conditions whereby agreements otherwise qualified by definition, may nevertheless be denied the Article's application where the external trade affects of the agreements raise new barriers overall to other GATT Parties. The logical way to approach a reading of the Article is to commence at the point where definitions are applied. This determines the scope of the Article in respect to the types of arrangements possibly exempted from GATT Article I.

2.4.1 *The first test: paragraph 8 definitional requirements*

Article XXIV:8 (paragraph 8) is the first to consider in any evaluation as it acts to identify the characteristics of those regional trade agreements which must be present in order to qualify for an exception to the MFN principle. Thus, either a free-trade area or a customs union,

> "… shall be *understood to mean* an area (or territory) where duties and other restrictive regulations of commerce are eliminated with respect to substantially all the trade between the constituent territories".[45]

This provision provides a definition for the two types of regional formations in terms of the amount of trade upon which action is to be taken (substantially all) and the actions that are to be taken regarding it (elimination of duties and other restrictive regulations of commerce). As drafted, an initial definitional requirement is imposed, since if a preferential arrangement would fail to eliminate the designated barriers on the appropriate amount of trade, then according to the paragraphs' own terms, such a formation *shall not be understood* to constitute either a free-trade area or a customs union. Therefore, the Article, and whatever exceptions it may accord, is expressly not intended to be applicable for an arrangement that does not fulfil these requirements, no matter its declared form or title as designated by its members. What is suggested is that some affirmative act of factual qualification is to be undertaken in order to determine that any particular arrangement meets the tests described so that it may be concluded that a free-trade area or customs union is being created. The subject of this qualification relates to the intra-regional or *internal* trade of the area or union. The paragraph requires that in order to be characterised as either a free-trade area or a customs union, that the trade to be considered is the trade between the members for their goods of origin.[46]

Other provisions support the proposition that the Article requires this initial definitional qualification. The provisions of paragraph 10 provide the additional mechanism whereby the Contracting Parties may approve proposals that do *not* qualify with the Article's other requirements by a 2/3 majority vote. This waiver is explicit however in only being available where, "such proposals lead to the forma-

---

[45] GATT Article XXIV:8(a)(1) for customs unions, and GATT Article XXIV:8(b) for free-trade areas (emphasis added). At this point we are not treating the listed Articles exceptions stated in paragraph 8(a) and (b). The complete text of the Article as provided in GATT-1947 is attached by Appendix.

[46] The term "free trade" is applied in this context to refer to the elimination of tariffs and quantitative restrictions. For now, the Article's term "other restrictive regulations of commerce" is applied here to indicate the removal of quantitative restrictions.

tion of a customs union or a free-trade area in the sense of this Article."[47] Thus, even Article XXIV's waiver provision makes a requirement that a paragraph 8 free-trade area or customs union must inevitably result. Further confirmation is found in the obligation imposed by paragraph 7 of the Article for proponents to submit a plan and schedule to demonstrate that the arrangements made are sufficient to meet the definitional test. Thus,

> "If, after having studied the plan and schedule...the Contracting Parties find that such agreement *is not likely to result in the formation of a customs union or of a free-trade area* within the period contemplated...the CONTRACTING PARTIES shall make recommendations ... The parties shall not maintain or put into force ... such agreement if they are not prepared to modify it in accordance with these recommendations".[48]

In this context, the principle reason why the Article would require a plan and schedule should be understood to provide the material for the Contracting Parties to review agreements proposed in order to apply the tests as stated in paragraph 8. On this basis, the Contracting Parties can then fulfil their stated obligation to make recommendations in those cases where an agreement does not result in either of the recognised forms. Thus, the Article requires an action by the Contracting Parties to distinguish between free-trade areas and customs unions on the one hand, and all other preferential arrangements on the other, and as a matter of fact.

There is a second aspect of the internal trade requirement that can be considered at this point. This requires that the removal of duties and other barriers be done so on a mutual basis. For customs unions, this is indicated by Article XXIV:8(a)(i) which refers to "...trade *between* the constituent territories of the union ..." For free trade areas, the comparable requirement is found in Article XXIV:8(b), which refers to, "... trade *between* the constituent territories in products originating in such territories".[49]

---

[47] The paragraph 10 provision is applicable for customs unions and free-trade areas between GATT parties and non-parties. GATT, **Analytical Index, Guide to GATT Law and Practice**, Geneva (6th Ed), 1994, p. 770. An Article XXV waiver, requiring for GATT-1947 for 2/3 majority "of the votes cast" would serve as the appropriate avenue for any formation which would not result in either a customs union or a free-trade area. The voting requirement is more strict than that provided by GATT Article XXIV:10, since the final formation, although not complying with other Article XXIV conditions, does eventually meet the definitional requirement of Article XXIV:8.

[48] GATT Article XXIV:7(b), emphasis added. A discussion of the effect of "non-decisions" concludes chapter 5.

[49] Emphasis added. It may be that the obligation would be better expressed as a "mutuality" requirement rather than that of reciprocity. The latter term is however consistently used to designate the requirement. Over the period of implementation there is no stated requirement that duties be reduced between the parties at the same rate. The inference is that within the time contemplated by the plan and schedule, a result shall be reached whereby both parties have eliminated their respective barriers to trade.

For customs unions only, there is an additional element of a definitional character that relates to the external aspects of the formation. This is found in Article XXIV:8(a)(ii) whereby, "substantially the same duties and other regulations of commerce are applied by each of the members of the union to the trade of territories not included in the union." This flows from the nature of a customs union as expressed by paragraph 8(a), "as it is understood to mean the substitution of a single customs territory for two or more customs territories ...". Although this requirement relates to the external aspects of a customs union, it is a requirement that yet remains formational and definitional in nature in prescribing the character of a union's regime which is to be attained in order to qualify for any exception under the Article.

2.4.2   *The second test: paragraph 5 requirements regarding external effects*

After meeting the definitional tests required by Article XXIV:8, then a consideration of how the formation will affect other GATT parties in implementation is made as according to Article XXIV:5. This paragraph grants the exception accorded by Article XXIV for customs unions and free-trade areas, provided that the effects of the implementation of the regional trade agreement do not impose higher barriers to trade upon other GATT Parties. Thus, it is required in respect to the trade of other contracting parties, that the duties and other regulations (maintained or imposed), "shall not on the whole be higher or more restrictive" than "prior to the formation".[50]

Any elimination of an internal barrier to trade between two parties is a preference and equivalent to a raising of the relative barriers to non-members. However, Article XXIV:5 does not require or suggest an interpretation that the overall effect of a qualified formation must leave the external trade in exactly the same position (or better) than prior to the formation. Otherwise, a partially preferential agreement could be more qualified for an Article XXIV exception where its effect overall was to raise fewer relative barriers to non-members. Any such reading would negate the Article XXIV:8 trade-coverage requirement outright.

This consideration reinforces the intended sequence to be applied to the Article's provisions. First, the proponents submit a plan and schedule which contains sufficient elements of commitment to demonstrate that a free trade area or a customs union can be realised. Second, they provide sufficient evidence according to the plan and schedule that they will not implement this otherwise qualified formation in any manner that would raise new trade barriers to the other GATT parties. Therefore, the second test, while certainly not incidental, must nevertheless be un-

---

[50]   GATT Article XXIV:5(a) for customs unions, GATT Article XXIV:5(b) for free trade areas. There is a difference for free-trade areas where the higher duties shall not be "maintained". For customs unions, they may not be "imposed at the institution".

dertaken only in regard to actual changes which occur in the external trade regimes of the regional parties and only for arrangements which are already qualified according to the definitional requirements of paragraph 8.

As we will see throughout the next Part, the interpretation and sequence of applying paragraphs 5 and 8 have formed primary fault lines for GATT Parties to disagree over the requirements of Article XXIV. As the first requirement outlined above requires regional parties to establish free trade between them, and since these benefits will not be granted to non-members, the GATT Article most directly affected by a regional formation is Article I, the Most-favoured Nation provision. But for the exception provided in Article XXIV, MFN would require that any preference offered by one regional party to another be likewise unconditionally granted to all other Contracting Parties.[51]

Understandably, the motives attributed to support or oppose regional formations are also typically viewed in the same dichotomous frame as is presented by the objectives of paragraph 8 and paragraph 5. As Snape has outlined the two positions,

> "(O)ne is that preferential discrimination permits countries to liberalize further than otherwise, by engaging in reciprocal reduction of barriers in agreement with like-minded countries. The other is that discrimination permits governments to raise, selectively, barriers against 'troublesome' exporting countries -- and thus to bow to domestic protectionist pressures -- in a manner in which they could not if the barriers had to be raised against all exporters, friends as well as foes".[52]

This statement summarises the two tests to be applied, and if they were applied in a manner consistent with the stated terms of the Article itself, it is likely that many of the objections on both sides would be met. For the first, paragraph 8 would require that parties do in fact liberalise further than otherwise. For the second, paragraph 5 would act to eliminate barriers overall from being raised against "troublesome" exporting countries.

However, it can be suggested that it is paradoxical for Article XXIV to require a high degree of internal free trade in the first instance, as this would certainly appear to aggravate the possible effects of external discrimination as to non-members. On its face, this is precisely what the Article appears to require. Since all preferences are discriminatory and raise relative barriers to trade, non-members can al-

---

[51] GATT Article I, reciting in relevant part, "... any advantage, favour, privilege, or immunity granted by any contracting party to any product originating in or destined for any other country shall be accorded immediately and unconditionally to the like product originating in or destined for the territories of all other contracting parties".

[52] Richard H. Snape, *History and Economics of GATT's Article XXIV*, in K. Anderson and R. Blackhurst, (Eds.), **Regional Integration and the Global Trading System**, Harvester Wheatsheaf, 1993, pp. 273-291, at p. 278.

ways support incomplete formations that will discriminate against less of their trade overall. If the provisions of paragraph 5 constituted the sole criteria for the Article, or were capable of overriding the definitional requirements of Article XXIV:8, then the result would be to increase the number of partial preference agreements operating under a claimed exception to MFN. Although any one such partial agreement may be causing less damage to the trade flows of non-members, the sum total of more such agreements may cause more damage overall in a systemic manner. As one proceeds to examine the application of the Article through GATT practice, a conclusion can be drawn that this is what has occurred, perhaps even to the point of constituting GATT's legacy for the common practice according to the Article.

Part Two:
REGIONALISM IN THE GATT (1947)

Part Two continues the story of legal developments occurring for free-trade areas under Article XXIV from the establishment of the General Agreement on Tariffs and Trade (1947). Chapter Three discusses the application of GATT Article XXIV in its first major application between developed and developing territories in the working group review of the EEC-Overseas Association (1958). The legal issues raised in this review set a pattern for most of the later GATT free-trade area reviews within which it became routinely difficult to apply the trade-coverage requirements for free-trade areas between territories exhibiting unequal development levels. This is demonstrated in the chapter by notation to a number of later GATT reviews, mainly dealing with EEC external regional formations through the 1960's and early 1970's. Many of the issues raised in the Overseas Association remain unresolved by the practice of reviewing formations to the present time.

The following Chapter Four discusses a number of "systemic" issues that were raised in the early GATT reviews. Not all identified issues are treated by the chapter. Rather, the selection is limited to those having a bearing on the failure of the GATT working groups to make recommendations for agreements notified. These include definitional issues, such as what constitutes sufficient coverage for the regional members. However, emphasis is placed upon arrangements between developed and developing territories, which have nearly all been intractable on reviews. This raises a treatment of the so-called "reverse preference" problem of exacting high coverage requirements for developing country members. Institutional aspects of working group reviews in the GATT are also discussed, particularly in regard to the consensus requirement and the Article XXIV paradox, which is really a conflict of interest problem, posed to reviewing parties who are charged with approving agreements that discriminate against more of their trade.

Chapter Five turns to the GATT "response" by reviewing the dispute panel jurisprudence prior to the WTO. This considers in chief two unreported 1990's GATT dispute panel cases concerning the legal qualification of the Lomé Convention (Bananas I and II). Although unreported, and therefore lacking designation of a source of WTO law, they also marked the beginning of a process whereby dispute settlement action could eventually bring the use of an Article XXIV exception under more meaningful legal control. They also hold interest for the expressed positions of regional members as they illuminate the GATT practice already covered in the working group reviews. They certainly retain importance for the quality of their reasoning regarding the qualification of free-trade areas between developed and developing countries, and as they inform the legal question of GATT review procedures that fail to result in recommendations on the question of compatibility of a regional arrangement with the Article XXIV requirements.

The Conclusion of this Part contains a single chapter with two components dealing with issues of law and economics. The first addresses the question of whether economic analysis regarding customs union theory should be considered as an aspect of the Article XXIV test. The position taken here is that an attempt to impose a trade creation or diversion analysis, or a "no harm done" test would contradict the Article's provisions as now drafted. The second aspect considers the traditional justifications raised for the high trade-coverage requirement, and determines that an economic test for Article XXIV need not necessarily undermine those rationales. However, the conclusion is made that the historical problem of country and market size would also not be resolved by an economic test for the Article, at least not for one dedicated to insuring only an absence of harm as to nonmembers. If states yet exhibit the capacity to employ preference as an instrument of national commercial diplomacy, then Article XXIV paragraph 8 requirements should be interpreted more rather than less strictly.

Chapter 3
ARTICLE XXIV IN PRACTICE: THE OVERSEAS
ASSOCIATION

"... if the percentage subject to protective duties reached 20 percent, the institutions of the EEC would then, but only then, ... apply for such waivers as they deemed necessary". *Delegate's statement, L/778, para.32.*

3.1   Introduction

Although the EEC Association of Overseas Territories was not the first free-trade area agreement to be submitted to the GATT for review according to Article XXIV, it remains a most important agreement for a number of reasons. Besides the sheer size of the arrangement, encompassing eighteen separate free-trade areas between former colonies of the original six and the declared European Economic Community, the reviewing parties were required to directly confront the most difficult interpretative issues regarding the requirements of Article XXIV in respect to free-trade area formations.

Complicating the review was the nature of the parties to the Association - the developed EEC economies on one hand, and a large group of lesser, if not least, developed territories on the other. Certain issues raised are distinct to this type of formation, particularly the question of whether the reciprocity (mutuality) requirement for free-trade areas should be imposed at all for such partners. This aspect of the Association made resolutions of the legal issues more difficult, particularly at this juncture of the early GATT practice. Since the EEC continued through the 1960's and 1970's to invoke Article XXIV for a number of Associations and agreements with developing countries, this Review remains a most valuable precedent as it tended to establish the overall pattern.

The approach taken here is to address the legal questions in the same order they were raised by the Working Group report, and then to summarise the recorded positions of the parties. The author's commentary is provided following.

3.2   Overview of Association issues

Of interest to the free-trade area requirements of Article XXIV was the work of Sub-Group D. This was established to examine the Association of Overseas Territories,[1] as arrangements were submitted to establish a number of bilateral free-trade areas between the Community as a single territory and the individual territories.[2] The plan was contested. As the report indicated, "most" of the Working Group members did not consider that the Overseas Association provisions as contained in the EEC Rome Treaty were compatible with the requirements of Article XXIV. Therefore the territories involved should not be entitled to a deviation from the Article I MFN requirement of GATT.[3]

The following reasons were listed in the report. First, the EEC Treaty provisions failed to contain an indication that such an association would constitute a free-trade area.[4] According to the reported EEC position, whether the Rome Treaty did or did not call the association a free-trade agreement would not alter the nature or legal structure of the resulting formation. Other matters such as investment were also to be covered in the association and the limitation of the terminology to that of a "free-trade area", as applied to these associations, would not be appropriate.[5]

Second, the internally restrictive aspects of the association were contrary to Article XXIV:4, which stated that the purpose of regional arrangements should be to facilitate trade between the constituent territories. This GATT Article requirement was contrary to EEC Treaty Article 134 authorising the six to take measures in respect to association member duties on imports.[6]

Third, Paragraph (8)(b) of Article XXIV required that a free-trade area formation must be accompanied by the elimination of the duties and other restrictive regulations of commerce on "substantially all the trade". This GATT sub-paragraph authorised where necessary the maintenance of certain regulations of commerce which were otherwise permitted under the GATT (from Articles XI-XV inclusive, and Article XX). These restrictions on commerce which were permitted between GATT parties generally according to certain requirements, were also therefore permitted between the parties to a free-trade area. However, this did not authorise oth-

---

[1]   The Overseas Association, The Treaties Establishing the European Economic Community and the European Atomic Energy Community, L/778 (1958), BISD 6S/70, 29 November, 1957.

[2]   Several arguments advanced by Working Group members have been long recognised as unsustainable under a current understanding of the Article's requirements. Except for passing reference a discussion of these questions is omitted. This includes particularly the question raised as to whether Article XXIV could condone the simultaneous establishment of a customs union (the EEC) and a free-trade area with the Association parties (the Ceylon note). The argument has a slight relevance in its bearing on another issue that was central to the review, that being whether the volume of trade between the parties could add intra-EEC trade. This is discussed below.

[3]   L/778, p. 91, para. 9.

[4]   Ibid., para. 10.

[5]   Dam has suggested that the arrangement was not initially conceived of as a free-trade area by the EEC, and the seeking of qualification under Article XXIV actually emerged as something of a "legalistic afterthought" Kenneth W. Dam, *Regional Economic Arrangements and the GATT, the Legacy of a Misconception*, University of Chicago Law Review, V. 30, No. 4, 1963, pp. 615-665, at p. 648.

[6]   EEC Article 134 permitted measures by the Community to avoid trade deflection. There is no identification in the report of a response particular to this concern.

er restrictions of commerce between free-trade area parties that were not listed in the paragraph. The EEC association appears to have deviated from these GATT requirement in several respects as enumerated:[7]

a) Association countries were not required to eliminate export duties on goods bound for the EEC six;
b) EEC Article 133(3) granted the overseas territories a latitude to install new duties, either for fiscal requirements or for purposes of meeting development goals;[8]
c) prior international obligations did not permit certain members of the EEC six to reduce duties discriminatorily in reference to the trade of particular association territories;
d) no provision was included in the Treaty for a complete and permanent elimination of quantitative restrictions on exports from the six to the association countries.

In view of the points made above, the construction was viewed by "most" of the Working Group members as a preferential agreement or an agreement to extend existing preferences, rather than as an agreement for the formation of free-trade areas.[9] In this view, existing preferences between several of the EEC six and certain associated countries should be permitted to be continued in force, but should not be permitted to be expanded according to GATT Article I:2. This Article and paragraph committed certain preferential arrangements to a standstill provision. The provisions of the Association necessarily extended the preferences on behalf of all of the six in the customs union contrary to the Article I:2 requirement.[10]

3.3   Issues regarding permitted exceptions

In the Overseas Territories report, the issues raised by the substantially-all trade requirement were central. For a more comprehensive treatment, they can be further divided for discussion.

---

[7]   L/778, para. 15.
[8]   EEC Article 133 stated, "The countries and territories may, however, levy customs duties which meet the needs of their development and industrialization or produce revenue for their budgets".
[9]   According to Dam, "(O)nly two members of the EEC were members of the Working Party: France and the Netherlands. Except for the United States and Greece, which apparently remained neutral throughout the discussions, the remaining members of the Working Party formed a solid front against the Six on most issues: Brazil, Ceylon, Chile, Dominican Republic, Ghana, India, Indonesia, Pakistan, Federation of the Rhodesias and Nyasaland, and the United Kingdom". K. Dam, Supra note 5 at p. 649, his note 101.
[10] L/778, para. 20.

3.3.1   *Permitted internal restrictions and the "exhaustive list"*

Article XXIV (8)(b) provides a list of GATT Articles that outline the restrictions to internal trade that are permitted to be retained in a free-trade area.[11] The primary exceptions contemplated by these listed Articles include,
1) export restrictions to prevent shortages of foodstuffs or other essential products;
2) restrictions connected with the classification, grading and marking of commodities;
3) restrictions necessary to safeguard the country's external financial position in balance of payments and related exchange control restrictions; and
4) the general exceptions to protect human, animal or plant life or health, etc.

By permitting the re-introduction of duties on behalf of the association territories for the purposes of development, some Working Group members took the position that the EEC was invoking an application of the GATT's development Article XVIII to the Associations. Since the development provisions of Article XVIII were not included in the listing of GATT excepted Articles permitted to be applied by regional partners under Article XXIV:8(b), it was argued that the re-imposition of duties for the purposes of development could not be entertained in a free-trade area.

3.3.1.1 The proponents' argument for a non-exhaustive listing
Dam singled out this line of argument particularly for his criticism of the "highly legalistic" nature of the report.[12] However, the passage of time has also revealed that the failure to reach a determination of the status of the listed articles as either exhaustive or non-exhaustive has remained a key element in the difficulties of applying Article XXIV. On a number of occasions it has also been a source of granting a degree of flexibility for regional members that may have extended well beyond what was contemplated by the drafters.[13]

The EEC's response to the objection also had a significant bearing on later developments regarding the qualification of free-trade areas. According to the EEC view, Article XXIV:8(b) requirements could not have been intended to be exhaustive in enumerating the only restrictions that could be permitted between members of a free-trade area. This was demonstrated *a contrario* by the fact that Article XXI, GATT's basic exception for national security measures, was also not listed under Article XXIV (8)(b). Given the omission of this important GATT exception from the listing,

---

[11] "... duties and other restrictive regulations of commerce (except where necessary, those permitted under Article XI, XII, XIII, XIV, XV and XX) are eliminated on substantially all the trade between the constituent territories in products originating in such territories". Article XXIV:8(b).

[12] K. Dam, Supra note 5 at p. 649, his note 98.

[13] The EC would affirm its 1958 position on the role of the development Articles as late as the first and second Banana panel cases in the 1990's, discussed infra, Chapter Five.

"(it) would be difficult ... to dispute the right of contracting parties to avail themselves of that provision ... and it must therefore be concluded that the list was not exhaustive".[14]

The report does not indicate that other Working Group members raised any effective rejoinder to the EEC position regarding the omission of the security exception. By implication, the EEC position that the Article XXIV:8(b) listing was not intended by the drafters to be exhaustive appears to have been tacitly accepted.

In addition, according to the EEC position, any restrictions that regional parties decided to impose upon their mutual trade that did not *cumulatively* detract from the substantially-all trade requirement should be permitted in any case. The GATT Article exceptions under XXIV:(8)(b), according to this view, could only then have been intended as an indicative listing.[15] The importance of this question is demonstrated when one considers that the Article XXIV:8(b) listing, if understood to be exhaustive, would provide the basis for a leading interpretation that other GATT exceptions to MFN could also *not* be applied between regional parties. Thus, as between regional parties, Article XXIV would not authorise the use of contingent measures such as anti-dumping and countervailing duties under Article VI and, although certain additional considerations would apply, the use of safeguards between regional members under Article XIX.[16] None of these Articles are listed in GATT XXIV:8(b). Thus, if the EEC's understanding of Article XXIV:8(b) would hold, this would also have significant implications for future practice, as it would necessarily follow that regional parties would have the flexibility to engage in any practice to restrict the trade of their partners, as long as some overall cumulative criteria of meeting substantially-all of the trade was met. Effectively, if the listing of GATT Article restrictions provided in the Article would be understood to be non-exhaustive, then they also must be considered to be essentially redundant.

3.3.1.2 Comment on the security exception argument

Völker also visited this question, but followed a somewhat different line of reasoning to reach a conclusion similar to that advanced by the EEC in the report.[17] He noted that GATT Article XXI is prefaced by the phrase, "Nothing in this Agreement shall be construed to prevent ..." This suggests that nothing in Article XXIV

---

[14] L/778, para. 26. The issue is still raised in the WTO. "With regard to the list of exception in Article XXIV:8, his delegation's position ... was that the fact that Article XXI (security exceptions) had not been included indicated that the list was not exhaustive ..." Committee on Regional Trade Agreements, comment by Japan representative, (CRTA) WT/REG/M/15, para. 18, p. 6.

[15] As though the clause was intended to read that duties and other restrictive regulations of commerce were to be eliminated on substantially-all trade, except where necessary in cases, *such as* Article XI, etc.

[16] For now we do not raise the question of whether such restrictions would be permitted in the interim period to formation.

[17] E.L.M. Völker, **Barriers to External and Internal Community Trade**, Kluwer, Dordrecht, 1993, p. 27.

shall prevent the operation of the basic security exception, which would infer that there would have been no need to include Article XXI in the listed Articles operating as exceptions under Article XXIV. However, since Article XX, which is listed as an exception in Article XXIV:8(b), also contains this same preamble language, one would reasonably conclude that the Article XXIV (8)(b) listing was not intended to be exhaustive.

A reading contrary to the EEC conclusion is possible, although it was not raised in the Report or by later commentary. This flows from the structure of the Havana Charter as it contained separately titled chapters, including the commercial policy chapter, but also a separate chapter for the ITO's general provisions. This *general provisions* chapter included the ITO security exception which applied to all of the Havana Charter. This would suggest at the outset that the security exception would have remained available as between regional members in the ITO framework. The resulting GATT contained consecutively numbered Articles and the security exception was not contained in a general and final provisions chapter or part. In point, the GATT Agreement contains no such chapter or part.

Article XXIV's predecessor in the final Havana Charter was numbered as Article 44. The restrictive regulations of commerce permitted between free-trade area partners in the Havana Article is listed as those, "under Section B of Chapter IV and under Article 45". Chapter IV of the Charter is titled "Commercial Policy" and is that part of the Havana Charter that later became the GATT. Section B of this Chapter IV contains Havana Charter Articles 20 through 24. These Articles match GATT Articles XI through XV and recount them in the same sequence.

Article 45 was also a part of the Commercial Policy Chapter IV and was titled, "General Exceptions to Chapter IV". With some other changes to the text, this Article later became incorporated as GATT Article XX, the General Exceptions Article for the General Agreement. In its original Havana position, this Article operated as an exception only to one part of the Havana Charter, the chapter on Commercial Policy, and, by its placement in the Commercial Policy Chapter, was not intended to operate as an exception to the ITO Charter provisions generally.

However, the GATT security exception of Article XXI, the non-listed Article raised by the EEC as the basis of its argument for a non-exhaustive interpretation, was not a part of the original Havana Chapter IV dedicated to Commercial Policy. Instead, the security exception was located under Chapter IX of the Havana Charter and numbered as Article 99. It was titled there as "General Exceptions". The rationale for its location outside the commercial policy chapter is quite clear from its preamble, as, "Nothing in this *Charter* shall be construed ..." (emphasis added). Thus, within the Havana drafting context, this exception was not likely placed before the Working Group of the sub-committee considering the provisions for free-trade areas and for customs unions. Nor would it likely have been placed before the Commercial Policy Committee, concerned as it would have been with its own chapter.

As Havana Charter Article 44 resided within the Commercial Policy chapter, it was reasonable that it would list only those articles within its own chapter which were intended to be excepted by its operation. Given the overall structure of the Charter, it would have been redundant for the Article to recite exceptions which were provided outside the Chapter on Commercial Policy and which in any case applied to the entire Havana Charter, as did Article 99. The most plausible interpretation for the absence of a security exception within the final Article XXIV is that of a simple incorporation error. In transferring the provisions from the ITO Charter to the GATT, the security exception, now also brought within the GATT as Article XXI, was simply omitted by oversight in failing to make a reference to an exception that was not originally located within the confines of the Commercial Policy Chapter. While this may only be a surmise, one notes the absence of any record to the contrary from the changes stated on behalf of the sub-committee report in outlining the changes to be effected for the Article.

In point, a referral by the drafting sub-committee at Havana that would have included a security exception would have had the effect of stating the exception two times. Thus, as recited from our earlier chapter on the Havana drafting, the referral to the larger Committee stated the following:

"(I)n paragraph 4 the definition of a customs union, which was contained in the second sentence of paragraph 4 of the Geneva draft, has been amended and a definition of a free-trade area has been added. This describes a free-trade area as a group of two or more customs territories within which tariffs, etc. (except where necessary, those permitted under section B of Chapter IV and under Article 43) are eliminated on substantially all the trade between the constituent territories … or at least on substantially all the trade in products originating in such territories".[18]

There would have been no reason for this listing of articles to include any of the provisions that would govern as exceptions to the Havana Charter as a whole and found outside the parameters of the Commercial Policy Chapter. Since Article 99 referred to the entire Charter in its preamble, Völker's point that it would have precedence over Article XXIV remains valid. If one considered the exceptions listed in the Havana Charter Article 44 as part of the overall Charter, then one would conclude that the security clause must also have been viewed to be an additional exception to the requirements, even though it was not listed in the Article.

---

[18] As cited in Supra, Chapter Two, section 2.2.4.

3.4   Issues regarding "Substantially-all trade"

3.4.1   *Internal-duty adjustments*

A second issue relating to the internal trade requirement was discussed in The
Working Group regarding permitted restrictions between regional partners. In response to the question of whether the GATT Articles listed in XXIV:8(b) were exhaustive or not, the reported EEC position was that,

> "In any case, the only question at issue was whether the *protective duties* that were
> authorized applied to a proportion of the trade of the area consistent with the require-
> ment that duties should be eliminated on substantially all the trade".[19]

This opinion was elaborated in more detail as,

> "... the representatives of the Six pointed out that the elimination of duties within the
> area -- as required by paragraph 8(b) -- could not be interpreted as meaning that a du-
> ty could not be reimposed or introduced. In the absence of any precise provision to
> that effect, such a restrictive interpretation could not be accepted ...The General
> Agreement merely provided that the duties in force at a given moment should not af-
> fect more than a fraction of the trade, so as not to jeopardize the requirement that sub-
> stantially all the trade should be liberalized".[20]

The net effect of providing for such flexibility for a completed free-trade area,
would be that,

> "...if the percentage subject to protective duties reached 20 percent, the institutions of
> the EEC would then, but only then, ... apply for such waivers as they deemed neces-
> sary".[21]

It is unfortunate that the issue of re-balancing sectors within a completed free trade
agreement was not resolved by the Working Group at this juncture. However, an
implicit EEC argument was also not addressed. This suggested that the substantially-all trade requirement *only* applied to the question of protective duties. Although
the report indicated earlier that concern was expressed regarding the use between
the regional parties of quantitative restrictions, the narrow question at hand during
the discussion above was the matter of re-establishing protective duties relative to
fiscal charges. In this regard, the EEC appeared to be making an interpretation of
the substantially-all trade test that would limit its scope only to the question of du-

---

[19] L/778, para. 26, italics added.
[20] Ibid., at para. 28.
[21] Ibid., at para. 32.

ties to be employed between parties, without consideration of the cumulative effects of other restrictive regulations of commerce.

Thus, even if one adopted a strict position that only those Articles listed as exceptions under paragraph 8(b) could be employed between the parties, the sum total of these restrictive regulations of commerce would also not be included in calculating the substantially-all trade requirement. Since the EEC had already determined that the list of Article exceptions were non-exhaustive, one can only conclude that a qualified free-trade area would permit the use of duties between parties and the adjustment of duties up or down to re-balance and exclude sectors as necessary within the parameter. In addition, whatever other restrictive regulations advisable to be applied between the members might not have any bearing on the substantially-all trade test.

3.4.2   The scope of the requirement as to duties and/or measures

This EEC position presented the Working Group with a question regarding the scope of the substantially-all trade requirement. Shall it be read to permit flexibility for the partners for both duties and measures, for duties only, or for measures only? The EEC view in the report can be read to support the notion that the requirement was being applied only to duties.

Commentators have not been active in making a response to the question of the scope of the substantially-all trade requirement. One can be reminded of Jackson's suggestion that the term "substantially" was not accidental but reflected the result of careful consideration in the negotiation and drafting of the text.[22] At the same time, Dam left us with a somewhat more cryptic definition of "substantial" in suggesting that it must refer to something less than "all of the trade", but certainly something more than "some of the trade". Neither offered an opinion as to whether the requirement is to be imposed upon only duties or only measures or both. This, however, was the concise issue that was presented by this aspect of the formation as a result of the EEC position taken.

The most restrictive interpretation that can be offered would state that duties are to be eliminated on all of the trade. Then, other restrictive regulations as measures would be entertained according to the Article XXIV(8)(b) listing of excepted Articles and as applied according to those provisions. In this reading the SAT requirement grants flexibility for the listed restrictive regulations but does not permit the continuing application or re-imposition of any duties after the interim period.

A "middle" view would permit duties together with other restrictive regulations to be counted together in determining whether substantially-all trade was being covered by the agreement. This could appear to coincide more closely with the

---

[22]   John H. Jackson, **World Trade Law and the Law of GATT,** the Mitchie Company, Charlottesville, Virginia, 1969, p. 608, citing UN doc. (1946) EPCT/C.II/PV.7, at p. 20.

punctuation of the text, which provides that, "duties and other restrictive regulations ... are eliminated." However, the text does not necessarily foreclose complete elimination of duties, since the clause providing for, "... except where necessary ..." refers to measures permitted to be undertaken, but not to duties. Further, the middle view, as does any other permitting maintenance of duties after formation, also forces the question of what exactly is an appropriate quantity of coverage to satisfy the SAT requirement. While the stricter view above does not provide flexibility for any duties, it does resolve the definitional problem of coverage by permitting only those measures that would be permitted between GATT parties as listed exceptions in any case. Although more rigorous, the stricter reading is easier to apply and confers a higher degree of legal certainty regarding the nature of the obligation to be imposed upon regional members.

It is not clear from the report whether the Working Group appreciated that the EEC was advancing a "least strict" interpretation. It is possible that the question of the scope of the SAT requirement was passed over by the group due to the overriding problem as to "how much" trade would be required to be covered in order to qualify for the Article XXIV exception.

3.4.3   *The extent of coverage required by "substantially-all trade"*

The EEC stated the position that if the Working Group was not able to advance a clear fraction of what constituted "substantially all the trade", then it was likewise not in a position to determine that a small volume of trade still operating by duties would violate the SAT requirement.[23] The EEC argued that only a small percentage of total trade (1.5%) would be affected by such duties. However, as noted in the report, this volume of trade appeared to include intra-EEC trade flows, a notation that was understood by the Working Group to be inconsistent with the formation of the customs union which would function as a single party to the Associations.

When challenged to present a better calculation to permit an analysis of how much trade was being covered, the EEC note indicated a refusal to provide such data unless the Working Group was prepared to first present its definition of substantially-all the trade.[24] Although it was somewhat disingenuous to attempt to apply the SAT standard to internal EEC trade, the EEC concern in revealing the actual bilateral trade between territories was that once revealed, the Working Group would retroactively determine that the volume of trade covered was inconsistent with the SAT requirement. Thus, the Working Group should "go first" in enunciating the percentage standard to apply, and then the EEC would supply the data.[25] Without such a definition being first provided, the EEC was prepared to consider (unilater-

---

[23]   L/778, para 29.
[24]   Ibid., at para 31.
[25]   Ibid.

ally) that a free-trade area covering 80% of the trade between the parties should be considered as a qualified agreement.[26]

In this exchange it is apparent that both parties were confronted with the problem of enunciating a quantity test which would then provide the other an opportunity to tailor the associations to the requirement. For the EEC's part, bilateral trade flows were not going to be disclosed since the Working Group could then set the fraction of trade at a level which would disqualify the association. However, given the inconclusive form of the agreements being reviewed with their lack of a clear plan or schedule showing reciprocity, and their retained right to re-impose future duties, one can also conjecture that the actual bilateral trade covered by the agreement might not have reached the 80% threshold advanced by the EEC. Later reviews of the Associations do tend to suggest that 80% may never have been reached. Moreover, given these other problems, one could also argue that coverage should have been the last thing to actually consider, and perhaps not considered at all until the other difficulties were addressed to the satisfaction of the Working Group. That however suggests a process that was not in application during this or later GATT Working Group reviews.

3.4.4 Reverse flexibility

While the Overseas Association review concentrated on the subject of reverse preferences, perhaps an impression has thereby been left that only the developing countries were granted flexibility in the preferences they were required to make. This is likely incorrect, and although the flexibility granted to the EEC as a party to the arrangements is not considered in the review, this aspect is also relevant to the legal criteria and forms a part of the necessary story that is to be disclosed in a review process.

Why there is such an absence of attention to the EEC's obligations under the Association is not clear from the review, but it is apparent that no adequate data to assess the EEC's market opening commitment was ever forwarded by the proponents. The EEC assertion that only 1.5% of the trade between the parties was uncovered by the commitment was correctly rejected outright not only for its inclusion of intra-Community trade flows. In this figure there was also the likelihood that "covered" referred to partial reductions of duties as well as to duty levels committed to be taken to zero. In the EEC's refusal to table the bilateral trade data the degree of trade affected by restrictive measures was also necessarily undisclosed.[27]

---

[26] Ibid., at para 30. This is the first reference in a GATT Working Group review report of the so-called 80% requirement. It has been occasionally applied in commentary to suggest that some type of finding was made in this Working Group that this percentage level met the requirement. There was no such finding in this review.

[27] L/778, para. 30-32.

As we know, the result of this exchange was the proponents' self-declared 20% designation, but how would review parties ever determine the meeting of that requirement in the absence of disclosure? From the EEC position, it appears that the proponents would apply for a waiver as necessary according to Article XXV if this 20% threshold were ever breached. Although not taken up by the Working Group, three ramifications are apparent. First, the EC never did concede that the 20% parameter would exclude intra-community trade. If the trade between member states was factored, then substantially all of the trade between the EC and the Association parties could be subjected to measures without breaching the 20% limit. Second, flexibility was intended by the 20% limit in regard to substituting one measure for another, or one sector for another. The EC made it clear that the parties intended to be free to open and close as they wish within the percentage parameter. This would supposedly apply to both measures invoked by the EEC and to measures invoked by the other partners. Third and related, the blanket limit as set made no allocation in regard to the limit to be applied by each party. If the 20% restriction referred to overall bilateral trade, The EC could avail itself of 19% of the limit, granting the partners 1%, or perhaps the limit could relate to 20% of each party's trade to the other.

3.5   Chapter Conclusion: commitment as a standard for review

An interpretation in favour of an exhaustive listing would have led to a somewhat stronger conclusion that other GATT Articles, notably Article VI and Article XIX, (antidumping and safeguards) were not listed in Article XXIV:8(b) because they were not intended by the drafters to be permitted as exceptions to the restrictions under Article XXIV. This view would admittedly have served as a basis for a far more restrictive exception granted by the Article than was advanced by the Overseas formation proponents, and by many regional proponents thereafter.

However, a strict view which would require the elimination of commercial defence and general safeguard measures for completed formations does derive some additional support from the conclusions in the previous chapter in regard to the alignment of provisions between customs unions as these were extended to free-trade areas. If we understand that free-trade areas and customs unions under Article XXIV were to be generally equated in their requirements regarding the substantially-all trade requirement, then a more coherent view of Article XXIV:8(b) is presented. The argument for preserving such measures in a completed customs union is questionable, as it appears inherently inconsistent with the formation of an external common tariff and supposedly, a common commercial policy.[28] In a com-

---

[28] While it is not inconceivable that members would retain internal authority while relieving themselves of external authority, such a situation would be not be easy to sustain beyond a transitional period. Just as deviations in the external application of a common tariff would cause the raising of

pleted customs union acting as a substitution for other customs territories, members would be met with inconsistency in employing continuing trade measures against goods originating in the other members, just as trade measures would be difficult to effect between provinces in a single national customs territory.

In a free-trade area where a constituent territory retain its sovereign commercial power, the possibility of directing trade measures between members remains real unless all the members are compelled by treaty to suspend their use, or otherwise agree to do so. As noted in the previous chapter, there was no prior pattern of practice before the GATT for any agreements known as free-trade areas. Therefore, it cannot be assumed that just because other pre-GATT preferential systems retained the use of contingent measures, that such a retention of country prerogative was considered either necessary or advisable for free-trade area partners. On the contrary, if a difference was intended to have been recognised between customs unions and free-trade areas in regard to internal measures, it would have been easy for the drafters to simply provide a different list of exception Articles for free-trade areas. Such a list would have acknowledged that these formations preserved commercial policy to other members. Instead, the provisions regarding customs unions, including its listed article exceptions were "extended" to the case of free-trade areas.

If Article XXIV:8(b) exceptions had been determined by decision at the time of the Overseas Association review to have been exhaustive, a rather strict equivalency between the internal requirements for the two types of formations would have been obtained at the outset. Neither type would have found a legal basis under paragraph 8 of the Article to apply internal contingent measures to other members for originating goods. Although GATT party practice according to the Article has not respected this line of interpretation in any manner, under different circumstances of review, Article XXIV(8)(b) could have been interpreted to deny the re-introduction of restrictive regulations of commerce other than those necessary as provided in GATT Articles XI through XV, the general exceptions according to Article XX recognising legitimate national objectives, and of course, the general security exception of Article XXI. This interpretation would have applied to the resulting formations after the completion of interim periods. Under what conditions certain

---

internal trade measures to avoid trade deflection, the application of internal measures would lead to a failure of free circulation. Origin determination would then be required for goods crossing internal borders in order to distinguish those subject to internal measures. In the EEC regime, Article 115 provided for such derogations, but restricted in application to problems incurred by the member states in reference to trade from third countries. As for internal trade, EEC Article 12 eliminated the use of customs duties and charges of equivalent effect, and EEC Article 30 eliminated quantitative restrictions and measures of equivalent effect. EEC Article 91 only authorised the Commission to redress dumping within the common market during the transition period. The placement of this Article in the Treaty's competition policy chapter indicates that the possibility of re-exportation of goods in a completed common market would alleviate the need for individual member-state anti-dumping remedies.

transitional measures would have been permitted would have been addressed on a case by case basis in reviewing the plan and schedule of the parties.[29]

It is conceivable that in a Review presented with different facts, that some progress toward formulating the application of Article XXIV to a free-trade area might have been realised. It is hard to imagine a worse set of facts to challenge the Article, devoid as it was of any previous interpretative framework for the tests to be applied. However, the Overseas Association Working Group did attempt to isolate the various standards to be applied to a submitted formation, and at least sought to determine whether or not the formation was compatible with the Article. One might suggest that but for the proponent's opinions, the balance of the Group might have well voted a resounding 'nay' on the Associations. Nevertheless, from this review forward, commentary has been normally quick to commence its criticism of the process by reference to the imprecision of the drafting of the Article and lack of clarity of the legal terms to be applied. After summarising the review, one is more inclined to lay fault on the lack of transparency in disclosure and upon certain institutional weaknesses in the process, an argument to develop in the next chapter.

For now, to demonstrate that the Working Group was in control of an appropriate line of analysis which could have led to the development of meaningful criteria over time, the following report statement is offered:

> "(M)any members of the Sub-Group said that each case of a proposed customs union or free-trade area had to be considered on its merits and that it was, therefore, inappropriate to fix a general figure of the percentage of trade which could be subjected to internal barriers without running counter to the definition in paragraph 8 (b) of Article XXIV. *A matter to be considered was whether the provisions of a free-trade area pointed towards a gradual increase of barriers affecting the trade between the constituent parties or a gradual reduction of such barriers".*[30]

The comment poses the foundation for a workable test in that it calls for a demonstration of whether regional members intend to reduce barriers over time. Absent documentation to support such a commitment, it is hard to imagine why Article XXIV should be available to grant an exception from GATT's other obligations. As indicated by paragraph 7 of the Article, this demonstration is required to be made by the submission of a plan and schedule. With reasonable disclosure, an initial determination can be exacted and examined in combination with the declaration of parties and the provisions of the applicable agreement.

---

[29] Non-members have tended to strenuously object to any interpretation of Article XXIV which would permit regional members to take measures against third country trade which would not likewise apply internally. This view is inconsistent with Article XXIV requirements as they are outlined here.

[30] L/778, at para. 34. (italics added).

The key element required to apply such a test is that of "commitment". The inquiry should be seen to revolve on the question of whether the parties have demonstrated a quality of commitment sufficient to pass the interim period with a gradual decrease of barriers. If the provisions of an agreement are silent on this point, or actually point to a possible gradual increase of barriers over time, then the commitment is low. The chances of completion are diminished and the agreement should not be supported according to the terms of the Article.[31]

As minimal as is this suggested test in imposing any precise criteria, arguably the Overseas Association did not even reach this first rung on the ladder. As a number of regional plans submitted after the Overseas Association also failed to exhibit qualities of commitment as suggested, it is not so difficult to understand why so many reviews failed to reach any consensus in support of the regional proponents. It is to a number of systemic problems flowing from this and later reviews that the discussion now turns.

---

[31] Article XXIV:8 together with Article XXIV:7 is an indication that GATT Contracting Parties are entitled to receive a credible demonstration of commitment.

Chapter 4
SYSTEMIC ISSUES IN GATT-47 REVIEWS

"But how many delegates could have foreseen that these provisions would be used also for forging closer commercial ties between developed and developing countries? Such a colonial-type pact was surely a thing of the past". *F.A. Haight, (1972)*.

4.1 Introduction

This chapter discusses some issues that have been identified to describe why the internal trade requirement for Article XXIV has not found a basis for a more strict coverage application. An impression that can be derived from the later dispute panel cases is that if only a legal interpretation of the qualification requirement in Article XXIV:8 had been adopted, then the problem of proliferation of agreements would be resolved to the benefit of the MFN principle. However, besides the question of legal certainty, there are also political, institutional and economic factors that would likely have an impact on whether the criteria could be applied in the actual practice. The point of this chapter is to raise these constraints in order to address the question of whether a more consistent application of Article XXIV requirements could be reconciled with these factors.

4.2 Coverage issues raised in later reviews

The flexibility demanded by the EEC and its Overseas Association partners established a precedent for an increasing leeway overall in the EEC's approach to free-trade areas. This flexibility, nearly always directed to the internal trade requirement, became a mainstay of later reviews. For example, in the 1972 Yaounde' II review, some Working Group members suggested that safeguard, budgetary and development measures, which were all capable of restricting trade between the parties, should be reported upon in the interim review in order to determine whether substantially-all trade was being accorded. The EEC responded that it was up to the regional parties and not to the Contracting Parties to determine if later-introduced measures degraded trade coverage below the substantially all trade level. The parties to the Convention promised to report to the GATT if such a lowering of trade occurred. It was, therefore, asserted that GATT parties should have no basis to conduct any independent determination of the requirements.[1]

From this perspective, one might conclude that having invoked Article XXIV, the EEC saw the exception as granting something of a free hand to the regional members to conduct the agreement according to their design without any meaningful oversight by the GATT Contracting Parties. As evidence, a call in this Yaounde review to have the Secretariat prepare an independent report to determine the status of restrictions imposed between the parties was also rejected by the EEC and also not permitted to go forward.[2]

Also in 1972 from the EEC-Israel review, another mark of flexibility was achieved where some working party members noted that there was no point in discussing the coverage of the agreement at all, since it did not provide for the elimination of duties but only for their reduction.[3] The inference made was that free-trade areas may be formed in the absence of a declaration of regional free trade. Similarly, in the 1972 report on the EEC Association with Tanzania, Uganda and Kenya, trade coverage before and after the Agreement was reported to be almost insignificant, perhaps affecting only 6-7% of the trade. The net effect was claimed to have simply accorded some preferences (one-way) without any commitment undertaken for reciprocity.[4]

In the EEC-Cyprus Association, a new concept of "provisional" agreement was introduced to distinguish between "interim" agreements permitted by Article XXIV. The EEC indicated that, "the agreement was not interim in the sense that it could be reversed." This inferred that no binding commitment was made at all between the parties, a point supported by the fact that although Cyprus' agriculture exports to the Community comprised 63% of all of its exports to the EEC, agriculture trade was excluded from the Agreement's coverage.[5] In the Egypt report, which was engaged after the GSP system was instituted and within which a complete alternative for granting developing country preferences had been created, duty free commitment was yet stated to be applied to only 45% of the bilateral trade.[6]

These samples indicate that whatever meaning the term "substantial" might hold for paragraph 8, it held little bearing over the regional proposals of the EEC through at least the early 1970s.

It also emerged more clearly over time that the EEC intended to reserve the right to impose safeguards on the trade of its regional partners, which safeguards would not necessarily be extended to other GATT parties unless and until the EEC invoked the provisions of Article XIX. This gesture was universally applauded by

---

[1]   1972 BISD, L/3465, para. 11 and 12.
[2]   Ibid., at para. 28.
[3]   1972 BISD, L/3581, para. 22-24.
[4]   1973 BISD, L/3721, para. 16.
[5]   1975 BISD, L/4009, para. 10-12 and para 21.
[6]   1975 BISD, L/4054, para 16.

reviewing parties since Article XIX offered certain procedural and compensatory guarantees for their trade. However, the reverse implication of the policy is also germane. For safeguards directed to the regional parties, the EEC did not intend to be bound by GATT rules to invoke Article XIX as to them, even where such regional members were also GATT Contracting Parties. This apparent conflict between GATT rules and the scope of the exception permitted by Article XXIV has escaped the attention of a number of Working Groups, at least as documented from the reports throughout the GATT-1947 era.[7] Rather, while the question of safeguards has been raised on a number of occasions within Working Groups, the discussion has tended to focus upon whether non-members' external trade would be detrimentally affected by the possible cessation of safeguards between members.

Non-members have remained understandably concerned that safeguards directed toward them would also be applied on a non-discriminatory basis to regional partners. Thus for the GATT, the issue has been whether or not regional partners would be relieved of safeguards, not whether safeguards imposed against regional members would be duly notified and treated under GATT Article XIX rules.[8] From a flexibility perspective, the free trade area plans would offer the EEC the capacity to execute selective safeguards in reference to the trade of its own regional partners (and vice versa). As a possible justification, one review discloses that the EEC, in noting that such safeguards would not necessarily be extended to non-members, indicated that the special safeguard language was necessary in order to adjust to certain "distortions of competition" that could occur under the free-trade area.[9]

4.3 Developed-developing territories and reverse preferences

Many of the formations causing difficulty for review parties on the coverage issues were those being established between developed and developing countries, combinations attempted by territories at occasionally extremely different levels of economic progress or national wealth. As noted earlier, the notion of a free-trade area did not pre-exist the GATT. While the inclusion of an exception for free trade areas was considered at Havana, the discussions, according to Haight, centred on their application either in the context of developing countries (Lebanon-Syria) or perhaps as to developed countries in reference to European integration. His reflection on events as they had transpired by 1972 is telling in this regard:

---

[7] For example, 1975 BISD, L/4054, para 19.

[8] For example, EC-Austria report, 1974 BISD, L/3900, para. 30-32.

[9] EC-Norway Report, 1975 BISD, L/3996, para. 31, but the agreement in question does not provide for such a criteria for the imposition of safeguards.

"(B)ut how many delegates could have foreseen that these provisions would be used also for forging closer commercial ties between developed and developing countries? Such a colonial-type pact was surely a thing of the past. For a backward territory to give better treatment of imports of manufactures from one or more industrialized countries than to those from other and possibly cheaper sources of supply was an arrangement sometimes imposed by colonial powers. One would not expect independent developing countries to enter voluntarily into such a new-colonial arrangement, thereby limiting their freedom to protect their own industrial development".[10]

Jackson also tended to support the view that for free-trade areas, the exception was understood to be a means of facilitating co-operation between developing countries as a method for assisting industrialisation.[11] Dam only ascribed the provisions to a mix of interest in European integration and the interests of less-developed countries.[12] Haight's opinion suggests that re-combinations of colonial-type trade arrangements within the frame of a new free-trade area exception were possibly not considered in the drafting of the Article.[13] This opinion finds some concurrence by Working Group member comments in later reviews which asserted that the Article could not possibly have been intended to be applied in any manner that would require developing countries to offer reverse preferences to the developed regional partner.[14]

---

10   F.A. Haight, *Customs Unions and Free Trade Areas Under GATT: A Reappraisal*, Journal of World Trade Law, V.6, No. 4, (1972), pp. 391-404, at p. 394.

11   John H. Jackson, **World Trade Law and the Law of GATT,** the Mitchie Company, Charlottesville, Virginia, (1969), p. 603, but not citing to a conference report or document.

12   Kenneth W. Dam, **The GATT: Law and International Economic Organization**, The University of Chicago Press, (1970), (Midway Reprint, 1977), p. 274. One could suggest that the customs union aspect certainly held interest for European governments interested in integration, as customs union formation had already commenced in the Benelux.

13   There is some support that the free trade area inclusion related also to European integration interests, although not so clear as to distinguish between the prospective employment of free-trade areas between European countries, or the maintenance of post-colonial systems within the context of possible future European integration. Thus, Haight notes that it was a French Representative, "who was credited with having thus developed and refined the Lebanon-syria proposal, said it would be of great interest to Europe, and so it proved to be". F.A. Haight, Supra note 10 at p. 394. He also appears to raise the post-colonial aspect for Europe in noting a possible French interest in reserving the capacity to match in its own post war relations to the type of standstill treatment that was obtained by the British Commonwealth system. A free trade area exception could be seen to provide such an avenue. However, the Overseas Association provisions of the Rome Treaty, and the Agreements themselves did not specify the formation of free-trade areas.

14   For examples, Yaounde' (first) Convention, 1966 BISD, L/2441, para. 13 and 25; Yaounde' II, 1972 BISD, L/3465, para. 20. Perhaps Haight and Jackson's understanding of the Article is consistent with other concessions made at Geneva on behalf of developing countries, including the draft Article 15 which would grant a 2/3 waiver for under-developed country regional preferences which would fall short of the more stringent free trade area requirements. However contra, Dam considered the issue as raised between industrialised and material producing countries in the Overseas Association review to be spurious. Kenneth W. Dam, *Regional Economic Arrangements and the GATT, the Legacy of a Misconception*, University of Chicago Law Review, V. 30, No. 4, 1963, pp. 615-665, p. 648, his note 97.

The question raised above by Haight was clearly at issue in the GATT Working Group review of the EEC's Overseas Association. If the Article was to be applied as it appeared to be written, the developing countries in the Association would be required to provide a full measure of reverse preferences to the EC as a condition for the free trade area formation. The result of these reverse preferences would be seen necessarily however to undermine the attributed motive of seeking to restrain colonial preference systems in the first place. GATT drafters may have viewed the role of the General Agreement to address (in part) the external discrimination posed by preferential colonial systems and thereby sought to constrain formations by raising the requirements. However, the free trade area exception together with its reciprocity provisions, when invoked by developed-developing countries, was likely seen to open the possibility for the reconstruction of these same disfavoured arrangements.

Whether or not the drafters contemplated limiting this aspect of the Article to developing country formations, the Article itself made no distinction between development levels of the parties, however requiring regional members to remove barriers between the parties, i.e., the reciprocity or mutuality requirement. However, in the context of developed-developing country relations, by requiring reverse preferences on behalf of former colonies, one can imagine a level of exasperation rising where Working Group parties were challenged to argue for the inclusion of these reciprocal exchanges between previous colonial formations. This would occur with the addition that combinations would be sanctioned in the context of GATT Article XXIV. To some of the parties, the use of the free-trade area exception in combination with reverse preferences between developmentally dissimilar territories must have appeared as though a colonial Trojan horse had been re-introduced to the GATT system.

As indicated earlier, there was objection by the review parties to the Overseas Association formation as presented. Most of it centred on the problem of reverse preferences not being required of the developing association countries. It is not difficult however to appreciate the dichotomous position that would have to be assumed by any non-member who would attempt to insist on a full measure of reverse preferences as a condition to these formations. This sentiment would be present whether taking the view of developing or developed non-members. Developing countries would understand that an extension of EEC member-state preferences to the wider Community diminished their market access.[15] Developed countries would also suffer exclusionary effects from developing country members as a result of any completed reverse-preference formation. For such objectors, exacting a full measure of mutuality between the EEC and its various regional partners must have been seen as a total contradiction, at least to the spirit of the GATT system

---

[15] This problem was dealt with in part by the resolution of the Working Group to provide a sector by sector study to determine if injury to this trade was being caused.

rules, as suggested by Haight. Further, exacting such reciprocity would probably have seemed damaging to their own direct interests in trade to the European market as well as the other regional members. In this context, one recalls Jackson's summary of the effects of the Overseas Association and its review:

> "Indeed, the EEC overseas territory arrangements were considered by many GATT members to be simply a continuation of the colonial preference schemes described in Article I annexes B and C of GATT, with the preferences expanded in the EEC setting".[16]

What is not clear from his statement or the reviews is whether the reverse preference problem would have also arisen in a situation whereby a truly complete exchange of reciprocity would have been created by all the partners. In other words, should one determine that an objectionable extension of colonial-type systems was being effected because preferences were being exchanged by developed and developing countries representing former colonial arrangements, or because the exchanges made were selective by nature and therefore partially preferential? The shading between these different possibilities is relevant if one considers that within a completed exchange the capacity of the developed territory to exercise a form of negative internal discrimination, i.e., to selectively offer and withdraw preferences as to its developing partner, is also markedly constrained. In a more flexible arrangement, the capacity to engage in selective internal discrimination is heightened. Thus, on the one hand we can argue that complete exchanges would have reinstituted a colonial arrangement in exacting a 100% positive preference in favour of the developed country. On the other hand, in exacting such a complete exchange, the developed country's discretion to deny market access to the developing country's trade is also eliminated.

It would seem that the more partial and tentative declarations between unequal partners would be the arrangements more likely to be associated with the effects of the colonial past. In this sense Haight and Jackson correctly summarised the opinions expressed by Working Groups toward the problem of reverse preferences, but perhaps did not go far enough in asking how these reverse preferences would have been viewed if exchanged for a full measure of access to the EEC market. Beneath the characterisation of colonialism, the underlying legal issue to raise may have not been only whether developing countries should have been granting reverse preferences, but rather whether they would be able to obtain fair value in return.

The manner in which this question was dealt with over time is also telling. Although later periodic reports by the participants projected the opinion that Association members were making progress toward establishing reciprocity, ultimately

---

[16] "Perhaps no case is more revealing of the danger of preferential arrangements contrary to Most-Favoured Nation creeping into GATT through the ambiguities of Article XXIV". J. Jackson, Supra note 11 at p. 609.

the illusion of reverse preferences was simply dropped in the reformation of the Association in the ACP-EEC First Convention of Lomé. By this time, it was reported that only one Working Group member objected to the disbanding of the formal reciprocity requirement as contained in the earlier Convention. As discussed in the following chapter, this decision to abandon the textual provision of the mutuality requirement of paragraph 8 of Article XXIV would provide the basis for a serious legal challenge to the Lomé's GATT status twenty years hence, at least as it was claimed to fall within the free-trade area exception of Article XXIV.[17]

Why would there be so little attention paid to the quality of the EEC's own commitments in these various developed-developing or large-small country free-trade areas? It seems logical after all, that for each agreement which did not call for a high degree of reverse preferences, that the EEC was also not being held to a very high standard of internal free trade. By reducing the obligations on the part of the developing countries, the EEC was also implicitly relieved from market opening commitments. One explanation by way of conjecture is that no one really cared if the EEC did not open its market. The regional members themselves could hardly object to their lack of market access when they themselves were not granting it. The developing country non-members could retain their trade from any incomplete formations as any absence of opening on behalf of the regional members would preserve the status quo. The developed country non-members may have gained the most from attempting to block incomplete formations, as this would preserve their MFN rights to developing markets in accordance with the GATT provisions. However, complete exchanges might also have been detrimental to their access to the EEC market.

Nevertheless, critical remarks concerning EEC regional developments did became more accentuated over time. For example, from EEC-Israel, "(t)he growing network of discriminatory agreements, many of which were not consistent with Article XXIV weakened the MFN trading system on which GATT was based".[18] From EEC-Egypt, one Working Group member noted that most of the Working Group members supporting the particular formation were already in similar arrangements and that virtually all such arrangements were by the EEC with some other party.[19]

---

[17]   1977 BISD, L/4369, para. 10. *EEC-Import Regime for Bananas*, 3 June 1993 and 11 February 1994, unreported.

[18]   EC-Israel, 1977 BISD, L/4365, para. 23.

[19]   EEC-Egypt, 1975 BISD, L/4054, para. 11.

4.4   Institutional factors in the review process

Besides the problem of attempting to review agreements that were never intended
to comply with Article XXIV terms in the first place, the weakening of the internal trade requirement was compounded by institutional deficiencies in the practice
of GATT reviews. It may be the case that the absence of independent control over
regional formations has contributed more to the slackening of the requirements
than has the interpretive problems associated with the provisions. This institutional deficiency also came to the surface in the Overseas Association review, particularly in light of the previous, albeit brief, Working Group review practice. Regarding this practice, GATT had reported in BISD three other regional formations. The
first two were reported in 1952 BISD, the first for the Customs Union between
South Africa and Southern Rhodesia,[20] and the second for the Free trade area between Nicaragua and El Salvador.[21] The third review was published in 1957 BISD,
concerning the Participation of Nicaragua in the Central American Free Trade
Area.[22]

4.4.1   *The earliest decisions*

All three of these reviews resulted in Contracting Party decisions and, as Sampson
has noted, this group of decisions constituted the first and last group of agreements
to ever receive a finding of conformity according to Article XXIV in the GATT
1947 by a consensus of the Contracting Parties.[23] In the Nicaragua-El Salvador review and decision, the Contracting Parties provided a decision memorandum for
the first free-trade area considered after the conclusion of the General Agreement.
The decision required that the regional members were to file an annual report and
declared a reservation to review the positive decision at any time if found that the
arrangement was not resulting, "in the maintenance of a free trade area in the sense
of Article XXIV of the General Agreement".[24] This condition was accompanied by
an unequivocal decision by the Contracting Parties that the government of Nicaragua was entitled to claim the benefits of Article XXIV relating to the formation of
this free trade area.

In the second decision relating to Nicaragua, the notification for this formation
was not based upon a completed treaty, but upon the country's decision to conclude
a treaty with other countries in the region. As such, no plan or schedule was submitted. Therefore, the decision, while taking note of the intent of the country to

---

[20]   1952 BISD p. 29.
[21]   Decision of 25 October 1951, 1952 BISD, p. 30.
[22]   Decision of 13 November, 1956.
[23]   G. Sampson, *Regional Trading Blocks and World Economy*, (mimeo), Address for Queen's University of Belfast, 2 June, 1994, p. 11.
[24]   1952 BISD, Supra note 21.

form the free-trade area within ten years, also noted the intent of Nicaragua to seek a plan and schedule for submission to the Contracting Parties within four years. On this basis, the Contracting Parties concluded that the country was entitled to claim the benefits of Article XXIV, however subject to a requirement that there would be a later review of the decision. This later review would take place if, based upon the filed plan and schedule, it was determined that the formation in the sense of Article XXIV was unlikely to be established within the ten year period. In this case the Contracting Parties seemingly provided flexibility for Nicaragua, but certainly due to the fact that the country made a notification prior to the completion of an actual agreement. A plan and schedule would constitute a declaration of the party's intentions, and would then provide a basis for review and be subject to review. The ten-year rule was clearly stated as not being waived for this formation.

4.4.2   *The power to make decisions and the power to block*

In both of these reviews there is a distinct inference in the decisions that the Contracting Parties had the power to determine whether or not free-trade area members could avail themselves of the provisions of Article XXIV. This suggests that the Contracting Parties would also have had the power to determine that a Contracting Party would not be entitled to avail itself of the Article XXIV exception. The components of the decisions which reserved the right to later deny the Article XXIV benefits if the regional agreement was not successfully completed can be cited to support the potential available under Article XXIV for the Contracting Parties to exercise control over free-trade area formations. The filing of an annual report, also dictated by the decisions, would assumedly provide the material necessary to determine whether such a later review was necessary.

However, Jackson appears to have disagreed at least in part with this characterisation. His interpretation was that authority for the Contracting Parties to declare the applicability of Article XXIV to a particular arrangement is valid only in those circumstances where a GATT party forms an arrangement with a non-Contracting Party. This is based upon his reading of paragraph 5 of Article XXIV, which limits the provisions of Article XXIV to the formation of regional arrangements to the territories of Contracting Parties. Both of the Nicaragua decisions involved arrangements with non-Contracting Parties. In the absence of this circumstance, Jackson concluded that the review of the operation of Article XXIV provided for an automatic exception, whereby no special action is required of the GATT. In this manner Article XXIV, in the absence of affirmative Contracting Party action, has been interpreted by him to be essentially self-declaratory in nature.[25]

---

[25]   J. Jackson, Supra note 11 at p. 582. However, paragraph seven of the Article does reserve to the Contracting Parties the right to make recommendations, and the proponents shall not place the formation into effect without adapting the agreement to the recommendations. This would seem to provide for the power of review outright.

It is not so clear that this was the prevailing view at the time of the Overseas Association report. There is no indication in the review that the Working Parties did not believe that they had an obligation to render a recommendation. Assumedly this recommendation would find its final expression as a Contracting Party decision. Given that the two earlier reports resulted in Contracting Party decisions, there may have been an understanding, or at least an anticipation, by the Working Group, that a decision either affirmative or negative would also result for this arrangement. In this first "contested" review, it is conceivable that arguments made for full preferences to be exchanged were done so with the intent to establish a basis for a Contracting Party decision along the earlier lines. Accordingly,

> "Some members of the Sub-Group pointed out that the Committee should be informed that a majority had advanced the view that the association ... was not consistent with the provisions of Article XXIV of the General Agreement ... The representative of the Six stated that in his opinion ... the Treaty could only be examined (or reported upon) *as a whole* by whatever body was instructed to carry out that examination".[26]

The EEC position was that consensus was required at each and every level of the process in order to pass any conclusion on to the next level. Recalling that paragraph 7 of the Article prohibits regional members from implementing a regional agreement in light of Contracting Parties recommendation for changes, the implications of the EEC view are clear. If no recommendations can advance from the Sub-Group level without the proponent's consent, then regional members exercise a true veto power over any possibility of receiving recommendations. In this sense, there is truth to Jackson's characterisation. As long as regional members hold the power to block a recommendation, the process is inherently self-declaratory overall. However, this view would only hold in the absence of any other process that could challenge measures undertaken by regional members in the course of implementation. As we shall see, the EEC did not perhaps factor the possibility of dispute resolution as a function of the process.

4.4.3   *The requirement of consensus*

While it was understood that the examination of the Rome Treaty and its association could not have been completed within a single session, it became clear by the following session that an attempt to obtain a decision on the larger question of Article XXIV consistency would not be forthcoming. By the first report of the Intersessional Committee on the Treaty Establishing the European Economic Communi-

---

[26] L/778, para 45, italics added.

ty,[27] the attempt to form some criteria for compatibility under these circumstances was abandoned outright; as,

"... the Committee felt that it would be more fruitful if attention could be directed to specific and practical problems, leaving aside for the time being questions of law and debates about the compatibility of the Rome Treaty with Article XXIV of the General Agreement".[28]

Even though a significant majority of the sub-committee had determined that the Association did not meet the qualifications of the Article, the lack of consensus even at this level prevented the larger committee from attempting to consider the majority opinion in the making of a recommendation.

Since any final Contracting Party decision would require a consensus in any case, and since those committee members in minority also were Contracting Parties for the purpose of a recommendation by the Contracting Parties, the heart of the institutional difficulty regarding non-complying regional agreements must be laid to rest on the requirement of consensus itself. Within this institutional context one should also consider the often-cited opinion that the term "substantially" has been the cause of the problem with the proliferation of non-complying agreements. Thus, one may consider the result obtained if the Article had been drafted absent the term, thereby leaving no possible doubt that coverage of all trade was required for the exception. Even in this hypothetical case, and with the process as described above, there would yet be a continuing absence of any recommendation or decisions disqualifying the compatibility of particular agreements with Article XXIV. By acting to reject a majority recommendation, regional members would continue to derive the "self-declaratory" basis to implement non-complying agreements regardless of the text of the Article.

A review of early Working Groups tends to confirm that the difficulty of application arose more from the absence of a more supra-national review mechanism that could make recommendations without regard to the position of the regional members. Such a mechanism could have developed a pattern of practice providing meaning over time for terms such as "substantially". Perhaps the absence of such a decision-making procedure was necessary at the outset to retain the underlying

---

[27] 1959 BISD, Seventh Supplement, p. 69.

[28] Ibid., para. 3 at p. 70. The Contracting Parties did make the following conclusion at page 71. Relating that postponement of final examination was called for as there was not sufficient information to enable the parties to complete an examination, pursuant to para. 7 of Article XXIV, that Article XXII procedures remained available for individual parties to address questions arising from the Rome Treaty, and that EEC members agreed to furnish information under Article XXII consultations in the future. Finally, noting other normal procedures available to Contracting Parties, "(I)t being open of course to such country to invoke the benefit of Article XXIV insofar as it considered that this Article provided justification for any action which might otherwise be inconsistent with a provision or provisions of the General Agreement". Ibid., para. f, at p. 71.

GATT political compromise between the principle of most-favoured nation and the pre-existence of preferential systems. Nevertheless, it is also a common feature of these Working Groups that regional members showed little inclination to amend formation plans to take into consideration Working Group considerations that were directly related to the Article's requirements.

4.5   The Article XXIV paradox

Related to the lack of an institutional grounding to impose the internal trade requirement is that aspect characterised by Haight as the Article XXIV paradox. This is the delicate point where legitimate non-member concern for trade flows confronts the internal trade requirement directly and the role of the parties in its enforcement. As the paradox is explained, Working Group members are said to be placed in the problematic position of objecting to a formation when it discriminates against only a portion of their external trade, but nevertheless be compelled to support it when discriminating against substantially all of their trade.[29]

What the paradox discloses is a divergence between the interests of non-members serving as GATT Contracting Parties as contrasted with their individual positions as trading countries, with issues being pressed regarding the sectoral concerns of proposed formations. This suggests that what is presented for consideration is not so much a paradox but rather a straight-forward conflict of interest. A possible resolution would acknowledge individual country interests and to provide a channel to express these positions which was separate from the process of compatibility determinations with the Article provisions. It could be suggested that reviewing parties should be relieved of the responsibility of simultaneously advocating on behalf of the GATT system. This would suggest establishing a separate mechanism to review the trade issues resulting from the implementation of formations that have been already qualified according to Article XXIV provisions. This would be in contrast to a review mechanism that takes up sectoral trade diversion issues at the outset of the process prior to any determination that legal qualifications according to Article XXIV have been or can be met by the regional members.

However, it has also been suggested earlier that the structure of GATT Article XXIV already accommodates this bifurcation. This is found in the provisions whereby a formation must first be determined to be either one leading to a free-trade area or customs union according to paragraph 8. Only after such a finding can be installed is there any necessity to proceed to the question of whether the qualified regional trade agreement raises new barriers to the trade of non-members. Thus it appears that the conflict of interest is resolvable by calling a forward a distinct two-step analysis as to paragraph 8 and then paragraph 5.

---

[29]   F.A. Haight, Supra note 10.

4.6   Chapter Conclusion

There are other aspects of the Overseas Association and the other early reviews that retain relevance for the interpretation of Article XXIV. At this juncture, what is learned from the reviews of the GATT-47 era is that free-trade areas and customs unions contained parallel restrictions in regard to the internal trade requirement. When presented with a large association concerning a number of linked developed/developing country preferential agreements, all of which presenting a conflict of requiring reverse preferences on the part of developing countries, the internal free trade requirement was disarmed overall. At the core of this action lay the EEC's continuing insistence that reciprocity would not apply for the developing parties of the Association.

While the most important legal questions posed by the Association and its successors remain unresolved to this very day, the cumulative effect of the arrangements brought forward during GATT's first twenty years should not be underestimated. In order to ameliorate the problem of institutional control, the problem of reverse preferences in developed/developing country arrangements, and the "Article XXIV paradox", a diminution of the requirement of mutual reciprocity covering a sufficient degree of trade was implemented as a matter of course. This flowed certainly from demands of regional proponents to institute their arrangements as declared.

While these systemic problems continued in the GATT and were reflected by many of its Working Group reviews, the dispute resolution process was eventually called into play, and slowly began to have bearing upon GATT parties' own impressions of the Article and the extent of the obligations imposed by it. The initial forays into this territory indicated at the outset that the legal provisions of the Article did in fact convey meaning in the form of actual legal requirements.

Chapter 5
THE GATT PANEL PRACTICE RESPONSE
(BANANAS I AND II)

"Had non-reciprocal agreements between developed and developing parties been considered justifiable under Article XXIV and Part IV, the decisions of the CP (contracting parties) on the GSP and the Enabling Clause would have been largely unnecessary. Developed countries could simply have formed a "free-trade area" with selected developing countries by reducing barriers unilaterally on imports from those countries". *DS38/R, para. 162 (unadopted, 1994).*

5.1   Introduction

This chapter discusses the GATT-1947 legal challenges that were made to regional trade agreements. As this has been a rarity in GATT legal practice, the material here is drawn from two unreported GATT dispute panel cases from the early 1990's. Unadopted cases are not officially reported by the GATT and are without any legal authority or status in GATT law. However, as later GATT and WTO panels have determined, the reasoning of unreported panels, where relevant, has the ability to provide useful guidance in later actions and may be called upon in that manner. Here, the interpretations of GATT Article XXIV as it is invoked as a type of defence, and particularly its relation to GATT Article I MFN, serve as first important benchmarks in the judicial development of a more restrictive criteria for the qualification of free-trade areas.

Both Bananas I and II ruled that where a regional party attempts to invoke the Article XXIV exception as a basis for extending selective preferences, that this defence is subject to some capacity for legal review according to dispute settlement procedures provided by GATT Article XXIII. This is the case at least where the text of the agreement by its own terms fails to establish a requirement of legal reciprocity according to Article XXIV requirements. While this holding can be viewed narrowly to the particular facts here as presented by the Agreement establishing Lomé, the implications have significance for future parties' practice, and for later rulings. As Lomé parties thereafter sought an Article XXV waiver for their preferences also suggests that they were not willing to assume the risk that later panelists in the WTO would affirm.

The impact of the cases flows from the view of the Article as a type of defence, and placing a burden upon the respondent party who has chosen to invoke it to demonstrate that the arrangement is a qualified free-trade area agreement. This overturns the previous view of the practice whereby regional members maintained that notification to GATT alone was sufficient to immunise their regional preferences from later challenges. Thus, although regional formations may yet be "self declaratory" in nature, they are not necessarily "self-qualified" upon declaration. A second implication drawn flows from the ruling that reciprocity (mutuality) between regional parties is a requirement of GATT Article XXIV:8(b). This undertaking must be explicit in the parties' declarations in order to survive a legal challenge. This rather directly confronts the view of regional proponents on the reverse preference issue raised first in the Overseas Association and those reviews of a number of later regional agreements between developed and lesser-developed territories.

5.2   First case: EEC-Member States' Import Regimes for Bananas, DS32/R (1993)

5.2.1   *Factual elements and terms of reference*

Consultations leading to this panel were raised in 1992 by Columbia, Costa Rica, Guatemala, Nicaragua and Venezuela.[1] The panel was requested in February of 1993. The following factual aspects regarding the EC import regime are noted. Since 1963, the EEC had maintained a common ad valorem 20% tariff for importation of bananas. However, discrimination in favour of Lomé bananas was granted by the Lomé Convention granting duty free treatment for these commodities. Protocol 5 of the Fourth Lomé Convention stated that the EC was committed to maintaining the traditional advantage of ACP suppliers on the EC member state markets. In addition, individual EC countries maintained certain national restrictions on non-ACP bananas. These were listed and reported to GATT as an annex to Regulation 288/82, the EC Regulation for Common Rules for Imports.[2]

The core of the complaint raised against the EC related to the restrictions imposed on the importation of Latin American (non ACP) bananas by the individual country regimes that were in operation at the end of 1992.[3] Four of the complain-

---

[1]   Besides these parties, permitted participation in the panel was agreed for meetings and submission of several countries of the Lomé Convention, particularly Cameroon, Cote d'Ivoire, Jamaica, Madagascar, and Senegal. A request to participate by Belize was made late and not granted by the parties.

[2]   All individual EC member state import regimes were scheduled to expire on June 30, 1993, as in February of 1993, the Council adopted Reg 404/93 to establish a common market organisation for bananas and a new import regime to be effective July 1, 1993. DS32/R, para 13-16. Individual EC countries maintaining national restrictions included France, Italy, Portugal, Spain and the UK.

[3]   National import regimes effective in the EC at the end of 1992 included, tariff free quota applied in Germany; 20% duty on non ACP bananas in Belgium, Denmark, Ireland, Luxembourg, Netherlands; various quantitative restrictions and licensing in France, Greece; Italy, Portugal and the UK; outright de facto prohibition of imports in Spain.

ants requested a panel finding that the country regimes were inconsistent with GATT Article I, II, XI, XIII and Part IV of the General Agreement.[4] The EC, aside from certain procedural objections, requested a finding that the regimes were in conformity with GATT as interpreted according to subsequent practice of the Contracting Parties. In addition, quantitative import restrictions were justified according to Article XI:2(c) and Article XXIV, in conjunction with Part IV of the GATT.[5]

Four countries raised Article II bindings in noting that the EEC had bound a 20% ad valorem import duty for bananas in 1963.[6] It was asserted by the moving parties that the concession held no reservations and therefore must be understood to be an unconditional concession which could not be impaired or changed for the worse without violating Article II of the GATT. The binding was therefore a contractual obligation by Article II:7 and the EC was obliged to refrain from applying any measure which impaired the concession.[7]

5.2.2   Party arguments, Articles I, XXIV and Part IV[8]

The application of 20% tariffs on non ACP bananas were claimed to be in contravention of Article I, since ACP like products were admitted on the basis of preferential tariff treatment, and as Article I applied to "customs duties and charges of any kind". Neither part IV nor Article XXIV could be used to justify the deviation from Article I. Part IV contemplated the granting of preferential treatment to developing countries as contrasted to developed contracting parties, but could not be interpreted as permitting any differential treatment between one group of developing countries and another. Article XXIV relieved Article I obligations in the case of customs union and free-trade area formations, but in this case there was present a "unilateral and non-reciprocal relationship". The parameters of Article XXIV precisely prevented the trade treatment in question (Lomé) from falling under the

---

4   Columbia raised Articles I, III, VIII, XI, XIII, XXXVI and XXXVII.
5   The panel discussion, for our purpose, is limited to the interpretation made of Article XXIV and its relation to other provisions of the GATT. Thus, Article XI, XIII, III, VII discussion is omitted. It is not clear from the Panel report why the challenge to the EC members' import restrictions were being advanced on the basis of the regime existing in 1992, when those rules had been passed on for a common import regime to be effective July 1, 1993.
6   This schedule had been resubmitted in 1973-4 on the accession of Denmark, Ireland and the UK to the EEC. The EEC schedule subsequently was restated on the accession of Greece, Spain and Portugal.
7   DS32/R, para 105. The EC indicated that the question of Article II had not been raised during the consultation and good offices and the panel should therefore refrain from ruling on this question. Two other arguments are passed-over in this summary, for now: subsequent practice, acquiesence and estoppel, Ibid., para 124, and existing legislation, Ibid., para 147.
8   Generally, from DS32/R, para 207.
9   DS32/R, para 210.

scope of Article XXIV.[9] The EC responded that preferences for France and UK followed from the explicit grant in Art I:2 together with its A and B annexes.[10] Preferential treatment to the whole territory was accorded by the Lomé IV and predecessor conventions in their establishment of a free trade area according to Article XXIV:5(b) and XXIV:8(b) in conjunction with Part IV of the GATT.[11]

The EC considered that this case was not merely directed to a market access issue, but rather constituted an attack on the contractual scheme of preferential arrangements made in the Lomé Convention. This discussion would necessarily be drawn beyond the panel's terms of reference, particularly as a working group was established to review Lomé IV and previous working groups that had reviewed earlier Conventions. Citing in support the earlier and unadopted Citrus panel report,[12] the EC argued in the present instance that,

"The legal certainty with respect to international contractual relations duly notified to the GATT would be severely affected, if many years after the coming into effect of an international convention which was examined by the appropriate GATT bodies, its conformity with the general agreement could be questioned anew".[13]

According to the EC, this re-examination of well-established practice would breach the legitimate expectations of the parties to be able to maintain their trade agreements without modification.[14]

On the question of reciprocity, the EC position was that as between developed and developing countries, reciprocity was not only *not* required, but if it was required, "this would mean that it would be nearly impossible to create a free-trade area between developed and developing countries."[15] As such, both the preferential

---

[10] The original negotiated exemptions for MFN. According to the EC, upon accessions to the EEC, these preferences were still covered by Article XXIV:9, at least while other member states during transition could collect the differences in rates at the internal borders of the EEC. See annotation to ad Article XXIV:9, DS32/R, para 216. The EC did not claim that this coverage continued on the same basis after the extension of these preferences to the entire territory of the EEC. Since formation of the EEC, it was not possible to collect internal duty differentials.

[11] DS32/R, para 217.

[12] *EEC-Tariff Treatment of Imports of Citrus Products from Certain Countries in the Mediterranean Region*, L/5776 of Feb. 7, 1986, para 4.16. As reporting the conclusion of the Panel, "(G)iven the lack of consensus among contracting parties, there had been no decision by the CONTRACTING PARTIES as to the conformity with Article XXIV of the agreements under which the EC grants tariff preferences to certain citrus products originating from certain Mediterranean countries, and therefore the legal status of the agreements remained open." Quoted in GATT, **Analytical Index, Guide to GATT Law and Practice**, 6th Edition, 1994, p. 762. However, the Citrus Panel also concluded, "that it could not investigate the conformity of the agreements with GATT Article XXIV, because this could be done only under Article XXIV:7 review proceedings." R.E. Hudec, **Enforcing International Trade Law: The Evolution of the Modern GATT Legal System**, Butterworth Legal Publishers, Salem, N.H., 1993, p. 161.

[13] Recited in DS32/R, para 220.

[14] Citing for support the last sentence of Article XXIV:7(b).

[15] DS32/R, para 221.

duty treatment and the use of preferential quantitative restrictions were justified under Article XXIV, as XXIV:5 contained an exception to Article I and to the XXIV:8(b) (permitted) restrictions which otherwise would contravene Article XI. Also, restrictive measures in force prior to the establishment of the free-trade area could be maintained. The establishment of the free-trade area neither created nor reinforced those pre-existing measures.[16]

The EC argument also raised the legal effect of Article XXIV:7(b). The position taken was that the last sentence of the Article permits a free-trade agreement with its notified features to be maintained and immune from later challenge as long as no recommendation to modify it had been addressed to the parties to the agreement. Relying upon the First Lomé Working Group Review,[17] the EC emphasised at that time that the Lomé complied with the obligation to eliminate duties and other restrictive regulations of commerce with respect to substantially all the trade with the ACP. However,

"In light of their development needs and the principles of Part IV of the General Agreement, the EEC had not demanded reciprocity in its trade with the ACP".[18]

The reference made to part IV was specifically intended to refer to GATT Article XXXVI:8. Other Lomé working group reviews were cited to support the EC position that a free-trade area could be formed according to Article XXIV without a reciprocity requirement, all in light of Part IV of the GATT.[19]

This argument requires some clarification at this juncture. Prior to the Lomé review cited above, the predecessor Overseas Associations and the Second Convention differed from the Lomé Convention at issue in that the EEC had previously maintained that reciprocity was a feature of those earlier agreements. This was refuted by other working group members, first on the merits, asserting that no reciprocity was being provided, and second, on the *undesirability* of requiring exchanges as between developed and developing countries. This issue has been characterised here as the "reverse preference" problem. Although Part IV did not exist in the first review for the Overseas Association, the EC did then argue that the development Article of the GATT could be applied to expand the listing of restricted Article exceptions permitted according to XXIV:8(b). This was made as a part of an argument on behalf of the Overseas Territories to permit them to re-impose duties after formation.

Thus, the EC argument also reflected the fact that, when the reciprocity require-

---

[16] It is not clear whether the restrictive measures were external as to outside parties or internal as to Lomé parties. If external, the argument is somewhat out-of-bounds. The XXIV:8(b) restrictions refer to permitted restrictive measures to be employed between parties to an FTA, not referring to those that would be continued or established as regarding non-members.

[17] BISD 23S/46, page 48, para. 4, July 15, 1976.

[18] Ibid.

[19] DS32/R, paras 227 & 228.

ment was dropped outright in the first Lomé Convention, many members of the Working group applauded this deletion, although some other members noted that the requirements for Article XXIV were not being met without a stated reciprocity requirement. As discussed below, the EC argument might therefore have been successful if the "fiction" of reciprocity that was provided in the earlier formations had been simply retained within the Lomé provisions. If this had occurred, the panel would have been in a position to determine under what circumstances, if any, the veil of a free-trade declaration could be pierced to determine whether reciprocity between parties was being applied *de facto*.

The complaining parties' response was directed to these elements. Lomé did not qualify as a free trade area according to Article XXIV, which required a binding commitment to establish a plan and schedule to eliminate the duties and other restrictive regulations on substantially all the trade. Part IV could not be interpreted to permit deviation from the reciprocity requirement of Article XXIV, as ad XXXVI:8 listed specific GATT articles permitted to be excepted by this provision. Article XXIV was not listed among these. In general, Part IV could not be relied upon as a means to discriminate against some developing countries in favour of others since, according to Part IV, benefits to be applied were to be available to all developing countries on an MFN basis.[20] Moreover, it was not the intent of the complainants to challenge the legal contractual structure of Lomé, rather only to challenge the banana regime preferences. It was after all, the EC and not the complainants that had raised an Article XXIV justification. The EC, having raised it as a defence to violating Article I, the panel was now obliged to rule on whether Lomé complied with Article XXIV in order to fulfil its terms of reference.[21]

Complainants also noted that reviews of the various Lomé Conventions all contained statements that some working group members considered it doubtful that compliance with XXIV was being effected. Further,

> "(I)t was also understood then in these working parties that these conventions would in no way be considered 'as affecting the legal rights of contracting parties under the General Agreement'."[22]

Columbia also raised a legal question on interim agreements. If an interim agreement was intended by the Lomé Convention, then the EC could have filed a plan and schedule which would have shown the arrangement leading to a free-trade area to be completed within a reasonable time. If the EC, however, intended to form a one-way reciprocal agreement, it could have also followed the US example in the Caribbean Basin and have submitted it for a waiver under GATT Article XXV.[23]

---

[20] DS32/R, para 230-234.
[21] DS32/R, para 235.
[22] DS32/R, para 236.
[23] DS32/R, para 240. As for differential treatment between developing countries, also citing *Norway, Restrictions on Textile Products*, BISD 27S/119 para. 15, 18 June 1980.

5.2.3 Panel findings on the Article XXIV Issues

The panel first responded to the EC argument that restrictions under Article XI were consistent if adopted according to an arrangement qualifying under Article XXIV. The panel interpreted XXIV:5 and XXIV:8 to mean that Contracting Parties could deviate from their obligations under the General Agreement for the purpose of forming a customs union, a free-trade area, or interim agreement, "but not for any other purpose".[24] Article XXIV did not provide a basis for justifying import measures as such, but only a basis for relieving another party to a trade agreement from those measures that were otherwise permitted under the General Agreement. In other words, XXIV could not be used as a basis for imposing quantitative restrictions on third parties that otherwise would not be lawful under Art XI or one of its exceptions. On the issues of subsequent practice and estoppel, the mere fact that parties did not exercise rights in the past did not modify those rights and did not prevent them from invoking those rights at this time.[25]

As for the relationship between GATT Articles I, XXIV, and Part IV of the GATT, the general question was first raised as to the relationship between GATT's consultation provisions, Article XXIII, and other GATT procedures. The Contracting parties had discussed this aspect in the past, but had not reached definitive conclusions. Specifically in regard to the previous (unreported) Citrus panel, where that panel concluded in the absence of a specific Council mandate that it would abstain from an overall examination of bilateral agreements otherwise subject to special review procedures, this previous panel ruling could now be read to mean that either Article XXIII was applicable to all disputes, or that Article XXIII was not applicable to *any* matters upon which the Contracting Parties had the power to take decisions.[26] If the latter interpretation were to be accepted, Article XXIV could prevail over XXIII only in those cases where Article XXIV was invoked *prima facie* for the type of agreement covered by the Article, "i.e., on its face capable of justification under the Article".[27] The result of this interpretation would be that,

"If preferences granted under *any* agreement for which Article XXIV had been invoked could not be investigated under Article XXIII, any contracting party, merely by invoking Article XXIV, could deprive other contracting parties of their rights under Article XXIII".[28]

---

[24] DS32/R, para 358.
[25] DS32/R, para 362.
[26] DS32/R, para 366, citing Citrus Panel, Supra, note 12 at para 4.16.
[27] DS32/R, para. 367.
[28] Ibid.

Therefore, the current panel would review the agreement to find out if it was *prima facie* an Article XXIV type agreement. Naturally, this would lead to a panel discussion as to the required elements of Article XXIV necessary to meet this test, at least in the context of the agreement in question. Continuing, XXIV:8(b) clearly defined a free-trade area as one in which duties and other restrictive regulations of commerce were eliminated on substantially all the trade *between* the parties, meaning not merely upon imports into only one of the territories. The panel noted that the EC also agreed with this interpretation by its invocation of Part IV provisions which would, if applicable, operate to amend this requirement.

The issue then presented for the panel was whether Part IV, read in conjunction with Article XXIV, provided a cover for agreements that liberalised imports into only one of its parties.[29] The conclusion was reached that,

> "Legal justification for the tariff preference accorded by the EEC to imports of bananas originating in the ACP countries could not emerge from an application of Article XXIV to the type of agreement described by the EEC ... but only from an action of the CPs (contracting parties) under XXV".[30]

Before commenting on this ruling, the second panel case will be introduced.

5.3   Second case: EEC-Import Regime for Bananas, DS38/R (1994)

This case[31] examined the consolidated EC banana import regime introduced on July 1, 1993.[32] In some respects this panel replayed identical considerations raised above for the first panel. However, there are also differences, which will be the subject of this summary.

5.3.1   *Party arguments*

For the Article XXIV and Part IV issue, an argument distinct from the first panel was made where the complainants characterised the EC's invocation of Part IV as

---

[29]   This may be a somewhat interesting expression of the issue to be treated, since for the sector concerned, bananas, no issue was being raised as to whether or not reciprocal trade was provided. The panel is looking instead to the general reciprocity provisions of the agreement in question.

[30]   DS32/R, para 372.

[31]   DS38/R, 11 Feb. 1994, Panel established 16 June 1993.

[32]   Regime under Reg. 404/93, which established external treatment for categories of suppliers: traditional imports from ACP, duty free up to maximum quantity; non-traditional imports from ACP; and imports from non-ACP subject to tariff-quota; EEC bananas. DS38/R, para 29.

inconsistent with certain other of its previous declarations.[33] The EC argument in response is also somewhat amended. Although a basis could be found in Part IV for the Lomé preferences, "... it was XXIV:8(b) alone, not Part IV or Article XXXVI:8 which in derogation from Article I permitted preferences granted in accordance with the Lomé IV Convention."[34] For the complainants however, the non-reciprocity requirement of Article XXXVI was inherently inconsistent with free-trade areas or customs unions under Article XXIV, as "(T)he very concept of non-reciprocity was fundamentally irreconcilable with the notion of a free trade area or customs union".[35]

The EC also submitted that the panel had no jurisdiction to examine the overall Lomé Convention in connection with Article XXIV of the GATT. Article XXIV:7 had a special procedure requiring expert evaluation of a trade agreement. Individual measures could be challenged as reservation of rights, but not possibly in such a manner as to call into question an agreement "as a whole".[36] The specific procedures applied in Article XXIV:7 should be seen in a hierarchy of norms that stood above the consultation provided in Article XXIII. Further, the duplication of procedures was contrary to the GATT. Thus,

"(B)y notifying the Lomé IV Convention to the GATT for examination by a working party, the parties to the Lomé IV convention had done all that was necessary and possible for them in order to obtain GATT clearance for this Convention".[37]

Clearance for an agreement is not possible to be either provided or denied under Article XXIII procedures since this article only arises in a dispute over a particular measure. Permitting consideration according to an Article XXIII procedure rendered the agreement made between parties able to be challenged in regard to its constituent elements. By way of example, a tariff preference granted under XXIV:8(b) should not be challengeable under XXIII.

Complainants stressed the legal insecurity that would result without a recourse to an Article XXIII review. In the face of nullification of a GATT right, a party would be left without the dispute resolution avenue to obtain any remedy. The panel need not engage comprehensive examination of Lomé to conclude that the EC's claimed Article XXIV exception was inapplicable to this dispute because the panel in any case was not being presented with an agreement that prima facie met the

---

[33]   DS38/R, para 34. If the Part IV had a political and non-binding character (citing citrus panel, para. 3.24), the EC could not have the interpretation both ways. Also noting in the Yaounde review that the EC had declared that Part IV did not aim to modify Article XXIV provisions. BISD 14S/106, para 14, adopted 4 April 1966.

[34]   DS38/R, para 37. The EC also said that GATT had accepted other non-reciprocal free trade areas, citing Papua New Guinea (BISD 24S/63).

[35]   DS38/R, para 37.

[36]   DS38/R, para 45 and 46.

[37]   DS38/R, para 49.

Article's test. In any event, an Article XXIV procedure should not be interpreted to be a replacement for the GATT dispute settlement process.[38]

5.3.2   Panel findings

The Lomé's external trade regime was generally validated, including the use of tariff quotas. The national treatment issues raised under Article III were found against the EC. The issue left to resolve was not the question of imposing higher barriers to external trade, but the preferences to ACP that were not likewise extended to third parties. The panel recalled that duty-free tariffs were applied by the EC to ACP countries and that this treatment was not granted immediately to like products originating from territories of complainants. This established the need for the Article XXIV exception to be reviewed.[39] The EC had invoked Article XXIV as it claimed that even if duties were due to be accorded to third parties on the basis of MFN, they were not required to be extended to others due to the establishment of a free-trade area under Lomé IV.[40]

First, what aspects could the panel examine? The EC argued that only specific measures were reviewable since Article XXIV:7 had its own procedure for evaluating free-trade areas in general. The panel noted on this that working groups for the various Lomé Conventions had not explicitly decided the issue of compatibility with the General Agreement. Notification of the Lomé arrangements made by the EC had not specifically invoked Article XXIV, and the terms of reference for the working groups had not referred to Article XXIV, instead, they were called upon to examine "relevant GATT Articles". No report had adopted a decision that Lomé was under the terms of Article XXIV because no conclusion was ever reached. Likewise, there were no Contracting Party decisions at hand establishing that Article XXIV:7 procedures applied at all to the Lomé Conventions.[41] Further, whatever the nature of the relationship between Article XXIII and Article XXIV, XXIV:7 could only apply to recommendations made for customs unions, free-trade areas, or interim agreements.

Article XXIV:7 does not therefore apply by its terms to *any* agreement notified, only to those provided for in Article XXIV. Therefore, before determining whether the special review procedure of Article XXIV:7 pre-empted Article XXIII, it must first be decided whether the agreement was of a type to be qualified for XXIV:7 treatment, i.e., that it was a customs union, a free-trade area, or an interim agreement leading to either. Thus, the following holding was made,

---

[38]   DS38/R, para 50.
[39]   DS38/R, para 155.
[40]   DS38/R, para 156.
[41]   This aspect of the ruling suggests that a decision by the working group that an agreement fell under the provisions of Article XXIV would eliminate the inquiry that followed. However, only a handful of all the notified agreements could possibly be placed into this category.

"(T)he Panel could not accept that tariff preferences inconsistent with Article 1:1 would, by notification of the preferential arrangement and invocation of Article XXIV against the objections of other contracting parties, escape any examination by a panel established under Article XXIII ... The Panel concluded therefore that a panel, faced with an invocation of Article XXIV, first had to examine whether or not these provisions applied to the agreement in question".[42]

Turning to examining the Lomé Agreement as to whether or not it was of a type of agreement falling under special review procedures of Article XXIV:7, the definition of XXIV:8(b) was recited. The terms "between" and "originating in constituent territories" made it clear that trade was to be liberalised in products from all the constituent territories. Then, citing Lomé Article 168 and 174 for products originating in ACP countries, these provisions indicated that the agreement "shall not comprise any element of reciprocity for those States as regards free access". Since the Convention did not provide for a requirement of reciprocity between the territories,

"This lack of any obligation of the sixty-nine ACP countries to dismantle their trade barriers ... made the trade arrangements set out in the Convention substantially different from those of a free trade area, as defined in the Article XXIV:8(b)".[43]

The next issue addressed was the EC argument that Article XXIV:8(b) requirements had to be read in light of Part IV, particularly Article XXXVI:8. This reiterates the Part IV analysis done from the earlier panel, except the second panel noted that Part IV history did not originally authorise the granting of preferences on a non discriminatory basis to developing countries. This came much later with GSP (1971) which were now carried by the GATT under the enabling clause of 1979. This led the panel to conclude that,

"Had non-reciprocal agreements between developed and developing parties been considered justifiable under Article XXIV and Part IV, the decisions of the CP (contracting parties) on the GSP and the Enabling Clause would have been largely unnecessary. Developed countries could simply have formed a 'free-trade area' with selected developing countries by reducing barriers unilaterally on imports from those countries".[44]

Finally, even if Lomé was to be covered by XXIV:8 in conjunction with Part IV, XXIV:5 must also be applied to consider whether discriminatory preferences could

---

[42] DS38/R, para 158.
[43] DS38/R, para 159.
[44] DS38/R, para 162. As above, the EEC's own declaration on Yaounde was also raised, which stated the Part IV could not modify XXIV. BISD 14S/100, para. 14, Ibid., para 162.

extend to non GATT members, which were also in the Lomé group. Here, Article XXIV:10 should apply with its drafting history to clearly indicate the appropriate procedure for permitting non member customs unions and free-trade areas.

5.4   Chapter Conclusion: the legal effect of non-decisions

Barely a handful of agreements submitted for review have resulted in a decision by the working group or by the Contracting Parties that an agreement is qualified according to the provisions of Article XXIV. However, a number of agreements submitted, unlike the Lomé, did ask for review according to the Article specifically, and not just to the application of GATT Articles generally. Few of these resulted in decisions. Where a decision was obtained that a declared agreement qualified under Article XXIV, the panel would not likely assert a basis to review the elements of that decision to determine whether or not the agreement was of a type to be subject to the exceptions provided by Article XXIV. A special procedure resulted in a determination and this would be recognised by the panel and inserted as a finding. Thus, a first effect of the rulings here is that an agreement submitted which was intended to seek the Article XXIV exception should clearly state the elements of Article XXIV:8 intended to be met by the arrangement, i.e., that a free-trade area or customs union was now being declared to be formed. This would clearly rebut earlier practice such as the Overseas Association for example, wherein the EEC had argued that declarations omitted from the agreement would not void a finding of a free-trade area formation, since the course of practice under the agreement could indicate the creation of the free-trade area.

For agreements specifically seeking to be covered according to Article XXIV:8, the panel holdings also suggest that the working group procedure according to Article XXIV:7 should first determine whether an agreement was of a type to be subject to Article XXIV, and that the proponent parties should seek to reach a positive decision on this point in order to prevent the type of challenge made here. This confirms that review parties should first apply Article XXIV:8 before considering external effects provided in Article XXIV:5 as argued previously. This approach would serve to reconstruct somewhat the dividing line intended between partially preferential agreements and qualified Article XXIV formations.

However, one must consider the great majority of examples where an agreement claimed to fulfil the Article XXIV:8 conditions were notified, but where no positive decision was reached. According to previous practice, the self-declaratory aspect of the review procedure would appear to have not prevented the parties from engaging in the preferences provided according to their plan and schedule. As expressed by the European Community in regard to the legal status of its own successive accession treaties,

"(I)t did not share the view that these earlier treaties constituted an open question or that their legal status was unresolved in GATT since the Contracting Parties had formulated no recommendation under Article XXIV:7(b) for any modifications to those arrangements".[45]

What may have changed in light of the panels discussed above, is that preferences could be subject to challenge in the absence of a compatibility recommendation from the working group or a Contracting Party decision. In this sense, the second panel's finding that Lomé was defective because it sought review only according to GATT Articles (generally) is not really material to the issue, for if a positive decision were obtained according to Article XXIV:7, then a panel would at least operate from the presumption, possibly irrebuttable, that the preferences accorded by the agreement were secured by Article XXIV. If a negative decision were obtained, then Article XXIV could not be invoked in any event. In the absence of any decision by Contracting Parties, it would seem, as a result of these panels, that the regional proponents assume the risk of later having to extend on an MFN basis any preferences exchanged according to their plan and schedule. Although this may not negate the inherent self-declaratory nature of regional trade agreements, it does shift the burden to proponents to establish that agreements declared are of a type to qualify under the definitional elements of Article XXIV:8. This aspect is taken up later in the context of contemporary developments in the WTO. For now, since the working group review process is still governed by consensus, it would seem that a result would have followed, even from these earlier cases, whereby proponents would need to satisfy all parties in the review process in order to obtain a positive recommendation.

One can note that the cases here were specialised on their facts as there was a clear facial defect in the declaration where Lomé parties were expressly exempt from removing barriers to EC trade. However, a variation of the claim can be constructed where a declaration is not defective, meets the Article XXIV:8 requirements according to its declared notification, but still no affirmative working group recommendation or other Contracting Party decision results. Complainants could then assert the claim, that in the absence of a decision, that the panel should beyond the mere facade of the parties' declaration to review the sufficiency of the plan and schedule according to the definitional elements. This would present the issue whether the rulings above turned upon the facially defective attributes of the arrangement considered or upon the absence of any affirmative recommendation forwarding from the Article XXIV:7 procedure.

A cautious interpretation should suggest that the failure to obtain a decision according to an Article XXIV:7 procedure retains the burden upon regional propo-

---

[45] "It was, however, always possible for any country to seek to resume discussions of these questions in another more appropriate context". L/5453, adopted on March 1983, 30S/175, para. 18, as quoted in GATT, **Analytical Index, Guide to GATT Law and Practice**, 6th Edition, 1994, p. 761.

nents to later justify their preferences. For, if a working party was unable to agree to qualify the arrangement overall, then the panel likewise has no finding to apply to its deliberations other than the declaration and assertion of the regional parties. On this point, the second panel rejected the EC's assertion that all that was required to be done had been done to qualify the agreement. Note again the panel's rejoinder on this point with italics added:

> "(T)he Panel could not accept that tariff preferences inconsistent with Article 1:1 would, *by notification* of the preferential arrangement *and invocation* of Article XXIV against the objections of other contracting parties, *escape any examination by a panel established under Article XXIII ...*".

One must accept the possibility of a later ruling that specialised procedures applicable to Article XXIV reviews are not invoked by mere notification. That while an affirmative decision would be sufficient to raise the Article's MFN exception, the absence of any decision retains the burden upon the regional parties in the event later preferential measures are challenged. In this case the regional members have chosen to proceed with preferential exchanges without the legal cover of a recommendation. A panel can likewise defer to the special procedure and indicate that it is unwilling to make any finding that an agreement is qualified where the working group had been unwilling or unable to do so.

An additional aspect of pre-WTO practice has also been affected, that being the failure of proponents to disclose sufficient information to working groups in order to conduct a review analysis. From these panels, one could conclude that if the proponents failed to provide the material sufficient for a meaningful working group review, as has allegedly occurred in so many previous reviews, then those parties could also be in the later position of finding it more difficult to argue that Article XXIV:7 has been sufficiently invoked by them, and that they have done all that was necessary to obtain an affirmative decision. This could suggest that an additional consensus from a working group must also be obtained at the outset in regard to the quality of the notification of the detailed plan and schedule submitted, and perhaps prior to any substantive review of the other Article requirements.

Chapter 6
ECONOMIC (CUSTOMS UNION) THEORY AND ARTICLE XXIV

"...since such a preferential arrangement by definition involves *less discrimination against nonmembers* than a customs union or free-trade area, the justification for proscribing such arrangements absolutely is not clear".
Kenneth Dam (1963).

6.1   Introduction

This Part has reviewed elements of Article XXIV as to its drafting history, its provisions, the practice established by GATT Working Group reviews parties examining agreements, and the GATT-1947 era dispute panel reports. To conclude it, a different systemic aspect is placed for discussion. This concerns the relationship between economic theory and the provisions of Article XXIV. The issue raised is whether an examination for compatibility with the Article XXIV requirements should entertain the consideration of economic welfare criteria? This deserves a treatment in simple recognition of the important role that economic theory and studies have played in framing the debate on the question of compatibility for agreements, and the continuing influence of economic literature on the subject of regional trade agreements generally.

Viner's original contribution has been highly refined over the years, but nevertheless remains central to the economics of regional trade agreements. Besides establishing the field of economic studies relating to regional economic integration, since 1950 his work has also has become a primary reference point for much of the analysis, economic and legal, on the compatibility issue. In point, many (or most) observers might consider the question posed above to be a simple misstatement, assuming incorrectly that economic welfare considerations are already incorporated into the text of Article XXIV. As such, the argument carried through this last Part that the qualification requirements flow first from an analysis of paragraph 8 of the Article can also be seen to have already posed as an implied rebuttal to a welfare-directed criteria.

A number of traditional justifications for the paragraph 8 requirements have been advanced over time. The chapter will conclude by comparing these with a "preservation of trade test" as it has also been raised in the chapter. An additional justification is submitted that relates to the notion of territorial differences as an elemental problem of commercial diplomacy. This brings us full-circle to a brief examination of most-favoured nation. If MFN can operate in practice to reduce certain power disparities as they appear between large and small countries, then the stricter requirements of the regional exceptions may also be validated in this light.

In treating the interface between law and economics regarding Article XXIV, the author also expresses a caveat. Since the point of the chapter is to show the divergence in interpretation raised by the application of a welfare perspective, the point of that divergence historically, and as it has developed, is more important in this context than is the development of the theory itself. Thus, it is recognised that a host of developments have occurred that are not based upon welfare analysis, but that this chapter is not intended to function as an update. Also, since the author holds a great respect for the field of international trade economics and its practitioners, the purpose of the chapter is also not to slight the science. Rather, it is dedicated to expressing some rationale as to why the legal requirements may express legitimacy even where they may not reflect economic considerations in all regards.

6.2   The divergent views of law and economy

The question of how the requirements of the Article XXIV should be interpreted in light of economic theory considerations has been an ongoing concern since the time of GATT's origin. As theory evolved to outline the application of welfare analysis to Article XXIV requirements, it is evident that the question also arose as to whether the Article's legal requirements respected these theoretical developments. If not, then considerations were raised as to whether the Article should be formally amended to validate these considerations, or in the alternative, should be functionally applied in practice to ameliorate the conflicts expressed by the provisions.

This conflict is demonstrated at the moment one suggests that Article XXIV provisions require the imposition of a high internal trade-coverage requirement. Since any agreement so qualified may be more trade diverting than a more partially preferential arrangement, a type of divergence between one interpretation of the legal text and the economic objectives is presented. Since both regional proponents and opponents have also argued that trade creation (or no trade diversion) is the final objective to be reached by the process of regional integration, they have also implicitly, and sometimes explicitly, argued for a lower internal trade standard to be applied on this basis. The result has been to add an economic argument for the weakening of the conditional and definitional requirements of paragraph 8. In its place, a greater emphasis can be placed upon the external effects of trade barriers as according to paragraph 5, and perhaps even paragraph 4, as this has also been argued on occasion to constitute a distinct legal requirement and for this reason. Whether intended or not, the economic insight forwarded by Viner, and as applied to the legal context by Dam, has probably made its own contribution to the proliferation of partial regional agreements, a result that neither would have likely approved.

6.2.1   Viner's customs union theory

The economic approach to the question of regional preferential trade formations has been to adopt a balancing approach in order to favour regional formations which would finally create rather than diminish global economic welfare.[1] In its most pure form, the result to be achieved by a wholly complementary arrangement is that each relatively efficient producer or source of supply, whether internal or external to the arrangement, shall be finally positioned to expand its production as a result of the formation. As such, preferences should only be permitted which reward regional producers who are more efficient than external producers. This presents a conflict with the legal requirements, as any such arrangement, while maximising welfare, is also likely to be incomplete in regard to its regional trade coverage. This result stands in conflict with an internal trade requirement imposed to cover substantially all of the trade between the regional parties.

   As such, it has been the position of a number of economic and legal commentators that GATT Article XXIV is economically irrational. This follows from the central point that an agreement which covers all the trade can result in a higher degree of trade diversion, resulting in the shifting of production from efficient to lesser efficient producers, than one which cover only a portion of the trade. Likewise, regional trade agreements which are only partially preferential, and therefore unqualified according to a more severe paragraph 8 test, may also result in lesser diversion of trade than a complete exchange of preferences. Simply stated, an incomplete formation may, in a given case, be economically superior to a complete formation.[2]

   It is generally agreed that the origin of this dichotomy rests with Viner and his 1950 treatise, **The Customs Union Issue**. Prior to his insight that customs unions were capable of diverting more trade than they created, it was assumed for the most part that all customs union were economically beneficial, and further, that Article XXIV arrangements reflected this by requiring completed formations. Viner illustrated the reasoning behind his argument by pointing out the absurdity of retaining

---

[1]   This is not to suggest that welfare analysis would favour any preferential arrangement over either unilateral free trade or multilateral trade liberalisation. For a succinct review of the evolution of customs union theory see, J. Bhagwati and A. Panagariya, *The Theory of Preferential Trade Agreements: Historical Evolution and Current Trends*, The American Economic Review, V.86, No. 2, May 1996, pp. 82-88, and L.A. Winters, *Regionalism versus Multilateralism*, World Bank Policy Research Working Paper, #1687. Although there is documentation that theory is moving away from a pure creation/diversion perspective, Panagariya also notes that, " ...the old concerns remain alive as well... ". *Preferential Trade Liberalization: The Traditional Theory and New Developments*, Journal of Economic Literature 38, June 2000, pp. 287-331, citing from page 3 of the World Bank paper, same title.

[2]   "The primary purpose of a customs union, and its major consequences for good or bad, is to shift sources of supply, and the shift can be either to lower -- or to higher -- cost sources, depending on circumstances." Jacob Viner, **The Customs Union Issue**, Carnegie Endowment, 1950, p. 44.

a legal distinction between the minimal difference of a 100 percent preference and lesser marginal preference. Thus,

> "Free-traders sometimes in almost the same breath disapprove of preferential reduction of tariffs but approve of customs unions, which involve 100 per cent preference, and this is the position at present of the United States Government and the doctrine of the Havana Charter. If the distinction is made to rest, as often seems to be the case, on some supposed virtue in a 100 per cent preference, which suddenly turns to maximum evil at 99 per cent, the degree of evil tapering off as the degree of preference shrinks, it is a distinction as illogical, the writer believes, as this way of putting it makes it sound".[3]

This follows from Viner's identification of the economic issue arising in determining the effects of the changes in "the national locus of production of goods purchased." As the shifting of purchases either to the higher or lower cost sources of supply is engaged by union formation, then such a shifting in its net effects is either positive or negative,

> "(a) for each of the customs union countries taken separately; (b) for the two combined; (c) for the outside world; (d) for the world as a whole".

Thus,

> "If the customs union is movement in the direction of free trade, it must be predominantly a movement in the direction of goods being supplied from lower money cost sources than before. If the customs union has the effect of diverting purchases to higher money-cost sources, it is then a device for making tariff protection more effective".[4]

6.2.2   Dam's interpretation of Article XXIV requirements

The juxtaposition of the GATT legal requirements with the 1950 economic analysis is often attributed to poor historical timing as Viner's contribution to the theory post-dated the drafting of the GATT Article responsible for the qualification of regional agreements. The position was shortly taken thereafter that Article XXIV, together with its substantially-all trade requirement, was more or less hopelessly outdated upon, if not shortly after, arrival.

---

[3]   J. Viner, Ibid., at pp. 49-50, and his note 6.

[4]   J. Viner, Ibid., at p. 42. "None of these questions can be answered a priori, and the correct answers will depend on just how the customs union operates in practice. All that a priori analysis can do, is to demonstrate, within limits, how the customs union must operate if it is to have specific types of consequences". Ibid., at p. 43.

The major legal contribution which applied Viner's theory to the Article XXIV requirements came from Dam in 1963, as he made a most extensive examination of the GATT reviews taken to date, and in light of Viner's proposition. Dam concluded that the Article was wanting in a most important respect,

> "Since the tariff reduction inherent in such a preferential arrangement might be considered to be a movement toward free trade, albeit not so dramatic as that produced by a customs union or free-trade area, and since such a preferential arrangement by definition involves *less discrimination against nonmembers* than a customs union or free-trade area, the justification for proscribing such arrangements absolutely is not clear".[5]

Dam's prescription was to conclude that the Article required revision.[6] Barring the practical difficulties of accomplishing a negotiated amendment to the Article, he recommended instead, a

> "'creative reinterpretation' of its provisions to emphasise that aspect of Article XXIV:4 which called upon the parties '... not to raise barriers to the trade of other Contracting Parties'."[7]

This was a call to interpret paragraph 4's requirements to provide for a trade creation standard, and effectively, to raise the paragraph into the position of an independent legal requirement. Implicitly, this would necessarily supersede the coverage requirements expressed by paragraph 8. It would also suggest a reversal of the examination sequence in order to impose paragraph 5 as the leading factor for qualification. This because the result to be achieved would be placed upon the final structure of barriers as to non-members, rather than upon the initial quality of internal free trade to be obtained by the regional parties at the outset. Amended in this way, qualified regional groupings would then serve the purpose of being a movement toward freer world trade by being individually rendered as trade creating, or rather non trade diverting.

5　Kenneth W. Dam, *Regional Economic Arrangements and the GATT, the Legacy of a Misconception*, University of Chicago Law Review, V. 30, No. 4, 1963, pp. 615-665, at p. 633, italics added.

6　K. Dam, Ibid., at p. 635.

7　K. Dam, Ibid., at p. 663.

6.2.3   *Implications for the review process and for MFN*

This view has also since tended to dominate the framework by which regional agreements are argued to be compatible with the GATT requirements.[8] Moreover, once it was understood that a strict internal trade requirement could do more damage to world trade than a less strict requirement, the requirement's objective of supporting a broader application of most-favoured nation treatment was also placed into consideration. As Johnson succinctly stated in 1976, the MFN principle,

> "...has absolutely nothing to recommend it on the grounds of either economic theory or the realities of international commercial diplomacy ... The speciousness of the principle of non-discrimination is only exceeded by the irrationality of permitting nothing less than 100 per cent discrimination in the case of customs unions and free trade areas".[9]

However, Johnson did recognise in the same instance that the justification for the MFN principle was not within the *economic* sphere at all:

> "(T)he principle has an important point and function, which can be loosely and inaccurately stated as the principle that if you pay your membership dues to a club you are entitled to decent treatment as one of the paid-up members.. " (Therefore), "... it seems the wiser course not to devise further exceptions to the principle or rewrite it, but instead to improve the framework of international economic relations within which countries receive non-discriminatory most-favoured-nation treatment".[10]

This acknowledges an agreed-upon notion of "fair play" as between members is also a function of a legal rule and may not necessarily express what can be stated to be the most efficient outcome. To place Johnson's point in a more legal context, the coherence of the principle rule of the club is obtained by its consistent application. Where efficiency considerations may argue for a more flexible set of exceptions in order to attain a higher welfare objective for the world as a whole, such flexibility also carries a certain risk. If members do not believe that the core rule of the club

---

[8]   Article XXIV:4, "The Contracting Parties recognize the desirability of increasing freedom of trade by the development, through voluntary agreements, of closer integration between the economies of the countries parties to such agreements". Only in the WTO 1994 Understanding on the Interpretation of Article XXIV is the "stepping stone" theory raised in, "(R)ecognizing the contribution to the expansion of world trade that may be made by closer integration between the economies of the parties to such agreements ...".

[9]   H.J. Johnson, *Trade Negotiations and the New International Monetary System*, Leiden: A.W. Sijthoff, for the Graduate Institute of International Studies, Geneva, and the Trade policy Research Centre, London, (1976), p. 30, quoted in R. Snape, in K. Anderson and R. Blackhurst, (Eds), **Regional Integration and the Global Trading System**, Harvester Wheatsheaf, (1993), p. 273.

[10]   H. Johnson, in R. Snape, Ibid., at p. 31, wherein Snape suggests an "economics of the club" approach.

is going to be applied consistently, then the value of membership is put into question.

The economic theory regarding the relationship between regional agreements and the multilateral system does not appear to have followed Johnson's prescription. In assessing whether regionalism is a "stumbling block or a building block" to the GATT/WTO, most emphasis continues to cast this question in terms of whether or not the end result is commensurate with the expansion of world trade, rather than the residual value offered by the MFN clause. According to Bhagwati and Panagariya, Kemp and Wan introduced a major addition to Viner's proposition, also in 1976. This demonstrated that any regional integration agreement could (in theory) be made to be welfare enhancing. Under certain conditions the external tariff for a customs union could be reduced overall to avoid the effects of trade diversion.[11]

6.2.4   *A modern test*

Kemp-Wan provided the foundation for a prescription that "compatibility" can be provided by a balancing test methodology to accomplish a "trade neutral" regional exception. McMillan offered a detailed expression of this view targeted precisely to the Article XXIV requirements. He proposed that a regional formation should be assessed by examining the resulting position of non-members in regard to the preservation of their trade flows. Thus,

> "(I) have suggested that the best test for judging whether a RIA (Regional Integration Agreement) is harmful is the simplest possible: does the agreement result in less trade between member countries and outside countries? If the answer to this question is no, then the RIA is consistent with open trade ...".[12]

While such a status quo approach presents obvious appeal for non-members (and would also permit members to restrict their intra-regional trade), it is a meaningfully divergent approach from that according to the provisions of Article XXIV. A complete removal of internal barriers between regional members will always present a greater difficulty for the resulting trade position of the non-members. This however was addressed directly by McMillan in his consideration of the value of the internal trade requirement:

---

[11]   M. Kemp and H. Wan, *An Elementary Proposition Concerning the Formation of Customs Unions*, Journal of International Economics, V.6, No. 1, 1976, pp. 95-97, at p. 95. Also referred to as the Kemp-Ohyamu-Kemp-Wan theorem by Panagariya, supra note 1 at p. 18. According to Bhagwati and Panagariya, the Kemp-Wan contribution consisted of showing, as a "possibility theorem" that, "one could always construct a welfare-improving CU (customs union) among any subset of countries while the non-members were left at their initial welfare." Bhagwati and Panagariya, Supra note 1 at p. 83.

[12]   John McMillan, *Does Regional Integration Foster Open Trade*, in K. Anderson and R. Blackhurst, (Eds), Supra note 9, pp. 292-310, at p. 306.

"(T)his, also, is not in general in the interests of either the member countries or the rest of the world. A zero intra-union tariff usually causes unnecessarily large amounts of trade diversion, as Meade (1955) showed".[13]

It would logically follow that an agreement providing for 100 percent tariff reductions upon all of the members' trade, while clearly in compliance with Article XXIV's paragraph 8 coverage provisions, could or should be substituted by a more partial agreement that is demonstrated not to harm the trade of non-members. The question raised by such a proposal is whether the GATT could accommodate such a change and still retain any basis of legitimacy for MFN.

6.3   Does GATT Article XXIV accommodate a welfare test?

What becomes evident from this brief review of the economic considerations is that there is a disagreement as to what "compatibility" of a regional agreement should be intended to mean. This concept is clearly not the same for economists as it was for the drafters. For some economists, the concept appears to focus upon the expansion of trade or at least upon the avoidance of trade diversion as it may relate to that objective. Whether this would be a good idea or not, it is clear, as Dam pointed out, that these economic considerations were not elevated to a primary position in setting the original parameters of the regional exception. Thus, Article XXIV:4 only provides that while the Contracting Parties,

"recognize the desirability of increasing freedom of trade by the development ... of closer integration between the economies of the countries parties to such agreements. *They also recognize that the purpose of a customs union or of a free-trade area should be to facilitate trade between the constituent territories* and not to raise barriers to the trade of other Contracting Parties with such territories". (italics added.)

The drafters may well have suffered under a type of primitive illusion that completed regional trade formations would contribute in all cases to an expansion of world trade, the very point invalidated by Viner. However, the experience of the interwar years and of the United States with the Commonwealth preferences should also be considered. There it was seen that the risk of exclusionary effects caused by preference was well known and a primary subject of commercial policy commentary. While this was not characterised in its time as trade diversion, it certainly centred upon the effects of preferences upon the losses occurring to third parties. In spite

---

[13]   J. McMillan, Ibid., at note 8. McMillan acknowledges that there are "broad systemic reasons" for the internal trade requirement, but as indicated in his conclusion above, the final test to be applied should refer first to the position of non-members regardless of whether or not internal trade is made free.

of this, the U.S. proposed and supported a customs union exception, which of course is a 100% trade coverage agreement. Thus, the italicised provision above also establishes the purpose of the exception as stated by the drafters in this light. That is to prefer those agreements that actually facilitate trade between the constituent territories as being worth some price to pay for the resulting diversion of non-members' trade.[14]

If GATT-1947 missed the emerging economic theory in establishing a welfare test for the exception, the drafters in the Uruguay Round also passed upon an opportunity to realign the provisions to the economic considerations. Instead, the original goal of permitting regional formations subject to an internal trade requirement according to paragraph 8 was not only restated by the GATT-1994 Understanding on the Interpretation of Article XXIV, but arguably strengthened from the original text. Although the Understanding does now refer to the idea that regional agreements may contribute to the expansion of world trade, such a contribution is also said to be decidedly *increased*,

"... if the elimination between the constituent territories of duties and other restrictive regulations of commerce *extends to all trade*, and diminished *if any major sector is excluded*...(and) *Reaffirming* that the purpose of such agreements should be to facilitate trade between the constituent territories...".[15]

Although Viner's insight has had years of development in the economic and policy literature, even to the point of creating specific prescriptions for determining compatibility in the GATT context, a criterion for applying trade creation has not yet found a place in the Article. One can only conclude, that given a choice between an MFN principle relegated in each case to a "preservation of trade" test, the club members have not yet given up the hope to reinforce a higher bar to MFN deviations rather than a lower one.

The occasional confusion between economic and legal objectives can trap even staunch opponents of regional proliferation. Thus, as Bhagwati commented (but only by way of a footnote),

---

[14] The General Agreement preamble can be raised for consideration as it would inform the objectives provided in Article XXIV:4. Here, the relevant text provides that relations should be conducted with a view to "expanding the production and exchange of goods" by entering into arrangements directed to the "substantial reduction of tariffs and other barriers to trade and to the elimination of discriminatory treatment in international commerce ..." (GATT 1947 Preamble). Trade expansion is not the sole objective of the GATT even while it might be a more predominant subject of economic inquiry.

[15] WTO Understanding on the Interpretation of Article XXIV of the General Agreement on Tariffs and Trade 1994, preamble, The Understanding modifies aspects concerned with Article XXIV:5,6,7 and 12. Article XXIV:8, which states the definitional internal trade requirement, was left entirely untouched from the original text of 1947. It is not suggested here that the preamble is raising a new legal standard. It does however enunciate a Members' consensus that more complete formations are compatible with the purpose of the exception.

"(A)side from the fact that NAFTA has its own holes, ... Ambassador Eisenstat has nothing but assertion on his side when he claims that full preferences are better than partial preferences. Indeed, some economic arguments suggest the opposite".[16]

Even if all economic arguments suggested otherwise, this would still remain beside the point, as the issue is whether any economic characterisation should frame the test for Article XXIV compatibility in the future, and particularly if it results in lower paragraph 8 requirements permitting more agreements to be formed. Further, whether there is a possibility of placing a welfare analysis, if necessary at all, into some aspect of assessing compatibility outside the domain of paragraph 8. That such a development is needed to occur is nicely indicated by the following characterisation by Jackson in regard to the use of contingent trade measures between regional members:

"(A) similar argument, or problem, arises with regard to unfair trade rules (anti-dumping and countervailing duty rules), but a practice has developed of tolerating preferential agreements *as long as they do not eliminate* such unfair trade rules between the preference parties".[17]

One can understand why non-members would make the argument that regional members should never be accorded a right by Article XXIV to suspend the use of trade measures between them, since certainly trade diversion should result. However, one would also ask customs union theorists to consider the economic results for regional agreements that may provide for very little in the manner of opening markets between those members. Any meaningful competitive pressures created by the process of regional integration can be closed between the members at any time by a domestic call for contingent protection. From a legal view, the retention of such trade devices between members should have a direct bearing upon whether a regional formation could sustain sufficient trade coverage as required by paragraph 8.

6.3.1 *Paragraph 8 requires a legal construction*

These examples are not raised to criticise the value of customs union theory for its concept of trade diversion, but to indicate how the theory is aligned with a view that considers compatibility with the trading system predominantly from the position of non-member welfare. What appears to have evolved is an "outsider-directed" perspective that equates the status of non-member trade with the larger inter-

---

[16] Jagdish Bhagwati, *Preferential Trade Agreements: The Wrong Road*, Law and Policy in International Business, Vol. 27, No. 4, 1996, pp. 865-872, at p. 868, his note 5.

[17] John H. Jackson, *Perspectives on Regionalism in Trade Relations*, Law and Policy in International Business, V. 27, No. 4, 1996, pp. 873-878, at p. 876, italics added.

ests of the multilateral system itself. In such a framework it is entirely possible to conclude that the highest-level regional integration schemes, such as completed customs unions providing for free internal circulation and disposed of all internal trade measures, should be concluded to be the most diverting and therefore the most incompatible of all possible arrangements.

In contrast, the more flexible form of a free-trade area where countries retain their individual commercial policies, as in Jackson's example above, can be tailored to serve the goal of net trade creation. Where sectors can so easily be omitted from internal coverage, this enhanced flexibility should permit outsiders a greater opportunity to preserve (or re-establish) their trade flows. Flexible organisational structure, like the free-trade area, provides a better instrument, which if properly composed, could far better meet the "no harm done" test as enunciated by McMillan. Partially discriminatory groupings suggest at least the possibility of creating a final result that is trade creating and therefore more compatible with the multilateral system.

That trade creation is not equated with the objectives of non discrimination is evident when considering together these following provisions from paragraphs 1 and 8 of Article XXIV:

"1. ... Each such customs territory shall, exclusively for the purposes of the territorial application of this Agreement, be treated as though it were a Contracting Party ...

8(a) ... A customs union shall be understood to mean the substitution of a single customs territory for two or more customs territories...".

Thus, the drafters remind us that a customs union in compliance with the coverage requirements of paragraph 8 *is* a customs territory. Since GATT's provision for territorial application of the Agreement requires that such a union *shall* be treated as though it were a Contracting Party, it must be considered an irony that a qualified union could be relegated by welfare analysis as a lesser compatible formation.

6.3.2   *Paragraph 5 accommodation of economic criteria*

Economic analysis of a sort does play a role for Article XXIV determinations in regard to the performance requirements dictated by paragraph 5. Although formations should first qualify according to paragraph 8, the paragraph 5 preamble grants the regional exception *provided that* the general incidence of duties and regulations of commerce shall not be higher or more restrictive on the whole. This suggests that an economic analysis be undertaken to determine such an overall effect. It does not suggest however that the condition to meet should turn upon whether the result is trade creating or trade diverting. A finding that a customs union was trade diverting on balance would not raise an argument that paragraph 5 requirements were not being met. It is not difficult to compose a hypothetical union consisting of high-tariff constituent members. Even while the resulting common tariff could be significantly lower than the previous individual tariffs to non-members, this union could yet be trade-diverting overall due to its complete elimination of internal barriers to trade. It may be better if such a union also ameliorated its diversionary tendencies. However, paragraph 5 does not demand such an amelioration, except where new barriers are raised overall.

What one concludes is that whether a customs union or free-trade area is diverting trade may well have negative implications for the welfare of non-members and for the expansion of world trade. This consideration, as important as it is, does not however equate with a conclusion that such agreements are incompatible with the trading system, at least as this concept is prescribed by Article XXIV. Thus, while the rules of the trading system regarding discrimination are established by the conjunction between Article I and XXIV, the result being sought is not only concerned with trade expansion. In addition, there is also the matter of providing a basis for equitable (non-discriminatory) treatment between GATT parties in respect to their goods of origin.

6.3.3   The implications of a flexible approach

It was suggested above, by considering regional compatibility only according to its external welfare effects, that any rationale for a higher internal free-trade requirement would be necessarily disregarded. Again from McMillan,

> "In practice it is possible that some member countries will not benefit from a RIA. But it seems reasonable to have a hierarchy of concerns: to put preventing harm to third countries ahead of preventing members from harming themselves".[18]

In practice, the equating of non-member interests with that of the trading system itself has influenced the discourse. The following European Commission statement responded to the charge that the rise in the number of regional agreements posed a threat to the WTO system.

> "WTO Secretariat analysis confirms the EU's view that, on the whole, the effect of regional integration agreements concluded since 1947 has been to create rather than divert trade, and has therefore tended to reinforce the benefits of the multilateral system rather than undermine them".[19]

The EC has made this argument before. In the 1970 Working Group Report of the EEC Association with Tunisia and Morocco, Working Group members attempted

---

[18]   John McMillan, Supra, note 12 at p. 295.
[19]   European Commission, (1997), *"Brittan Memorandum" on European Union Preferential Agreements*, Europe Documents, No. 2025, 27 Feb. 1997, p. 3.

to draw a linkage between the proliferation of developed/developing country regional agreements and the larger framework of international trade and development. The EEC's response at that time was that previous similar agreements had not led to any finding of damage to non-members, that a majority of the Contracting Parties had entered into such agreements over the previous twelve years, and that (nevertheless) world trade had expanded.[20]

There are several points by which to contest this reasoning, not the least of which is to inquire what growth for world trade would have occurred according to MFN in the absence of any regional agreements? One may also suggest the reverse inference for consideration. If there would occur a period within which world trade would fail to expand overall, would regional proponents then conclude that preferential agreements were no longer compatible with the multilateral system? Underlying, there remains a persistent assumption that trade creation is the context within which the question of compatibility should be determined. This is maintained without reference to the particular quality of the agreements themselves, as though all regional agreements were the same.[21]

Article XXIV could be redrawn to drop the definitional requirements free-trade areas and customs unions altogether. This would permit the parties to freely engage a sector by sector examination and then permit all preferences between members for those sectors that do not interfere with the existing trade of non-members. This would encapsulate a preservation-of-trade test as proposed by McMillan and in point, it would complement Dam's original prescription to address the Overseas Association problem on a sector by sector basis.[22] In light of such a possibility, we turn now to consider what justifications have been offered for a high internal trade requirement.

6.4   Justifying internal trade

6.4.1   *A first justification: avoiding trade-diverting preferences*

Although trade creation is not a part of the Article XXIV legal test, there remains a thread of commentary asserting that paragraph 8, by expressing a requirement for complete preferences to be exchanged, tends to eliminate the possibility of only trade-diverting preferences being selected. Hudec identified this aspect in respond-

---

[20]   1972 BISD, L/3379, p. 149, para 5-11.

[21]   For examples, how much of the expansion was caused by customs unions as compared to free-trade areas, and how much was caused by free-trade areas in their differing varieties? Was more or less expansion caused by free-trade areas that omitted agriculture and textile coverage? Was more or less expansion caused by free-trade area plans between developed territories or between developing territories, or between developed and developing territories?

[22]   Sectoral examination was endorsed by Dam for the Overseas Association, in reference to the Haberler Report. Supra note 5 at p. 652.

ing to those who, "charge that the present all-or-nothing rules are economically unsound ..."

> "(I)n addition, once governments are allowed to select some products and not others,
> political forces will inevitably exert enormous pressure to choose trade-diverting
> preferences first. Trade-diverting preferences are the ones that result in the greatest
> net political gain for governments; the political gains arise from pleasing local pro-
> ducers who displace third-country producers, while political losses are entirely avoid-
> ed because third-country producers do not vote".[23]

Jacob Viner also made this point, perhaps even expressing a qualification to his
own assertion that a 100% preference was economically unsound. Thus,

> "(T)here is one ground only on which it can consistently be held that preferences are
> economically bad and are increasingly bad as they approach 100 per cent...Customs
> union, if it is complete, involves across-the-board removal of the duties between the
> members of the union; since the removal is non-selective by its very nature, the ben-
> eficial preferences are established along with the injurious ones, the trade-creating
> ones along with the trade-diverting ones. Preferential arrangements, on the other
> hand, can be, and usually are, selective, and it is possible, and in practice probable,
> that the preferences selected will be predominantly of the trade-diverting or injurious
> kind".[24]

Although requiring 100 per cent preferences may be economically inferior to partial exchanges that select only trade-creating preferences, in actual practice such a
beneficial partial exchange is not at all likely. Therefore the all-or-nothing approach installs the good with the bad, as contrasted to only installing the bad.
Roessler recounted this same justification for the stricter requirement in suggesting
that formations dedicated to the purpose of diverting external trade can be avoided
by such an application of GATT Article XXIV:

> "(D)omestic protectionist pressures will tend to favor trade diversion over trade cre-
> ation, and governments negotiating RIAs will therefore be under pressure to avoid
> preferences in those sectors in which they are likely to increase imports. If the GATT
> were to permit governments to accord preferences selectively for certain products on-
> ly, trade-diverting preferences would tend to prevail".[25]

---

[23] R. Hudec, comment on M. Finger, *Gatt's Influence on Regional Arrangements*, in De Melo,
Jaime, and Panagariya, Arvind, (Eds), **New Dimensions in Regional Integration**, Center for Economic Policy Research, Cambridge University Press. 1993, p. 155.

[24] J. Viner, Supra note 2 at p. 51.

[25] Frieder Roessler, *The Relationship Between Regional Integration Agreements and the Multilateral Trade Order*, in K. Anderson and R. Blackhurst, (Eds), Supra note 9, pp. 311-325, at p. 314.

Roessler's comment also suggests that, but for such a requirement, regional parties would have no inclination to exchange any preferences that would truly create regional competitive conditions. This infers that there is inherent in the requirement also an accommodation for the possibility that regional trade creation should also occur as a result of the preferences. Paragraph 4 of the Article suggests as much in indicating the purpose of customs unions and free-trade areas should be to facilitate trade between the regional members and not to raise barriers to other contracting parties.

Although this limited view of trade creation may not be optimal from a global perspective, it may be preferable to the absence of any other liberalisation. Although the efficient external producer offers the best trade creation potential if it attains access to the market of the regional members, this point also begs the question if there is no market presence for such a producer prior to the regional formation. Viner also entertained this prospect as,

> "(T)here will be commodities, however, which one of the members of the customs union will now newly import from the other but which it formerly did not import at all because the price of the protected domestic product was lower than the price at an any foreign source plus the duty. This shift in the locus of production as between the two countries is a shift from a high-cost to a lower-cost point, a shift which the free-trader can properly approve, as at least a step in the right direction, even if universal free trade would divert production to a source with still lower costs".[26]

In these examples, it appears that the internal trade requirement of Article XXIV:8 has been cited to appear to serve a trade creating goal, albeit within a limited framework, and from a viewpoint based upon the prospective conduct of regional members and some natural inclination to select injurious preferences.

6.4.2 *A second justification: preventing proliferation*

Roessler has also suggested that the purpose of the requirement is to reduce the number of regional agreements, as,

> "... the political forces behind RIA's that cover substantially all trade are such that a quasi-universal organization such as the GATT must permit them lest it lose its members. RIAs covering a small portion of trade are unlikely to have as strong a political support. The substantially-all-trade requirement can therefore be seen as a require-

---

[26] J. Viner, Supra note 2 at p. 43. This scenario should be more rare over time due to the tariff reductions in the successive rounds. It may remain a feature for sensitive sectors and even in regard to developed country markets. These are also the sectors where developing countries tend to claim advantage.

ment that helps differentiate between politically unavoidable and containable deviations from the most-favoured-nation principle ...".[27]

Here it may be suggested that GATT parties will be more inclined to accept the deviations from MFN when the regional parties are themselves serious enough to consider meeting the internal trade requirements. This suggests that GATT can limit proliferation by proscribing those regional endeavours that would not carry significant political support anyway. This also raises a type of systemic interest that appears to inure to non-members even while their trade may be more greatly affected by completed internal agreements. If permitting agreements to form with a lower threshold of coverage means that a greater number of agreements will be formed overall, then the net result for all parties is that less international trade is governed by MFN.[28] In this context, the internal trade requirement can be understood to prevent proliferation of regional systems.

6.4.3   Challenging the traditional justifications

The justifications noted above reflect well-established views supporting the substantially-all trade requirement. However, they can also be countered by a "no harm done" approach. For the first, it was suggested that members would only exchange trade-diverting preferences and those that do not likely provide for internally competitive openings. However, while such minimal exchanges would not lead to regional trade creation, they would also not diminish external welfare to any particular degree. If such exchanges are economically neutral, i.e., if they do not hurt anyone, then there is no particular reason why GATT Article XXIV should be viewed as preventing them from occurring. For the cases where meaningful preferences are exchanged and regional trade creation has occurred, then the pre-GATT environment as described by Viner, where non-members did not have market access in the first place, is not really so applicable now. Non-members are more likely now to have established trade. Where bilateral preferences are exchanged, real market access is diminished and the preferences are therefore trade diverting. Thus, as barriers have come down overall, completed preferential exchanges may be more likely to divert pre-existing external trade. As for the point raised by Hudec regarding the regional selection of only externally trade-diverting preferences, McMillan's approach would seem to confront this problem directly by simply

---

27   F. Roessler, Supra note 25 at p. 314. "RIAs" refers to regional integration agreements.

28   This consideration was nicely expressed by a member of the working group in the review of the EEC-Agreement with Egypt, who considered that the additional expansion of the EC network of regional agreements would render the few remaining outsiders "least favoured nations". 1975 BISD, L/4054, para 11.

requiring the preservation of pre-existing levels of external trade for the benefit of non-members.[29]

The proliferation argument is also challenged by a preservation-of-trade approach. If within this proliferation environment, trade flows for non-members were preserved on an agreement by agreement basis, then external trade diversion would be in check. This result would permit regional parties to advance integration when actual trade creation resulted, and would prohibit them from advancing regional integration when world external trade was harmed. This seems to go to the point of the Kemp/Wan construction, that it is possible to acknowledge the benefits of regional integration without reducing world welfare. In order to respond in kind, one turns now to the question of national prerogative as it finds expression in regional commercial diplomacy.

6.5 Part Two Conclusion: restraining national prerogative

A persistent point remains that some countries and territories have a greater power to initiate regional exchanges than others. The largest of them, upon which most other territories rely for markets, are in the most advantageous position to derive the benefit from a less stringent regional exception. In a more flexible system, they would derive the enhanced capacity to select among a larger number of potential partners who may likewise be competing against each other to be favoured by preference, or perhaps to regain some balance lost by the granting of preference to others.[30] Among all of these potential candidates, it may also be apparent that some countries are more desirable regional partners than others. For both the largest players and the most favourable regional candidates, the acceptance of a more flexible regional exception could be favourable. More agreements could be formed with more partners and under less restraint from GATT's more rigid substantially-all trade requirement.[31]

However, if one considers that country and market endowments actually differ, then it also becomes evident that GATT most-favoured nation operates as a type of restraint upon more powerful players for its tendency to compel equal treatment among otherwise unequal actors.[32] From this it is drawn that that the core justifi-

---

[29] However, attempting to accord MFN on the basis of quantity is historically problematic. See, Henry J. Tasca, **World Trading Systems**, International Institute of Intellectual Cooperation, League of Nations, 1939, Paris, p. 25.

[30] Regional agreements may be subject to a type of domino effect. For an example, recipients of the US preferences in the Caribbean Basin Initiative have necessarily sought to redress later preferences granted to Mexico in the NAFTA. The EC-Turkey customs union was sought to be completed by Turkey, in part, to redress new preferences being granted by the EC to the countries of Central and Eastern Europe in the Europe Agreements.

[31] Some countries appear to specialise in accumulating regional attachments.

[32] GATT Article I applies to those like products, "*originating in* or destined for the territories of all other contracting parties".

cation for non-discrimination, and for its specified regional exception, is not economic in rationale. It rather reflects the resolution of an historical problem of international commercial diplomacy by the use of a legal rule employed within a contractual undertaking.

The Article XXIV internal trade requirement is an important element in this MFN construction as it restrictively sets conditions for the exception. As suggested by Roessler, the lesser desirable regional partners may find some basis to curtail the ambitious regional designs of others by seeking to delineate those with sufficient political support and those without. Further however, if one examines the manner in which preference may function within a regional setting, there is an additional possibility that MFN is also capable of affecting the commercial policy problem of the quality of treatment accorded between unequal regional partners within regional systems.

6.5.1   *Preference and dependency*

Hirschman's thesis demonstrated the need for such a requirement in isolating the components and instruments of dependency. He offered the case example of Germany and Bulgaria. In 1938 this bilateral trade represented 52 and 59 per cent of Bulgaria's total imports and exports respectively. However for Germany, Bulgarian trade represented less than 2 percent of its total trade for both imports and exports. Even while the trade was monetarily balanced, he raised the proposition that, "... it will be much more difficult for Bulgaria to shift her trade with Germany to other countries than it will be for Germany to replace Bulgaria as a selling market and a source of supplies".[33]

For Hirschman, the granting of a positive preference by one territory to another served a first purpose in inducing the conditions of trade dependency. This strategy required an initial deviation from MFN and was a prerequisite to exercising influence. However, once dependency was established by the inducement of trade generated by these positive preferences, a second application of discrimination then became possible whereby the dominant territory could dictate additional terms by exercising, or threatening to exercise, the termination of this dependent bilateral trade. This second act would require the application of a negative preference, but would also require a deviation from MFN since otherwise, a threat to terminate the trade of one party must also be threatened against all.[34] As Hirschman summarised,

---

[33]   Albert O. Hirschman, **National Power and the Structure of Foreign Trade**, University of California Press, Berkeley, 1945, (expanded edition, 1980), p. 31. If all countries were created the same, this would not be an issue.

[34]   In Hirschman's words, "... the power to interrupt commercial or financial relations with any country, considered as an attribute of national sovereignty, is the root cause of the influence or power position which a country acquires in other countries ...". This served as the definition of trade policy for him. A.O. Hirschman, Ibid., at p. 16. He also distinguished this strategy from mercantilism or autarchy, as the influence effect of trade cannot be achieved without engaging in trade.

"The idea could come to its full fruition only after commercial policy had been provided with the weapons necessary to influence the geographical distribution of foreign trade. As long as the most-favoured-nation clause was prevalent in commercial treaties and trade was regulated mostly by tariffs, governments had relatively little influence upon the geographical course of trade, or, at any rate, were not fully conscious of possessing this influence".[35]

Therefore, the restoration of an MFN clause for international trade would contribute to the solution.

"An argument *a fortiori* applies to the simple abolition of discriminating treatments such as quotas, preferential or discriminating duties...This program is much less ambitious than that of universal free trade...it admits general tariffs and outright prohibitions. The most-favoured nation clause is one of the typical expressions of this system which is generally implied in such phrases as 'equality of trading opportunity'...".[36]

Hirschman could be understood to be stating that MFN was intended to diminish the power of a large nation's economic diplomacy apparatus from being exercised selectively as to economically dependent states. In the modern era, we rarely (if ever) conceptualise MFN in these terms, but there does not appear to be anything inherent to the principle itself to suggest that its application should be necessarily so limited. On the contrary, to the extent that MFN could be said to serve the GATT's preamble objective of eliminating discrimination in international commerce, it is possible that such an objective extends even to the preferential relationship established between regional members.

6.5.2   The basis for MFN's legitimacy

Franck has suggested that the MFN rule derives the basis for its legitimacy as a function of its own inherent coherency. As he summarised,

"(GATT's) most basic provision is the most-favoured-nation (MFN) clause which (contrary to its name) seeks to preclude favouritism. It prohibits members from giv-

---

[35]   A.O. Hirschman, Ibid., at p. 8.

[36]   A.O. Hirschman, Ibid., at p. 76. His prescription went beyond MFN to call for the re-organisation of international trade to eliminate the power of national sovereignty as, "... the exclusive power to organize, regulate, and interfere with trade must be taken away from the hands of single nations. It must be transferred to an international authority able to exercise this power as a sanction against an aggressor nation." Ibid., at pp. 79-80.

ing benefits to some but not all trading partners. As long as this rule is applied consistently, it appears to be coherent and thus legitimate".[37]

As Franck's statement raises the notion of favouritism, one may go on to consider that differences between states in their capacity to grant or demand favouritism may also be considered as an aspect of this legitimacy. Since MFN prohibits distinctions between like products on the basis of their territory of origin, the principle displays an ability to equalise the conditions of entry as between the different sources of supply. If the ability to employ favouritism is also a reflection of a country's political or economic strength or size, MFN can then appear to sever the potential of exercising this power from other permissible commercial policy measures. As MFN acts to eliminate discrimination by precluding such favouritism, the economic and political advantages held by some territories could be seen to be somewhat contained by the principle. In the absence of MFN, favouritism in the form of preferences, the ability to control the geographic course of trade, would tend to be employed most by those territories most likely to employ it successfully.

Franck's interest was to outline the notion of "fairness" as such a concept might be evident in the field of international economic law. For MFN, this might be expressed as providing a recourse whereby the powerful should, by operation of the principle, be restricted from extracting more favourable treatment from the weak.[38] If this is the core of what forms legitimacy for MFN, then it can also be suggested that the principle should find an application across a wider range of preferential activities. These would include the traditional understanding of MFN as it protects the interests of a third state "C" from the preferentially extracting activities of State "A" as directed to "B".

It also seems plausible that the principle could also apply as between two territories "A" and "B" in reference to the quality of their own exchanged preferences and in light of the paragraph 8 requirements of Article XXIV. Thus, if paragraph 8 required only a low threshold of exchange between parties, then "A" could pursue the extraction of preference from "B", without "B" having any basis to obtain a mutual exchange in return from "A". In addition, there would be little likelihood that "C" might also have a basis for a legal intervention. In contrast, by requiring a high degree of exchange (and mutuality), "A's" capacity to pick and choose the

---

[37] According to Franck, "a rule is coherent when its application treats like cases alike and when it relates in a principled fashion to other rules of the same system". Thomas M. Franck, **Fairness in International law and Institutions**, Clarendon Press, Oxford, (1995), pp. 38 and 39.

[38] Franck goes beyond this position in arguing that fairness also requires a corrective equity in trading arrangements. For MFN, "(A)fter it became clear that such a regime would produce further erosion of the developing world's share of world trade, GATT parties agreed to the GSP". (General System of Preferences) T. Franck, Ibid., at p. 58. However, unlike bilateral preferences, GSP may well respect the coherency of MFN since GSP is also intended to treat all cases of like-developing countries alike.

terms of the schedule of preferential concessions as to "B" is greatly reduced. Likewise, "B" must also be given mutuality for all of the trade originating from its territory. In the strictest interpretation, only an "all or nothing" exchange between " A" and "B" can foreclose the possibility of an MFN challenge by "C". This outline suggests a purpose for paragraph 8 for Article XXIV that is directed to the relationship between the regional members, and not just to the effects of this relationship as to non-members.

Franck also considered that the principle retains coherency, "as long as the rule is applied consistently."[39] The record on Article XXIV formations through the years of GATT-1947 is arguably poor on this account. That occasional periods have seen proliferation of regional preferences would seem to suggest that there have been times when the MFN rule as it is intended to protect non-members has been honoured only in the breach. However, under WTO this may change. Throughout the GATT years, working groups reviewing agreements made statements as to what the GATT provisions appeared to require and whether or not any particular agreement was perceived to be meeting these requirements. As WTO dispute settlement practice has come to the fore, these recorded statements have found a new venue to refute the notion that the old GATT practice constituted acquiescence and/or an established pattern of subsequent practice. Although it has taken 50 years, one can now see the possibility emerging wherein the application of MFN and the regional exception becomes more consistent with the expressed terms of the provisions themselves.

As the WTO has come into force, the groundwork may also be laid for a view of MFN not so different than that held by Hirschman. Large regional systems continue to be implemented by the major trading partners in the WTO. Attention is being directed not only to the welfare implications of a particular bilateral arrangement, but rather to the relationship of such systems as a whole to the WTO, and to the relationships between the large and small territories within the regional systems. As the WTO practice develops, one can see that the issue continues to turn upon the meaning to be accorded to the requirements of paragraph 8 of Article XXIV. It remains a distinct possibility that GATT MFN may increasingly derive its sense of legitimacy in a type of restatement of the concept of the "open door". This would affirm that competition between great powers for preference upon third territories inures to the detriment of all the Members.

---

[39] Thus raising the question of institutional power to enforce the rule.

Part Three:
REGIONAL PRACTICE IN THE WTO

The resurrection of MFN in the GATT era can be claimed to have had the effect of reducing the power of any one country to control the geographical distribution of its trade. Necessarily, where an exception to this rule was granted by GATT Article XXIV, the restrictions imposed by the Article can also be seen in this same context. In this view, the purpose of the Article would be to require such a high degree of trade coverage between regional proponents that the opportunities to exercise the control of geographic distribution would be reduced. For those meeting the higher thresholds for coverage, the capacity to exercise a power to close intra-regional trade would also be minimised.

Thus, one objection to raising Hirschman's considerations in modern times is that GATT has already installed MFN on a multilateral basis for over fifty years, and has therefore rid the trading system of the onerous geographic strategies. MFN's establishment in the GATT is conceded. Nevertheless, the characterisation above depends not only upon the existence of the legal rule, but also upon the capacity of the institution and its Members to require adherence to it, i.e., whether MFN is being coherently applied. To this point, it has already been noted that the capacity of GATT-47 to contain deviations was limited. Also, as indicated in the last chapter, much criticism of Article XXIV has not been advanced from the view that regional members should be required to make more complete exchanges, but rather that such a requirement is not economically rational in the first place.

The legal and political setting within which Hirschman described the potential for dependency must certainly be different after 45 years of MFN application within the GATT. Large and developed countries are not prohibitively closed. In the old setting, selected positive preferences could quickly induce dependency where the recipient's production was expanded to seize export opportunities in otherwise closed markets. WTO[1] has come into force in a dramatically lower tariff environment, and one wherein quantitative restrictions have also been prohibited and actionable. Where quotas continue to persist by meaningful exceptions, they nevertheless do not serve as the predominant mechanism by which world trade is regulated.

Nevertheless, there still are a great, if not greater, number of regional formations continuing to be established even since the conclusion of the Uruguay Round

---

[1]   The Final Act Embodying the Results of the Uruguay Round of Multilateral Trade Negotiations, including the Agreement Establishing the World Trade Organization, MTN/FA II, signed in Marrakesh, 15 April 1994, reprinted in 1994 OJ L 336/1; 33 I.L.M. 13, 1994; *The Results of the Uruguay Round of Multilateral Trade Negotiations, The Legal Texts*, GATT Secretariat, Geneva, 1994.

in 1994, and one must wonder what now constitutes the motivation for the continuing persistence of regional trade agreements? Regional proponents suggest a
number of relatively benign possibilities. Some say that the increase is a response
to the risk of GATT failure to liberalise international trade at a sufficient pace.
However, many new regional members are also developing and/or developing transition economies. They should not likely be the parties making this point, since
most also complain that more time is needed to enact new WTO obligations and assumedly, such regimes are mandating liberalisation at a slower pace than their own
regional plans. Related, regional endeavours are also said to seek to stimulate
GATT progress. This appeared to make a deal of sense during the frustrating eight
years of the Uruguay Round, but then, why would the number of regional agreements continue to accelerate after the WTO was formed? Others suggest that regionalism allows countries to achieve higher thresholds of integration or to exper-
iment with new approaches without having to obtain the larger GATT consensus.
To the contrary, advanced examples of advanced integration are few. At least in the
treatment of complex non-tariff barriers, the free-trade area examples offered by
the EC external arrangements point to the extension of the Community's regimes
rather than identifiable new approaches. The NAFTA does not appear to treat regulatory barriers in depth. Neither are being cited yet for impressive achievements
in regional integration innovation.

A popular explanation claims that regional agreements act to "lock-in" the
process of economic liberalisation occurring in developing countries. However,
GATT rules arguably succeeded also in this task, and even prior to the WTO if one
considers that the economic miracles of Asia through the 1970s and 1980s were
generated in the absence of regional agreements. Moreover, where new regional
partners have had recourse to raise protection levels to non-members, any "lock-
in" if evident, may inure more to the benefit of the other regional partners.

This Part examines certain elements of internal practice between regional members
as it occurs in the WTO. By focusing separate chapters on rules of origin and safeguard mechanisms, it is hoped that these examples will establish at least a question
as to whether internal trade requirements for regional agreements in the WTO need
to be examined for a stricter application. The following Part Four will concentrate
on the WTO's response as it is developing in the dispute settlement cases and in the
reviewing of regional trade agreements.

For this Part, the introductory chapter raises issues concerning the so-called
new regionalism, mainly focusing upon U.S. and EC initiatives and an introductory critique made of their role as regional players in the WTO. The following two
chapters spell-out the use of restrictive measures as may be employed in current
practice as between regional members. Chapter Eight will consider the choice of a
legal form at the outset as free-trade areas are ubiquitous and possibly constitute a
more receptive vehicle for employing negative preferences between regional members. A problem unique to free-trade areas is the requirement of rules of origin.

While it has long been argued that the formulation of such rules can divert external trade, and should therefore be examined according to GATT Article XXIV:5, this chapter is rather oriented to viewing origin rules as they might fall under an examination according to GATT Article XXIV:8. The question of examining cumulation of origin among multiple free trade parties is also raised.

Chapter Nine considers especially the situation of regional safeguard measures. This appears to be a primary loophole in permitting regional members to re-establish restrictions upon internal trade. Most free-trade areas employ so-called *lex specialis* regimes to address the problem of increased imports. The position taken here is that GATT Article XIX and the WTO Agreement on Safeguards should retain validity as between these members and should not be waived or otherwise modified by special regional safeguard regimes. Examples of safeguard measures and regimes arguably modifying GATT/WTO safeguard rules are drawn from the EC-CEEC Europe Agreements and the NAFTA.

Chapter 7
MODERN REGIONALISM

"(I)f the logic of regionalism often makes less economic sense in an era of globalisation, why are we witnessing such a dramatic expansion of regional initiatives? Perhaps part of the answer could be that in some cases these initiatives are less about advancing regional economic efficiency or cooperation…and more about securing regional preferences, even regional spheres of influence, in a world marked by growing competition for markets, for investment and for technology". *Runato Ruggiero, (1997).*

7.1   Introduction: is new regionalism the same as the old?

In attempting to characterise regionalism developments since the entry of the WTO, one must first pay homage to the repeated assertions that the new regionalism is at variance from the old due to the less "closed" nature of the regional systems being formed. The new systems are not attempting to shield themselves from the global economy and are rather trying to maximise their participation in it. Thus, external barriers to the rest of the world should not be as high and preferences are not selected to only eliminate outside participation in the markets. This characterisation may be most apt in comparing regional formations made between developing countries now to those of the earlier wave. What is more in focus for this study is the nature of regional developments as they occur between the developed territories, like the U.S. and the EU, and their less developed regional partners. Here a question of terminology is also raised, as we may describe these agreements as "north-south", or "developed-developing" or as "developed-transition market", or even as "large-small". No attempt is made here to isolate the particular characteristics that would try to validate the use of one expression over another, or to attempt to delineate between these differing possibilities. Thus the reader is cautioned that a certain amount of interchangeability occurs here in the use of the terms. Instead the emphasis is upon the notion of "unequal" partners in regard to market size and level of development generally.

More important, the emphasis placed is not on the external reflection of these arrangements as to whether they are more or less open to non-members as compared to previous generations of regional agreements. Rather, the focus remains upon internal characteristics and the degree of flexibility sought to be retained by the members to the agreements. In this regard the primary question asked is whether there is anything "new" about the new regionalism, or is it merely a revival (or continuation) of the same motives that promoted the use of preferences in the past? To open the discussion on this, several characterisations are now set forth to demonstrate what may or may not be different about regionalism in the WTO era.

7.1.1   The remaining trade barriers

The margin of preferences granted relative to MFN is not completely irrelevant in the modern setting. The large and developed territories bound rates of duties are historically low overall, suggesting that their capacity to re-direct imports from one partner or another is limited. However, the external trade regimes of many of developing or transition-market regional partners do not exhibit such low tariffs nor are they anywhere near as comprehensively bound as their more developed partners. The developing country member can grant meaningful positive preferences that might well have the power to favour the trade of a developed member relative to other suppliers. Such market openings would also suggest the possibility of an increasing dependency upon the developed territory by the less developed or smaller member.

7.1.2   Regional trade dependency

Trade dependency among members is evident in the new regionalism. Even before the NAFTA was formed the U.S. market absorbed 81% of Mexico's exports and acted as the origin for 80% of Mexico's imports. For the U.S. however, Mexico received only 7% of U.S. total exports and only provided 6% of its total imports.[2] For the EC, so-called asymmetrical trade flows to central and eastern Europe countries (CEECs) so characterised the development of early trade that the matter was raised as a problem at the European Summit level. Thus,

> "(S)ince 1989 trade patterns between the Union and the associated countries have changed radically. Although the European Union now absorbs over 50% of the associated countries' exports they still only account for 4.2% of total European Union imports. In spite of the rapid rise in their exports to the Union, the Union's exports have risen even faster causing concern about the large trade deficit (5.6 billion ECU in 1993)".[3]

---

[2]   Directory of Trade Statistics Yearbook, 1991, for the year 1990. Cited in M. Akman, and M. Darton, *The Political Economy of Regionalsim in World Trade*, Marmara Journal of European Studies, V. 5, No. 1-2, 1997, p. 30.

[3]   According to Eurostat in 1993, the total of all CEEC exports as a portion of total imports to the EU was under 4.5%. CEEC imports as a share of all EU exports was 5.3%. Recited in European Commission, Com (94) 361 Final, 27-04-94, ANNEX II, and at p. 7. For the more advanced of the CEECs, 1995 exports to the EU comprised 62% of their total exports. Their imports from the EU equalled 61%, of which Germany generated 26%. Source, *Commerzbank Focus on German and European Economic Issues*, The Economist, (Europe Edition) 23 Aug 1997, after p. 47. The summary data includes six CEEC countries, Poland, Czech and Slovak Republics, Hungary, Bulgaria, Romania.

7.1.3   Investment attraction and security

A difference from previous periods of regional activity is the heightened role of capital and investment across borders. The inter-war period was dominated by exchange controls whereas now the cost of relocating capital has decreased enormously. There is also recognised to be competition between developing and transition-market countries to attract inward flows from the primary sources of investment held by firms located in the United States and Europe, but also from other developed countries. Perhaps regional agreements are a part of this process of attracting investment by making one potential location more desirable than another, by guaranteeing the free-trade channels for the inputs and outputs of established investment and by providing certain legal guarantees to secure the treatment of investors.[4] It is the case that a number of regional agreements in the modern times are hybrid in nature and include investment provisions of various sorts.

In this setting, positive trade preferences may not be an end in themselves, but rather serve as a means of facilitating the process of development. However, even while this suggests that there is something contemporary about the new regionalism, as it may be more in tune with the reality of globalisation, it also may not say very much about the accorded treatment of partners within a regional relationship. Since investment itself is not subject to a multilateral MFN obligation, preferences can be freely extended or exchanged on a preferential basis and without regard to mutuality. One might conclude that dependency in the new regionalism may be more comprehensive across a broader range of traded factors than just goods.[5]

7.1.4   Regional strategies as lobbied by firms

A conclusion is still possible that the new regionalism differs too much from the era of Hirschman to allow any comparisons to be drawn. In the 1930's, regional political hegemony was in vogue and trade policy was an instrument of national power, allegedly used to relegate the small and neutral to one regional zone of influence or another. In the modern era the reality is supposed to be global and more economic rather than political. Thus, much attention is drawn to the global nature of competition between multinational firms as they are seen to compete in all markets, each other's as well as upon third markets. However, this also belies a differ-

---

[4]   Ethier employs this consideration in his North-South stylised facts, although concluding that the process is supportive of multilateral trade liberalisation. Wilfred J. Ethier, *Regionalism in A Multilateral World*, The Journal of Political Economy, Volume 106:6, December 1998, pp. 1214-1245.

[5]   Occasionally the relationship between the elements of trade and investment is raised in the regional setting. As the European Commission noted the view of some of the Europe Agreement parties, "(T)he use by the Union of these commercial policy instruments (anti-dumping and safeguard actions) is perceived by the Europe Agreement countries as both a political and an economic problem; they believe that the existence of these instruments is likely to have a dampening effect on trade and inward investment". European Commission, Com (94), 361 final, at p. 8.

ent truth as support for new regional agreements also tend to be identified with proposals generated and then lobbied by the multinational firms themselves. If competitive life for them is global, then query what is the role of regionalism in the process of globalisation? The answer to this may lie in the fact that large developing and transitional markets are important growth markets. Regional preferences together with the investment factor provide the possibility for developing a meaningful competitive edge for firms receiving a more favourable treatment. Thus, while firms may compete globally they may do so by also enacting regional strategies. Likewise, they may choose to defend markets regionally.

7.1.5   *The factor of territory size*

In assessing the consequences of regional arrangements for international trade, Pomfret appeared to reject the risk of emerging trading blocks as the primary threat. Rather, the proliferation of agreements between a large country and smaller clients caught his attention.

> "Individually such PTAs may be of minor significance, but collectively they undermine the non-discrimination principle. The threat is more serious because the small country enjoys analloyed economic benefits even if the scope of the scheme is unilaterally restricted by the large country, while the large country sees unquantifiable (and hence difficult-to-challenge) political benefits for which it is willing to pay small economic costs. Such arrangements proliferate because they face no checks and they tend to take the hub-and-spoke form which is least economically justifiable".[6]

Whatever other difference may describe the difference between the trade diplomacy environment of the 1930's and the late 1990's, Hirschman would have likely recognised some of the elements set forth in Pomfret's statement. The large/small factor also appears to have been a factor in raising a certain level of WTO concern regarding the new regionalism.

7.2   The WTO in the post cold-war era

While the new wave of regionalism in the later years of the Uruguay Round emerged in force, the GATT Secretariat was otherwise primarily occupied with the difficulties of concluding the Uruguay Round, and then later, with the administrative difficulties of establishing the new WTO as an international organisation. The

---

[6]   Richard Pomfret, **The Economics of Regional Trading Arrangements**, Clarendon Press, Oxford, 1997, pp. 358-9. In addition, "(T)he danger sign for GATT in the 1980s lay in the diminishing number of important trading nations that accepted its principles as applying to their own trade policies". Ibid. at p. 367.

first Secretariat statement on the issues concerning regionalism in the multilateral system did not surface until 1995. The conclusions were tentative but tended to emphasise the potential for compatibility of regional arrangements with the multilateral trading system, but while noting that certain aspects might undermine compatibility.[7]

7.2.1   Committee on Regional Trade Agreements (CRTA)

Institutional developments however followed. The Singapore Ministerial Meeting (1996) called for an end to the ad hoc Working Party Review system of the GATT practice by establishing a standing review committee for regional trade agreements, the Committee on Regional Trade Agreements.[8] The terms of reference made for the CRTA included the examination of new agreements and the reviewing of the operation of existing agreements, to improve the examination process and,

> "(d) to consider the systemic implications of such agreements and regional initiatives for the multilateral trading system and the relationship between them, and make appropriate recommendations to the General Council …".[9]

Over the first years of the Committee's operation, there was solid progress made in outlining the systemic issues. However, while the parties could identify which aspects required clarification, they nevertheless continued to disagree on the substance of the answers that would free the process of evaluating particular agreements. Thus, while a large number of agreements continued to be notified since 1996, only the Czeck-Slovak customs union was able to receive an affirmative recommendation.[10]

7.2.2   Ruggiero's comments on U.S. and EU regional activities

Thus, aside from a bit more clarity as to what was at issue for interpreting Article XXIV, one could reasonably have assumed that WTO practice would go along to imitate, more or less, the pattern set in GATT-1947. For observers, it then came as some surprise when a far more critical WTO viewpoint was expressed in 1997 in a

---

7   See Overview and Conclusion, pp. 1-3, WTO, *Regionalism and the World Trading System*, Geneva, April 1995.

8   Decision of the General Council of 6 February 1996, WT/L/127, 7 February 1996. The CRTA convened its first meeting on the 21st of May, 1996. Minutes reported as WT/REG/M/1.

9   Drawn from the 1999 report of the CRTA to the General Council, WT/REG/8, 11 October, 1999, attached here as appendix three.

10   According to the Synopsis of "Systemic" Issues Related to Regional Trade Agreements, Note by the Secretariat, WT/REG/W/37, 15 February, 2000, p. 10. According to the 1999 CRTA Report, 118 RTAs have been notified to the GATT/WTO.

Rome speech delivered by the Director-General of the new Organisation, Runato Ruggiero. As he addressed the participants of the Transatlantic Business Dialogue, his comments revolved around the same question posed above as he asked, "(I)f the logic of regionalism often makes less economic sense in an era of globalisation, why are we witnessing such a dramatic expansion of regional initiatives?" As he responded,

> "(P)erhaps part of the answer could be that in some cases these initiatives are less about advancing regional economic efficiency or cooperation…and more about securing regional preferences, even regional spheres of influence, in a world marked by growing competition for markets, for investment and for technology. This, in my view, is potentially the most worrying feature of the new regionalism we see unfolding around the world today".

His reference to a world of regional spheres of influence is striking in its resemblance to the lexicon of the 1930's, and certainly not how the economic superpowers of the modern age would choose to see their role characterised as major partners in the WTO. However, the behaviour of the U.S. and the EU was central to Ruggiero's critique as,

> "(W)hat makes this competition more worrisome is that at its heart lies the world's two major economic players -- the United States and the European Union. What we see when we look at the pattern of regional expansion in the world today is essentially two focal points with concentric circles of preferential trade arrangements radiating outwards -- almost as if they were competing to see who can establish the greatest number of preferential areas the fastest. If it is true that the strength of the multilateral system for fifty years rested on the strength of the transatlantic partnership, it is also partly true that the sudden proliferation of regional arrangements reflects a certain inability of the transatlantic community to co-ordinate its trade interests and vision".[11]

The MFN implications of these regional developments were also considered. Thus,

> "(F)irst, we must ensure that the foundation of the trading system remains non-discrimination as embodied in the two fundamental principles of National Treatment and Most-Favoured-Nation. Regional agreements which are preferential by nature represent an exception to the most-favoured nation treatment".[12]

---

[11] Runato Ruggiero, *Regional Initiatives, Global Impact: Cooperation and the Multilateral System*, Address to the 3d Conference of the Transatlantic Business Dialogue, Rome, 7 November 1997, reported by NAFTA & Inter-American Trade Monitor - Vol. 4, Number 24, November 28, 1997, citing, "Ruggiero Says U.S., EU Drive for Influence Fuels Regional Initiatives", Inside U.S. Trade, November 21, 1997.

[12] Ruggiero address, Ibid.

The manner by which MFN acts to delineate the distinction between liberalisation undertaken within the regional preferential setting as compared to the multilateral system does provide the key to framing the question of the compatibility of regional endeavours with the rules of the WTO. It may seem remarkable for the WTO, as keeper of the non-discrimination rule, to have taken so long to initiate a response to the new regionalism. But considering the inherently diplomatic and intergovernmental nature of the organisation and the important role the U.S. and EU play within it, it is perhaps more surprising that any criticism from the Director General was made at all.

Since the commentary was directed to the two economic superpowers, and since these territories were founding parties of the GATT, they should most of all appreciate the value of MFN. So then, what possible changes occurred in this relationship to permit the promotion of regionalism and the apparent expense of the principle? The answer to this question could have a bearing upon the question of whether the interwar experience can ever be repeated in the WTO era.

7.2.3   The end of the cold war and the end of constraint

While GATT 1947 imposed only a weak form of institutional restraint, real constraints on national prerogative were relaxed only as the conclusion of the cold war has translated into new political and economic realities. According to Drestler,

> "The global geopolitical transformation has left three economic power centres - America, Europe, Japan -- with no common adversary to bind them. This does not necessarily make them enemies to one another -- indeed, continued global well being depends on their continued cooperation. But the security imperative no longer constrains them; the United States is no longer motivated to mute its economic demands to strengthen its alliances, and our allies are no longer driven to yield economically because they are dependent militarily".[13]

The establishment of the GATT in 1947 coincided with the initiation of this period of imperative constraint, or perhaps more accurately, with the economic version of it, in being portrayed at that time as necessary to defend the market economies

---

[13] I.M. Drestler, **American Trade Politics**, 2d edition, Institute for International Economics, Washington, 1992, pp. 210-212. An example of the role for governments in competition for global markets is the implementation of market opening strategies in both the U.S. and the EC. In both, firms are provided a streamlined and administratively assisted access to complain of foreign market barriers. This type of assist is arguably healthy where the national procedures are required to invoke GATT/WTO rules for dispute resolution determinations. For the EC, Council Regulation No 3286/94 of 22 December, "Laying down Community procedures in the field of the common commercial policy in order to ensure the exercise of the Community's rights under international trade rules, in particular those established under the auspices of the World Trade Organization", a/k/a the New Trade Barriers Regulation. 1994 OJ L 349, p. 71.

against the growth of state socialism. That GATT was eventually viewed in this manner was demonstrated by the arguments made by Cortney to reject its more conciliatory predecessor, the Havana Charter for the International Trade Organisation (ITO):

> "(T)he Havana Charter attempts to reconcile fundamentally conflicting ideas or objectives. It claims to make possible normal business relationship between countries dominated by state-socialism (and using planning for 'full employment') and countries where the individual competitive capitalism is prevailing. The Charter hopes to promote at the same time 'full employment' and free multilateral trade".[14]

If the GATT and its non discrimination rules derived any legitimacy from the imperative to defend the market system from the rise of Communism, then the demise of the Soviet model could also suggest that a re-examination of this legitimacy would also be set into motion.[15] On reflection, one can suggest that the multilateral MFN principle over this last century has not yet been tested for its capacity to bind the major actors in an economic environment other than that of the cold war exigency. That such a re-evaluation commenced in the closing years of the cold war is also shown by a number of commentators who claimed that the GATT and its principles had already outlived their usefulness. Bhagwati summarised their critique in 1991 as,

> "(T)he facile views of GATT's impotence are fashionable in the United States among several lobbies and in Congress. They principally reflect panic at the payments deficit and at the rise of Japan. Quick fixes on the trade front, using American muscle to extract trade concessions unilaterally and quickly from others, regardless of the im-

---

[14] Philip Cortney, **The Economic Munich**, Philosophical Library, New York, 1949, p. 23. The ITO charter and its provisions made reference to accommodating full employment policies that were not carried over to the GATT. An anti-Soviet argument did not succeed to create support for the later attempts to upgrade GATT to full organisation status. By this time, other activities which related more directly to the Soviet threat were also set in place, notably the Marshall Plan and NATO. Richard N. Gardner, **Sterling-Dollar Diplomacy in Current Perspective**, Columbia University Press, New York, 1980, p. 73. Much later in the 1970's, the U.S. administration actively viewed the GATT and its MFN clause as a political instrument in the policy known as "differentiation", undertaken to promote the GATT accessions of several central European countries. See generally, Leah Huis, **Globalizing the GATT**, The Brookings Institution, Washington, D.C.,1992.

[15] For definitional purpose, "When it is asserted that a rule or its application is legitimate, two things are implied: that it is a rule made or applied in accordance with right process, and therefore that it ought to promote voluntary compliance by those to whom it is addressed. It is deserving of validation." Thomas M. Franck, **Fairness in International Law and Institutions**, Clarendon Press, Oxford, 1995, p. 26.

pact on the world trading regime, therefore have a superficial but compelling appeal".[16]

By the mid-1990s however, the Japan "problem" had also outlived its usefulness. Absent the competitive Japan threat, Bhagwati's categorical concerns about US policy for its obsession with unfair trade, managed trade, aggressive unilateralism, and regionalism could all have been fairly claimed to have been only episodic events.[17] If Japan was no longer a popular threat to the United States' economic power, then one could have safely concluded that the era of U.S. disillusion with the GATT should also have been at an end. However, if as Bhagwati suggested, the GATT 1947 was being subjected to a strong challenge during the period when imperative constraint controlled U.S. behaviour, then what factor would serve as a constraint on U.S. policy upon the conclusion of the cold war?[18]

7.2.4   New-world regionalism

The case for developing a critical view of regionalism in the WTO should rest upon factors other than the sheer volume of agreements notified to the GATT/WTO during and after the conclusion of the Uruguay Round.[19] Rather, the focus could be

---

[16]   Jagdish Bhagwati, **The World Trading System at Risk**, Harvester Wheatsheaf, New York, London, 1991, p. 6; citing as examples, Michael Finger 1989, *Picturing America's Future: Kodak's Solution of American Trade Exposure*, The World Economy, V.12, No. 4, pp. 377-380; Rudiger Dornbusch, et al., *Meeting World Challenges: United States Manufacturing in the 1990's* (pamphlet written for Eastman Kodak Company, Rochester, N.Y.; and Lester Thurow's declaration at the 1988 Davos Symposium that the "GATT is dead". Bhagwati, ibid., at p. 7.

[17]   This is shown by Bhjagwati's equation of the US situation to the position of Britain at the end of the nineteenth century, as both were victims of the "diminished giant syndrome". "'Fair trade' and 'reciprocity' were the buzz words in Britain then, and they are in the United States now". J. Bhagwati, Ibid., at p. 16. "Perhaps the most important factor, responsible in particular for the American conversion to neurosis on this front, has been the relative decline of the United States within the world economy, leading to what I christened some years ago the diminished giant syndrome." Ibid., at pp. 15-16.

[18]   To trace the evolution of a position in favour of US bilateralism, see Rudiger W. Dornbusch, *The Case for Bilateralism*, in Salvatore, D., (Ed.) **Protectionism and World Welfare**, Cambridge University Press, Cambridge, 1993, pp. 180-199, "The case made here for bilateralism in no way questions the usefulness, past, present and future of the GATT system. Rather it advocates that there is room for, and indeed a good reason for a parallel track (to) move on to a bilateral basis." Ibid., at p. 181.

[19]   The European Commission reported that of the 69 preferential trade agreements notified to the GATT since 1947, and currently in force as of the end of 1996, 39 of these agreements were notified since 1990. European Commission, *"Brittan Memorandum" on European Union Preferential Agreements*, Europe Documents, No. 2025, 27 Feb. 1997. According to the Director-General of the WTO, "Since the entry into force of the GATT in 1947, 163 regional trade agreements were notified to the GATT or the WTO. In the period 1986-1991 only five agreements were notified to the GATT; the equivalent number for the period 1992-1996 is 77. Of these 163 agreements, around 60 per cent are currently in force. Thus over three quarters of the operational regional agreements in existence today have entered into force in the last four years." Ruggiero Speech, Supra, note 11. The WTO Secretariat indicated that as of 31 July 2000, there were 172 RTAs in existence, "a number which will increase to 240 after five years despite significant consolidation of some agreements in that period. This illustra-

placed upon the quality and legal character of the agreements being entertained and upon the goals sought to be achieved by the proponents in light of their other rights and obligations within the WTO. For this purpose, it is noteworthy that many of the regional trade agreements notified under the WTO appear either as initiatives of the U.S. and the EC, or as a type of response to their earlier initiatives.

The focus of regional attentions is also evident as many parties to the agreements appear to be transition market economies.[20] Not every country in market transition has become a signatory to a regional trade agreement with one of these leaders. But, free-trade area agreements, together with services and investment provisions, do appear to have become a primary mechanism applied to relate former centralised economies to the market system participants.[21] Not all of these agreements retain geographic proximity. Examples of out-of market initiatives include the EU-Mexico free-trade area and the increased preferences being granted to certain African countries by the U.S.[22] Both the U.S. and EC are active in negotiating free-trade agreements in South America. The FTAA hemispheric construction is inherently a U.S. conception and the EC has attempted to negotiate a free-trade area with the MERCOSUR.

tes the robust dynamism in the whole phenomenon of RTAs after the Uruguay Round." WTO (CRTA) Annual (2000) Report to the General Council, WT/REG/9, 22 November, 2000, paragraph 16, citing, WTO Secretariat, *Mapping of Regional Trade Agreements,* WT/REG/W/41.

[20] Defined here as territories formerly closed to trade or investment due to government ownership of production or restrictive government controls upon trade and foreign exchange. The WTO Committee on Regional Trade Agreements (CRTA) of the WTO, organised to report on notified agreements posted its work schedule for 1996. Of 32 reviewed for that period, the 20 following notifications are suggested here to fit this characterisation: NAFTA, goods & services; EC agreements with the Czech Republic, Slovak Republic, Hungary, Poland, Romania, Bulgaria, Latvia, Estonia, Lithuania, Turkey; EFTA agreements with Poland, Hungary, Romania, Bulgaria, Slovenia; Switzerland agreements with Estonia, Latvia, Lithuania. Source, WTO Focus Newsletter, June-July 1996, No. 11, p. 10. The CRTA 1999 Annual Report provides a later listing of notified agreements. Supra note 9.

[21] Neither Russia nor India is in a preferential trade agreement with either the U.S. or the EU. According to Fred Bergsten, regional trade agreements formed or forming constitute 60% of total world trade. He provides the following summary table for 1994 showing each arrangement's share of total world trade: APEC (exclusive of its subregional agreements) -- 23.7%; European Union -- 22.8%; NAFTA -- 7.9%; (other arrangements not shown). Intra-EC trade should probably be omitted from his account. His list does not include the FTAA, Free Trade for the Americas. According to Bergsten, India and Russia have both applied to the APEC (Asian Pacific Economic Co-operation). China is already an APEC member. Fred Bergsten, *Open Regionalism*, The World Economy, August 1997, pp. 545-566, at p. 555 (Table 1) and p. 551.

[22] "EU-Mexico update on declaration for negotiation principles", Institute for Agriculture and Trade Policy (IATP), Bridges, 10 August 97; Prospects for Congressional passage of the African Growth and Opportunity Act (AGOA), "Republicans see Africa floor vote in July", *Inside US Trade*, Inside Washington Publishers, Vol. 17, No. 26, 2 July, 1999.

7.2.5   EC initiatives

Regional formations are not new for the European Community and the increase in EC regional agreements over the last decade does seem to reflect the changes in the European landscape. This is associated with the demise of Soviet authority over the Central and Eastern European Countries (CEECs), specifically, the demise of the COMECON system over individual state external relations, and the resulting openings to the west. The primary reference point for these changes is the Europe Agreement (Association Agreements) framework for the establishment of free-trade areas with ten of the Central and Eastern European countries.[23] The choice of regional trade arrangements in this context is justified by reference to the endpoint of European integration by accession to the European Union. This movement has set in motion a number of revisions and demands for revisions to the pre-existing universe of EC regional agreements. By now, most have been either upgraded, the EC-Turkey and Mediterranean Agreements for examples, or are in the process of re-negotiation (EC-Lomé Convention). The pattern of upgrading these relations to reflect the EC's new approach of utilising free-trade areas with investment and services provisions is apparent.[24]

7.2.6   U.S. initiatives

The United States also employs free-trade areas as its primary legal regional vehicle, but unlike the EC, the U.S. is a new regional actor. Although the projection of a consistent regional trade policy has met with difficulties in Congress and in the public domain, a commitment to a regional strategy has remained steadfast for the Executive Branch over the last three presidents.[25] Early justifications for the US to

---

[23]   The Europe Agreements evolved from the context of cold war relations between the EEC and those countries within the Soviet sphere of influence, and in the context of the GATT, See, A. M. Van den Bossche, *GATT: The Indispensable Link Between the EEC and Hungary?*, Journal of World Trade, V. 25, No. 3, 1991, pp. 141-155; D. Horovitz, *"The Impending 'Second Generation' Agreements Between the European Community and Eastern Europe--Some Practical Considerations*, Journal of World Trade, V. 25, No. 2, 1991, pp. 55-80. Existing Europe Agreements are in force with Estonia, Latvia, Lithuania, Poland, The Czeck Republic, The Slovak Republic, Hungary, Romania, Bulgaria, Slovenia. Likewise, individual member countries of the European Free Trade Association (EFTA) have also initiated free trade area agreements with most of these countries. In addition, a number of CEECs have entered into the Central Europe Free Trade Area (CEFTA). In all, the CEEC connected agreements account for a good portion of the agreements notified to the GATT since 1990.

[24]   Arrangements with Turkey are historically bound in the customs union framework, but the transition market aspect is apparent as the renewed EC-Turkey customs union formalises, primarily on Turkey's part, an intent to open its market to the EC and to apply a number of essential EC internal market legal regimes. The formative proposals for a new European Union approach to the Mediterranean also have the aspect of upgrading the relationship by encouraging (or requiring) these territories to open to each other and to the EC. Proposals for Lomé at this writing, appear to encompass a number of free-trade areas for the more developed Members of the Convention.

[25]   Presidents Reagan, Bush and Clinton, two Republicans and one Democrat. The Office of the United States Trade Representative is within the Executive branch of government.

become a regional actor were often based on the case for pressuring the European Community and others to make settlements in the Uruguay Round. However, the policy in favour of regional agreements has continued since the conclusion of the Round and the entry into force of the WTO. Thus, by accident or otherwise, the end of the cold war has coincided with the emergence of the United States as a new purveyor of the free-trade area model.[26] Two of the US regional proposals deserve note. The countries of Central and South America have formed a continental centre of regional attention even while they have set upon unilateral and conventional market reforms. For this region the U.S. and Canada act as developed-market anchors within the Free Trade Area of the Americas (FTAA).[27] More ambitious, if only geographically, is the promotion of a free-trade area to be concluded within the framework of the Asian Pacific Economic Cooperation (APEC). By its 1994 Jakarta Declaration, the governments comprising nearly all of the countries which border the Pacific Ocean, including the U.S., Japan and China, have indicated a ministerial commitment to establish free trade on the Pacific Rim by the year 2010.[28]

7.2.7   Regional competitions

Between the United States and the European Union, although EU-related arrangements form the largest number of individually notified regional agreements to the WTO, the cause of concern for the upsurge in regionalism is viewed by some to be mainly attributed to the entry of the United States. According to Bhagwati,

---

[26]   During the cold war, the U.S. refrained from such agreements and acted as a primary critic of other territory formations. The United States did not oppose the formation of the EEC. This formation was presented to the GATT as a customs union plan and met most of the traditional elements maintained as consistent with GATT territory formation. Objections were made regarding member state preservation of quantitative restrictions and agriculture provisions. L/778, 1958 BISD, 6th Supp., pp. 68-89.

[27]   Summit of the Americas: Declaration of Principles and Plan of Action, December 11, 1994, 34 I.L.M. 808. Sixth Ministerial Meeting in Buenos Aires, Argentina, April 7th, 2001. 34 countries of North, Central and South America are included in the negotiations. Canada and Chile have commenced a bilateral arrangement along the lines of the NAFTA model, for now without the participation of the U.S. The U.S. program as of this writing, is awaiting renewal of executive fast track authority. This authority for the Executive to obtain Congressional approval without amendments attached was rejected in 1997. Whether or not the US Congress finally endorses such authority, the regional plans are indicated to remain an aspect of the new (G.W. Bush) Administration's foreign economic diplomacy.

[28]   With extensions to 2020 for developing members. Asia Pacific Economic Co-operation Forum (APEC), Declaration of Common Resolve, November 15, 1994, 34 I.L.M. 758. See also, Achieving the APEC Vision, Second Report of the Group of Experts, 1994. According to the WTO, APEC comprises 40 per cent of the world's population, some 54 per cent of the world's GDP, and 42 per cent of its trade. Ruggiero speech, 7 November 1997, Supra note 11. A difference between FTAA and APEC is that the former is intended explicitly to qualify as a free-trade area under GATT Article XXIV. While APEC members have made tariff-cut commitments, the treatment of any cuts in excess of Uruguay Round bindings is not settled. In order for APEC to leverage other GATT parties conditionally, the agreement would have to be qualified first by Article XXIV.

"The main driving force for regionalism today is the conversion of the United States, hitherto an abstaining party, to (GATT) Article XXIV...(T)he conversion of the United States is of major significance. As the key defender of multilateralism through the postwar years, its decisions now to travel the regional route (in the geographical and preferential senses simultaneously) tilts the balance of forces at the margin away from multilateralism to regionalism".[29]

In the same exchange, Baldwin agreed with the implications raised by the change in U.S. policy, but drew a wider picture by noting the rise of U.S. non tariff measures and the use of its unfair trading laws during the 1980's. Together with its interest in regional trade agreements, these,

"... are all efforts aimed both to bring pressure on GATT members to change the rules as the United States wishes and to explore whether the country can do better outside of the GATT multilateral framework".[30]

Pomfret noted that the EC was first in the accumulation of its "special cases" and recited Patterson's earlier predictions on the fundamentals of discriminatory preferences. As he summarised Patterson, each new discriminatory trade policy weakened the international system based on non-discrimination by eroding the share of world trade carried out under MFN conditions; by increasing conflicts among beneficiaries of complex preferential systems; by encouraging dissatisfaction in countries sticking to the non-discriminatory policies (because other countries were seen as stealing a march on them); and by undermining the legitimacy of GATT.[31] For Pomfret, the shift in U.S. policy in the early 1980's was an important step along this course as it had been the bulwark against discrimination since the late 1930s.

"Symptomatic of the erosion of the MFN principle's standing was the cavalier manner in which US officials talked of exploring new trade policy paths in the early 1980s; even after the CVERA and USA-Israel free trade area had been finalized, they were referred to as 'tentative tests' of a new approach".[32]

---

[29] Jagdish Bhagwati, *Regionalism and Multilateralism: an Overview*, in J. De Melo, and A. Panagariya, (Eds), **New Dimensions in Regional Integration**, Center for Economic Policy Research, Cambridge University Press, 1993, pp. 22-51 at p. 29.

[30] Discussion by Robert Baldwin, Ibid., at p. 53. According to Baldwin, these policies are responsive to the increased foreign competition facing import competing industries (textiles, apparel, steel, autos) as well as by the demands of export-oriented sectors such as computer chips and other high technology products. Contrary in part, Richard Blackhurst takes the view that the Bhagwati opinion regarding the U.S. conversion to regionalism understates the country's commitment to a successful Uruguay Round completion. Discussion by Richard Blackhurst, Ibid., at p. 55.

[31] R. Pomfret, Supra note 6 at p. 367, citing, Gardner Patterson, **Discrimination in International Trade – The Policy Issues, 1945-1965**, Princeton Universtiy Press, 1966, p. 356.

[32] R. Pomfret, Ibid., at p. 368. "The language could not be in starker contrast to Cordell Hull's zeal for a non-discriminatory trade regime." Ibid., and citing Weintraub (1986) for the absence of reaction in the U.S. regarding the policy change. The reference to CVER is not specified.

While the United States has received some attention for its shift in policy, the aspect relating to the differences in size or market development between regional members has not received much attention even from those who ascribe political-economy factors as primary to the phenomena. For example, Krugman attributed the rise of trading blocks (his term) to four factors: the excessive number of participants in the GATT; the difficulty of the negotiation space and the absence of reliable monitoring tools (i.e., grey area measures); the institutional differences between countries, especially Japan where tariff reductions are not perceived to actually open markets; and finally, an American position no longer preoccupied with trade, "as a binding agent in a political and military struggle". According to him, regional trading arrangements became favoured as a means to reinstate the bargaining environment where all of these problems could be diminished.[33]

What is evident in only the few years since Krugman's summary is that these factors have become less relevant, except for perhaps the last one. Monitoring orderly marketing arrangements is expressly required by GATT Article XIX as revised. If anything, unsupervised safeguard measures may now pose more of a problem when applied between regional members. The view of Japan's trade policy may continue to be an issue, but perhaps not a very important aspect as its economy and global competitiveness have slumped through the 1990s. The desire to negotiate in smaller groupings can continue to be cited as a valid motive, but then again, the diversity of the APEC and the FTAA groupings also do not suggest that the United States is only seeking smaller pools of like-minded parties.

Krugman's final factor does remain persistent in suggesting that the United States no longer views itself as the party primarily responsible for the multilateral system and its MFN clause, or if it does, that it no longer associates this task with restraint upon its own regional agenda. If so, then the idea that this change has also generated a new regional competition for spheres of influence between the US and the European Union should not be so surprising. That the end of the cold war opened the prospects for new competitions would also seem to follow.

7.2.8   The question of "open regionalism"

The role of MFN as it applies to regional preference represents an old issue that apparently requires periodic revival. As such, a first mythology that is confronted by recalling the role of MFN is the notion that regional overtures are always compatible with the goals of the trading system merely because both processes deal with the reduction of trade barriers. As stated, since free trade is a good thing, a free-trade agreement with a particular territory (Mexico, Chile, South Africa, etc. ...) is likewise also good and should therefore be promoted by government policy. Unfor-

---

[33] Paul Krugman, *Regionalism Versus Multilateralism: Analytical Notes*, in J. De Melo, and A. Panagariya, Supra note 29 at pp. 74 and 75.

tunately for the multilateral system, the same reasoning is also adopted in reverse and the WTO is jeopardised as a result. Thus, the dislocation effects of a particular free-trade arrangement are bad, free trade is therefore bad and WTO must also be bad.[34]

The GATT/WTO is probably accurately attributed with maintaining as a goal the formation of an integrated global economy. This objective should be open to debate on the value of its own merits. However, whether or not one supports this goal, it is also clear that the GATT/WTO system of legal rules seeks to impose upon the process a condition that developments should occur according to the non-discrimination principle. Thus, GATT's purpose is all about the matter of not permitting special advantages to accrue between territories, except according to certain excepted circumstances. To contrast, regional formations are really all about the business of developing special relationships and advantages by one territory one behalf of another, no matter the degree of historical or cultural propinquity that may be raised to validate them.

A number of new regional endeavours openly hedge the MFN problem as they are self-dedicated to the support of the multilateral rules via the expressed concept known as "open regionalism". While this innovative term remains wholly undefined in GATT legal practice, it can not be presumed that this theory of open preferences will find endorsement as compatible with the Article XXIV rules if and when it is ever tested. Historically, the notion of a "low tariff club" appears to be analogous.[35] In those systems, members exchanged preferences and then offered them to other territories on the condition that they would also reduce their barriers. While low-tariff club models were known to the GATT drafters to examine for their possible application in a new multilateral system, they were never adopted as a legal model for the exception provisions. Instead, Article I MFN was settled to be an unconditional obligation. Article XXIV also makes no accommodation for a conditional open regionalism approach, unless of course a grouping would first be validated as either a free-trade area or customs union. Only then may members choose to offer positive preferences to non-members on a reciprocal basis as they may wish. However, MFN will also apply to the reductions made by any outside party who has determined to reciprocate. So, they too must grant their new tariff cuts on an MFN basis to all other WTO Members or alternatively, formally accede to the grouping by the use of a free-trade area or customs union. This "rolling" form of trade liberalisation was passed-over in favour of provisions for multilateral negotiation rounds intended to include all Members. One may offer as a reason, that the low tariff club concept permits groupings of parties to form together to dic-

---

[34] Many opposing U.S. adoption of NAFTA also opposed the Uruguay Round implementing legislation, even though GATT rules provide the only treaty law limitations on the formation of regional trade agreements.

[35] Recalling Whidden's terminology from Chapter and section 1.4 of this book.

tate the terms of liberalisation to be adopted by the other Members. MFN becomes a conditional obligation rather than one unconditional.

7.3   Chapter Conclusion: new regionalism as a WTO system loophole

The new regionalism is certainly not conducted in the same legal environment as that described in the 1930's and 1940's. While Hirschman's thesis was brought forward prior to the restoration of MFN in the GATT, his view was retrospective to the era when MFN was not predominant, and when applicable, was often attempting to be applied to the allocation of quantitative restrictions in an environment of nearly prohibitive tariff duties. In the GATT era, MFN has been installed as a point of legal reference for regional endeavours. The results of the Uruguay Round also show that MFN has been reinforced throughout the annexed Agreements, both in the detailing of legal regimes and for traded sectors such as agriculture and textile products. Thus, where new regional agreements fail to accommodate MFN as a form of minimum treatment between partners, a major difference posed by the WTO is that the resulting levels of treatment between them may now fall below a level which has evolved to provide for actual market access. As Roessler has noted,

> "A zero-tariff commitment incorporated in a regional agreement leaving broad scope for the unilateral imposition of other import controls, or providing for no effective dispute settlement procedures, may therefore generate less trade than a tariff binding at a moderate level under the GATT".[36]

This comment confronts the apparent conventional wisdom that regional agreements are only instigated to provide for deeper liberalisation than that able to be accorded by the GATT/WTO. Rather, what is suggested directly by Roessler's statement is that instead of instigating "WTO plus" regimes, regional members may be able to develop a formidable means of avoiding them. As the WTO develops to provide less flexibility for discrimination in regard to national policies generally, the regional solution may offer an escape avenue for the continued exercise of national prerogative that can be directed at the regional level. Although this result is inconsistent with our understanding of the legal security understood to be provided for the Members of the WTO, it is also evident through the period of GATT-47, that the MFN principle, as well as other GATT provisions, have never been determined authoritatively to govern intra-regional regimes. Rather, the

---

[36]   Frieder Roessler, *The Relationship Between Regional Integration Agreements and the Multilateral Trade Order*, in K. Anderson and R. Blackhurst, (Eds), **Regional Integration and the Global Trading System**, Harvester Wheatsheaf. 1993, pp. 311-325 at p. 318.

record is full of references to the nature of regional formations as *lex specialis*. If the major parties view Article XXIV as a type of waiver from GATT obligations generally, then who is to say what GATT rules are supposed to remain in force between members?

All can agree that the multilateral system has matured and that large country actors are now constrained in a manner that would have appeared utopian to Hirschman. The WTO's integrated dispute system now permits the small to challenge the large with an increased certainty that the effort, when successful, will not be merely blocked. Powerful unilateral selective instruments, like the U.S. section 301, have been subject to challenge, even if there remain practical constraints upon the smaller territories to raise such challenges on their own behalf. The other instruments traditionally cited for their unilateral, discriminatory and non-compensatory characteristics have also been tightened in the WTO. A new safeguards understanding for Article XIX appears to expressly prohibit grey-area measures and requires notification and multilateral supervision of safeguards by an established WTO Committee. Injury and conditions for compensation are clarified, by and large to the benefit of the smaller parties. Even anti-dumping procedures are said to have become more regular and transparent, eliminating certain troublesome accounting regimes that were alleged to have led to inflated injury margins. The concept of *de minimis* has been imposed and sunset rules are now coming into force to retire older antidumping actions.

In light of these and other improvements to the system, one could argue that for the purpose of re-establishing selective discrimination, Article XXIV formations present one of the last great system loopholes for national prerogative. Thus, it is posited here that while many of the conditions have been greatly altered over the years, that the motive for regional formations in this era may not be so much different than that of the pre-GATT era. What appears to finally be common to both is the presence of intent to affect trade flows along geographic lines by the use of preferences, positive for sure, but also possibly negative as well.

Chapter 8
THE CHOICE OF FRAMEWORK: ORIGIN RULES AND IN-
TERNAL TRADE

"The solution to these problems will not only condition the functioning of a free trade area; it will also, to some extent, govern its actual scope. The volume of goods which can circulate free of duty within the area will depend on whether these "mixed" products are given exemption from duty in a more or less liberal manner". *OEEC, (1957).*

8.1   Introduction: the choice of a legal framework

Without a point of reference to country differences, there would be no particular reason to find that heightened dependency resulting from a regional trade agreement should inure to any one member relative to another. Likewise, neither party would derive any superior position to threaten the termination of trade or otherwise act to affect the bilateral terms of trade.[1]

For the GATT, there are three possible avenues offered for regional trade agreements according to Article XXIV: customs unions, free-trade area formations, or an interim agreement leading to either.[2] In comparing the two completed forms, it is not difficult to conclude that both can establish higher levels of trade dependency between members. The customs union form may however go forward institutionally to create the conditions of free circulation between members, suggesting that an even higher dependency can be realised by this form.[3]

---

[1]   "Terms of trade" in this context refers to the rate at which the territory's exports exchange for the imports which survive the tariff. "The greater the economic area of the tariff-levying unit, the greater is likely to be, other things being equal, the improvement in its terms of trade with the outside world resulting from its tariff." J. Viner, (1950), at p. 55.

[2]   Interim agreements are recognised by the rules to be a distinct form and have been necessarily treated as such due to the tendency of a number of them to have failed over time to be resolved into completed formations. Since they are transitional by definition, there are a number of opportunities for flexibility possible in an interim arrangement. See generally, F. Schoneveld, *The EEC and Free Trade Agreements, Stretching the Limits of GATT Exceptions to Non-Discriminatory Trade?*, Journal of World Trade, V. 26, No. 5, 1992, pp. 59-78.

[3]   The conclusion above is subject to the caveat that a customs union formation is not required to create free circulation. GATT Article XXIV:8 requires a common tariff be provided for customs unions, but elimination of duties only as to goods originating in constituent territories. The key difference that is presented by the concept of free circulation benefit is that the origin of the goods need not be established as goods cross borders between member countries. Also, a free-trade area can act to align the members' external tariffs and create similar conditions permitting free internal circulation.

A more significant distinction between the two forms may refer to the degree of discretion left to the members to terminate or threaten to terminate the trade of other members. Here, the same elements referred to above, that appear to heighten trade dependency between members, operate in reverse to restrict the capacity of any one member to restrict the trade of another. Thus, where a customs union provides for a common external tariff, the power to exercise internal trade measures by single members can only be given effect if the internal policy is somehow divorced from the external policy. This means that members must retain a commercial policy separate from that of the customs union, or that the custom union must somehow authorise individual member actions. Either way, there would be two sets of commercial policies. This may not be an impossible arrangement within the context of a customs union plan, but it is not a very likely occurrence in a completed customs union, given a result that the internal trade regime could be potentially more restrictive than the external trade regime.[4]

The free-trade area by its legal form provides for a reserve of national commercial policy, that policy governing the measures employed to provide for economic protection. Since each territory in a free trade area has the capacity to retain separate commercial policies externally, this power will also be resident as to other members unless it is affirmatively restricted by some express provision of the agreement or by other decision of the members. Therefore, sectors already liberalised or declared for free trade may later fall in treatment according to the exercise of the individual commercial power of any of the members. This need not happen in the free-trade area context, but a commitment between the parties to not apply their individual commercial policies to the trade of other members would be required. While there are examples of free-trade area formations that exhibit such characteristics, they are the exception rather than the rule. By adopting certain commitments however, any free-trade area could be elevated to suspend the commercial policy of its members in regard to internal trade. Thus, one should avoid generalisation in drawing distinctions between the two forms. In theory it is possible to design a free-trade area which provides for a high degree of internal free movement which is legally bound, as it is also possible to design a customs union that fails to obtain free circulation and retains member to member commercial policies. It is also difficult to generalise from the practice, since the number of completed customs unions in the modern era are few.

The EEC Treaty provided for free internal circulation as according to EEC Article 11, stating that third-country goods shall be placed into free circulation after the common duty is paid and other formalities of importation have been met. Individual members may yet impose marketing requirements and maintain certain inspections on the passage of goods where such requirements have not been harmonised.

[4]   An intergovernmental customs union could obtain this result. The parties could agree on a common external tariff, but then fail to reach internal free movement via the reservation of their individual territory controls in respect to each other. As a supranational authority represents a passage of sovereign power to a common institutional structure, small members could tend to favour this aspect as it would tend to curb practices by the larger members in regard to internal trade.

For the EC, the common (external) commercial policy *shall* be based on uniform principles as according to EC Article 133 (ex. Article 113). For this customs union, there are two possible exceptions to the principle. The first would occur in any situation where the external regime for admission of goods fails to be uniform. If uniformity is not obtained or retained, then internal controls would likely result to compensate for the varying conditions of entry to the less restrictive territory.[5] A second situation raising the requirement of internal barriers to trade can also be identified where there is no difficulty in the application of external uniformity for the admission of goods. However, for some reason or another, a member state has acted to restrict the trade of the goods from another member. Where the enforcement mechanism would fail to sanction this member action, internal controls upon the trade of members would occur as a result whether "legal" according to the agreement or not.

In actual practice, the conditions required for establishing internal free movement of goods do suggest that a free-trade area is a somewhat weaker form of integration in this regard and upon several counts. First, without the requirement to apply substantially the same duties and other regulations of commerce as to the trade of third parties, it is more difficult to imagine by what circumstances free-trade area members would commit to align their external provisions, and thereby permit truly free internal circulation for goods covered. More to the point, as long as members retain national commercial policies generally, the quality of internal-trade coverage must always be dynamic as it remains a function of individual member behaviour in regard to other members' goods. Even while a free-trade area may attempt to impose a common external regime by harmonising tariff lines, any later variation in the application of individual territories' instruments will necessarily result in new internal controls to reflect the difference in entry conditions. This would suggest that, not only is an external common tariff a prerequisite for free internal movement, but that individual territory discretion must also be overcome by some institutional mechanism.

That it may be more difficult for free-trade areas to achieve internal free movement over time may also explain, in part, their attraction as a legal form for so many regional proposals. The degree of flexibility retained permits members to enunciate free-trade objectives, thus satisfying whatever agenda is motivated by them, but at the same time preserve the options to restrict trade accordingly between members at a later time. Haight was more severe on this point, as he believed

---

5   This also necessarily impedes free circulation as confirmation of origin of goods would be required. Although, this requirement would not undermine the legal status of the customs union. For the EC, this problem has been reflected by EC Article 115, now EC Art. 134, as amended. This provides for certain protective measures in regard to third-country products. The resolution of Article 115 measures became a necessity with the completion of the internal market , established with all of the characteristics of a single national market and by the removal of internal frontiers. See preamble, Council Regulation, EC No. 518/94 of 7 March 1994, on Common Rules for Imports, OJ No. L 067, 10/03/94. See Infra, Chapter 9, note 21.

that the legal form of free-trade areas dictated that they were inherently preferential, as contrasted to formations that were intended to create customs territories.[6] Here, it would be suggested that the potential for formations to result in partial preferences over time does remain a distinct possibility with the larger majority of free-trade areas now in operation or declared for formation. In this the role of preferential origin rules must also be considered. It is suggested by the above that neither form of regional agreement is disqualified by the application of preferential origin rules. A uniform external tariff permits the conditions for internal free circulation without the use of origin rules, but this level of integration is not an apparent requirement of GATT Article XXIV. However, since preferential origin rules fall outside the considerations of the provisions of Article XXIV, they should also be observed for the effects their application may have in regard to the quality of trade coverage obtainable by regional members. Since free-trade areas remain exempt from the necessity to apply uniform conditions for entry does suggest that preferential origin rules play a far more important role in their establishment and operation. In this, the design of such rules may also appear to operate as a key internal instrument for regulating the conditions of preference between free-trade area members.

8.2   Origin rules in preferential formations, bilateral coverage

Preferential rules of origin are a required aspect in the establishment of a free-trade area in the absence of a harmonised tariff.[7] The rules established serve in practice to determine the scope of the free trade area, including the volume of trade that is actually freed between the parties. As indicated by an early OEEC report on origin rules,

> "The solution to these problems will not only condition the functioning of a free trade area; it will also, to some extent, govern its actual scope. The volume of goods which can circulate free of duty within the area will depend on whether these "mixed" products are given exemption from duty in a more or less liberal manner".[8]

---

[6]   "To drop the term 'free-trade area' from the vocabulary of commercial policy and, in practice to limit the use of Article XXIV to customs unions would reinforce the very foundations of the GATT." F.A. Haight, *Customs Unions and Free Trade Areas Under GATT*, Journal of World Trade, V.6, No. 4, 1972, pp. 391-403 at p. 401.

[7]   "The need to define the origin of products stems from the fact that, in a free trade area, each participating country retains its national tariff on imports from third countries. This is a special problem, therefore, which does not arise in the customs Union when the common external tariff has come into force." OEEC, Special Working Party for the Council, *Report on the Possibility of Creating A Free Trade Area in Europe*, C(57)5, 67 pages, Paris, (1957), at p. 11.

[8]   OEEC, Ibid., at pp. 11-12.

Thus, if a narrow definition is adopted whereby products incorporating only a small proportion of imported materials are permitted, the volume of trade will be more restricted between the parties.[9] Above all, the importance of the rules is also established as they determine which products shall receive preferential treatment and which products shall not.[10]

Since the purpose of preferences is to shift sources of production, the manner in which the rules are set between preference parties determines the extent of that shift. In this respect preferential systems generally intend to accord the preference for products that have made a (last) substantial transformation within the territory of a preference-receiving country. The techniques employed to identify this transformation vary between agreements, and combinations of different approaches are common within single arrangements. The primary categories employed to effect this include value added, specified (list) processes, and change in tariff classification. Each approach presents its own policy considerations and has particular implications for internal trade.[11]

8.2.1   The evolution of EEC preferential rules

For the EEC's external regional trade agreements, the approach taken for its regional preferential rules was evolutionary but not necessarily from a restrictive view to a liberal one. The first EEC preferential agreement to contemplate such rules was the Yaounde I Covention of 1963.[12] The impetus to establish a more formal approach came with the expiration of the first Yaounde Convention in 1968 with the simultaneous negotiations of new preference areas with the first generation of Mediterranean Agreements, together with the expansion of the African associations to three English speaking newly independent states.[13] This need was raised to deal with manufactured goods as these products, unlike agricultural and other tropical products, were not able to be designated as wholly obtained within the origin country of their production.

Although the Community already employed certain general rules of origin on a non preferential basis, as found in Council Regulation 802/68, these rules were not determined to translate well to the preferential situation. According to Forrester,

---

[9]   OEEC, Ibid., at p. 33.

[10]   Ian S. Forrester, *EEC Customs Law: Rules of Origin and Preferential Duty Treatment--Part One*, European Law Review, V.5, (1980a), pp. 167-197, at p. 167.

[11]   See generally, David Palmeter, *Rules of Origin in Regional Trade Agreements*, Leige Conference Papers, 1996, in P. Demaret, J.F. Bellis, and G. Garcia, G, (Eds), **Regionalism and Multilateralism After the Uruguay Round**, European University Press, 1997, Brussels. For free-trade areas, the tariff shift approach is suggested to be the least distortionary, although it is also subject to industry lobbying and capture.

[12]   1964 OJ 1431, granting duty free treatment to a limited number of products, "originating" in the Associated states. I. Forrester, (1980a), Supra note 10 at p. 175. Protocol 3 to the Convention contemplated adoption of rules within six months, but this adoption was not accomplished. Ibid.

[13]   I. Forrester, Ibid., at pp. 175-6.

the notion of last substantial transformation as it was incorporated in the Regulation for non preferential rules was not seen to be strict enough for the regional setting, as

> "any product essentially made in the United States or Japan could be finished in the beneficiary country, shed its United States or Japanese origin and thus gain preferential access to the EEC".[14]

In order to avoid distortion to trade caused by deflection, the EEC resolution disregarded the idea of providing separate rules for each product (too complicated), as well as the use of a generalised 50 per cent value added test as applied in the European Free Trade Association (EFTA). Forrester stated that the EFTA approach was rejected due to its unfairness as to cheaper labour countries. He offered the example that if a Swiss worker applied a single-day's labour to an imported leather product, the test could be met. The same labour added by a Saharan worker would fail to raise the product value to the same degree.[15]

The EEC solution was to retain the overall concept of substantial transformation but to indicate this change by comparing the tariff heading of the finished product with that of the non-originating components. Where the heading had changed, with exceptions for certain listed processes, there would be an indication that a new product had been formed. This new product was therefore entitled to receive origin by this final producing country. This was understood to be an easily understandable means of conferring the principle of last substantial transformation, although it did also necessarily raise the issue of the mixing of inputs and therefore the question of cumulation. According to Forrester, this new problem of mixing inputs from differing sources presented both a negative (loss of origin) and a positive (gaining of origin) facet. Thus, he phrased the salient legal questions as follows:

> "If a product originates in one country, should processing in another country involving non-originating parts or materials *deprive* the product of origin, and if so under what conditions? Should origin be acquired gradually in several countries, or should each country have to satisfy the rules individually in order for the end product to be originating?"[16]

What is revealed by this two-part description of the origin question is that there is present an internal aspect (gradually acquired in several countries), as well as an external dimension (involving non-originating parts) to origin rule constructions.

---

[14] I. Forrester, Ibid., at p. 176.

[15] I. Forrester, Ibid. However, see Matthew McQueen, *Lomé and the Protective Effect of Rules of Origin*, Journal of World Trade, V. 16, No. 2, 1982, pp. 119-131, p. 125, documenting the inclusion of such a test in later Lomé I and citing the use of value added as an internally discriminatory instrument.

[16] I. Forrester, (1980a), Supra note 10 at p. 176.

In the process of analysing the effects of rules, it also occurs that a single rule can have implications for both external and internal dimensions. This point is developed below when discussing the primary methods for conferring preferential origin. For the external aspect, a core consideration is that of deflection to the normal flow of trade caused by maintenance of different tariffs by member countries on imports from sources outside the area.[17] An externally protective origin regime would be according protection in excess of what is needed to remedy deflection.[18]

8.2.2 Origin rules and effects upon internal trade

For internal trade the question should be related to the trade coverage that is sought to be accorded by the agreement. This can be expressed by directing attention to the question of preference as in, which goods shall be considered to be of origin to the preference member and which goods shall not be so qualified? As a preliminary matter, there is also the question of how origin rules by their technical sectoral nature are subject to capture in order to limit the range of goods which may be otherwise qualified. Palmeter recounted a list of "Directly Unproductive Profit Seeking Activities" as provided by Bhagwati.[19] As he described, lobbying in free-trade agreements is oriented to 1) increasing one's own exports at the expense of outside competitors; 2) blocking increased competitive imports from within the free trade area; 3) tailoring the rules so that one's own multi-country rules benefit from the preference while competitors do not; and 4) to support rules which effectively block trade as a last resort.[20]

This suggests that origin designation rules appear to be susceptible to domestic capture and may be designed upon occasion to reduce the coverage of internal trade. While a rule may be decipherable upon its face, its underlying intent may be not transparent. The rules are complex by their nature and where designation is made sector by sector, only firms handling the particular commodities have the energy or resources to have actual insight into the effect of the rules on local production. While the design of rules may naturally seek to provide the entire regional grouping protection from external sources, it stands to reason that changes in competitive forces internally also may be sought to be affected by the rules.

---

[17] OEEC, (1957), Supra note 7 at p. 31.

[18] There is a relationship between origin rules which are externally protective in excess of what is required to address deflection and a resulting internal distortion to trade, since third-party inputs can be denied to a regional partner's production. This aspect is considered below.

[19] The four activities provided included, 1) tariff-seeking lobbying, which is pecuniary seeking in the shifting of factor incomes, 2) revenue-seeking lobbying which is government transfer of revenues to oneself as recipient, 3) monopoly seeking activities to create artificial rents, and 4) tariff evasion and smuggling. Bhagwati, Jagdish, *Directly Unproductive profit-Seeking (DUP) Activities,* in J. Eastwell (Ed.) **The New Palgrave Dictionary of Economics**, Stockton Press, 1987, pp. 845-847.

[20] D. Palmeter, Supra note 11 at p. 21.

A brief survey of the leading categories of designating origin will assist in understanding how these questions may be raised for the context of internal regional trade. As the focus is upon origin designation related to the internal shifts of production, the problem of according preference in a bilateral setting is taken up first. A separate section follows to deal with the added problems of area-wide designation between two or more regional partners.

8.2.2.1 Value added

An origin rule may be enacted which is so restrictive in its criteria so as to not permit the flow of goods between the parties in spite of a zero-tariff preference committed as an aspect of the free trade plan. While the parties may have declared such an intent within the context of a free-trade area, the origin rule as applied to any particular commodity may operate instead to provide a single party a domestic protective effect from the goods originating in the other member state. This prospect has been raised as a criticism when value added criteria is applied between territories of differing development levels. Generally, it appears to be understood that value or content added requirements tend to favour the higher-cost producer, or to generalise further, the higher-developed regional partner. For an example, in the First Lomé convention, a value added criteria was applied across a range of products in addition to change of tariff heading criteria. While this value added requirement did not exceed 60 per cent, and would have been considered to be a neutral criteria between developed trade partners, "by the same token, they are inappropriate for countries at the level of development and with the small size of domestic market previously outlined for the ACP countries".[21]

McQueen suggested that while a restrictive rule may be necessary to avoid trade deflection, that there is possible for each rule an examination of what level of restriction is actually necessary to eliminate the risk of deflection, and not more. As he explained it, where the producing partner's country tariff was relatively high, or where tariffs between the partners were similar, then deflection should not be an issue in any case. If so, it would follow that a rule operating in excess of a measured requirement to eliminate deflection would be indicative of an internally diverting origin construction.

Palmeter came to a comparable conclusion in his analysis of the application of value added criteria in the North America Free Trade Agreement (NAFTA) where he claimed that preference eligibility would more easily confer origin in higher cost U.S. and Canadian operations than in Mexico.

"In this way, a value added rule may distort economic efficiencies and divert investment from where it might otherwise occur, and where it may be most needed".[22]

---

[21]   M. McQueen, Supra note 15 at p. 125.
[22]   D. Palmeter, Supra note 11 at p. 11.

Palmeter's comment also introduces the notion that the imposition of value-added criteria raises considerations of investment and production location, as capital movement would otherwise be shifted as a result of preference. Where parties are dissimilar in cost structure, an origin rule can be made to either respect or undermine the comparative advantage of the lower-cost member producer. Thus, it is possible that the same rule may act in two ways, first to fashion an external diversion in favour of the region, and then second, to allocate the benefits of diverted production to one regional member relative to another.

8.2.2.2   List processes or technical test

The use of denoting specific production or sourcing requirements as applied for the general rule to confer preferential origin has increased in recent years.[23] A technical test can be either a positive or negative test, positive where production or sourcing requirements conferring preferential origin are specified, negative where processes that do not confer origin are specified.

Examples of how list-processes criteria may be employed to shift internal sources of supply have not been offered in the literature, but examples have been raised to demonstrate the externally diverting possibilities for the use of technical tests. That such a rule can play both an external and internal diverting role can be shown from an example for origin-sourcing rules taken from a WTO study. A NAFTA "yarn forward" rule requires that for many clothing products, 100 per cent of all inputs must be obtained from within the free-trade area in order to qualify for the preference. The rule is indicated in the WTO study as externally trade diverting as it shifts supply from external sources to those of the regional partners since outsiders can no longer supply a partner manufacturer without that internal producer foregoing its regional preference.[24] However, it also seems possible that an internal shift of production can also be accomplished by the same rule in two possible ways. First, internal diversion could be derived in favour of the end product (downstream) producer in the higher cost regional partner market. This could occur where the lower cost producer of the end product was diminished without access to the cheaper foreign input as a result of the rule. This raises the second possibility, that the higher cost producer of the input might also extend its production throughout the region as the sole regional supplier at least, "up to the point where the origin rule becomes so restrictive that producers opt for the second option."[25]

---

[23]   WTO, (1998), Committee on Regional Trade Agreements, *Inventory of non-tariff Provisions in Regional Trade Agreements,* WT/REG/W/26, Geneva, p. 11. Comment from the representative from Australia, "He also noted that the analysis seemed to indicate that the test most often used in RTA's for rules of origina was a technical test rather than a change in tariff heading ... it was his understanding that a change in tariff heading was usefully regarded as the clearest and least complex way of determining origin ...". WTO, Committee on Regional Trade Agreements, Note on the Meeting of 6-7 and 10 July, 1998, WT/REG/M/18, 26 July 1998, para. 20, pp. 4-5.

[24]   WTO Secretariat, (1996), **Regionalism and the World Trading System**, Geneva, p. 48.

[25]   "The second option being the obtaining of the materials from an outside supplier and foregoing the preference." WTO, (1996), Ibid.

8.2.2.3 Change of tariff heading

Although change of tariff heading is considered to be less distortionary for trade and investment then the above categories, the same type of result can be obtained via a rule designating transformation by change of tariff heading. Also offered by Palmeter as a NAFTA example, as between the headings as applied to tomato paste (HTS 2002.90) and which is turned into tomato catsup (HTS 2103.20). The previous Canada-U.S. free-trade area rule provided that a change in heading between the two chapters, 20 to 21, was sufficient to confer origin. The NAFTA rule however provides an exception for the particular subheading of tomato paste. The result is that third-party imported tomato paste processed into catsup within the region will not accord origin for preferential treatment. Only paste produced within the NAFTA area can be transformed into catsup in a way that will confer free movement for catsup from one member to the other.[26] While Palmeter raises this example to demonstrate the external trade diversion possible, as for example, Mexico will now replace Chile as a supplier of paste, as above, it is not difficult to consider conditions that would also generate an internally diverting result. Thus, if only one regional party produces paste, the effect of the rule would also be to secure the market regionally as to outsiders, but to also capture the end-product market locally. Likewise for downstream diversion, if Mexico's catsup production relied upon Chilean paste, the same rule which excludes Chile would also then restrict Mexico's catsup production as it would now be required to source its paste from higher cost NAFTA members for all catsup intended for the NAFTA market. The result would be that, even while tomato catsup might be a product declared to receive zero-tariff treatment according to the free-trade area, the preferential origin rule applied upon its primary input might effectively eliminate regional sources of competition.

Although these examples can only be posed here as hypothetical cases, what should be apparent is that all of the primary categories of origin transformation can be operated in a manner that would restrict internal producers as effectively as third-country suppliers. For many GATT review parties, even where new tariff levels were not seen to raise barriers to trade, restrictive origin rules have long been charged to effectively raise new barriers to trade in derogation of the requirements of GATT Article XXIV:5.[27] More recently, the internal prospects have also been noted. For an example, the representative of Korea posed the following in a CRTA meeting held to discuss non-tariff provisions:

---

[26] D. Palmeter, Supra note 11 at pp. 5-7.
[27] First raised in 1961 BISD, Ninth Supplement, *European Free Trade Association Examination of Stockholm Convention*, Report adopted 4 June 1960, (L/1235), pp. 70-87 at paragraphs 4 through 10.

"... his delegation wished to advance one thought for colleagues' reflection: that the use of preferential rules of origin in RTAs related to the definition of "substantially all the trade: (SAT). It could be argued that the use of preferential origin rules should have a bearing on determining whether the SAT criterion were met; that is, concern that the stringency of preferential rules of origin might have added effect on the patterns of trade and economic co-operation amongst RTA parties themselves and between RTA parties and third parties. Therefore to prevent unwarranted disruptions to trade patterns, there was a *prima facie* case for relating the use of preferential rules of origin to the definition of SAT".[28]

The comment recognises the role that preferential rules of origin play in determining that actual scope of a free-trade area as it relates to the substantially-all trade requirement. It suggests the direction that developments could take in assigning a rule of origin review feature to the question of internal trade coverage, but also highlights the absence of such a review feature up to the present time. The manner by which GATT reviewing parties for both external and internal aspects have been unable to address the questions raised by preferential origin rules is also indicated, but no more clearly than in the case of overlapping free-trade areas and the issues raised by them regarding the concepts of area treatment and cumulation.

8.3　Origin designation and area definition

The question of what type of "area" is being suggested by regional proponents has both a dimension that is geographic as well as legal in regard to trade coverage. For this aspect the concept of cumulation for either inputs for processes must also be considered. According to Forrester, cumulation rules,

"state the terms on which an end product may enjoy originating status even (al)though the normal origin rules would not confer origin on the basis of the work done in the country of last processing".[29]

---

[28]　WTO, CRTA, Supra note 23, para. 19, p. 4. For the recommendation on a framework for measuring in conjunction with an Australian proposal for determining SAT see, WTO, CRTA, Statement by the Delegation of Hong Kong, China on Systemic Issues, WT/REG/W/27, 8 July 1998, Geneva. The proposal is discussed below.

[29]　Ian S. Forrester, (1980b), *EEC Customs Law: Rules of Origin and Preferential Duty Treatment--Part Two*, European Law Review, V.5, pp. 257-286, at p. 266: "A simple problem would concern a stone handicraft, made from marble quarried in Italy, carved in Switzerland and reimported into the EEC. A more complex example would involve a German electric motor shipped to Switzerland for incorporation in the manufacture of a washing machine which is assembled from components originating in Finland, Portugal, Japan and France, then exported to the EEC: on what basis may the washing machine receive preferential treatment?"

8.3.1 *Donor country and bilateral cumulation*

The consideration of cumulation must arise initially between any two parties as a matter of whether donor country benefit will be extended by both members so that bilateral cumulation, or bilateral area treatment will be a result. The most restrictive treatment possible is where there is no bilateral cumulation provided between two parties which would permit origin to be obtained. As such, the preference granted is restricted to the wholly-obtained products of party A or B, as the materials of A may not be processed in B for the purpose of obtaining preferential origin in respect to the other partner. The second designation is known as bilateral cumulation. Between two countries A and B, the inputs provided by either are added to the origin calculation. Bilateral cumulation creates "area treatment" between two parties.[30]

8.3.2 *Area constructions, diagonal or full cumulation*

Although it remains conceivable that bilateral free-trade areas may be formed under the GATT rules providing for no bilateral cumulation, the primary contemporary issue regarding area designation is where a single party is common to separate bilateral free-trade area agreements. For these arrangements, the question that arises is whether or not the resulting regional system could be devised, or should be compelled, to form an area whereby inputs can be traded and/or processes combined across all of the markets concerned. This determination is made by reference to the degree of cumulation that is provided among its members, *bilaterally* with the common member (the hub country), and *diagonally* among the partners (the spoke countries). Generally, in the absence of positive cumulation rules connecting the bilateral areas, there is not a legal basis for inputs to be accumulated between the lateral partners.

This question of area-wide design received new attention as an aspect of the North American Free Trade Agreement (NAFTA -- U.S., Canada, Mexico) from the Canada-U.S. Free Trade Area (CUSTA). As according to Wonnacott,

"... an important case arose in North America soon after the 1989 Canada-US free trade agreement came in effect. Would Mexico join the FTA ... or, to get a quicker and simpler agreement, would it negotiate a bilateral FTA with the United States

---

[30] I. Forrester, (1980b), Ibid., at p. 267. Making an earlier characterisation that no longer applies, "(U)nder the GSP, products of Community origin are treated as if they were third country products". In the absence of a general non-cumulative provision, the same effect could be obtained by list processes which were insufficient to confer origin. Donor country benefit can also extended to the goods of only one partner.

alone... thus creating a hub-and-spoke system (H&S), i.e., a system in which the US hub would have had two overlapping bilateral agreements".[31]

In such a system of overlapping bilateral agreements without an overall area designation, the trade effects are said to favour the hub relative to the spokes. Again according to Wonnacott,

"In a H&S, the hub would get two special trade advantages which it would not get under an FTA: (1) the hub would benefit from the preference it would get in the market of each spoke in competition with the others; and (2) only firms in the hub would be able to acquire duty-free inputs from each spoke. In short ... a H&S offers special preferential advantages for the hub because of the trade barriers it would leave between spokes".[32]

This construction, by accident or design, of a series of bilateral agreements with a single large country at the hub can present certain negative implications for the resulting quality of internal trade coverage between the parties, primarily at the expense of the spoke countries. Moreover, Wonnacott, and Enders and Wonnacott, suggested that such a system also has implications, perhaps political, for reinforcing an already dominant party as,

"An examination of only the obvious special preferences that would be created could lead to criticism throughout the region of the hub for participating in the development of such a system that would allow the relatively wealthy US or EU hub to increase its already dominant position in its hemisphere by benefiting at the expense of its relatively poor neighbours ...".[33]

However the selection of the choice of forms, bilateral or multilateral, can also not be presumed to be merely accidental. If one country has bargaining power in the first place, then its choice of bilateral agreements at the outset is already an expres-

---

[31] Ronald J. Wonnacott, *Trade and Investment in a Hub-and Spoke system Versus a Free Trade Area*, The World Economy, Vol. 19, No. 3, 1996, pp.237-252, at p. 237. According to Wonnacott, Canada's decision to engage in the NAFTA turned upon the negative consequences of not participating, wherein the result would be a U.S. hub with two spokes, Canada and Mexico. Rotterdam Interview with the author, 1995.

[32] R. Wonnacott, Ibid., at p. 241. In addition, "The hub's special advantages in trade would translate into an advantage in attracting investment: other things being equal, firms would prefer to locate in the hub because this is the only location that would give them free access to inputs and markets in all participating countries." Ibid., at p. 246.

[33] ·R. Wonnacott, Ibid., at p.249. From Enders and Wonnacott, "... a strong hub like the United States or EU will have its already dominant bargaining power increased if it is negotiating with one partner at a time, and may use this to maintain more protection (perhaps contingent protection) against its spoke partners -- at a cost not only to the spokes, but also in many cases, to the hub itself." Alice Enders and Ronald J. Wonnacott, *How Useful is the NAFTA Experience for East-West European Integration?*, (1995, draft version), p. 4.

sion of this prerogative, perhaps to the extent that the partners find it necessary to co-operate with this choice. This suggests that considerations can be effected to determine which level of area treatment if any, should be provided, and that the decision to form a series of bilateral agreements can be reflective of a conscious choice to not establish an area-wide treatment.

8.3.3   The Multilateral European Area proposals (1957)

This insight did not surface on first impression in the course of the NAFTA analysis. Rather, the question of overall area construction was a central issue in the early days of European regional integration. Prior to the formation of the EEC, the OEEC sponsored a working party to consider the feasibility of a free trade area that would include the developing EEC Customs Union and the other member countries.[34] At that stage, the desired solution by the OEEC working party was to preserve a multilateral framework for Europe, even while regional integration would proceed within the EEC. Although there was little prior experience with free-trade area formations, the OEEC group contemplated the creation of an overall area, whereby a product would obtain satisfactory origin,

> "if it undergoes successive processing in several countries of the area and if the total of such operations is sufficient, according to the definition of origin adopted, to confer the nationality of the area on that product".[35]

This early reference precisely contemplated a European-wide treatment for the production and trade of goods throughout the region as defined by its OEEC members. This element was sought to be preserved as the six moved to form their own customs territory. The response of the non-EEC countries within the OEEC to form a "little" free-trade area was further specifically directed toward the desire of those members to seek yet a multilateral European wide formation. In assessing the potential for what would later become the European Free Trade Association (EFTA),

> "A number of reasons are put forward in support of the conclusion that the plan will help achieve an accommodation with the Six. It will keep the Seven together and thus maximise the bargaining power of those who want a free trade area, while at the same

---

[34] "By July 1956, political and economic factors had coalesced to the point where formation of the EEC was imminent...Because several OEEC members were anxious to counterbalance the formation of the EEC common market, the (OEEC) Council established a working party to examine the feasibility of forming a free-trade area in Europe." James B. Dunlap, and Robert N. King, *Regional Economic Integration and GATT: the Effects of the EEC EFTA Agreements on International Trade*, Law and Policy in International Business, V.6, 1974, pp. 207-235, at p. 208.

[35] OEEC, (1957) Supra note 7 at p. 33.

time forestalling the development of a trading pattern that would rule out a multilateral settlement".[36]

Although the formation of the European Free Trade Area would finally not succeed to provide the basis for multilateral settlement as sought by its advocates until the formation of the European Economic Area (EEA) in 1992, there is little doubt that the desire to avoid individual bilateral agreements with the newly formed EEC was a paramount goal:

> "(O)nce some countries began making bilateral agreements with the Six, others would be tempted to follow suit and, if this happened, a multilateral association would soon become impossible. Instead of a broad free trade area in which each country maintained similar relations with every other country within the group, a new pattern of trading would be established based on an inner group of countries (the Six) at the centre of the web with ties radiating out to the surrounding countries".[37]

This quotation presents perhaps a first description of a hub and spoke system, like that described by Wonnacott, for what could have transpired in the NAFTA. It was joined with a forewarning of the potential negative effects on the smaller partners:

> "(N)ot only would the small countries, acting individually, be in a weak initial bargaining position, but they would also be denying themselves, for the future, the increased strength that can be gained from acting together or in concert with the United Kingdom. Furthermore, the resulting network of bilateral agreements would not only be inherently discriminatory against the United Kingdom, but would tend to increase trade with the Six at the expense of the considerable trade carried on by the outer countries with each other".[38]

---

[36] Miriam Camps, *The European Free Trade Association, A Preliminary Appraisal*, Britain and the European Market, Occasional Paper No. 4, PEP publications, 1959, p. 27. The reference to a free-trade area refers to a European free-trade area whereby the customs union would be one constituent territory. "Although it is probable that Sweden, and perhaps Switzerland, would have been in favour of the establishment of the free trade association on economic grounds alone, it seems clear that in most of the countries concerned the determining factor was not the prospect of economic advantage, but the belief that the formation of the new association would improve materially the chances of an accommodation (sic) with the Six." Ibid., at p. 27. For an overview of the European Free Trade Area and its developments over time, see F.W. Weiss, *The European Free Trade Association after Twenty-five Years*, Yearbook of European Law, Vol. 5, 1986, pp. 287-323; and, F.W. Weiss, *The Functioning of the Free Trade Agreements*, in Oliver Jacot-Guillarmod, (Ed.), **L' avenir du libre-e'change en Europe: vers un Espace économique européen?** Schulthess Polygraphischer Verlag AG, Zurich, 1990, pp. 61-78.

[37] M. Camps, Ibid., at p. 24.

[38] Ibid. The concern expressed was not with EEC formation per se, but the manner in which the new customs territory would relate to its partners in either bilateral or multilateral agreements.

At the 1969 Hague Conference of the EC Heads of State, the decision was made to reconsider the membership applications of certain EFTA states and to begin discussions with those EFTA members who had not applied. Participants realised then that when the United Kingdom and Denmark would enter the EEC, that they would adopt the EEC common tariff and re-impose tariffs on the former EFTA partners. Thus, "it was evident that some accommodation would have to be reached between the enlarged community and the remaining EFTA countries."[39] At that time, three special concerns to be advanced in the negotiations by the EEC and EFTA countries were raised. First, the EEC emphasised that only industrial products should be covered by future agreements. Second, "(T)he Community was also anxious to protect those of its industries in which EFTA countries held dominant positions, such as Sweden in the paper industry."[40] Third, "(T)he Community sought to tighten EFTA's liberal rules of origin, while EFTA members wanted to retain the existing rules in order that the agreements would cover more products."[41]

In retrospect, one can easily say that EFTA parties miscalculated that they could avoid bilateral country agreements by the formation of its own free-trade area. Having determined not to form a customs union, the retention of individual EFTA member external policies effectively eliminated the possibility of a single external commercial policy and therefore a single bilateral agreement between two territories.[42] What is also indicated in the history is the manner in which bargaining power was finally reflected between unequal parties both in the selection of a framework for regional trade, i.e., a series of bilateral rather than a single multilateral configuration, and the manner in which rules of origin were intended to provide for internal domestic protection. This latter aspect becomes more visible as the EC-EFTA territory arrangements were examined in the GATT.

Besides the question of bilateral cumulation between two partners, it is evident that two other forms of cumulation also relate to the composition of area-wide treatment when two or more bilateral agreements provide for a common member. Multilateral (total or full) cumulation occurs where all members are permitted to add inputs and processing which will act to designate the product as one deriving

---

[39] J. Dunlap and R. King, Supra note 34 at p. 215.

[40] J. Dunlap and R. King, Ibid., citing 5 Bull. EEC July-Aug 1972 at p. 15.

[41] J. Dunlap and R. King, Ibid., citing The Economist (magazine), Jan. 20, 1973, at p. 62.

[42] The assessment of the country positions makes an interesting historical footnote and reveals the tensions between bilateral and multilateral approaches which are evident in the consideration of free-trade areas and as perhaps reflected by the relative market power of the respective members. Thus, "... attempts to influence or isolate the French by pressure on, or appeals to, other members of the Six were conspicuously unsuccessful and the belief that the German Government gave a high enough priority to the free trade area to ensure eventual agreement proved to be disastrously optimistic ... But within the Six, the Dutch have always been the strongest advocates of the broad free trade area and no economic pressure is needed to stimulate their interest." M. Camps, Supra note 36 at pp. 28 and 29.

origin in respect of the larger area.[43] This occurs normally by designation to the country of last processing those operations that were carried out in the other recognised countries. Cited as an early form is the preferential trade agreements between the Community and the Maghreb countries, which were said to allow for total cumulation.[44]

The far more common and intermediate form for relating multiple agreements with a common member provides for diagonal (or triangular) cumulation. In contrast to full cumulation, diagonal cumulation allows origin to be achieved by adding together originating materials, but not the value added contributed by processing. In the absence of any other provisions and in the case where bilateral or donor country origin would already be provided, the conditions for obtaining origin must be met in the last country of export. This raises a discriminatory hardship where between two lateral partners, the degree of processing in the first country is sufficient to confer its preferential origin, but where admission is not granted based upon the fact that the second country's contribution was individually insufficient to confer its origin.

8.3.4 *Diagonal forms in early European regional arrangements*

Diagonal provisions can be expansive or restrictive. While the trend now has been developing to provide for a more expansive diagonal cumulation throughout the EC, EFTA and CEEC regional network, the earlier formations were heavily criticised for their restrictive diagonal limitations. For an EEC-EFTA member state example, a product processed in Norway would have obtained Norwegian origin as to the EEC, but it is exported first to Sweden for additional processing. This processing is insufficient to meet the test for Swedish origin which would allow it to have the preference to the EEC market. Therefore,

---

43 "'Full cumulation' is the system which represents a more advanced form of economic integration between the partner countries. Full cumulation provides for the cumulation of processing between two or more countries. Account is therefore taken of all processing or transformaiton of a product within the trade zone without the products being used necessarily having to originate in one of the partner countries. One of the results of "full" cumulation might lead to an origin common to all partners (i.e., the EEA Agreement). EC Commission, Communication to the Council Concerning the Unification of Rules of Origin in Preferential Trade Between the Community, the Central and East European Countries and the EFTA countries. Restricted and non cited, at p. 5.

44 P. Kelly and I. Onkelinx, **EEC Customs Law**, ESC Publishing, Oxford, 1986, T-188 (S5/8/93), citing for Algeria: Regulation 2210/78, OJ 1978 L263/40; Morocco: Regulation 2211/78, OJ 1978 L264/38; Tunisia: Regulation 2212/78, OJ 1978 L265/38, as amended. For description, "As regards the application of the value added test, this implies that all value added in any of the Maghreb countries and the community will count in favour of Maghreb origin, while the value of any components or materials from a third country will count against preferential origin, unless these third-country components and materials are incorporated in a semi-finished product having obtained the preferential origin of one of the Maghreb countries or the Community which is later used in the manufacture of the finished product." **EEC Customs Law**, Ibid.

"It will - under the general rules of origin -- have neither Swedish nor Norwegian origin and therefore would not qualify for the preferential duty treatment on importation into the Community (or any EFTA country except Norway)".[45]

Thus, the necessity for examining the diagonal rules in multiple free-trade area constructions occurs in either granting (or failing to grant) an initial area-wide treatment so that components of origin can be counted together for export to either the common member, or to other lateral members. However, the creation of diagonal possibilities for the lateral partners requires affirmative action. As long as free-trade area partners initiate separate bilateral agreements with a common member, in the absence of special provisions, there will not be any legal basis for cumulating the inputs, let alone value added by processes, of its various members.[46]

The EEC-EFTA country solution to this absence of cumulation was to devise a most complex series of rules.[47] While a number of aspects contributed to this complexity, for Forrester, the most difficult aspect resided in their approach to neutral calculation as stated in Article 2.1.A.b of the EC-EFTA Origin Protocols, This stated,

"where a percentage rule limits...the proportion in value of non-originating products that can be incorporated under certain circumstances, the added value has been acquired in each of the countries in accordance with the percentage rules and with the other rules contained in the said lists *without any possibility of cumulation from one country to another*".[48]

The rule applied when a percentage value added test was in place in addition to a change in tariff heading. The difficulty arose in its interpretation by the Commission and EEC national officials which disregarded any EEC contribution to the product for the determination of its origin on transfer to another EFTA country for later processing.

"To apply the principle, the value of the EEC component is deducted from the ex-factory value of the machine in Austria and the resultant diminished value must then be compared with the value of any third country parts or components. The result is that the amount of third country components which may be incorporated into the machine in Austria without detracting from eligibility for Austrian preferential origin is lower

---

[45] **EEC Customs Law**, Ibid., at T-172.

[46] I. Forrester, (1980b), Supra note 29 at p. 267.

[47] Generally, I. Forrester, Ibid., at pp. 270-277; EC Law Handbook, Supra note 44 at T-172-181. Originally, Article 2 of the Origin Protocols of each EEC-EFTA agreement, revised by Decision 5/88 applied by Regulation 4274/88, OJ 1988 L381/13, for Norway.

[48] Origin Protocal, Ibid., italics added.

than would be the case if the EEC component counted 'in favour' of preferential origin".[49]

Forester concluded that this application of the rules was not accidental as,

> "The decision to structure the diagonal cumulation rules in this fashion, and to adopt the neutral cumulation system was not inadvertent. It was a political decision not to accord full access to preferential treatment to triangular trade touching two EFTA countries and one EEC".[50]

The apparent effect was to give EFTA parties an option to either compute origin bilaterally between an individual EFTA member and the EEC, or to compute two EFTA contributing states together but minus any EEC contribution. The result of the bilateral agreements and the construction of diagonal origin provided was precisely what the EFTA parties were attempting to avoid in the first instance: a pattern of agreements which would promote trade to the centre country at the expense of trade and processing between the lateral parties in respect to the centre.

This result flowed not from the diagonal rules themselves since in the absence of any rules there would have been no basis for any diagonal cumulation. Rather, the choice of the legal form of the arrangements designating bilateral agreements with a common member was the source of the problem. As the EEC was the largest partner, so did it also have an interest and the power to conclude a hub and spoke system. As the EFTA parties were smaller trading countries, so was it also in their interest to reach a multilateral solution.

In this sense the proposals made to extend the Canada-U.S. arrangement to NAFTA, and Wonnacott's recognition of the inferior position of Canada if it failed to engage the Mexico triangle to match any U.S.- Mexico agreement, presents an analogous situation. As the largest partner, it would not have been adverse to a narrower set of U.S. interests to see a resulting construction operate as a hub and spoke system. It would certainly however have been adverse to Canada.

8.3.5   The unveiling of the EEC-EFTA rules in the GATT

The first full examination of the EEC's origin approach to EFTA was provided in the review of the formation of the EEC-Austria free-trade area.[51] The first objection to the origin rules was based on GATT Article XXIV:4 on the basis that they

---

[49] I. Forrester, Ibid., at p. 274.
[50] I. Forrester, Ibid., at p. 275.
[51] GATT, 1974 BISD (covering 1972-73) Twentieth Supplement, *European Communities --
Agreements with Austria*, Report 10 October 1973, (L/3900), BISD p. 145. Additional identical reports:
(L/3902) Iceland, p. 158; (L/3901) Portugal, p. 171; (L/3899) Sweden, p. 183; (L/3893) Switzerland &
Lichtenstein, p. 196.

would operate to frustrate the goal stated to permit free-trade areas as a means of facilitating trade between the constituent parties. This was raised due to the potential of the rules to frustrate intra-area trade in products that could not meet the various origin criteria. In addition, by depressing this internal trade, it was claimed that there would necessarily be raised new barriers to third-countries in their exports of intermediate products. In this way, the origin rules to be applied were also claimed to violate Article XXIV:5(b) because their effect was more restrictive to outsiders as in the manner of raising new barriers to trade of other GATT parties. As one working group member was quoted, the rules "...were so complex and cumbersome as to be a barrier to trade in and of themselves ...".[52]

In this characterisation, the ability of restrictive rules to frustrate internal trade as well as external trade was easily recognised as well as the linkage between imposing internal barriers which result in the loss of external trade. In the more detailed examination of the objections, allegations were posed that some of the rules required content as high as 96 percent (microphones); on one-fifth of total industrial headings (BTN 84-92), the parties permitted only 5% non origin. In other headings a restrictive 20% rule was applied. Origin sourcing was alleged to have been obviously promoted by the design of the rules.[53]

The EEC defence on these working group comments was reported to have relied upon the necessity of origin in order to avoid trade deflection. However, others noted that where the countries involved had similar tariffs, then deflection should not have been at issue and such restrictive rules would have served no purpose in this respect. Also, observers claimed that the rules were more restrictive than the comparable EFTA rules in 335 out of 338 tariff headings.[54] As to the general allegation that the rules were operating in a manner that was not trade neutral, the EEC response was that a comparison to the EFTA rules was not valid and that the parties were free to adopt any system of their choice.[55]

---

[52] GATT, L/3900, Ibid., at para. 5. A non violation complaint argument was also raised. By restricting third country products, bound tariffs would be nullified by the application of rules of origin. According to Forrester, the EEC-EFTA agreement was subject to working group criticism not only by outsiders but also by EFTA countries themselves, including Austria. I. Forrester, Supra note 29 at p. 283, his note 16.

[53] Article 23 of Protocol 3 also appeared to exclude the possibility for drawback.

[54] Stressing the complicated nature of the rules, sometimes four criteria were necessary to meet together with eight movement certificates. Article VIII of the GATT was also suggested to apply to this situation. Although no rule in GATT applied to preferential Rules of Origin, GATT Art. XXIV:5(b) was also brought into the discussion as "other regulations of commerce more restrictive".

[55] GATT, L2300, para 27-28. The discussion on the EEC-EFTA rules was developed incrementally in the report on the EEC Agreement with Norway. GATT, 1975 BISD (covering 1973-74). Twenty First Supplement, *EC Agreements with Norway*, Report 28 March 1974, L/3996, BISD p. 83. Here, the objections were made more on the basis of a legal issue raised as to whether or not Article XXIV:5(b) should be interpreted more restrictively than paragraph 5(a) for customs unions, since it does not include the phrase "on the whole" in reference to a free-trade area.

The result of the EFTA association's attempts to reach a multilateral accommodation with the EEC was a series of bilateral agreements upon which positive action was required to install some basis for cumulation. The system that resulted emphasised the bilateral constructions and failed to achieve a cumulation system that would rise to the level of European-area treatment. The review of these agreements in the GATT failed to disclose a legal basis to clearly challenge the constructions either on their external diverting effects or for their internal diverting effects. For the EFTA partners, this issue would not be resolved until the conclusion of the European Economic Area (EEA).

8.3.6   *Development of the European diagonal area*

The EC external regional system developed in the 1990's by a large number of new agreements with the CEEC's, in the form of the Europe Agreements. These free-trade area agreements were matched by agreements between EFTA parties and several of the CEEC's initiated their own free-trade areas. The resulting fragmentation of an overall non-cumulative system began to press upon European producers. Their capacity to seek lower cost production sources in the wider European area was likely frustrated by the very bilateral structures that were generated on behalf of the Community itself, and the issue was raised in two European Councils, Copenhagen in 1993 and Corfu in 1994.[56] In a non-cited Commission Communication, the advantages of extending diagonal cumulation were described as facilitating EC manufacturers to source components in CEEC countries, to spread production processes to two or more involved areas or countries and to export the end-products to EFTA countries and other CEEC without loss of origin.

What has resulted from this recognition in final form is a communication to the WTO notifying the Committee on Regional Trade Agreements of a System of European Cumulation of Origin.[57] According to the notice, the implementation of a "new origin network" has two major consequences.

"First, semi-finished products originating in any country of the system and which are further processed or assembled in any other partner country may always be consid-

---

[56]   This resulted in two Commission Communications which included discussion of diagonal cumulation for the CEECs. European Commission, *The Europe Agreements and Beyond...*, COM (94) 320 final, 13.07.94. *Follow-up to the Commission Communication on the Europe Agreements and Beyond...*, COM (94) 361/3, 26.07.94.

[57]   WTO, Committee on Regional Trade Agreements, Joint Communication to the WTO on the System of European Cumulation of Origin, WT/REG/GEN/N/1, 16 November, 1998. The list of affected free-trade agreements is too long to duplicate here. Included are Fourteen EC agreements including the European Economic Area, ten EFTA member state agreements, the EFTA Stockholm Convention, and 13 intra CEEC agreements, 38 agreements affected in total.

ered as originating products. Secondly, originating products can be traded between any of the countries involved in the system".[58]

At this time, there is only preliminary comment in published CRTA documents regarding the new system regarding its external implications, although some detailed analysis will certainly be likely to emerge as to the system's impact on outside producers. An analysis of the internal aspects may not emerge, but it is apparent in light of the above that the new system is an attempt to provide for a comprehensive diagonal system for all of the "European" parties that are connected by one bilateral agreement or another. As such, it must represent an important improvement on the earlier situation and may even be determined to actually resolve the historical problem of a non-multilateral Europe raised at the time of the EEC formation by the other OEEC parties, also as discussed above. It may be now possible to make reference to a multilateral European area.

However, before this characterisation is attached, additional features will need to be explored. One is the interaction of harmonised protocols and their annexes. For this it would need to be determined whether any amendments are being formed which introduce new list-process criteria that, while likely to receive attention for external trade diversion, may also raise the issue of internal shifting of sources of supply to provide for protective effects. This may also be exhibited if there are changes made to value added or content requirements. Thus, one indicator of internal diversion would be demonstrated by annexes that are not harmonised even while the protocols that establish the diagonal cumulation are identical through all of the agreements. A second area of investigation would relate to the system's effects on other EC external regional agreements some of which may also be emerging as diagonal systems, including the EC-Turkey customs union, but also the new generation of Mediterranean Agreements and the EC-ACP Convention in the post-Lomé. This process of consolidating a large number of bilateral arrangements into several multilateral systems with a common centre in the EC may also have implications for internal movement overall. It may reflect the inexorable process of globalisation whereby producers seek to source production at ever-lower cost. It may also reflect in part a type of defensive response to that same process, as where producers within one regional system are inclined to support cumulation, but not cumulations between different systems. Thus, the same issues raised above regarding the protective effects that were obtainable by the use of single bilateral agreements may yet be seen to emerge over time by the divisions that are maintained between separated regional systems.

A final aspect to be addressed is the question of whether this development toward an integrated diagonal system has implications for the prospects of full or

---

[58] Joint Communication to the WTO, Ibid., at para 2. "Before the introduction of European cumulation, trading of originating products was seriously limited."

multilateral cumulation. Advancing from recognition of accumulating origin of goods toward a system permitting origin to be attached to non-originating goods by the accumulation of processing would appear to be unlikely. While it appears that multilateral cumulation presents the largest opportunity for third parties to introduce their non-originating components into the European market, it is not clear whether the new proposal reduces prior possibilities, or as claimed by the Joint Communication, enhances them by granting a general tolerance rule. Likewise, the delineation of the effects between diagonal regional systems and multilateral systems on the internal trade of the regional parties has not been discerned in the literature. As a starting point, it is probably suggestible that an integrated diagonal system increases competition between lateral partners for inward investment for production from outside sources, as harmonised protocols would allow inputs to be sourced across the internal frontiers without reference to the location of final assembly facilities. This would appear to reduce the relative advantage of one regional member that has already secured a large assembly production to demand that input manufacturing must also occur within its territory. This is a positive development.

As to the comparison of diagonal with full cumulation, in the NAFTA case a number of commentators suggested a diversionary effect in favour of inward investment and production overall. One can assume that there is a certain tendency for a larger integrated diagonal system to also divert a certain amount of external trade and investment. This is clearly an external consideration that may or may not be able to be taken up for discussion under the provisions of GATT Article XXIV:5. However, even while the linkages between external and internal effects caused by origin systems are not yet so clear, an Article XXIV:8 consideration should also be engaged.

8.4   Chapter Conclusion: an Article XXIV requirement for origin and cumulation

A concluding point to raise in regard to the creation of regional diagonal systems is the absence of meaningful control exercised over the developments by the GATT/WTO review process. If the evolution is determined to be positive both internally as well as externally, it is noteworthy that market forces have apparently made more of a contribution to calling forth the new integration than has any point of reference derivable from GATT Article XXIV, either (5) or (8). This, in spite of the recognised fact that the use of preferential qualifying rules are definitional as to the nature of the area being created, its scope of trade coverage, and its implications for raising new trade barriers. As noted from the early review of the EEC-EFTA arrangements above, members have argued for years that Article XXIV conditions are affected by rules of origin designations within the regional proposals. However, Article XXIV itself does not state as much for either internal or external requirements and this omission has always provided a basis to argue, on behalf of proponents, that preferential rules of origin do not fall under the purview of GATT review.

In the context of the CRTA, much discussion in the systemic negotiations has turned on the question of whether origin rules in the preferential setting should be included in the definition of "other regulations of commerce" (ORCs) as these are prescribed according to Article XXIV:5 regarding external effects; or in the alternative, "other restrictive regulations of commerce" (ORRCs) as this term is used for the internal requirements of Article XXIV:8. While no final opinion is offered at this point regarding the applicability ORC's to rules of origin, it is hoped that the discussion above could contribute to the simple proposition that preferential rules of origin should be initially considered as having a bearing on the paragraph 8 requirements. To the extent that the rules act to define the scope of a free-trade area, the substantially-all trade test would appear to be raised for consideration.

This consideration leads one to consider how a test would actually be applied. For this, a Hong Kong proposal provides a starting point, as the following was suggested:

> "(iii) … in measuring SAT as a percentage, as proposed by Australia, the base (100 per cent of trade between the RTA parties) should comprise all intra-RTA trade measured according to MFN rules, while the qualifying proportion of trade (to meet the SAT requirement to be set at a specified percentage) should be measured according to preferential rules of origin".[59]

This raises the concept that a comparison is drawn between trade before and after formation as a result of the operation not only of declarations for duty reductions, but also considering the operation of the rules of origin on those trade openings. It also raises intentionally the linkage between internal and external effects of rules. Where MFN trade is the pre-defining measure applied, then reduction of trade from this level within a free-trade area would indicate that a restrictive rule has been applied internally. This has been suggested above to have potentially adverse effects also on non-members.

McQueen proposed that a rule more restrictive than necessary to counter trade deflection is one that is internally discriminatory. This would suggest comparing the degree of protection offered by the origin rule with the difference in individual member tariff rates. Within the matrix of a free-trade area, one can also imagine a complimentary test that would provide a basis to challenge internally restrictive rules, at least from a GATT system perspective. This test would attempt a compar-

---

[59] "Thus, the less stringent the preferential rules of origin are for a RTA, the higher percentage of their members' intra-RTA trade will be included towards meeting the SAT threshold." WTO, Committee on Regional Trade Agreements, Statement by the delegation of Hong Kong, China on Systemic Issues, WT/REG/W/27, 8 July 1998, Geneva.

ison between the origin rules internally applied between members and the quality of internal treatment applied as analogous to GATT Article III, National Treatment. Thus, one would ask whether the treatment of an input by a domestic enterprise is more favourable than the treatment given to the like input that is applied to a regional partner's production. This comparison could be suggested whether or not the inputs were of origin to the regional partner, and in respect of any difference in duty treatment as to third parties. At the outset this would require that whatever is deemed to be "locally obtained" in the first member must also be recognised as "locally obtained" as it may be derived from the second member's territory. This would negate the right of a free-trade area member to impose a duty upon another member's inputs of origin as this would be a form of discriminatory treatment "internal" to the area. It may likewise suggest a requirement that the listed processes that do not deny origin domestically should not also deny origin regionally.

For these cases there is no issue of deflection, but only the issue of whether or not the input is going to be covered or uncovered trade to meet the Article XXIV:8 test. Any rule applied that eliminates or frustrates trade between partners of goods that are wholly obtained should be presumed at the outset to be a trade barrier, just as quantitative restrictions are trade barriers. Thus, rules should be examined according to Article XXIV:8 as an aspect of determining whether regional parties are covering substantially all of the trade. Just as a plan and schedule discloses the sequence for the intended removal of trade barriers, the plan would also be required to disclose the list of products of individual partner territory origin that will not freely exchange as a result of the preferential rules.

Shifting to the problem of deflection caused by differing duties applied by members to third-party goods, the additional concept of adopting adjustments only as necessary for the purpose of avoiding trade deflection could be considered. This suggests a framework for origin rules that is derived from the non-discriminatory concept of a border tax adjustment. Thus, for an example. Non-member input X is charged a duty of 30% by member country 'A'. Once admitted, X is freely used in commerce and production within 'A'. Member 'B' imposes a duty of 10% on the same input and likewise applies it for domestic production. The end-product, as produced in either member territory, is a free-trade item as according to the plan and schedule of the regional trade agreement. Thus, where the 'A and B' free-trade area requires a rule of origin to prevent trade deflection or distortion, an internal duty charge on the input would act to equalise the external duties without rendering 'B's final product non-originating. This is what rules of origin in principle should seek to achieve, when they are necessary. Obviously there are complexities in any scheme to effect tax equalisation, especially given the quantity of inputs that go into modern products. However, at least in theory, a tax equalisation method can be applied where regional members use external tariff duties. More difficult is for those sectors which are treated differently by each member and not on the basis of tariff duties. Where list-processes or change of tariff heading are applied to equalise these external differences, these approaches may also not provide a ready basis to determine precisely what measure is necessary to offset the deflection, and no more.

The question of overlapping free trade areas is difficult, if for no other reason, than that the limitations of the review function that has treated each declaration as a distinct formation to be qualified under the GATT Article XXIV rules. It is easy to imagine that two regional members would strenuously object to any review assessing the regional-systemic implications for pre-existing free-trade areas. As the GATT rules now stand, it would appear that the CRTA would have the right to review a free-trade area proposal as submitted by the members. Between two members, this would not apparently permit a consideration of whether or not bilateral cumulation (donor-country benefit) was being accorded by each member to the trade of the other. Likewise, in spite of the potential for abuse discussed above in regard to hub and spoke systems, there certainly appears to be nothing in Article XXIV that compels members to qualify multiple free-trade areas as a single area. However, as in the case of the European area-wide proposals, where members do seek to create a diagonal cumulation between two or more free-trade areas, it would seem that a new free-trade area formation is being proposed *de facto*. Reviewing parties should then arguably have the right to determine the geographical scope of this new area and to apply the Article XXIV tests accordingly to it, including the substantially-all trade test as applied to the larger area.

Chapter 9
REGIONAL SAFEGUARDS AND RESTRICTIVE MEASURES

"Canada has committed to reduce its softwood lumber exports to the United States in exchange for a U.S. commitment to refrain from trade action in this sector" *United States Trade Representative Kantor, (1996).*

9.1   Introduction

The chapter discusses safeguard measures as applied between regional members and addresses the applicability of GATT Articles, such as Article XIX, to the members of regional trade agreements. It may be recalled from Chapter Three that an argument was made that the Articles listing found within Article XXIV:8 (XI through XV and XX) is an exhaustive listing. By treating the question now as whether GATT Article XIX may also apply to the trade of regional members, one is not conceding that position already taken on the exhaustive listing. Rather, it has to be recognised that there is a significant body of opinion that considers the listing of the Article to be non-exhaustive, and that safeguard and anti-dumping actions (not treated here) are permissible as between regional members.

What is attempted is to demonstrate first that the regional safeguard regimes established can be at divergence from the GATT rules on emergency measures, including the WTO Agreement on Safeguards. Rather than being more restrictive in permitting internal measures, they may well be less restrictive both on the substantive injury test to be applied and upon the procedures. The chapter will first provide a brief note on the GATT-1947 provisions and revisions introduced by the WTO Agreement on Safeguards. Whether or not MFN applied to the application of a safeguard under the original Article XIX, a point debated throughout the GATT years, the regime established in the WTO is nevertheless prescriptive as to certain non-discrimination obligations for WTO Members. Further, the WTO Agreement expresses the intent that all safeguards should fall under its control, including the notification obligation and the oversight of the Committee on Safeguards. Next, it will be shown by an overview of the EC Europe Agreement regime that specialised provisions within regional agreements have deviated in their legal form from the GATT rules. An example is also raised from U.S. Canada trade in softwood lumber to show the likelihood that a safeguard was also employed in that context without reference to the WTO Agreement on Safeguards. The later chapter developing the treaty law aspects of regional agreements will address the legality of these specialised regimes as they act within regional trade agreements as modifications to the general obligations contained within the GATT.

9.2   GATT-1947 Article XIX provisions

GATT-1947's Article XIX, titled "Emergency Action on Imports of Particular Products" provides what is known as GATT's general escape clause. The Article permits a party, in regard to a particular product, to suspend an obligation or to withdraw or modify a concession. This is possible for such time as may be necessary to prevent or remedy an injury, caused, "... as a result of unforeseen developments and the effect of the obligations incurred by a contracting party under this Agreement, including tariff concessions." The injury required for implementation is that a "product is being imported in such increased quantities and under such conditions as to cause or threaten serious injury to domestic producers in that territory ..."[1]

Before taking action, a party seeking to raise emergency measures must notify the contracting parties in writing and afford them an opportunity to consult in respect to the proposed action.[2] If agreement in regard to the action is not reached, the party seeking the measure shall be free to act. However, the affected parties shall then be free (within 90 days) to suspend equivalent concessions that are not disapproved by the contracting parties.[3] In addition, there is a provision for critical circumstances whereby delay would cause damage difficult to repair. In this case, although the measure may be introduced without prior consultation, consultation shall in any case be effected immediately on taking action.[4] In this case, the affected party remains free to suspend equivalent concessions as may be necessary to prevent or remedy injury.[5] To summarize, GATT-1947 provided a basis for a contracting party to enact emergency measures according to GATT Article XIX. An import country might raise its tariff or impose a non-discriminatory quantitative restriction when domestic producers were threatened by an unanticipated surge in imports as a result of GATT negotiations.

While the Article was significantly neglected by the practice of GATT parties favoring bilateral export restraint arrangements, orderly market agreements and other so-called grey-area measures, its requirements remained in place. The affected party was granted a right, subject to some contracting party oversight, to retaliatory measures as necessary to adjust the balance of concessions between the parties. In this manner, GATT Article XIX was distinguished by its provisions which

---

[1]   GATT Article XIX:1(a).
[2]   GATT Article XIX:2.
[3]   GATT Article XIX:3(a).
[4]   GATT Article XIX:2.
[5]   GATT Article XIX:3(b), explaining provisions for preference, Article XIX:1(b).

granted an affected party the right to draw compensation for the measure invoked, an aspect that is not found in other contingent measures permitted by the GATT, such as antidumping or actions for countervailing duties.

9.3   GATT-1994 Agreement on Safeguards

The WTO Agreement on Safeguards (the Safeguards Agreement) introduced significant changes to the way Article XIX is applied. Overall, a framework for handling emergency measures in the GATT is designated by the Agreement. Aspects of this framework include required notification to a Committee on Safeguards, conditions for conducting national investigations, more concise injury tests to be applied, a surveillance mechanism under the authority of the committee, and a series of provisions that balance the issue of discriminatory application and compensation.[6] A striking feature of the Agreement is its declared prohibition on grey-area measures. As contained in Article 11 of the Agreement,

> "Furthermore a Member shall not seek, take or maintain any voluntary export restraints, orderly marketing arrangements or any other similar measures on the export or the import side".[7]

Bronckers has suggested that this provision constitutes a "flat out prohibition of grey area measures".[8] As discussed below, the viability of this ban must also be considered in light of other GATT regimes which would allow parties to achieve a similar result. One avenue indicated as remaining open by him is that of resolving anti-dumping actions by the use of these similar measures as, "… the new anti-dumping agreement still permits certain grey area measures (price undertakings and export bans) as a means to settle anti-dumping investigations."[9]

---

[6]   WTO, Annex 1A: Multilateral Agreements on Trade in Goods, Agreement on Safeguards. The Committee on Safeguards is established by Article 13 of the Agreement. According to sub-paragraphs (b) and (d), it is granted the authority to determine if the procedural requirements of the Agreement have been complied with on request of a Member, and to examine measures covered by Article 11 of the Agreement.

[7]   WTO, Safeguards Agreement, Article 11(b). Footnote 4 to the Agreement lists additional "similar measures" as, " export moderation, export-price monitoring systems, export or import surveillance, compulsory import cartels and discretionary export or import licensing schemes, any of which afford protection." However, footnote 3 does permit import quotas that otherwise comply with GATT-1994 to be administered by the exporting party.

[8]   Marco Bronckers, *Voluntary Export Restraints and the GATT 1994 Agreement on Safeguards*, in H.J. Bourgeois, F. Berrod, E. Fournier, (Eds), **The Uruguay Round Results, College of Europe**, European Inter University Press, Brussels, 1995, pp. 273-279 at p. 274.

[9]   M. Bronckers, Ibid., at p. 276, and citing Article 8 of the WTO Agreement on Implementation of Article VI of the GATT (Agreement on Anti-dumping).

A factor complicating a discussion of regional safeguards is the change noted above in the rules from the GATT-1947 to GATT-1994. This also bridges a large number of notified but interim free-trade areas. For safeguard measures, GATT parties rarely invoked the GATT regime provided in Article XIX formally. With the likely application of MFN and the Article's compensation provisions, a generation of grey-area measures designed to avoid the Article was the apparent result. If parties acted to provide a tailored safeguard mechanism within a free-trade area, it would not necessarily be observed that they were also avoiding GATT Article XIX. This regime was being avoided by the more general practice as a matter of course.

With the changes brought by GATT-1994 for emergency measures, the question of whether WTO law sanctions the non-application of this regime via provisions contained within a regional trade agreement becomes more pressing as the new regime has eliminated many of the old loopholes. The question however remains unsettled. In point, the relationship between Article XIX and XXIV on this question could be said to be explicitly unsettled. As Footnote 1 to the WTO Agreement on Safeguards states, "(N)othing in this Agreement prejudges the interpretation of the relationship between Article XIX and paragraph 8 of Article XXIV of GATT 1994." Thus, there is no clear intention directed at the outset to interpret paragraph 8 of Article XXIV as either permitting or not permitting the use of safeguards as between regional members. One can conclude that, as far as the Safeguards Agreement is concerned, the question has simply been left open for the future.

Similarly, the text of the Agreement on Safeguards has also not provided, in the case that safeguard measures are lawful to apply as between regional members, that they then must also go on to fulfil the requirements of Article XIX and as elaborated by the WTO Agreement. Since the question of the legality of regional safeguards does not appear to have been resolved by the entry of the WTO Safeguards Agreement, certainly this second question as to regional members' compliance with the Agreement is also left open. Thus, one can also commence from the proposition that that there is nothing in the Safeguards Agreement (or footnote 1) that exempts regional members from complying with the GATT-1994 requirements regarding the use of safeguards.

There are a number of Safeguard Agreement provisions that can be raised to illustrate the importance of this last point. A first one is notification, as to whether or not regional members must notify their safeguards to Committee on Safeguards as per Article 12 of the Agreement. A second is the application of the test to determine injury, as to whether regional parties can modify this test as between them and provide a less strict basis for adopting intra-regional safeguards. The GATT Article XIX test has been significantly developed by Article 4 of the Safeguards Agreement. Another consideration relates to the requirement of applying MFN treatment in determining whether non-members who might also be contributing to serious injury should also be compelled to be included in the investigation and application of a safeguard. Since the Safeguards Agreement also provides requirements for the duration and review of imposed safeguards by its Article 7, the question of whether these provisions should continue to control regional safeguards can also be raised.

A final consideration relates to the legality of certain remedial measures that are now prescribed as between GATT parties generally. The Safeguard Agreement's Article 11(1)(b) prohibition on grey-area measures, as recited above, also applies to, "actions under agreements, arrangements and understandings entered into by two or more Members." While footnote 1 does not pre-judge the relationship between GATT Article XIX and paragraph 8 of Article XXIV, the simple meaning of the text quoted here could suggest that regional agreements are not excluded from this prohibition. This must remain a possibility in light of paragraph 1(a)'s direct requirement that,

> "(A) Member shall not take or seek any emergency action on imports... as set forth in Article XIX of GATT 1994 unless such action conforms with the provisions of that Article applied in accordance with this Agreement".

Thus, without pre-judging the question of whether Article XXIV:8 prohibits the use of safeguards between regional members outright, one necessarily goes on to inquire whether GATT Article XIX and the Safeguards Agreement can be considered as suspended for those regional members who have invoked a specialised, or *lex specialis,* safeguard regime.

Regional members have argued on occasion that certain specialised safeguard mechanisms are made necessary as the parties advance toward actual free trade, as contrasted to merely conducting trade at MFN tariff levels. Since the risk to domestic markets of new competitive forces is greater while tariffs are reduced to zero, the safeguard mechanism employed must also be tailored to accommodate these varying and unpredictable circumstances. In order to validate this possibility, some attention should be paid to the specifics of such a regime, and an attempt should thereby be made to determine whether the conditions designated for intra-regional safeguards reflect these unusual competitive circumstances. The following case study regarding the Europe Agreements concluded between the EC and the Countries of Central and Eastern Europe provide evidence of a mechanism that, by design or accident, deviated from the emerging WTO Safeguards Agreement provisions. Demonstrating the points of divergence is not so difficult. Justifying the specialised regime on the basis of unforeseen competitive pressures incurred in a tariff-free environment is not however so easy to distil from the overall scheme.

9.4   EEC safeguard regimes – Central and Eastern Europe

9.4.1   *CMEA and EEC safeguards in the GATT*

A number of Central and Eastern European countries of the Council of Mutual Economic Assistance (CMEA) acceded to the GATT during the first half of the 1970's.[10] A central issue on the GATT accession of these state-trading countries, and thereafter, was the continued application of quotas by the western economies upon CEEC exports. The outline of what came to be a significant dispute in the GATT between a number of GATT parties and the EEC, and between the EEC and the CEEC countries, was centred on this problem. It remains documented in the annual and biennial reviews of working parties relating to the Hungarian accession to GATT.[11] In the Hungarian case, its protocol of accession to GATT called for the progressive removal of quantitative restrictions on Hungarian exports other than for exceptional reasons for the maintenance of quotas by the date of 1 January 1975.[12] The issue of removal was subjected to a series of biennial reviews in the GATT.[13] However, the resolution of the quota problem was not successful in the GATT reviews, which increasingly became a forum for third parties to criticise the EEC on this issue.[14] The issue between Hungary and the EEC was ultimately resolved in the context of bilateral negotiations outside of the GATT framework and the attentions of third parties in the working group reviews. While this route had been proposed by the EEC since 1974, Hungary had long resisted this bilateral solution. According to Van den Bossche, there was a general concern about bilateralism in the GATT, and a specific concern by Hungary that,

> "...only the GATT rules could provide Hungary with the necessary protection against unfavourable conditions imposed by the EEC, in the sense that concluding a separate trade agreement outside the GATT would deprive Hungary of its contractual and legitimate rights".[15]

---

[10]   See generally on this history, Leah Huis, **Globalizing the GATT**, The Brookings Institution, Washington, D.C., 1992.

[11]   A.M. Van den Bossche, *GATT, the Indispensable Link Between the EEC and Hungary?*, Journal of World Trade, V. 25, No. 3, 1991, pp. 141-155.

[12]   GATT, 20 BISD, protocol 4, 1974.

[13]   As cited by Van den Bossche: GATT, BISD S22 (1975), sub 19, p. 57; GATT BISD S25 (1978), sub 10, p. 158; GATT BISD S27 (1980), sub 6, p. 157 and sub 15, p. 160; GATT BISD S29 (1982), sub 10, p. 130; GATT BISD S31 (1984), sub 9 and 15, pp. 157 and 159; GATT BISD S33 (1986) sub 22, 142. See Van den Bossche, Supra note 11 at p. 146 and her note 27.

[14]   Van den Bossche, Ibid., at p. 160, reciting a number of EEC justifications posed for the quantitative restrictions, but most of them oriented to the "exceptional economic situation prevailing, particularly in sensitive sectors." Citing, GATT BISD S27 (1980), sub 4.

[15]   Van den Bossche, Supra note 11 at p. 151.

Ultimately the resolution was drawn into the provisions of the 1988 Trade and Co-operation Agreement between the EEC and Hungary.[16] In resolving the Community's interest, Van den Bossche cites as one of the goals to be achieved, a safeguard clause to be included to, "provide adequate protection to the Community's internal market in cases of market disruption."[17] She also segregated the agreement's provisions for those situated into the GATT context and, "clearly indicating that the bilateral agreement basically provides an additional, complementary framework and the GATT remains the *lex generalis* for relations ..."

This is to contrast with those aspects of the agreement intended to be *lex specialis*. "In cases of this type the Agreement is not a complementary, but a substituting, framework in the sense that the Agreement (the *lex specialis*) has preference over the GATT (the l*ex generalis*)."[18]

Thus were provided the "made to order provisions" which reflected the resolution of the EEC-Hungary particularities which could not be accommodated under the General Agreement. Her conclusion on this point is that both the inclusion of the safeguard clause and the provisions for dealing with quantitative restrictions were both *lex specialis* to the GATT Agreement. For safeguards, Article 7 of the EEC-Hungary Agreement provided that a bilateral system of consultations leading to the measures to be taken and their duration, be implemented in full between the two parties prior to any recourse to the GATT.[19] In regard to removal of quantitative restrictions for the most sensitive products, the safeguard clause applied unilaterally in favour of the Community and, "recourse to GATT is plainly excluded."[20]

These characterisations provide a clear example of how a bilateral agreement may act to suspend the operation of the General Agreement as it would otherwise apply between two parties. As one takes this example forward in time, it is also il-

---

[16] The Agreement on Trade and Commercial and Economic Cooperation between the European Economic Community and the Hungarian People's Republic, signed 26 September, 1988. (popularly known as known as the "new generation" or "first generation agreement", see generally, Dan Horovitz, *EC-Central/East European Relations: New Principles for a New Era*, Common Market Law Review, V. 27, 1990, pp. 259-284.

[17] Van den Bossche, Supra note 11 at p. 153, citing the Committee on External Economic Relations of the European Parliament, Zarges Report, P.E. Doc A 2-88/86; Article 4 and protocol of the EEC-Hungary Agreement.

[18] Continuing, "(T)hese references indicate how indispensable the GATT has been for concluding the bilateral agreement. In other words, the ultimate reasons for concluding a bilateral agreement on – to use early Hungarian terminology – 'already contracted rights and obligations' appear perfectly clearly here." Van den Bossche, Supra note 11 at p. 153.

[19] "(a)ll specific bilateral remedies must have been exhausted first." Van den Bossche, Supra note 11 at p. 154.

[20] Van den Bossche does not consider that the provisions of this agreement would form a pattern for other CMEA arrangements. While she notes that the Czechoslovakian government also made a demand to eliminate quantitative restrictions, this country's position in GATT as an original contracting party suggested that the solution for Hungary which grew out of the biennial reviews on its GATT accession might be unique to Hungary. Van den Bossche, Supra note 11 at p. 155.

lustrative to see how the deviation is accommodated in the European Community import regime with its implementing legislation enacting GATT Article XIX. Here the evidence of an approach *lex specialis* is confirmed by the separate regulatory framework established by the EC for dealing with the CEEC Europe Agreement context, the successor agreements to the first generation trade and co-operation agreements noted above.

9.4.2   *The general Community safeguards regime*

At the time of the trade and co-operation agreements, the EC legislation authorising the use of emergency measures according to EEC Article 113 was Council Regulation (EEC) No. 288/82, titled, Common Rules for Imports.[21] This Regulation provided two procedures for safeguards. The first was the "normal" procedure providing for internal consultation between Member-state authorities and the Commission,[22] and following that consultation, the opening of investigation by the Commission.[23] This investigation would be accompanied by publication in the Official Journal and, where a safeguard was found to be necessary, action by the Commission within nine months of the opening of the investigation. Within certain restrictions, interested parties were given a right to investigate information supplied and to supply information. A limited right to be heard was provided.[24] The injury test stated as necessary to justify a safeguard was provided by Article 14 and copied the GATT Article XIX text,

---

[21]   Council Regulation, (EEC) No. 288/82 of 5 Feb 1982, repealed by Council Regulation (EC) No. 518/94 of 7 March 1994 on Common Rules for Imports, Official journal NO. L 067, 10/03/1994, pp. 0077-0087. The purpose of the repeal of 288/82 was not directed to a change in the GATT regime, as the regulation was promulgated prior to the conclusion of the Uruguay Round. Rather, the legislative program for the completion of the EC internal market made amendments necessary. As according to the preamble of Reg. 518/94: "Whereas in order to achieve greater uniformity in the rules for imports it is necessary to eliminate the exceptions and derogations resulting from the remaining national commercial policy measures and in particular the quantitative restrictions maintained by Member States under Regulation (EEC) No 288/82. By this time the CEEC countries were not subject to state trading provisions. "It is worth noting that in the application of EC safeguard measures the passage from the NME (non market economy) to the common rules was already effected for reference periods which largely predated the entry into force of the relevant IA's (Interim Agreements). M. Maresceau, and E. Montaguti, *The Relations Between the European Union and Central and Eastern Europe: A Legal Appraisal*, Common Market Law Review, V. 32, 1995 pp. 1327-1367, at p. 1351, their note 79.

[22]   Council Regulation, (EEC) No. 288/82, Article 4.

[23]   Council Regulation, (EEC) No. 288/82 , Articles 5-7.

[24]   Council Regulation, (EEC) No. 288/82, Article 5(4). "The Commission may hear the interested parties. Such parties must be heard where they have applied in writing within the period laid down in the notice published in the Official Journal of the European Communities, showing that they are actually likely to be affected by the outcome of the investigations and that there are special reasons for them to be heard orally."

"(W)here a product is imported into the Community in such greatly increased quantities and/or on such terms or conditions as to cause, or threaten to cause, serious injury to Community producers of like or directly competing products".

An alternate "fast track" procedure permitted a response by the Commission within five days. Within a month following, a member state had an option to refer such a decision to the Council, which could then confirm the Commission by qualified majority, or choose to amend or revoke the Commission decision. If after three months there was no Council decision (inactivity), the Commission measure was deemed by the Regulation to be revoked.[25] Thus, even according to this express procedure, an affirmative action of the Council would be required to continue the temporary measure in force.

While the Regulation was dedicated by its Preamble to respect the GATT Article XIX provisions, "... with due regard for existing international obligations ...", it was also not intended to apply to bilateral trade agreements made between the Community and third countries. Article 18(1) stated that,

"(T)his Regulation shall not preclude the fulfilment of obligations arising from special rules contained in agreements concluded between the Community and third countries".

1992 would see the publication of the interim agreements for free-trade areas negotiated between the EC and the first of the CEECs. These provisions were severed from the Europe Agreements as they could be given an early effect by a vote of the Council according to the Common Commercial Policy (EC Article 113, now 133). The latter and comprehensive agreements were mixed and required EC member state ratification, a process taking several years to complete. The safeguard provisions contained in the interim agreements did indeed vary from those provided by Regulation 288/82 and the GATT-47 Article XIX. They developed upon the *lex specialis* orientation of the original EEC-Hungary bilateral settlement.

9.4.3 Safeguards in (CEEC) Interim Agreements for Association

The test provided for the EC-CEEC interim agreements is stated in Article 24, using the EC-Poland agreement for example.[26] There, safeguards would be permitted to be taken where, as in the EC Regulation 288/82 and GATT Article XIX, products are imported in such increased quantities as to cause or threaten to cause serious injury to domestic producers of like or directly competitive products. In addition however, safeguards could also be established where there were, "... serious

---

25   Council Regulation, (EEC) No. 288/82, Article 14(4)-(6).
26   The provisions here are drawn from EC-Poland Interim Agreement, OJ 1992 114/1. The Article number is also indicated as "EA 30" showing its position in the final Europe Agreement once ratified.

disturbances in any sector of the economy or difficulties which could bring about serious deterioration in the economic situation of a region."

This test for injury is broader than GATT Article XIX as it contemplates a sectoral (agriculture?) injury, and even recourse for a broad deterioration of a regional economy, perhaps without any particular sector or producer-group identification. As a safeguard remedy under the Interim Agreement, a party may take "appropriate" measures, but Article 27 of the agreement does require that they must be the least disturbing and be accompanied by a timetable for their abolition. Without any further provisions, "appropriate measures" would suggest those also accorded by GATT Article XIX, the suspension of a concession (suspension of a preference) in the form of a duty increase, or a quantitative restriction, or perhaps a minimum price or price undertaking.

Besides the broader injury possibilities, what appears to also be divergent is that there is no requirement contemplated for any compensation to be paid by the enacting party. What is made explicit in GATT Article XIX:3(a) does not appear to be accorded to the regional parties in any manner. This suspension of Article XIX could be said to flow from the lack of agreement by GATT parties generally on how compensation was to be handled in a safeguards case. It may also be said to follow from the nature of the free-trade commitment, as it differs from the contractual binding of a GATT negotiated and bound tariff. In the GATT, concessions are said to be reciprocal and reflecting mutual advantage. This contractual aspect is demonstrated where, if one suspends a commitment by application of a safeguard, the other party has a right to withdraw a comparable concession if compensation is not forthcoming. Free-trade agreements may not exhibit the same type of contractual relationship. Both parties are supposed to be dedicated to achieving an end-goal of free trade. Safeguard provisions are agreed upon to allow flexibility to render this achievement without undue market disruption along the way. Thus, it may not be reasonable to require compensation and/or retaliation that would act to unwind the course of positive preferences already scheduled to be established.

On the other hand, retaliation, or the threat of it, also reflects the mutuality of GATT provisions, that what is breached is then capable of being redressed. While all parties retain such a power, this should tend to confine the number and intensity of initial suspensions undertaken. This restraining factor is removed between the free-trade parties in this regional setting. This suggests not only that a greater flexibility to apply safeguards has been sought to be obtained by the regional members, but that one party's unilateral determination of imposing a safeguard can never operate as a breach of the agreement. This may well reflect the end-point of seeking to establish free trade together with the recognition of the difficulties of adjusting domestic protection along the way. At the same time, however, it also calls into question the degree of commitment in meeting the substantially-all trade test within the regional framework since the additional flexibility would permit parties to restrict more trade without incurring the risk of retaliation or the need to generate compensation.

The MFN aspect is also subject to identification for possible divergence. The interim agreements do not say that MFN is being suspended as to the necessity of enacting investigations for like products from third parties (non-members). Parties disagreed under GATT-47 as to whether non-injuring parties should be captured in a safeguard measure in any case. But, GATT parties did not disagree as to whether a safeguard would require MFN as to those parties contributing to injury. For the interim agreements, there appears no provisions requiring that a notice of prospective intra-regional safeguards should be also accorded to the GATT Contracting Parties (Article XIX:2). If the regime overall is considered *lex specialis*, as Van den Bossche has suggested, then one can certainly imagine an interpretation going forward arguing that there is no obligation by a regional member to consider any third-party exports as a possible contributor to the domestic injury. This leaves open the possibility that a regional member would be required to pay the full price of the injury especially where the WTO Safeguards Agreement has later evolved to strike a certain balance on the MFN issue. With the addition of a more disciplined administrative regime, the gap between what is provided in the free-trade agreement and that which is provided in the WTO has widened.

9.4.4 *Procedural variations*

Divergence is also documented for the procedural and institutional arrangements provided between the Europe Agreement parties. These aspects are not found within the Interim Agreement, but are provided by further detail for each individual CEEC party according to Commission Regulations.[27] According to the Regulation for Poland, an EC member state is provided a right to request a safeguard of the Commission. If the Commission decides unfavourably on this request, the member-state may then appeal to the Council, which shall consider the application on the basis of qualified majority. If the Council decides against the Commission (and in favour of the safeguard), then the Europe Agreement party is then notified for the purposes of joint consultation. The Council can reverse its decision 20 days after consultation, but apparently not thereafter.

This procedure varies from that provided by the general Regulation 288/82 (and later Regulations). While Council action is to be taken by qualified majority in both instances, in the general 288/82 procedure inactivity by the Council for three months terminates the measure. There is no corresponding provision in the special

---

[27] For Poland, Reg. 518/92 of 27 Feb. 1992, OJ No L 56/3, "on certain procedures for applying the Interim Agreement on trade and trade-related matters between the EEC and the ECSC, of the one part, and the Republic of Poland of the other part". The Poland provisions are cited for convenience. They do not vary as to the other Association agreements as far as this author can validate.

CEEC provisions. Also, where the Council does reverse the Commission and endorses the measure, a twenty-day period of consultation is only possible prior to the Council losing its right to reverse its decision or assumedly to modify it. This 20-day limit is not raised in the general procedure and there is no indication that the Council cannot reverse or modify its own decision at any time.

This procedure also involves a significant variation from GATT Article XIX in that the Europe Agreement procedure permits one party to first determines the necessity of the safeguard and its application prior to consultation with the affected country. The emphasis is not on the joint undertaking to resolve the difficulty, but on a unilateral action taken by one party that must then be addressed by the other prior to implementation. As the non-EC party is notified after the measure is passed, it would seem that the only reasonably response would be to seek to convert the measure, already approved, into some type of export control.

9.4.5   Europe Agreement safeguards conclusion

The evolution of the safeguard clause applied by the Community toward Central and Eastern Europe was derived in the context of the GATT accessions of these countries. This was resolved essentially in favour of the preservation of the clause in the "New Generation" trade and co-operation agreements concluded between the EC and several CEEC countries in 1990 and 1991. As these agreements became outdated by political events, the Europe Agreements, containing the interim agreements, were then initiated to form free-trade areas between the Community and the CEECs, as individual signatories. These agreements have been submitted for examination according to Article XXIV. The provisions for regional safeguards, as they vary from GATT Article XIX and the expanded WTO Safeguards Agreement should be of interest in the process of review. However, judging from past working group experience, the emphasis on safeguards is likely to remain on whether or not regional parties can apply external safeguards while exempting regional partners. Given the differences in the applicable legal regimes, the opposite scenario may be more likely. From a "preservation of trade" perspective this may also be desirable, since it indicates a lesser likelihood of external trade diversion. However, the divergence in regimes favouring intra-regional safeguards is systematically problematic. If WTO Article XIX procedures are bypassed by regional safeguard actions, then the facility to enact grey-area measures and the like is also enhanced. The transparency and discipline that the WTO Safeguards Agreement has sought to bring to the global problem of evasive measures is undermined. Overall, there should always be a question of whether a regional formation covers substantially all trade. The number and intensity of safeguards enacted between members should be relevant to that determination, particularly after the conclusion of the interim period.

Since the European Community is not the only customs territory that is a party to a regional safeguards framework, we turn now to another example in the NAFTA context. Here the attention is on the failure to notify and asking whether WTO Members retain a right to self-characterise measures so that WTO Safeguards Agreement disciplines may be avoided.

9.5 NAFTA Countervailing duty action: Canadian softwood

9.5.1 *Introduction*

The Canadian softwood trade issue with the United States has been the basis of a number of distinct actions before and after the formation of the Canada-U.S. free-trade area (CUSTA), and then NAFTA.[28] The first action commenced in 1982 with a filing of a formal countervailing duty complaint with the United States International Trade Commission (USITC) by the U.S. Coalition for Fair Canadian Lumber Imports. In May of 1983 the International Trade Administration (ITA) rejected the preliminary ruling of the USITC in finding that the stumpage fee program did not constitute a countervailable subsidy according to United States law.[29] According to the ITA, since Canada's stumpage program was generally available, it could not be construed as a domestic subsidy.

A second complaint was filed by the Coalition in 1986 in order to seek reversal of the earlier finding. Although there had been no change in either the nature of the industries or the management of the program by the Canadian provinces, in this second action the ITA made a positive finding that softwood lumber imported from Canada was subsidised through administratively set stumpage prices and via the provision of public resources.[30] The subsidy was calculated to equal 15% ad valorem. A material injury finding was made and the CVD duty of 15% was to be applied as from December 30, 1986. According to Meilke and Sarker, the market

---

[28] Canada-U.S. Trade Agreement, North American Free Trade Agreement, the latter signed at various dates in Washington, Ottawa and Mexico City in December of 1992. **International Legal Materials**, Volume 32, pp. 289 and 605. The history of the countervailing duty actions is drawn in part from Karl Meilke, and Rakhal Sarker, *National Administered Protection Agencies: Their Role in the Post-Uruguay Round World*, International Agricultural Trade Research Consortium, Working paper #96-1, January 1996, pp. 13-19.

[29] This finding of no countervailable subsidy by the Department of Commerce is commonly known as "Lumber I". The alleged subsidy related to the Canadian provincial stumpage program. The Department found that the advantage of the system did not inure to the benefit of any specific industry or group in Canada and did not provide goods at preferential rates. See for summary, *In the Matter of: Certain Softwood Lumber products from Canada*, Extraordinary Challenge Committee Memorandum Opinions and Order, (U.S-Canada Free-trade Agreement), ECC-94-1904-01USA, August 3, 1994, Introduction.

[30] Extraordinary Challenge Committee, Ibid. This determination is known as "Lumber II". The finding was based upon a "purported comparison between revenues from stumpage charges and the provincial government's cost of administering their stumpage systems." Ibid.

share of Canadian softwood equalled 33% of the U.S. market at the time of the second complaint. No other producer country exported to the U.S. market. In 1991, 70% of Canada's production was exported to the U.S.[31] This CVD duty did not go into effect as a result of a bilateral negotiated settlement, known as the Memorandum of Understanding on softwood lumber between the two governments.[32] Effective January 8, 1987, Canada agreed to impose an export tax of 15% on softwood. On September 3, 1991, Canada renounced this arrangement after review of the programs and declared that stumpage fees had risen so that there was no longer a need to collect the export tax. As a response, the United States Trade Representative self-initiated the third CVD case. While pending, a 15% import duty would be applied for contingency protection prior to administrative findings to be made in the case. These actions resulted in a subsidy and injury determination on May 28, 1992 that led to an imposed CVD of 6.51% ad valorem.[33]

By this point in time, the Canada-US free-trade area (CUSTA) was in force and Canada appealed the US agency determinations to the newly established binational panel as according to Article 1904 of that Agreement.[34] On July 26, 1993, this panel remanded (in part unanimously and in part by majority) the factual and legal findings, and requested the U.S. Department of Commerce to consider a number of factors, including clarification of the appropriate legal standard. After the Commerce Department made its remand determination (and increasing its countervailable duty) the binational panel ruled again by majority on January 28, 1994 that the subsidy determination was "unsupported by substantial evidence and otherwise not in accordance with the law(,) and the countervailing subsidies could not be maintained."[35] Thus, the binational panel dismissed the CVD case against Canada.

This rejection of the third CVD action by the binational panel led to a period of unilateral gestures by the United States, including the threat, not acted upon, to bring the dispute under the GATT (Tokyo Round) Subsidies Code dispute settlement procedures. Finally an export restraint was agreed upon by negotiations that

---

[31] Meilke and Sarker, Supra note 28 at p. 13. They attribute the difference in findings between the first and second actions to a change in U.S. law permitting subsidised inputs to be considered, and possibly, to a new U.S. provision providing for assistance to complainants in the preparation of their actions.

[32] "The Department thereupon terminated its investigation and declared its preliminary determination to be without legal force and effect. " Extraordinary Challenge Committee, Supra note 29, Introduction.

[33] This determination is known as "Lumber III". This Decision by the Department of Commerce is characterised as a "final affirmative countervailing duty determination." According to the Committee, the Department found that the programs were specific and provided for preferential rates. Extraordinary Challenge Committee, Supra note 29, Introduction.

[34] Prior to the free-trade agreement, Canada's recourse would have been made according to a review of the Decision by the Court of International Trade (U.S.), and then the U.S. Appellate Court system. Under the U.S.-Canada FTA, a binational panel of five experts would review the Decision. According to the Agreement, there is no basis for appeal from the panel and their decision is binding upon the parties. Extraordinary Challenge Committee, Supra note 29, Introduction.

[35] Extraordinary Challenge Committee, Supra note 29, Introduction.

were completed as announced on April 2, 1996.[36] According to the United States Trade Representative, the five-year agreement provided that,

"Canada has committed to reduce its softwood lumber exports to the United States in exchange for a U.S. commitment to refrain from trade action in this sector".[37]

To administer the export restraint,

"Canada began implementing on April 1 a nationwide program for export licensing and permitting, allowing both countries to track volumes and province of origin".

9.5.2   The U.S-Canada measure according to GATT rules

In determining whether or not the export restraint as agreed by the parties is GATT legal, there is first a need to characterise it. Given that Canada promised by the agreement to implement a control system for export licenses and permits, it would seem reasonable that the action taken was an export quantitative restriction in the form of a voluntary export restraint. As such, GATT's provision of Article XI prohibiting measures other than duties should apply in the first instance, subject only to Article XI's stated exceptions. However, "undertakings" are permitted by Article 18 of the WTO Agreement on Subsidies and Countervailing Measures. This would permit a voluntary undertaking by the exporting government agreeing to either eliminate or limit the subsidy or, "take other measures concerning its effects." According to Article 18.3 of the Subsidies Agreement, if the U.S. has made its preliminary affirmative determinations regarding the subsidy and its injury, then perhaps Canada's undertaking in the form of a quantitative restraint might fall under the remedies permitted by way of an undertaking.[38]

However in this case, although the U.S. Department of Commerce had made a determination, this determination was not accepted upon review, and the action itself was no longer pending as the binational panel had not adopted the U.S. determination. As provided according to Article 1904 of the U.S. and Canada Free-trade Agreement, "the Parties shall replace judicial review of final antidumping and countervailing duty determinations with binational panel review." Thus, as required by Article 18 of the Subsidies Agreement, countervailing duty proceedings were not being "suspended or terminated" by the acceptance of a voluntary undertaking.

---

36   Office of the United States Trade Representative, Statement of Ambassador Kantor on *Finalizing the Softwood Lumber Agreement*, Press Release, Tuesday April 2, 1996.

37   The specific volume commitment from combined shipments of 16.2 billion board feet to 14.7 billion board feet, plus provision for additional imports to enter at a tax rate of $50/1000 board feet. Kantor statement, Ibid., at p. 1.

38   WTO Agreement on Subsidies and Countervailing Measures, Article 18 titled "Undertakings". "18.1- Proceedings may be suspended or terminated without the imposition of provisional measures or countervailing duties upon receipt of satisfactory voluntary undertakings …".

As indicated by the USTR above, the measure was being agreed upon, "to refrain from trade action in this sector.." This reference must refer to future trade action, perhaps in the WTO under the Subsidies agreement itself. It seems clear from the facts that the previous trade action, of which the U.S. determination had been a part, had already been resolved in Canada's favour.

Thus, one is presented here with either a violation of GATT Article XI or with a safeguard action that should fall under the provisions of GATT Article XIX. The WTO Safeguards Agreement, including its prohibition against grey-area measures in Article 11, is said according to Article 1 to apply to those measures provided for in Article XIX of GATT 1994. GATT Article XIX permits emergency action for two types of circumstances. As according to paragraphs 1 (a) and (b), either to address the result of unforeseen developments and the effect of the obligations incurred by a contracting party under this (GATT) Agreement, or alternatively, for a product which is the subject of a concession with respect to a preference. Thus, whether the problem caused to the U.S. resulted either from the operation of GATT bound tariff rates, or due to a preference possibly extended in the Canada-U.S. free-trade area, Article XIX should apply to the measures undertaken.[39]

9.5.3   *Conclusion on Canada softwood: Article XIX notification*

This raises the question of whether the voluntary export restraint should have been notified according to the Safeguards Agreement and then regulated according to its procedures. One argument against notification would refer to the illegality of the agreement made. Since the WTO Safeguards Agreement prohibits these arrangements according to Article 11, it could be suggested that that notification would never be required since the arrangement was unlawful. This would seem to be a difficult construction since without a requirement of transparency, the Safeguards Agreement and its provisions for monitoring would be rendered non-effective. Since the expressed intent of the Agreement according to its preamble is to "re-establish multilateral control over safeguards and eliminate measures that escape such control", a conclusion that prohibited measures need not be notified would easily undermine the objective of the Agreement.

A second argument against notification, and submission of the measure for control by the Committee on Safeguards, would relate to the existence of the CUSTA (later NAFTA) as it might have controlled with speciality the rights and obligations between these regional members. Here it could be argued that NAFTA provides its own safeguards regime which did not in this case result in a referral to the Article XIX procedure. This is the *lex specialis* argument. Such an interpretation if correct,

---

[39]   This, unless the measure undertaken was "sought, taken or maintained" according to some other provision of GATT-1994, an annexed Agreement or, "pursuant to protocols and agreements or arrangements concluded within the framework of GATT 1994." WTO, Safeguards Agreement, Article 11.2 .

would provide the widest latitude for regional members to activate restraint arrangements outside the purview of the WTO Agreement on Safeguards, and further outside the purview of its prohibition on grey-area measures. For NAFTA Emergency Actions in particular, Article 801 of the Agreement provides a set remedy for imports causing injury during the transition period. The parties are permitted to suspend the rate of duty reduction as scheduled by the Agreement, and then to impose an increase in the rate of duty to the MFN rate applicable at the time action is taken or to the time immediately prior to the Agreement, whichever is lesser.[40] Thus, according to NAFTA, an export volume restraint would not in any case comply with the NAFTA provisions of the Chapter on Emergency Action.

Whether or not *lex specialis* applies to permit regional members to except the application of the Safeguards Agreement turns also on the issue of notification. If notification is required, then the Agreement's monitoring provisions and tests and rules governing application among WTO Members should also apply. It is clear that the Safeguards Agreement establishes rules for application of "safeguard" measures, which are, "understood to mean those provided for in Article XIX (GATT 1947)". What types of measures are at hand? The original Article XIX does not use the terms "safeguards", but paragraph XIX:2 of GATT-1947 requires that before any party shall take an action pursuant to the provisions of paragraph 1, it shall give notice in writing. As indicated above, paragraph 1 (a) and (b) contemplates application both for tariff concessions in accord with the GATT and concessions in respect of a preference. Preference granted within Article XXIV arrangements is not excluded by GATT Article XIX, rather referring only to the action undertaken by a contracting party. Article 11 (c) of the WTO Safeguards Agreement subjects the application of the Agreement and its prohibition of certain measures only to those measures which are not authorised by other GATT provisions and protocols and agreements and arrangements concluded within the framework of GATT 1994.

It can be suggested that a safeguard regime which excepts the application of Article XIX and is concluded within an Article XXIV agreement is such an "agreement or arrangement". Except however, that Article XXIV itself provides explicitly for the adoption of restrictions only within the context of application of GATT Articles XI-XV and XX. In other words, there is no express authorisation within Article XXIV to adopt measures according to Article XIX. Likewise, there is also no express authorisation in the Article to adopt measures that would fall outside of Article XIX's control.

An additional question is raised as to what substantive types of suspensions should be notified. By Article XIX, Members have arguably obliged themselves to notify (at the latest) upon a decision to suspend an obligation or withdraw or modify a concession. However, this may not be occurring in the case of a regional

---

[40] NAFTA, Article 801, para. 1, Supra note 28.

framework where a regional preference that is not a GATT concession is at issue. Thus for example, between GATT parties a bound tariff duty of 20% may be at issue for suspension, while between regional parties a 0% duty may be under consideration. If the preference has gone beyond the GATT concession, the entire Article XIX Agreement may not be seen to apply in any manner unless regional parties have incorporated it or have failed to designate a *lex specialis* provision.

However, there is an additional question where the preference being suspended also acts to suspend the underlying GATT MFN concession. Thus as above, if the 0% preference duty is being suspended in favour of an import or export quantitative restriction, then both the preference and the GATT concession are affected. Likewise, if the suspension has been made in favour of a duty increase, then any increase above the GATT binding would also impinge the underlying concession. Perhaps this consideration indicates one possible dividing line between the operation of Article XIX and Article XXIV for these types of cases.

9.6   Chapter Conclusion: safeguards and regionalism

Footnote 1 to the WTO Safeguards Agreement states that, "(N)othing in this Agreement prejudges the interpretation of the relationship between Article XIX and paragraph 8 of Article XXIV of GATT 1994." This does not say either that Article XXIV:8 formations are exempt from Article XIX procedures or that Article XIX procedures apply to regional formations. What can be said is that the Agreement applies to WTO Members and does not by its terms exclude any of them. Article 12 of the Agreement requires a WTO notice on commencements of investigations, the finding of injury, or the taking of a decision to apply a safeguard. Both the U.S. and EU have provisions for these procedures in their regional agreements. At the point in time when these procedures are invoked according to the regional framework, arguably a WTO notice is then required, at least if the action contemplated might result in the suspension of a GATT obligation or in "modifying or withdrawing a concession." Finally, even while the negotiators did not pre-judge the relationship between the two regimes as noted above, the Safeguard Agreement's prohibition against the use of grey-area measures in Article 11(b) provides that prohibited measures include "actions under agreements ... entered into by two or more Members." Article XXIV agreements were not excluded from this provision.

The threat of terminating internal trade is most aptly considered in cases of protective measures employed where an exclusion occurs during the operation of an agreement. This may occur between regional partners after the interim period because Article XXIV:8(b) has not been interpreted by any consensus decision of the GATT Contracting Parties or the WTO Members to exclude the use of contingent protective instruments between regional partners.[41] However, where regional parties do reserve the right to apply contingent measures internally, there is little question that the effect of this reservation would serve as a basis to eliminate trade from the coverage of the free-trade area that otherwise would be subjected to a free movement commitment. Working group reviews have traditionally passed on considering this problem, although retention of contingent commercial power between partners does relate to the legal capacity of partners to eliminate barriers to trade for substantially all the trade. A number of free-trade area working group reviews have raised the collateral concern of whether regional partners have a right to relieve each other from safeguard measures which remain in place against outsiders, thereby providing for more favourable treatment between regional partners relative to other GATT partners. Here, attention has been drawn to the reverse scenario where outsiders are not made subject to a measure that is applied by regional partners to their trade internally.

Since dozens of WTO members are parties to regional agreements with special safeguard provisions, it is not a trivial question to inquire whether such provisions are under the jurisdiction of the WTO, and therefore covered by the GATT and its Agreement on Safeguards. As indicated in a 1998 background note by the WTO Secretariat, emergency safeguards are found in virtually all of the 68 regional trade agreements, and for all of these, only 6 limit the use of safeguards to the interim period. In nearly all of the 68, increased imports alone can trigger a safeguard. The majority of agreements allow safeguards based on more than a single criterion, and many criteria posed in agreements are less stringent than the multilateral rules. Regional trade agreements in general do not specify whether the measure may be imposed as linked to concessions granted in the agreement. Only a few agreements are said to include parameters referring to prevailing GATT disciplines.[42]

This is the environment within which the new WTO Agreement on Safeguards has taken effect. Since 45 of the 68 agreements listed have also taken effect since 1990, one may conclude that GATT parties, if not actively opting out of Article XIX, certainly have provided for themselves a certain legal framework by which this may be accomplishable. If *lex specialis* is designated to relegate the WTO safeguard regime, then one would expect the bulk of such actions to be taken up at the

---

[41] The use of anti-dumping actions between regional partners has not received treatment here, but the author has treated the issue in a similar context in other publications. See, Peter Holmes, and James Mathis, *Europe Agreement Competition Policy for the Long Term: an Accession Oriented Approach*, in **Rules of Competition and East-West Integration**, M. Fritsch, and H. Hansen, (Eds.) Kluwer Academic Publishers, Dordrecht, 1997; and, Phedon Nicolaides, and James Mathis, *European Community Competition Rules in the Associated Countries of Central and Eastern Europe: How to Ensure Effective Enforcement*, Aussenwirtschaft, V. 51:4, 1996, pp. 485-512.

[42] WTO, Committee on Regional Trade Agreements, *Inventory of non-tariff Provisions in Regional Trade Agreements,* WT/REG/W/26, 5 May 1998, Annex VI, paras. 41-44.

regional level and likewise, notices and the control of the WTO Safeguards Committee to become somewhat more rare over time as to regional members.

Regional safeguard regimes probably do require some response that can address unanticipated surges of imports which occur as a result of scheduled tariff decreases. However, this does not make an argument that regional measures should be exempt from GATT Article XIX and its procedures. If the regional preference is in fact the cause of the injury, then other GATT parties need not be caught by the measure in any case where the new procedures permit a certain selectivity for absolute increases in exports. If external trade is a contributing factor, then the WTO Article XIX procedures are designed to allocate the application between all affected WTO Members, regional members and non-members alike. In the alternative, if Article XIX has no lawful application to regional parties, then the prospect remains that regional members will be compelled to pay for the adjustment costs for injuries that should have been remedied elsewhere. The cause for this diversion of treatment to members rather than non-members would be found in the relative ease of invoking a regional procedure as contrasted to the more rigorous multilateral procedures within the WTO.

Finally, and again without pre-judging the Article XXIV legality of any safeguard measures between regional members to a completed agreement, one may also draw upon the NAFTA provisions described above. It is perhaps possible to conceive of an interim regional framework that would omit reference to the WTO Safeguards Agreement where a preference was suspended between regional parties only to return to the level of MFN. Injury occurring beyond that first corrective measure would require invocation of the WTO Agreement on Safeguards and the participation by the balance of the WTO Members.

As the discussion turns to consider the dispute resolution cases in the WTO, one can determine that legal developments are occurring which appear to press new interpretations of GATT Article XXIV. These will be argued to have a bearing on the heretofore-presumed flexibility of regional members regarding the availability of internally trade-restrictive measures.

Part Four:
THE WTO RESPONSE

Chapter Ten turns to the dispute settlement practice in the WTO and brings the discussion to contemporary events. Two WTO panel and Appellate Body reports concerning Article XXIV are detailed. These cases are viewed as building upon the unreported panel cases from the GATT era, discussed in chapter 5. However, in going beyond those earlier panels, the power of panels to address the compatibility of a regional trade agreement with the conditions of Article XXIV is also found to be a ruling of the Appellate Body Report regarding the Turkey-EC customs union. There is also a clear ruling on the position of Article XXIV paragraph 4, in that it expresses 'purposive' language rather than a distinct legal obligation. The second WTO case concerns Argentina safeguards on footwear products. While the Appellate Body in that case does not rule on the question of whether safeguards may be prohibited between regional members, there is a clear outcome that Article XIX and the Safeguards Agreement continues to apply to the external applications of safeguards by regional members. We draw from this the possibility that the test enunciated for permitting the violation of GATT rules as to non-members may also be applicable to members.

The following Chapter Eleven attempts to integrate the WTO dispute settlement developments with the ongoing reported work of the WTO Committee on Regional Trade Agreements (CRTA) in regard to the discussion of the systemic issues. This chapter uses the template developed by the WTO Secretariat's itemisation and organisation of systemic issues. Thus, "both sides" of an interpretive question regarding paragraph 8 are outlined, and then prescriptive in attempting to resolve the question in light of the cases and other materials as drawn from the chapters. An important consideration for the CRTA is the manner in which recommendations are, or more often not, made. In the conclusion to Chapter Five and Part Two, a discussion was made of the legal effect of "non-decisions" in the review of regional agreements. Chapter Eleven concludes this Part on the same consideration as it has been affected by the WTO Appellate Body rulings in regard to the competence of panels to qualify an Article XXIV defence by determining the compatibility of an agreement with the Article's provisions. It is argued here that the effect of this ruling will effectively shift the burden to regional proponents in the review process in order to obtain the necessary affirmative recommendations for their regional systems.

Chapter 10
ARTICLE XXIV PANEL AND APPELLATE BODY PRACTICE IN THE WTO

> "... we caution that the degree of "flexibility" that sub-paragraph 8(a)(i) allows is limited by the requirement that 'duties and other restrictive regulations of commerce' be 'eliminated with respect to substantially all' internal trade." *Turkey Textiles Appellate Body Report, para. 48.*

10.1   Introduction

In the previous Chapter Five we discussed the two unreported GATT panel cases which applied the legal requirements of GATT Article XXIV to the Lomé Convention.[1] As the WTO and its Dispute Settlement Understanding came into force, it was perhaps only a matter of time before a preference or measure enacted in the context of an Article XXIV formation, whether free-trade area or customs union, would be met with a legal challenge. Ironically perhaps, the first WTO challenge did not arise in the context of an MFN complaint regarding the preferences exchanged between free-trade area members. Rather, a customs union formation between the European Community and Turkey provided the context. The question concerned the GATT legality of new quantitative restrictions installed by Turkey on the trade of a third party, India, all in furtherance of the customs union plan.[2]

While this issue concerned the application of *external* rather than *internal* measures taken by a regional party, both the Panel and the Appellate Body dealt at length with the legal nature of Article XXIV as it may serve as a type of exception to other GATT Article violations. The legal position of the Article within GATT and the requirements necessary for a party to successfully invoke its exceptional nature have been established, arguably for the first time. As an aspect of this development, the relationship between the various paragraphs of Article XXIV, in particular paragraphs 4, 5 and 8 have also been discussed. The ordering of these paragraphs is especially of note in the Appellate Body's ruling that paragraph 4 is *purposeful* by nature but does not establish an independent legal test for the examina-

---

[1]   *EEC – Member States' Import Regimes for Bananas*, DS32/R, 3 June 1993; *EEC – Member States' Import Regimes for Bananas*, DS38/R, 11 Feb. 1994. The other non-reported GATT panel regarding Article XXIV is, *EEC-Tariff Treatment of Imports of Citrus Products from Certain Countries in the Mediterranean Region*, L/5776 of Feb. 7, 1986.

[2]   *Turkey – Restrictions on Imports of Textile and Clothing Products*, Report of the Panel, WT/DS34/R, Report of the Appellate Body, AB-1995-5, WT/DS34/AB/R. For purpose of abbreviation, text references throughout will refer to the Turkey Panel or Turkey Appellate Body.

tion of regional trade agreements. In addition, both the panel and the Appellate Body have commenced the process of judicial interpretation of some of the substantive terms provided in the Article's paragraphs. By so doing, the direction of interpretation for future reviewing parties has been spelled-out for even difficult expressions such as, *other regulations of commerce*, and *substantially all of the trade*.

Finally, in a complex and likely controversial determination, the Appellate Body has also arguably established a requirement that future panels must undertake a compatibility assessment of a regional trade agreement when a member is seeking to invoke the Article XXIV defence. While this ruling has a number of institutional implications, one such inference, as discussed below, concerns the WTO Committee on Regional Trade Agreements (CRTA) in those cases where the CRTA does not form an affirmative recommendation regarding the compatibility of a regional trade agreement with the Article's substantive requirements. Such a *non decision* can no longer be presumed to grant a self declaratory avenue for regional parties to obtain the benefit of the exception. Rather, invoking regional parties must be prepared to make their entire case for compatibility before the panel. If so, the practical legal effect of notification of a regional trade agreement before the Council on Trade in Goods may be limited. Regional parties may only be deriving for themselves a future right, together with the commensurate burden of proof, to affirmatively establish Article XXIV compatibility as a matter of first impression before a panel. Perhaps time will tell whether any regional party will ever choose to invoke the Article XXIV defence subject to these terms.

Shortly following the Appellate Body Report in the Turkey textiles case, another Article XXIV case came to light, this one dealing with safeguard measures upon footwear taken by Argentina. This case also received Panel and Appellate Body treatment with a reversal specifically on the question of whether Argentina's individual safeguard measures could be attributed to the MERCOSUR customs union. Since the Appellate Body dealt in depth with the requirements of Article XIX as they might apply to a member of a customs union, this case outlines some significant terrain for the relationship between GATT Articles and Article XXIV. It does not however resolve the question of the legality of applying safeguards between regional members, even while the Appellate Body reversed the Panel's finding that Article XXIV granted a permissive approach to the question, up to some point where substantially-all trade would be undermined. For the Appellate Body, the question of eliminating safeguards between regional members was expressly not ruled upon.

The chapter discussion will proceed by outlining the factual aspects as presented in the Turkey Textiles case and then moving on to the Argentina Footwear case. A brief conclusion on each case will be provided. The commentary seeking to integrate these rulings will be made in the following chapter of the book, together with a treatment of the remaining systemic issues presented for WTO Members in their review of regional agreements.

10.2 Turkey Panel – Restrictions on Imports of Textile and Clothing Products [3]

India requested the panel in February 1998 in light of the GATT and the WTO Agreement on Textiles and Clothing (ATC), claiming that quantitative restrictions (QRs) imposed by Turkey on Indian products were inconsistent with Turkey's obligations under GATT Articles XI and XIII, and were not justified by Article XXIV.[4]

The WTO Agreement on Textiles and Clothing requires, by 1 January 2005, that import countries will thereafter be barred from discriminating between exporters in the application of safeguard measures via the Multi-fibre Arrangement (MFA). Although Turkey was a member of the MFA from 1981, at the time of entry into force of the ATC Turkey did not maintain quotas on imports of textiles and clothing (T&C) products. Therefore, Turkey was not able to notify any pre-existing safeguards for preservation under the ATC until 2005. The EC however did notify and therefore retained certain quantitative safeguards according to the provisions of the ATC. Between the two parties, Turkey's exports of T&C products were also under a restraint as to the EC market, and in accord with the MFA provisions.[5]

10.2.1 *The Association Agreement, Turkey-EC customs union*

The contested measures originated in the context of the Turkey-EC Association Council Decision 1/95 of March 1995, setting out certain modalities for the final phase of Association between Turkey and the EC for the completion of a customs union.[6] This Decision required the elimination of customs duties, alignment of the common customs tariff, and provisions for the harmonisation of certain other policies. The entry into force of the "final phase of the Customs Union" was notified to the WTO in December of 1995 under Article XXIV GATT.[7] The Council for Trade in Goods referred the notice to the Committee on Regional Trade Agreements (CRTA). No finalised examination or finding, either negative or affirmative, was made by the CRTA prior to the dispute being brought by India before the panel.

---

[3] Report of the Panel, 31 May 1999, WT/DS34/R.
[4] Discussion of Article 2.4 of the ATC is generally omitted in this summary.
[5] Turkey Panel Report, paras. 2.29 and 2.30.
[6] Ankara Agreement, 1963, Turkey Panel Report, para. 2.16.
[7] Turkey Panel Report, para. 2.17.

10.2.2 *Measures undertaken*

Turkey applied quantitative restrictions from January of 1996 on imports from India for 19 categories of textile and clothing products.[8] The QRs for 1996 were allocated on a quarterly basis, upon a semi-annual basis for 1997, and annually for 1998. The actions taken to impose the QRs were made by Decrees issued by Turkey's Council of Ministers and published in the Turkish Official Gazette.[9] This resulted following proposals made by Turkey to India to negotiate on a draft memorandum in July of 1995 for the purposes of completing, prior to the formation of the customs union, a series of measures similar to those already existing between India and the EC.

India declined to negotiate on this basis. Turkey went on to effect restraints similar to those applied by the EC with 24 other countries. The unilateral measures described above were installed for T&C products originating from a total of 28 countries, including India.[10]

10.3   **Preliminary Issues Before the Panel**

The Panel made preliminary rulings on a few points that contribute to an understanding of the legal identity, for WTO purposes, of regional parties and the measures undertaken by them as individual WTO members.

10.3.1 *Compelled joinder of parties*

As a first question, Turkey asserted that the EC should have been named as a party to the action as brought by India.[11] Turkey based its claim here on the point that the Turkey-EC customs union had been notified to the CRTA as a customs union, and therefore should be represented as such by its constituent members. The Panel noted that the EC had declined to participate and found that the Dispute Settlement Understanding does not allow for any procedure to join a party other than third-party rights under Article 10 of the DSU. Thus, "We consider that we do not have

---

8   A formula used by Turkey corresponded either to (1) the arithmetic average of imports into Turkey during the period 1992-1994; or (2), annual amount based on EC imports multiplied by the percentage of the "basket exit threshold" laid down in an EC and India bilateral agreement for 1994, multiplied by the percentage share of Turkish GDP in the EC 15 (2.5 percent). Generally, Turkey Panel Report, paras. 2.37-2.39.

9   Turkey Panel Report, para 2.33.

10   Turkey Panel Report, paras. 2.35 and 2.36.

11   Other preliminary issues were resolved in favour of India and affirmed the preliminary rulings made by the panel in the present case. These included an allegation of insufficient description of the measures in order to permit defence and whether India had properly followed consultation rules as required by the DSU. See generally, Turkey Panel Report, para. 9.1.

the authority to direct that a WTO Member be made a third-party or that it otherwise participate throughout the panel process."[12] In addition, the panel noted that the Turkey-EC customs union was not a member of the WTO and could not therefore be subject to any DSU procedure, "as it lacks WTO legal personality".[13]

10.3.2 *Attribution of measures, customs union legal personality*

A related issue presented asked whether the measures enacted were attributable to Turkey, to the EC, or to the Turkey-EC customs union. On this the panel provided a discourse on the conditions by which a customs union may be viewed to have a legal personality distinct from that of the constituent territories for purpose of the attribution of its measures. Such a question should not be seen to turn on quality of movement within the territory, but rather upon the degree of sovereignty actually retired by the parties, and as determinable on a case by case basis.

For the Turkey-EC customs union, there were no arrangements made for a legislative body with constitutional authority. While there was an Association Council provided for the customs union, its powers were understood to be limited to action according to unanimity. This indicated an intent by the constituent parties to preserve each party's sovereign right to act independently. Therefore, the measures must have been undertaken by Turkey alone and were attributable accordingly.[14] In enunciating what appeared to be general ruling on this point, the Panel made reference to the existence of the EC customs union and noted,

> "In WTO terms, unless a customs union is provided with distinct rights and obligations (and therefore some WTO legal personality, such as the European Communities) each party to the customs union remains accountable for measures it adopts for application on its specific territory".[15]

10.3.3 *Panel jurisdiction to investigate Article XXIV measures*

Turkey raised a final preliminary issue. It argued that the Panel was without power to assess the WTO compatibility of any specific measure adopted in the context of the formation of a regional trade agreement, separately, and in isolation from an assessment of the overall compatibility of the agreement with Article XXIV. Such

---

12 Turkey Panel Report, para. 9.5, quoting the preliminary ruling.

13 In support, the Panel cited ICJ cases including the Nicaragua case, *Military and Paramilitary Activities in an Against Nicaragua* (1984), p. 431; and *Certain Phosphate Lands in Nauua* (1992), pp. 261-262. Turkey Panel Report, paras. 9.6, 9.8-9.10.

14 Turkey Panel Report, para. 9.40. Examples of similar situations are provided in the Panel Report's note 272, citing ICJ, the customs regime of Germany and Austria, for definition, plus the particulars of the Czech and Slovak customs union as an example of regional parties retention of individual independence.

15 Turkey Panel Report, Ibid.

a compatibility assessment was argued to be exclusively within the province of the Committee on Regional Trade Agreements and according to the procedures established in Article XXIV.[16] Turkey argued further that the WTO compatibility of an Article XXIV agreement, together with all of its related measures, is a matter to be determined exclusively within the confines of Article XXIV itself and not by any other provisions of the WTO.[17] By this argument, the role of a panel to review individual measures was called directly into question by Turkey. If a compatibility finding is a pre-condition to examining the legality of measures undertaken to form a customs union, and if the panel does not have any jurisdictional basis to make an overall assessment of compatibility, then it would follow that the Panel can not take up the question of the legality of any particular measure.

The panel found that WTO dispute settlement can be invoked to challenge a measure adopted on the occasion of a customs union formation. The source for this ruling is found in Article XXIV:12 of GATT-1994, providing that a panel may examine,

> "*any matters arising from the application* of those provisions of Article XXIV relating to customs unions, free-trade areas or interim agreements leading to the formation ...".[18]

For the Panel, this language meant that it had authority to examine, "one or several measures 'arising from' Article XXIV types of agreements...".[19]

However for the Panel, this conclusion was not the same as suggesting that a Panel should also undertake an overall compatibility assessment of a regional trade agreement with the GATT. This larger assessment appeared to the Panel to remain the responsibility of the CRTA together with its special procedures. Thus,

> "(W)e consider that regional trade agreements may contain numerous measures, all of which could potentially be examined by panels, before, during or after the CRTA examination, if the requirements laid down in the DSU are met. However, it is arguable that a customs union (or a free-trade area) as a whole would logically not be a "measure" as such, subject to challenge under the DSU".[20]

---

[16] Turkey Panel Report, para.9.45.

[17] India characterised this as an argument for waiver in asserting that Article XXIV provisions do not constitute a waiver from other WTO obligations. Turkey Panel Report, paras. 9.46 and 9.47.

[18] Turkey Panel Report, para. 9.49, emphasis provided by the Panel in its quotation.

[19] Turkey Panel Report, Ibid.

[20] Turkey Panel Report, para. 9.53. Thus, the Panel basically ruled that the term "matters" as they may arise from application of the Article is limited in its definition by the concept of "measures", a limitation on authority rejected outright by the Appellate Body, as below.

In the case at hand, the panel also determined that it was not necessary to rule explicitly on the question of whether a panel can assess the overall compatibility of a regional agreement. Judicial economy was raised to suggest that the panel need not address the question. Rather, the issue could be treated as whether,

"...in this case, on the occasion of the formation of the Turkey-EC customs union, Turkey is permitted to introduce WTO incompatible quantitative restrictions against imports from a third country, assuming arguendo that the customs union in question is otherwise compatible with Article XXIV GATT".[21]

10.4   Violations of GATT Article XI, XIII and 2.4 ATC

On the substance of India's complaint, the panel found that the quantitative restrictions violated Article XI and XIII as, "the measures at issue, on their face, impose (QRs) on imports and are applicable only to India.[22] In so ruling, the Panel reiterated an earlier ruling on the persistence of QRs through the era of GATT-1947, and dismissed the notion that QRs could ever attain the status of permitted subsequent practice in derogation or modification of Article XI.

"Certain contracting parties were even of the view that (QRs) had gradually been tolerated and accepted as negotiable and that Article XI could not be and had never been considered to be, a provision prohibiting such restrictions irrespective of the circumstances specific to each case. This argument was, however, rejected in an adopted panel report EEC- Imports from Hong Kong".[23]

The panel went on to list the newly-devised mechanisms installed during the course of the Uruguay Round in order to assist in the elimination of QRs, including provisions made for the areas of agriculture, textiles and clothing, balance of payments, and safeguards. Obviously, "Participants ... recognized the overall detrimental effects of non-tariff border restrictions ... and the need to favour more transparent price-based, i.e., tariff-based measures ...".[24]

---

[21] Turkey Panel Report, para. 9.55.
[22] Turkey Panel Report, para.9.66. The discussion of the ATC violation is omitted.
[23] Turkey Panel Report, para.9.64.
[24] Turkey Panel Report, para. 9.65.

10.5   Party Arguments and Panel Treatment of Article XXIV

Upon finding of the violation of GATT Articles, the Panel undertook to examine
the defence raised by Turkey that these prohibited measures were permitted by the
operation of GATT Article XXIV. For this analysis, the Panel first established an
interpretative framework to guide the examination of the Article's provisions, as
found in general principles of public international law and the law of treaties.

10.5.1   *General interpretative framework*

As recited by the Panel, Article 3.2 of the WTO Dispute Settlement Understanding
requires that the examination of GATT Article XXIV must be guided by the principles of customary rules of interpretation of public international law, which includes Articles 31 and 32 of the Vienna Convention on the Law of Treaties. Thus,
the Panel determined that Article XXIV should be first interpreted by using the
ordinary meaning of the terms as elaborated by the GATT-1994 Understanding.
This should be done in the context and in light of the object and purpose of the
relevant WTO agreements. If needed for the purpose of clarification, reference to
negotiation history including the historical circumstances that led to the drafting of
Article XXIV should also be made. In addition, Article XVI of the WTO
Agreement indicates that the WTO shall be guided by decisions, practices, and
customary practices followed by the contracting parties to GATT-1947 and those
bodies established in GATT-1947. [25]

Another principle raised was that of the need to avoid conflict in interpretation
in the context of the WTO as a single undertaking.[26] Thus, the panel chose at the
outset to consider that if Article XXIV appeared to authorise measures which
GATT Article XI, XIII and 2.4 ATC otherwise would prohibit, that a resolution
must bear, "in mind that to the extent possible, any interpretation of these provisions that would lead to a conflict between them should be avoided."[27]

---

[25]   Turkey Panel Report, para. 9.91.
[26]   Turkey Panel Report, para 9.92. The Panel recounted public international law materials and
earlier WTO cases to establish the presumption against conflict in the interpretation of WTO obligations. This proposition appears to have played a significant role in framing one of the Panel's primary
later findings, that Article XXIV:8(a)(ii) should be interpreted in a sufficiently flexible manner in order
to permit regional formations without causing violation of other GATT Articles. This in light of
Turkey's (conditional) right to form a regional trade arrangement.
[27]   Turkey Panel Report, para. 9.95. Also, by footnote 324, the distinction between the issue of
conflict and that of *lex specialis* is mentioned, as the latter , "which is inseparably linked with the
question of conflict" does not apply if two provisions deal with the same subject from different points
of view, are applicable in different circumstances, or one provision is more far-reaching, but not inconsistent, with those of the other (citations provided therein).

Finally, the Panel made reference to the principle of effective interpretation in noting that all treaty provisions should be given their full meaning to the extent possible. Application of this principle would prevent a panel from reaching conclusions that would lead to a denial of either party's rights or obligations.[28]

10.5.2 Panel overview of Article XXIV

The Article XXIV recognition of the desirability of regional trade agreements is not without certain qualification, as Article XXIV:4, and as re-iterated by the GATT-1994, both indicate that the purpose of arrangements is to facilitate trade between the parties "and not to raise new barriers of trade to other Members ..." According to the terms of Article XXIV, Members "have a right, albeit conditional, to conclude regional arrangements."[29] The linkage between Article XXIV:4 and Article XXIV:5 is made by the word "accordingly" in the first sentence of paragraph 5. This relates back to the previous Article and provides the framework for interpretation of Article XXIV:5. Thus,

> "the conditional right to form a regional trade agreement has to be understood and interpreted within the parameters set out in paragraph 4".[30]

While the Panel was not so explicit on the point, the strongest inference that can be drawn from this reference to paragraph 4 is that the Panel made a finding that the purpose of an agreement "not to raise new barriers" constituted a GATT legal requirement not to do so. Having established such a requirement, the issue of conflict between provisions would arise between the paragraph, as interpreted, and especially the requirements of paragraph 8 dictating the degree of internal trade liberalisation to be achieved. Prior to that analysis the Panel proceeded to extensively interpret paragraph 5 in light of the paragraph 4 interpretation.

10.5.3 Treatment of Article XXIV:5(a)

Turkey claimed that Article XXIV:5(a) should be read as permitting parties to introduce new measures in the form of other regulations of commerce (ORCs) as long as the overall incidence of duties and ORCs resulting were not higher or more restrictive after the completion of the formation. The GATT-1994 Understanding confirmed this view by indicating that an assessment is to be made of the incidence of ORCs. Therefore, such measures undertaken as applied to third parties were

---

[28]   Turkey Panel Report, para. 9.96. It is somewhat clear from the Panel's later application of this principle that it led to an error of law in the interpretation of the relationship between paragraphs four and eight of Article XXIV.

[29]   Turkey Panel Report, para. 9.103.

[30]   Turkey Panel Report, para. 9.105.

not intended by the GATT provisions to be outright prohibited by Article XXIV:5.[31]

A second argument by Turkey referred to Article XXIV:5 as it establishes a derogation, but not confined to any particular GATT rule (such as MFN), but to all GATT rules from which a derogation would be necessary in order to permit the formation of a legal customs union. This was demonstrated by the opening language of Article XXIV:5, and as it is similar to GATT Article XX (General Exceptions) in that, "the provisions of this agreement shall not prevent …"[32]

India responded that XXIV:5 authorised the formation of a customs union but does not go further in providing any legal basis for adoption of measures otherwise incompatible with GATT/WTO rules. The article's terms only exempt those measures that are necessarily inherent to the formation of a qualified trade agreement, MFN in Article I for example. There is nothing provided in Article XXIV that would otherwise require a regional member to impose any new restrictions inconsistent with GATT XI, XIII and 2.4 ATC.[33] India cited Article XXIV:6 to support this view as a process for re-negotiation and compensation for duty increases is provided there. But, no such comparable provision for compensating third parties in regard to quantitative restrictions is indicated by that paragraph. This should suggest that the imposition of QRs was not contemplated by the provisions as being a permitted ORC under the terms of Article XXIV:5.

The Panel recognised that paragraph 5(a), and as elaborated by the GATT-1994 Understanding on Article XXIV, provides an "economic" test for assessing whether a customs union is compatible with Article XXIV.[34] Although there is no agreed-upon definition of the term *other regulations of commerce* by WTO members, it is nevertheless clear that the term includes quantitative restrictions. As determined by the Panel,

> "(M)ore broadly, the ordinary meaning of the terms 'other regulations of commerce' could be understood to include any regulation having an impact on trade (such as measures in the fields covered by WTO rules, e.g., sanitary and phytosanitary, customs valuation, anti-dumping, technical barriers to trade; as well as any other trade-related domestic regulation, e.g., environmental standards, export credit schemes). Given the dynamic nature of regional trade agreements, we consider that this is an evolving concept".[35]

---

[31] Turkey Panel Report, para. 9.110.
[32] Turkey Panel Report, para. 9.112.
[33] Turkey Panel Report, para. 9.113.
[34] Turkey Panel Report, para. 9.120. This element of the ruling was affirmed by the Appellate Body, but it does not say that all elements of an Article XXIV assessment are inherently subject to an economic assessment.
[35] Turkey Panel Report, para. 9.120.

The Panel went on to characterise Article XXIV:5(a) as general rather than prescriptive. It authorises regional formations but it does not contain any provision that authorises or prohibits the adoption of import restrictions that are otherwise GATT/WTO incompatible. In the overall assessment to be made, while the wording of paragraph 5(a) assumes that duties and other ORCs may be more restrictive than before, it does not specify whether such a situation may occur only through GATT/WTO consistent actions or may occur through GATT/WTO inconsistent actions.[36] Thus, "… we consider that the terms of paragraph 5(a) do not address the GATT/WTO compatibility of specific measures that may be adopted on the occasion of the formation of a new customs union."[37]

Similarly, the assessment required by the CRTA of a regional trade agreement in regard to its compatibility with Article XXIV:5 also does not require the determination of the compatibility of specific measures with GATT rules. On this point the Panel looked to the standard terms of reference granted to the CRTA, "that the CRTA in its overall assessment, shall not determine the WTO compatibility of specific measures."[38]

In regard to whether paragraph 5 authorised new QRs upon third-party trade, the Panel employed a type of parallel analysis of both subparagraphs (a) and (b) to conclude that the Article did not so authorise. For free-trade areas, paragraph 5(b) is seen to provide an identical scheme, excepting that duties and ORCs shall not be higher in each *constituent territory*. This reflects the absence of a single tariff formation in a free-trade area. For free-trade area members, they would never have an occasion to argue that a formation entitled them individually to impose new QRs on other GATT members in harmonizing external trade, since they are not required to do so in any case. It follows that the provisions of the terms of 5(a) and 5(b) should not lead to different interpretations in terms of what the GATT rules require.[39]

---

[36] Turkey Panel Report, para. 9.121.

[37] Turkey Panel Report, para. 9.122.

[38] Turkey Panel Report, para 9.122, and note 338. The Panel thus makes a demarcation in jurisdictional responsibilities between the CRTA and an Article XXIII Panel. The CRTA is not to be concerned with legality of particular measures and panels are likewise not concerned with overall assessment of the resulting economic effects of all regional measures taken together. It follows that a successful overall compatibility assessment by the CRTA should not exempt a challenge as to any particular measure as it may violate a GATT/WTO rule. For support, the Panel cited an Understanding indicating that the purpose of examination under paragraph 5(a) is not to determine whether each individual duty or regulation existing or introduced is consistent with all the provisions of the WTO Agreement. Understanding read out by the Chairman of the Council for Trade in Goods, 20, February, 1995, (WT/REG3/1).

[39] Turkey Panel Report, para. 9.125. The same argument can be applied to XXIV:8(a) and (b) in terms of the Article's internal requirements, since that language is also identical for both customs unions and free-trade areas in regard to other restrictive regulations of commerce (ORRCs). See, Infra note 49.

After referring to aspects of paragraphs 4 and 6, and together with a discussion whether or not the location of Article XXIV in Part II of the GATT carried any legal significance,[40] the Panel made its conclusion as based on the ordinary meaning of the terms included in paragraph 5:

"(C)onsequently, we find that there is no legal basis in Article XXIV:5(a) for the introduction of quantitative restrictions otherwise incompatible with GATT/WTO; the wording of sub-paragraph 5(a) does not authorize Members forming a customs union to deviate from the prohibitions contained in Article XI and XIII of GATT or Article 2.4 of the ATC".[41]

10.5.4 *Treatment of Article XXIV:8*

Turkey argued that Article XXIV:8(a)(ii) requires it as a regional party to impose the same conditions to third countries that are applied by the EC to its external trade. This is why the Association Council Decision of 1/95 envisaged the wholesale adoption by Turkey of the EC commercial policy instruments as well as its customs code, all prior to the completion of the customs union.[42]

India's contrary view was that paragraph 8(a) merely acts to define the requirements to be fulfilled in order to qualify as a customs union within the meaning of the Article. India noted that Turkey had reserved the right in its Association Council Decision to apply differential external measures in other areas, including agriculture, steel and other industrial products, as well as differential regimes from the EC in measures undertaken for actions concerning anti-dumping, countervailing duties and safeguards. Further, there is no stated requirement in paragraph 8(a) that conditions necessary to qualify a trade agreement must be fulfilled by the regional parties immediately.[43] Turkey responded that the India view of paragraphs 5 and 8(a)(ii) was overly restrictive as,

"... any interpretation of Article XXIV which could lead to the conclusion that in certain circumstances, WTO Members with diverging external trade regimes were legal-

---

40 Turkey argued that the position of Article XXIV in Part II of the GATT indicated a "self-contained" regime for the formation of trade agreements (Article XX and XXI are in Part II). According to the Panel, there is no drafting history to illuminate a legal effect of an Article's placement other than the fact that Part II and Part III entered into effect at different times. In the Havana draft, Article XXIV's predecessor was listed in the Commercial Policy chapter along with the other special provisions, including Article XX. Panel Report, para. 9.132.
41 Turkey Panel Report, para. 9.134.
42 Turkey Panel Report, para. 9.135.
43 Turkey Panel Report, para. 9.136.

ly inhibited from forming a customs union, is in contradiction with the objective clearly stated in Article XXIV:4".[44]

Turkey relied upon paragraph 8(a)(i)'s obligation to cover substantially all trade in its customs union formation with the EC. In order to meet this requirement, turkey must obviously be required to cover textiles and clothing products as they together represent 40 per cent of Turkey's exports to the EC. For these goods to be covered, the constituent members of the customs union must have common tariffs and a common foreign trade regime with third countries in accordance with paragraph 8(a)(ii).[45]

The Panel determined that Turkey was raising two distinct points in this argument. The first was that Turkey was being required to adopt EC external rules in order to form a custom union compatible with XIV:8(a)(ii). The second was the requirement that Turkey adopt EC external policies as a matter of its own agreement with the EC.

The Panel determined that XXIV(8)(a)(i) was not directly on point in consideration of the case as India's claim itself was not directed to the *internal* preferences of the formation. As India's claim related to the *external* regime of Turkey, as it was to result from the customs union formation, Paragraph (8)(a)(ii) was the appropriate sub provision to be considered, since it provides the external customs union requirement.

For sub-paragraph (8)(a)(ii), since the panel would interpret in a manner to avoid conflict between provisions, the question at hand was how to interpret the sub-paragraph (8)(a)(ii) together with GATT Article XI and XIII so as to avoid one being required to yield to the other. The Panel was of the opinion on this point that there was an inherent flexibility within sub-paragraph (8)(a)(ii) that permitted a harmonious interpretation.[46] This flexibility was discerned in the use of the term "substantially" within the sub-paragraph as the parties are required to apply *substantially the same duties and other regulations of commerce.*[47] This flexibility may be exhibited further in the relationship between the sub-paragraphs (a)(i) and (a)(ii), which address distinct but "inter-linked" policies. Thus, while the first sub-paragraph may require certain goods in trade to be covered as to the internal requirements, it did not necessarily follow that identical external trade policies in regard to third countries need necessarily result.

---

[44] Turkey Panel Report, para. 9.138. The objective being referred to would assumedly be that reference in paragraph 4 which indicates that the purpose of a regional trade agreement should be to facilitate trade between the parties to a formation.

[45] Turkey Panel Report, para. 9.139.

[46] Turkey Panel Report, para. 9.147.

[47] Turkey Panel Report, para. 9.148. … Also, "while parties have never reached agreement on the meaning of the term, its ordinary meaning appears to provide for both qualitative and quantitative elements to be considered, the quantitative aspects perhaps more emphasised in relation to duties." Ibid.

"Therefore, the inclusion of a sector within the coverage of a customs union, i.e. the removal of all trade barriers in respect of products of that sector between the constituent members of the customs union, does not necessarily imply that those constituent members must apply identical barriers or barriers having similar effects to imports of the *same products* from third countries".[48]

What can be said to underlay this ruling by the Panel is that the concept of "removal of trade barriers" for the purpose of a customs union formation does not include the required elimination of individual member rules of origin and the associated use of movement certificates. Free circulation is not therefore a requirement of Article XXIV for a customs union.[49]

The Panel also took up the role of the listed GATT Article exceptions in sub-paragraph 8(a)(i). This provision contemplates that certain quantitative restrictions could be maintained between regional parties, as necessary and as described by GATT Articles XI through XV and XX. This suggested for the Panel that even where substantially all trade is provided by the parties, that certain WTO compatible restrictions in the form of quantitative restrictions can be continued to be maintained between them. In relating this to the external requirements of sub-paragraph (8)(a)(ii),

"This implies that internal quantitative restrictions can be used in the event that only one of the constituent territories has in place a restriction on imports from third countries. If such pre-existing import restrictions were WTO compatible, the maintenance of an internal import restriction between the two constituent countries would ensure that the protection afforded by the original WTO compatible quota would not be circumvented. The maintenance of such an internal restriction can obviate the need for identical external trade policies".[50]

Finally, the Panel made its holding on interpretation of the second sub-paragraph itself:

"Considering this wide range of possibilities, we are of the view that, as a general rule, a situation where constituent members have "comparable" trade regulations having similar effects with respect to the trade with third countries, would generally

---

48 Turkey Panel Report, para. 9.149, emphasis added for clarity.
49 Earlier the Panel employed a parallel interpretation of paragraph 5 (a) and (b) to draw a conclusion that customs unions could not apply new restrictions upon third parties. The same analysis was foregone on the point made in the text. If the substantially all trade requirement of paragraph 8 as applied to free-trade areas could not be interpreted to require the elimination of member rules of origin and the use of movement documents, then the identical provision should not be viewed as creating such a requirement for customs unions.
50 Turkey Panel Report, para. 9.150. Although, there is not an exception listed in Article XI-XV and XX to maintain internal quantitative restrictions as result of a customs union formation.

meet the qualitative dimension of the requirements of sub-paragraph 8(a)(ii). The possibility also exists of convergence across a very wide range of policy areas but with distinct exceptions in limited areas".[51]

In this, the Panel emphasised that a number of administrative means were also available to insure that no trade deflection would occur while respecting the parameters of paragraphs (8)(a)(i) and (8)(a)(ii). It recalled that the two sets of policies under the paragraphs were distinct and the relationship between them a flexible one. It was also noted that the Turkey-EC agreement contemplated itself the use of origin certificates where agreements with third parties could not be concluded. Therefore, Turkey was apparently able to establish its internal coverage obligation under sub-paragraph 8(a)(i) without abridging the obligation imposed by the following paragraph, or without violating other GATT Articles. Thus, in the Panel's view, "the terms of Article XXIV:8(a)(ii) do not provide any authorisation for Members forming a customs union to violate the prescriptions of Article XI and XIII of GATT or Article 2.4 of the ATC."[52]

The panel went on to consider the wider context in forming its final ruling. After referring to a number of preamble provisions in the GATT, Article XXIV and the 1994 Understanding,

"(W)e read in these parallel objectives a recognition that the provisions of Article XXIV ... do not constitute a shield from other GATT/WTO prohibitions, or a justification for the introduction of measures which are considered generally to be ipso facto incompatible with GATT/WTO".[53]

10.5.5 *Additional and final considerations by the Panel*

Having reached this conclusion, the Panel then addressed some final arguments which might be characterised as affirmative defences. This included the issue of subsequent practice, the absence of a recommendation according to Article XXIV:7, and the argument of necessity of violating GATT rules for the constituting of the Turkey-EC customs union.

Turkey had made the argument that GATT inconsistent measures as to third parties had been implemented and tolerated in previous customs union formations.[54] Article 31.3(b) of the Vienna Convention (VCLT) provides that the context of interpretation of a treaty provision also includes, "any subsequent practice in the application of the treaty which establishes the agreement of parties regarding its interpretation." Consistently, Article XVI of the Agreement Establishing the WTO pro-

---

[51] Turkey Panel Report, para. 9.151.
[52] Turkey Panel Report, para. 9.154.
[53] Turkey Panel Report, para. 9.163.
[54] Turkey Panel Report, para. 9.164, with reference to paras. 6.58 to 6.61.

vides that the WTO shall be guided by the customary practices followed by the Contracting Parties.[55]

For the Panel, the more precise standard to be applied in regard to subsequent practice on this point was enunciated by the Appellate Body in *Japan – Alcoholic Beverages*. This requires a,

> "... 'concordant, common and consistent' sequence of acts or pronouncements which is sufficient to establish a discernable pattern implying the agreement of the parties regarding its interpretation. An isolated act is generally not sufficient to establish subsequent practice; it is a sequence of acts establishing the agreement of the parties that is relevant".[56]

The panel reviewed aspects of the record of working group reviews in the GATT and found that no consensus had ever been reached on the interpretation of Article XXIV in relation to certain other GATT provisions.[57] As indicated by the quotations from working group reviews, expressions such as, "some members felt", or "most members were of the opinion" established the absence of consensus on these practices. In addition, a particular reference to arguments made within a non-adopted GATT panel report confirmed that there was outright disagreement among GATT parties as to whether the absence of a previous challenge to a regional formation (and the measures undertaken) constituted a tacit acceptance that such agreements were in conformity with Article XXIV.[58]

As the absence of challenge did not confer compatibility, so should GATT rights also not be denied from the absence of a previous recommendation under Article XXIV:7. Thus, the absence of recommendations to change or abolish import restrictions as they might have been adopted in previous regional formations did not have a bearing on whether third parties could assert their GATT claims. Citing *EEC- Imports from Hong Kong*,

> "(T)he Panel considered it would be erroneous to interpret the fact that a measure had not been subject to Article XXIII over a number of years, as tantamount to its tacit acceptance by contracting parties".[59]

---

[55] Ibid.

[56] Turkey Panel Report, para. 9.165, and citing the sources of Sinclair and Yasseen from the original notes of the Appellate Body.

[57] Turkey Panel Report, para. 9.1666, and citing EEC examination, Sub-Group B, working groups on EC accession of Denmark, Ireland and United Kingdom, Greece, Portugal and Spain.

[58] Turkey Panel Report, note 372, quoting, *EEC-Tariff Treatment of Citrus Products from Certain Mediterranean Countries*, L/5776, paras. 3.12-3.22. "The United States' statement in response to the European Communities' argument was that the failure of the Contracting Parties to reject the agreements did not imply acceptance nor did it constitute a legal finding of GATT consistency with Article XXIV."

[59] Turkey Panel Report, para. 9.173, quoting EEC-Hong Kong paragraphs 28 and 29. No citation to the EEC-Hong Kong panel was provided by the Panel.

The adoption of paragraph 12 of the GATT 1994 Understanding on Article XXIV also informed this question, as prior to that time it was not so clear whether specific measures adopted upon formation of a customs union could be challenged under Articles XXII and XXIII.

Turkey argued that it was required to adopt the WTO compatible import measures of the European Community. In the Panel's view, "a bilateral agreement between two Members...does not alter the legal nature of the measures at issue or the applicability of the relevant GATT/WTO provisions."[60] Also drawing upon Bananas III, the argument that a panel should defer to a common understanding of the parties rather than examine the content of the trade agreement was rejected there. In this context, the Panel raised for consideration Article 41 of the VCLT, stating,

> "Two or more parties to a multilateral treaty may conclude an agreement to modify the treaty as between themselves alone if ... (b) the modification in question is not prohibited by the treaty and (i) does not affect the enjoyment by the other parties of their rights under the treaty or the performance of their obligations".[61]

The Panel did not elaborate on the applicability of this VCLT provision, as it may be applied or not applied in its relation to the GATT Article XXIV. However, the Panel did appear to conclude that the Article XXIV exception does not establish an autonomous regime outside the WTO.

> "We have considered the proposition that Article XXIV is *lex specialis* and is purported to be a self-contained regime insulated from the other provisions of GATT and the WTO Agreement. We are not convinced by this argument. The relationship between Article XXIV and GATT/WTO seems to us to be self-evident from the wording and context of Article XXIV."[62]

10.6 Turkey Textiles Appellate Body Report [63]

10.6.1 *Panel findings and issues appealed*

The Panel found that the wording of GATT Article XXIV does not authorise a departure from the obligations found in GATT Articles XI and XIII, and Article 2.4 of the ATC. While paragraphs 5 and 8 of GATT Article XXIV do not specify which

---

60 Turkey Panel Report, para. 9.178.
61 Turkey Panel Report, para. 9.181.
62 Turkey Panel Report, para. 9.186. The relationship between this VCLT article 41 and Article XXIV is discussed at length, Infra, Chapter Twelve.
63 22 October, 1999, AB-1999-5, WT/DS34/AB/R.

measures may or may not be adopted on the formation of a customs union, they nevertheless do not act to authorise violations of GATT Article XI and XIII. Therefore, the Panel, "draw(s) the conclusions that even on the occasion of the formation of a customs union, Members cannot impose otherwise incompatible quantitative restrictions."[64]

Turkey claimed on appeal that the panel erred in its interpretation of GATT Article XXIV on a number of points. As Article XXIV permits (or requires) the common regulation of commerce by customs union members, the adoption by one member of another's legal quantitative restrictions should be lawful as long as unified regulations were not overall more restrictive than those applied before the customs union by these constituent members.[65] This flowed in part from Turkey's assertion that Article XXIV, unlike GATT Articles XX and XXI, does not grant an "exception" from other GATT obligations, but rather accords an autonomous right to form a customs union.[66] There was no basis in law therefore for the panel to conclude that Article XXIV granted derogation only for GATT Article I, most-favoured nation, but not from other GATT Articles as well. Rather, the text of the chapeau of Article XXIV:5 provided according to its ordinary meaning that, "the provisions of this Agreement" shall not prevent the formation of a customs union. Therefore, other provisions besides Article I can be excepted in the course of customs union formation.[67]

According to Turkey, this allegation of Panel error was further supported by the inherent nature of the test required under Article XXIV:5(a). There, an assessment must be made on the resulting duties and other regulations of commerce *as a whole*. The requirement to assess in this manner would be rendered a nullity by a panel interpretation that the "introduction of an otherwise inconsistent measure could disqualify the customs union even though trade flows were, on the whole, facilitated by the conclusion of the regional formation."[68]

10.7   Appellate Body findings and supporting argument

The Appellate Body adopted Turkey's arguments in part and reversed the Panel on the specific question of whether GATT Article XXIV could justify measures that were inconsistent with other GATT Articles. Following the Appellate Body's reasoning, a type of "defence" for customs union parties to violate GATT Articles as

---

[64]   Turkey Panel Report, paras. 9.86, 9.188 and 9.189, as recited in the Turkey Appellate Body Report at para. 42.

[65]   Turkey AB Report, para. 8.

[66]   Turkey AB Report, para. 9.

[67]   Turkey AB Report, paras. 10-13.

[68]   Turkey AB Report, para.14. In addition, the Panel was claimed to have misinterpreted the context of Article XXIV:5(a) in relation to Articles XXIV:5(b), XXIV:4, XXIV:5(a) and (b), and as to the location of Article XXIV in Part III of the GATT. AB Report at para. 15. Additional arguments made by Turkey are not detailed here.

to other WTO Members could arise where two requirements were demonstrated. First,

> "...that the measure at issue is introduced upon the formation of a customs union that fully meets the requirements of sub-paragraph 8(a) and 5(a) of Article XXIV. Second, the party must demonstrate that the formation of that customs union would be prevented if it were not allowed to introduce the measure at issue".[69]

Both conditions must be fulfilled. In this case, Turkey had failed to demonstrate the necessity of violating GATT Articles XI and XIII as other means were available to accommodate the internal trade requirement imposed by Article XXIV:8(a)(i). On this there was concordance between the Panel and the Appellate Body in noting that Turkey could have adopted rules of origin with certificates of movement as necessary to avoid the potential deflection of third-country goods. This would have allowed Turkey to distinguish between textile and clothing products that were of external origin and not subject to any harmonised external trade regime. In point, the Turkey-EC Association Decision of 1995 contemplated this possibility by providing for use of origin certificates for Turkey-EC trade if needed.[70]

In its overview of Article XXIV, the Appellate Body took a different course than the Panel. Rather than viewing the Article as sequential, and primarily flowing from paragraph 4, the pivotal position of the exception as it is enunciated in the head paragraph of Article XXIV:5 was first established. Then, other provisions were referred into the exception as it was stated in order to fill out the meaning of the requirements. Rather than establish the need to avoid conflict between paragraph 4 and paragraph 8, it appears that the Appellate Body demoted paragraph 4 back into the position of a "purposive" or informative position. The sequence of discussion here will follow that of the Appellate Body Report.

10.7.1 *The role of the chapeau of Article XXIV:5*

The Appellate Body determined at the outset that the Panel had not given sufficient weight to the role of the chapeau of Article XXIV:5, as the introductory paragraph of this Article functions as the key provision for resolving the issues at hand.[71] In respect of its ordinary meaning, the provision "shall not prevent" is to be read to mean, "shall not make impossible". It was clear therefore that under certain conditions, Article XXIV could grant the possibility of adopting measures that otherwise would be considered as inconsistent with other GATT Articles. Article XXIV may

---

[69] Turkey AB Report, para. 58.

[70] Turkey AB Report, para. 62, citing Panel Report, para. 9.152.

[71] Turkey AB Report, para. 43, reciting Article XXIV:5 in part: "(A)ccordingly, the provisions of this Agreement shall not prevent, as between the territories of contracting parties, the formation of a customs union ...; Provided that ..." (emphasis as supplied in the Appellate Body quotation).

therefore be invoked as a possible "defence" to a finding of inconsistency.[72] The elements of other Article XXIV provisions were drawn into the chapeau by its own terms. These elements were then taken up by the Appellate Body in turn to assist in the interpretation of the chapeau's requirements for permitting the exception.

10.7.2 *The definitional requirements of Article XXIV:8*

The chapeau of Article XXIV:5 makes reference to the "formation of a customs union". Therefore, any inconsistent measures sought to be defended by invoking Article XXIV must be undertaken upon the actual formation of a customs union, and then, only to the extent that such a formation would be prevented if the measure were not allowed to be implemented.[73] Therefore, reference to the definition of a customs union as provided by Article XXIV:8(a) is required in order to determine the interpretation of the Article XXIV:5 chapeau.

The definitional provisions governing a customs union indicate that there are both internal and external aspects to be considered. For the internal trade requirement, Article XXIV:8(a)(i) requires the elimination of "duties and other restrictive regulations of commerce" (ORRCs) in respect to "substantially all the trade" between the constituent parties. While neither GATT Parties nor WTO Members have ever reached agreement on the meaning of "substantially all trade", the term refers to something "considerably more" than some of the trade, even while it is not the same as "all of the trade". Thus, some flexibility was intended for parties in order to meet this internal aspect.[74] This is indicated by the deviations from internal trade coverage that are accorded by the availability of GATT Articles XI-XV and Article XX, and all within the text of sub-paragraph 8(a)(i). However, such flexibility is not unlimited as,

> "... we caution that the degree of "flexibility" that sub-paragraph 8(a)(i) allows is limited by the requirement that 'duties and other restrictive regulations of commerce' be 'eliminated with respect to substantially all' internal trade".[75]

An *external* trade requirement is also established for customs union members, as "substantially the same" duties and other regulations of commerce must be applied to the external trade with third countries, as according to Article XXIV:8(a)(ii). In terms of qualifying this definitional element, the Appellate Body affirmed and reversed the Panel in part. It agreed with the Panel that the requirement has both

---

[72] Turkey AB Report, para.45, and note 13 therein, reciting scholars supporting the point that Article XXIV operates as an exception or a possible defence to claims of other GATT provisions.

[73] Turkey AB Report, para 46.

[74] Turkey AB Report, para. 48.

[75] Turkey AB Report, para. 48. The question of whether GATT Articles XI-XV and XX form an exhaustive list in describing the parameters of flexibility was not addressed on point by the Appellate Body.

qualitative and quantitative aspects, and that flexibility was also available here for parties to meet the requirement. However contrary to the Panel's view, the Appellate Body found that provisions made for "comparable" trade regulations by regional parties would not be sufficient to meet the requirement. Rather, a higher degree of "sameness" was called for, as the term "substantially" was seen in context to qualify the word "same".[76]

10.7.3 The proviso requirements of Article XXIV:5(a)

Returning then to the requirements of Article XXIV:5, the chapeau also indicates that the provisions of GATT 1994 shall not prevent the formation of a customs union "provided that" the proviso of Article XXIV:5(a) is respected, in that the duties and other regulations of commerce (ORCs), "shall not on the whole be higher or more restrictive than the general incidence" of the duties and ORCs applicable in the constituent territories prior to the formation. On the question of duties, the 1994 Understanding on Article XXIV had already clarified that this examination would be engaged as to the actual applied rates of duties rather than designated bound rates.[77]

For "other regulations of commerce", the Appellate Body agreed with the Panel, "that the effects of the resulting trade measures and policies of the new regional agreement shall not be more trade restrictive, overall, than were the constituent countries' previous policies." Further, and as also determined by the Panel, the assessment on this point requires an "economic" test for determining whether a specific customs union is compatible with Article XXIV."[78]

10.7.4 The "purposive" requirement of Article XXIV:4

Finally, the chapeau of Article XXIV:5 must also derive its interpretation by reference to the wider context provided by Article XXIV:4. As indicated by the Panel, this linkage is disclosed by the use of the term "accordingly" which introduces paragraph 5 as it follows paragraph 4. This earlier paragraph reveals that the purpose of a customs union is to facilitate trade between the constituent members and not to raise new barriers to the trade with third countries. The Appellate Body noted that this was affirmed by the 1994 Understanding on Article XXIV. As to the legal nature of this provision in its relation to other paragraphs of Article XXIV, the Appellate Body stated that,

---

[76] Turkey AB Report, para. 50. We discuss below whether the same argument can be made in parellel to the use of the term "substantially" as it modifies the word "all" in sub-paragraph (8)(a)(i).

[77] Turkey AB Report, paras. 51-53.

[78] Turkey AB Report, para 55, reciting the Panel Report, para. 9.121.

"Paragraph 4 contains purposive, and not operative, language. It does not set forth a separate obligation itself but, rather, sets forth the overriding and pervasive purpose for Article XXIV which is manifested in operative language in the specific obligations that are found elsewhere in Article XXIV".[79]

Thus,

"... the chapeau of paragraph 5, and the conditions set forth therein for establishing the availability of a defence under Article XXIV, must be interpreted in the light of the purpose of customs unions set forth in paragraph 4. The chapeau cannot be interpreted correctly without constant reference to this purpose".[80]

Whatever else may be inferred from the obligation to make a constant reference to this purpose, the other provisions of the Article are also understood by the Appellate Body to have already incorporated these concerns. Therefore, there is no need to consider paragraph 4 as a separately constituted legal requirement in order to apply the exception.

10.7.5 *Appellate Body conclusion on the Article XXIV:5 chapeau*

As indicated above, the Appellate body concluded that Article XXIV might justify a measure inconsistent with certain other GATT provisions, providing two conditions would be fulfilled. First, the party claiming the defence must demonstrate that the measure being challenged was introduced upon the formation of a customs union that fully meets the requirements of Articles XXIV:8(a) and XXIV:5(a). Second, a party would have to show that the formation would be prevented if it were not allowed to introduce the inconsistent measure.[81] Going further at this point, a sequential relationship between these two requirements to be established was then noted, as the second condition may not be able to be met in the absence of meeting the first. As stated,

"(I)n other words, it may not always be possible to determine whether not applying a measure would prevent the formation of a customs union without first determining whether there *is* a customs union".[82]

This appears to suggest a certain sequence of examination, as has been suggested throughout the text, which would require regional proponents to establish the definitional elements of Article XXIV:8 compatibility at the outset. However, in

---

[79] Turkey AB Report, para. 57.
[80] Turkey AB Report, Ibid.
[81] Turkey AB Report, para. 58.
[82] Turkey AB Report, para. 59, emphasis in original.

posing such a requirement, an institutional question of whether panels can make such a determination under paragraph 8 would now necessarily arise.

10.7.6 *Turkey Appellate Body Ruling on the scope of review*

In considering its two-step test, the Appellate Body noted that the Panel did not address the question of whether the Turkey-EC arrangement constituted a customs union meeting the requirements of Articles XXIV:8(a) and XXIV:5(a). On this point, it noted the Panel's expressed opinion that panels may not have the jurisdiction to assess the overall compatibility of a customs union with the requirements of Article XXIV. While the Appellate Body explicitly noted that it was not being called upon to rule this question, since neither party had raised the issue on appeal, it then went on to cite its previous ruling in *India – Quantitative Restrictions on Imports of Agricultural, Textile, and Industrial Products*. This August of 1999 Appellate Body Report addressed the similar question of the jurisdiction of panels to review the justification of balance of payment (BOP) restrictions under Article XVIII:B of the GATT and the GATT-1994 BOP Understanding.[83]

To clarify the reference made to this earlier case, the Appellate Body in the India BOP case concluded that,

"... the Panel in the present case was correct in interpreting GATT practice as permitting the member concerned to choose either course of action. Should a member decide to have recourse to dispute settlement procedures under Article XXIII, such action would in no way prejudice the competence of the BOP Committee and the General Council to consider the same matter in accordance with Article XVIII:12".[84]

This would indicate that panels have retained authority according to GATT Article XXIII and relevant provisions of the DSU to rule upon matters arising from the application of the provisions of Article XXIV. This would include those aspects examinable by the special procedures applied by the Committee on Regional Trade Agreements as according to its granted authority.[85] However, the India BOP Panel had also found in reference to the BOP Committee that,

"By finding that panels can review the justification of balance-of-payments measures, we do not conclude that panels can substitute themselves for the BOP

---

[83] Turkey AB Report, para. 60 and note 25 therein, citing WT/DS90/AB/R, Adopted 22 September, 1999, paras. 80-109.

[84] WT/DS90/AB/R, para. 97, and holding, "(w)e conclude that panels have the competence to review the justification of balance-of-payments restrictions". Ibid., at para. 109.

[85] As according to Article XXIV:12, "with respect to any matters arising from the application of those provisions of Article XXIV ...". The India-BOP AB Report defined "application" as used in footnote one of the BOP Understanding to mean "use or employment". Ibid., at para. 92.

[86] Ibid., at para. 81, as reciting the India-QR Panel Report at its paragraph 5.114.

Committee ... It is also clear that panels could not ignore determinations by the BOP Committee and the General Council".[86]

A brief comment is offered at this juncture. The CRTA is authorised to receive notifications and to make assessments on the question of Article XXIV compatibility. Where it has made such a determination as to a particular regional trade agreement, such a recommendation should be honoured by a panel in assessing the elements of the first test recited above. Where the CRTA has made no such recommendation, one can conclude that a regional party's capacity to assert the Article XXIV defence is directly related to its ability to establish the required Article XXIV elements before the panel.[87]

10.8   Conclusion on the Turkey Reports

Both reports discussed above can be compared and contrasted to those rendered in Bananas I and II, as discussed in chapter Five. Those reports concerned MFN Article I, as an exception was not granted for an incomplete free-trade area agreement. There, the emphasis was upon interpretation of the internal trade requirements required under Article XXIV(8)(b), particularly the requirement that barriers be removed *between* the parties to the formation. Here we have a customs union plan and a complaint deriving not from MFN but from Article XI's prohibition against certain measures.

Both sets of reports addressed the role of the dispute settlement procedures as they may be invoked to challenge preferences exchanged or measures enacted in the course of regional trade formations. With the undoubted assistance of the WTO Dispute Settlement Understanding, and a revised Article XXIV:12, the development on this front is substantial. While the two Banana panel reports made reference to the necessity of a *prima facie* review of a trade agreement's provisions, for those facts at hand, no more was required. Arguably the same can be said of the facts presented in the Turkey case. But rather than draw a narrow view of the panel's authority to oversee a regional formation's invocation of the Article XXIV exception, the Appellate Body in particular has determined a panel's obligations more ambitiously. At the extreme, this would be something akin to "dual track" authority, this term introduced by the Appellate Body in the BOP case. Additional comments on these developments are made below.

---

[87]   While one could form an argument that a later panel could reject an Article XXIV defence in the absence of any CRTA recommendation, there is no indication in the Appellate Body Report that such an avenue has been left open for a later panel. One caveat on the interpretation presented in the text above is in order. In arguing in the BOP case for a principle of institutional balance between panels and committees, India cited unadopted Article XXIV cases in support of the point. The Appellate Body noted that those cases referred to the relationship between Articles XXIII and XXIV, and not as between Articles XXIII and XVIII. Ibid., at para. 100.

In outlining the Article XXIV elements drawn into the paragraph 5 chapeau, the Appellate Body has not only affirmed Article XXIV as exceptional in nature, but has also arguably informed the process of an examination to be applied in order to qualify for the exception. This can be seen to vary somewhat from the approach followed by the Panel, which perhaps emphasised more the desire for paragraph 8 definitions to be interpreted in a flexible manner in order to avoid conflict between the various GATT Articles in question.[88] The Appellate Body appeared to shift attention to the core definitional requirements provided in Article XXIV:8, as they were found to be incorporated as required legal elements by the paragraph 5 chapeau, and in conjunction with that paragraph's own proviso regarding the overall effect of duties and other regulations of commerce.

It can be suggested that the facts at hand in the Turkey case reflect a rather uncommon situation in comparison to regionalism in the WTO generally. Most regional agreements are free-trade area formations. In these cases the issues of externally-applied measures pursuant to the adoption of a common external policy are not at issue. GATT Articles XI and XIII would not in these circumstances be called into play. Rather, the more likely basis for a challenge would be concerned with the obligation of Article I for most-favoured nation as WTO Members might seek to obtain the positive preferences exchanged between free-trade parties. In the absence of a CRTA recommendation to insert on the issue of compatibility, a consistent interpretation of this Appellate Body Report would appear to require that the future panel must find whether or not a free-trade area has been formed within the meaning of sub-paragraph 8(b). This suggests that a future panel must be prepared to enunciate in more detail the meaning of "substantially all trade", at least as applicable to the particular case at hand.

As for Article XXIV:5(b), a free-trade area does not by definition require the establishment of a common external trade regime. One could conclude that the difficulties suggested for this proviso assessment in the case of a free-trade area would also not arise. However, a future panel will not derive much comfort on this point if it recalls the current Panel's definition provided above for "other regulations of commerce". As free-trade areas become more ambitious in their treatment of regulatory matters, the examination for such external effects could also be challenging. Interestingly, as broadly as the definition was framed, it also did not include the term "rule of origin". One is left to question whether such rules cannot be determined to be ORCs, no matter their impact upon trade. This question is explored in some more detail in the following chapter.

According to the Panel, Article XXIV is not *lex specialis* to the WTO and does not constitute a self-contained regime. The WTO is a single undertaking and Article XXIV is a part of it. Although the Appellate Body does grant regional proponents a conditional right to derogate from GATT obligations, a central basis of

---

[88] For example, Turkey Panel Report, para. 9.147, "... the flexibility inherent in sub-paragraph 8(a)(ii) allows for harmonious interpretation."

Turkey's case throughout was the notion that Article XXIV constitutes a special regime allowing parties to invoke a type of waiver as to GATT obligations owed to other WTO members. While the Appellate Body trimmed the panel conclusion on this point, both reports are in substantial agreement and travelled some length to extinguish this interpretation of Article XXIV in the practice. Regional parties who invoke Article XXIV as a defence in the absence of a CRTA determination of compatibility as to their particular formations run a certain legal risk by subjecting themselves to the juridical process when they choose to invoke this defence. Any criteria evolving from a panel or the Appellate Body in regard to the meaning of the internal trade requirement may be stricter than that which might evolve from the CRTA process. The CRTA is intended to reflect the circumstances of Members' diplomacy functioning on the basis of consensus. A dispute resolution panel is not so charged. This suggests that regional parties should now have some greater identifiable interest in determining the successful establishment of criteria within the CRTA process itself.

Finally, the Panel may have also introduced a new tool in the determination of what measures may be permitted in the course of intra-regional trade. This is captured in the final paragraphs dealing with Article 41 of the Vienna Convention (VCLT) governing the conditions by which two parties may modify as between them the obligations contained in a multilateral convention. The Panel recited the Article to indicate that two parties do not have a right to make a bilateral waiver if the modification is prohibited by the multilateral agreement governing the subject matter. Here, the adoption of discriminatory quantitative restrictions by Turkey as to India was found to be a violation of Article XI of the GATT, as such measures are prohibited by the GATT. Consider by analogy the situation for internal trade. If a bilateral modification cannot be permitted which would infringe the rights of third parties as guaranteed by GATT Article XI, then it may follow that regional members may not likewise modify the obligation imposed by the same Article XI in regard to intra-regional trade.

Although it would be easy to dismiss this legal theory of action for the likely absence of complainants, one can also recall from the GATT-1947 practice that challenges to externally applied measures undertaken by regional formations were also somewhat rare. Nevertheless, an absence of cases did not deter this Panel from concluding that no precedent of subsequent practice or acquiescence had ever been established. Just as the Panel relied upon GATT-1947 working group reviews to establish an absence of consensus on the legal point, some of these same reviews can also be recalled to identify a lack of consensus regarding the legality of intra-regional trade restrictive measures.

As the WTO jurisprudence developed, an additional case arose concerning the exemption between regional members for measures in the form of safeguards. The discussion now turns to this action between the EC and Argentina.

10.9   Argentina Footwear Appellate Body Report

10.9.1   *Introduction and factual background*

According to the Appellate Body summary,[89] this action resulted from safeguards on certain footwear products applied by Argentina as a result of an investigation and a resolution adopted in 1997. The investigation undertaken and the provisional duties imposed were notified by Argentina to the WTO Committee on Safeguards. On September 1 of 1997, the Committee was notified of the country's intent to impose a definitive safeguard measure. The EC commenced the action before the Panel arguing that Argentina's measures were inconsistent with a number of Articles of the WTO Agreement on Safeguards. The Panel determined that Argentina's measures were inconsistent with Articles 2 and 4 of the Agreement and that there was nullification and impairment of the EC's benefits to be derived under the Safeguards Agreement within the meaning of Article 3.8 of the WTO Dispute Settlement Understanding. On September 14, 1999, Argentina made notification of its intent to appeal certain issues of law. The EC also raised certain points relevant to Article XXIV. During the course of the appeal, Indonesia and the United States each filed third participant's submissions.[90]

10.9.2   *Issues presented on appeal relating to Article XXIV*

Argentina argued on appeal that the Panel had made errors in its legal reasoning concerning the interpretation of the WTO Agreement on Safeguards as it related to Argentina's claimed right (or obligation) according to Article XXIV of the GATT. For Argentina, this Article operated so as to exclude its MERCOSUR trading partners from the application of safeguard measures. As the Panel itself framed this issue,

"... the essential question is whether Argentina was permitted under the Safeguards Agreement to take imports into account in the analysis of injury factors ... and was at the same time permitted to exclude countries from the application of the safeguard measure imposed".[91]

According to Argentina on appeal, the Panel misinterpreted footnote 1 to Article 2.1 of the Agreement by imposing a requirement to apply safeguards to other customs union members when the investigation of the safeguard action was based

---

[89] *Argentina – Safeguard Measures on Imports of Footwear*, Report of the Appellate Body, WT/DS121/AB/R, 14 December, 1999.

[90] Generally, Argentina AB Report, paras. 2-6.

[91] Argentina Panel Report, para. 8.75, recited in Argentina AB Report at paragraph 100.

upon all sources i.e., including custom union member sources.[92] The Panel had identified the first and third sentences of footnote 1 to apply to the Argentina safeguards, and had also found that the context of Article 2.1 and its footnote was that of Article 2.2, providing that, "(s)afeguard measures shall be applied to a product being imported irrespective of its source."[93] As the Panel found,

> "The ordinary meaning of Article 2.2 would appear to imply that, as a result of a member-State-specific investigation, safeguard measures have to be imposed on a non-discriminatory basis against all sources of supply, regardless of whether they originate from within or from outside of the customs union".[94]

On appeal, Argentina claimed that Article 2.1 of the Agreement comprehensively addresses all the conditions applicable to a safeguard investigation made by a Member who is also a party to a customs union.[95] That there is no stated requirement to impose the measures on customs union members is indicated by footnote 1, where the fourth sentenced indicated an absence of consensus in the drafting of the Agreement as regarding the relationship between the Safeguards Agreement and Article XXIV.[96] Argentina cited negotiating history to indicate that while a proposal had been made to require customs unions to apply measures upon its own members, this proposal was not accepted for the final text of the footnote. Thus, the Panel made an error in incorporating into the Agreement a requirement that had been rejected outright in the process of negotiation.[97]

On a related issue of appeal, Argentina argued that the Panel, by requiring a match between the sources investigated for the determination of injury and the sources subject to the application of a safeguard, had introduced a new "parallelism" requirement into the Agreement. No such requirement could be validated in the provisions of the Agreement. Article 5 of the Agreement only required that a

---

[92] Argentina AB Report, para. 12.
[93] Argentina Panel Report, para. 8.84, recited in Argentina AB Report at paragraph 102.
[94] Ibid.
[95] Article 2.1 of the Safeguard Agreement reads, "(A) member (footnote 1) may apply a safeguard measure to a product only if that Member has determined, pursuant to the provisions set out below, that such product is being imported into its territory in such increased quantities, absolute or relative to domestic production, and under such conditions as to cause or threaten to cause serious injury to the domestic industry that produces like or directly competitive products."
[96] Footnote 1 of Article 2.1 reads as follows. "A customs union may apply a safeguard measure as a single unit or on behalf of a member State. When a customs union applies a safeguard measure as a single unit, all the requirements for the determination of serious injury or threat thereof under this Agreement shall be based on the conditions existing in the customs union as a whole. When a safeguard measure is applied on behalf of a member State, all the requirements for the determination of serious injury or threat thereof shall be based on the conditions existing in that member State and the measure shall be limited to that member State. *Nothing in this Agreement prejudges the interpretation of the relationship between Article XIX and paragraph 8 of Article XXIV of GATT 1994* ". (italics added).
[97] Argentina AB Report, para. 13 with note 27.

measure may not exceed what is required to remedy the injury. "In Argentina's view, the only "parallelism" on which the Members agreed is that only the market where injury is found can apply safeguard measures."[98]

For its part, the European Communities endorsed the Panel's conclusion that a parallelism requirement existed as an aspect of the Agreement. Summarising its position,

> "(B)y taking into consideration imports from MERCOSUR countries for the purposes of making its injury determination, even though it never intended to impose measures on those imports, Argentina violated its obligation under the Agreement on Safeguards and Article XIX of the GATT 1994".[99]

However, at the oral hearing before the Appellate Body the EC objected to the manner in which the Panel had interpreted GATT Article XXIV and Article 2.2 of the Agreement, as it argued that the analysis made of Article XXIV was unnecessary in order to conclude that a parallelism requirement existed. Since no claim relating to the legal status of MERCOSUR was made in the case before the Panel, it was not necessary for the Panel to engage in an analysis of the safeguard measures at all within the context of an Article XXIV arrangement.[100] This course undertaken by the Panel resulted from Argentina's argument that Article XXIV (and certain MERCOSUR regulations) prevented it from imposing safeguard measures on other MERCOSUR countries. As summarised by the Appellate Body, following an analysis of Article XXIV, the Panel concluded that Article XXIV:8 did not prevent Argentina "from applying safeguard measures to all sources of supply, i.e., third countries as well as other member States of MERCOSUR."[101]

Indonesia concurred with the EC opinion in its third-party appellate submission stating that Argentina's interpretation of footnote 1 was incorrect, as no safeguard action had ever been taken *by a customs union*. Rather, Argentina had acted independently and on its own behalf. Footnote 1 says nothing about the obligation of a member of a customs union acting individually.[102] Indonesia further questioned whether Article XXIV could apply at all to the circumstances at hand, since the members of MERCOSUR had never notified the customs union under Article XXIV of either GATT 1947 or 1994.[103]

---

[98] Argentina AB Report, para. 14. The Panel's reference to parallelism is found at paragraph 8.87 of the Report. It states, "… the two options offered by the footnote to Article 2.1 in conjunction with Article 2.2 imply a *parallelism* between the scope of … *investigation* and the scope of the *application*. (emphasis in original), as recited in Argentina AB Report, para. 103.

[99] Argentian AB Report, para. 27.

[100] Ibid. The Report states that this matter was raised by the EC at oral hearing and stating that EC had indicated there that no parties had appealed on the apparent presumption made by the Panel that Article XXIV was applicable to the case.

[101] Argentina Panel Report, para. 8.101, recited in Argentina AB Report, para. 104.

[102] Argentina AB Report, para. 53.

[103] Ibid.

In its third-party submission, the United States referred to the drafting history of the agreement, as spelled out by the Panel, and noted that footnote 1 followed the word "Member" as contained in Article 2.1. This was done in order to deal with the status of the European Community in the GATT. The United States also argued that the Panel made an error in referring to Article XXIV, as the MERCOSUR had been notified under the Enabling Clause providing for differential and more favourable treatment of developing countries.[104] Thus, the reference made by the Panel to footnote 1 of Article 2.1 of the Agreement was, "legally irrelevant in this case."[105]

10.10   Appellate Body treatment of Article XXIV issues

Based upon the submissions, the Appellate Body stated the legal issue relating to Article XXIV as,

> "whether the Panel erred in its interpretation and application of Article 2 of the *Agreement on Safeguards* and Article XXIV of the GATT 1994 as these provisions relate to the application of the safeguard measure at issue in this case".[106]

10.10.1 *Whether measures were attributable to Argentina*

Central to this question is the role of the non-discrimination requirement on the application of a safeguard. As stated in Article 2 of the Agreement, would this requirement prevail or be inferior to a possible exception from MFN provided in Article XXIV for certain regional trade agreements? For the Panel, Article 2 appeared to prevail, at least for member specific investigations, as it concluded that,

> "... in the case of a customs union the imposition of a safeguard measure only on third-country sources of supply cannot be justified on the basis of a member-state specific investigation that finds serious injury or threat thereof caused by imports from all sources of supply from within and outside a customs union".[107]

One should clarify that the Panel did not rule that a customs union is prevented from excluding other members from the application of a safeguard when it acts on behalf of a single member State. Rather, since footnote 1 permits a customs union to investigate on behalf of a single member, the parallelism requirement raised by

---

[104] Argentina AB Report, para. 64 and 65. The Enabling Clause, "Decision on Differential and More Favourable Treatment, Reciprocity and Fuller Participation of Developing Countries", L/4903, adopted 28 November 1979, BISD 26S/203, as cited in the AB Report, note 57.

[105] Ibid.

[106] Argentina AB Report, para. 70 (c).

[107] Argentina Panel Report, para. 8.102, recited in Argentina AB Report, para. 105.

the Panel throughout would require that, as long as other member sources were excluded from the investigation, other members could also then be excluded from the application. The difficulty for the Panel in this case appeared to be a use of an Article XXIV exception that would allow customs union members to contribute to an injury that would then be remedied only by non-members. The Panel ruling does not suggest that a customs union acts unlawfully in all cases if it excludes application of the measure on other customs union members.

The Appellate Body took a more pre-emptive course in line with the EC, Indonesia and United States' submissions. It ruled that footnote 1 did not apply at all to the facts at hand. According to it, the investigation and the application of the safeguards were never undertaken by the MERCOSUR customs union *on behalf of* Argentina, but rather only by Argentina and on its own behalf. The Appellate Body did recognise that the transitional measures undertaken by the MERCOSUR decision delegated the investigation and application of safeguards to the member states individually.[108] It also recognised that according to the same transitional measures, MERCOSUR had established and had exercised the authority of WTO notification for the investigation and application.[109] These actions were considered irrelevant in the determination of the application of footnote 1 since,

> "(I)t is Argentina that is a Member of the WTO for the purposes of Article 2 of the *Agreement on Safeguards*, and it is Argentina that applied the safeguard measures after conducting an investigation of products into *its* territory and the effects of those imports on *its* domestic industry".[110]

To comment, this is a difficult construction if one considers that footnote 1 expressly contemplates the notion that a customs union may act on behalf of an individual member also in regard to *its* territory and the injury effects on *its* domestic industry. To the extent that these elements have been chosen to be emphasised by the Appellate Body, this does not appear to create a meaningful distinction between an action to be covered according to footnote 1, and one that would not fall under that footnote. Rather, the distinction being made by the Appellate Body must be oriented to the question of which party acted to investigate and implement the measure, i.e., a customs union or an individual member. It is, however, unclear as to what bearing this distinction should actually have when in the presence of a legal customs union and in the course of determining whether the measure has been

---

[108] Argentina AB Report, para. 107, citing Common Market Decision 17/96. "According to these transitional provisions, the investigation procedure for the adoption of safeguard measures was to be conducted by the competent authorities of the State Party in question, applying relevant national legislation."

[109] Argentina AB Report, note 96. The measures were so notified by Uruguay acting as Pro Tempore President of MERCOSUR, as indicated by the Appellate Body.

[110] Argentina AB Report, para. 108.

investigated and applied in a parallel manner. If a customs union is present, then the heart of the issue would appear to be the parallel application as far as the question of discriminatory investigation and application is concerned.[111] However, by eliminating the consideration of footnote 1, the Appellate Body also conveniently avoided any need to determine whether or not MERCOSUR actually is a customs union, a point contested by both the Indonesia and United States submissions, but not the EC. This question is not so easy to answer, if for no other reason, than because of the types of transitional arrangements employed by MERCOSUR. These demonstrate a significant, although perhaps temporary, residual commercial power held by the individual members. Here, these retained powers may have appeared in any case to be sufficient to have the measure assigned to Argentina rather than to MERCOSUR.

10.10.2 *The application of Article XXIV to the Argentina measures*

Having reversed the Panel and eliminated footnote 1 from any consideration, the Appellate Body went on to treat the possibility of an Article XXIV exception for Argentina's actions as a distinct legal issue. Argentina appeared to have claimed that Article XXIV either excused or mandated the selective application. The difference between the two issues can be highlighted. Footnote 1, if applicable, would have only gone so far as to authorise a customs union to act on behalf of an individual member in investigating *for whom* the measure may be applied (which territory may enact the safeguard). It does not say anything regarding *upon whom* a measure may be imposed. The Article XXIV question takes up this *upon whom* aspect by addressing whether members may be exempted from the application of the measures. As the Appellate Body restated,

> "(T)his issue, as the Panel itself observed, is whether Argentina, after including imports from all sources in its investigation of "increased imports" into its territory and the consequent effects of such imports on its domestic footwear industry, was justified in excluding other MERCOSUR member States from the application of the safeguard measures".[112]

The Appellate Body ruled that the resolution of this question was to be found in the context of the rule enunciated by its earlier Report in the Turkey textiles case wherein it had been found that "Article XXIV may justify a measure which is inconsistent with certain other GATT provisions."[113] In the instant case however,

---

[111] This can be shown by modifying the facts wherein the customs union framework would allocate investigation to the individual member, like in the case at hand, but then retain the power of approval of the measure in a customs union institution. Then a measure authorised by the customs union would be applied by the individual member.

[112] Argentina AB Report, para. 109

[113] Ibid., citing Turkey AB Report, para. 58.

"As Argentina did not argue before the Panel that Article XXIV provided it with a defence against a finding of violation of a provisions of the GATT 1994, and as the Panel did not consider whether the safeguard measures at issue were introduced upon the formation of a customs union that fully meets the requirements of sub-paragraphs 8(a) and 5(a) of Article XXIV, we believe that the Panel erred in deciding that an examination of Article XXIV:8 of the GATT 1994 was relevant to its analysis of whether the safeguard measures at issue in this case were consistent with the provisions of Article 2 and 4 of the Agreement on Safeguards".[114]

To identify the particular GATT violation in question, a WTO Member, whether a customs union member or not, would have the power to investigate imports for the purposes of undertaking a safeguard measures from all sources. Therefore, the inconsistency referred to above must be based upon the investigation and application of the measures upon some WTO Members and not others, whether or not fashioned in a parallel manner. As the Appellate Body continued on to investigate the Panel's conclusion of "implied parallelism", the violation became apparent from its reading of Article 2.2 of the Agreement. Argentina violated this provision since its safeguard was not "applied to a product being imported irrespective of its source."[115] Thus, the Agreement required that Argentina, "apply those measures to imports from all sources, including from other MERCOSUR member States."[116] Finally,

"... we find that Argentina's investigation, which evaluated whether serious injury or the threat thereof was caused by imports from *all* sources, could only lead to the imposition of safeguard measures on imports from *all* sources. Therefore we conclude that Argentina's investigation, in this case, cannot serve as a basis for excluding imports from other MERCOSUR member States form the application of the safeguard measures".[117]

This constitutes the facial violation. A remaining point to clarify was whether this ruling included a conclusion that customs unions were without a legal right under Article XXIV to exclude members from a parallel application of safeguard measures, either on behalf of the entire union or for an individual member. In either case all customs union members would be excluded from the investigation of sources. As the Appellate Body indicated,

---

[114] Argentina AB Report, para. 110.
[115] Argentina AB Report, para. 112. See additional discussion on this point, Infra, Chapter Eleven, section 4.
[116] Ibid.
[117] Argentina AB Report, para. 113 (emphasis in original).

"... we wish to underscore that, as the issue is not raised in this appeal, we make no ruling on whether, as a general principle, a member of a customs union can exclude other members of that customs union from the application of a safeguard measure".[118]

That the possibility remains for a customs union to so exclude one of its own members from a safeguard is also exhibited by the Findings and Conclusions wherein the Appellate Body,

"(d) reverses the Panel's findings and conclusions relating to footnote 1 to Article 2.1 of the Agreement on Safeguards and Article XXIV of the GATT 1994, and concludes that Argentina, on the facts of this case, cannot justify the imposition of its safeguard measures only on non-MERCOSUR third country sources of supply on the *basis of an investigation* that found serious injury or threat thereof *caused by imports from all sources*, including imports from other MERCOSUR member States".[119]

10.11 Conclusion on the Argentina Reports

The Conclusion leaves open the possibility that Article XXIV acts to permit the exclusion of member sources from the application of a safeguard. The next question to raise is how would members validate a selective application in light of this Appellate Body Report and as it incorporated the test formulated in the Turkey Appellate Body Report. The next chapter will attempt to address this by seeking to integrate the two reports as they also reflect upon the systemic issues outlined by the WTO Committee on Regional Trade Agreements. Assuming that the investigation and application of the safeguard action are handled by the customs union either on behalf of a member or on behalf of itself in its entirety, this issue drops out of the discussion since footnote 1 to Article 2.1 of the Agreement is properly applied. As we will see, that the case concerns Article XIX safeguards raises some distinct issues for Articles XXIV and XIX that have not been resolved by either the Safeguards Agreement, the CRTA in its systemic treatment of Article XXIV issues, or by any consistent practice developed by regional parties. Finally, although the Argentina Panel was reversed on its treatment of Article XXIV, some issues discussed by the Panel would likely be revisited where an Article 2.2 violation was initially found and the customs union member then properly asserted its Article XXIV defence.

---

[118] Argentina AB Report, para. 114.
[119] Argentina AB Report, para. 151 (emphasis added).

Chapter 11
SYSTEMIC ISSUES IN THE CRTA

"If the General Agreement on Tariffs and Trade is to retain a significant influence in world trade policy, a new understanding of the meaning and application of Article XXIV is one of the issues that must be resolved. That Article, permitting the formation of customs unions and free-trade areas, is probably the most abused in the whole agreement and the heaviest cross the GATT has had to bear". *F. A. Haight, (1972).*

11.1 Introduction

As some WTO cases have now gone through both Panel and Appellate Body review, one might begin to outline the features of an interpretive framework for Article XXIV. The pattern could be set where judicial developments have moved ahead of the stumbling blocks that have infested the GATT review process since the earliest notified agreements. Although many of these stumbling blocks have represented the mutual interests of regional members to establish more flexible arrangements within autonomous regional regimes, others reflect honest and complex differences of opinion regarding the interpretation of the Article's requirements.

As these dispute settlement events have transpired, the WTO standing Committee on Regional Trade Agreements (CRTA) has also continued its assignment to attempt to qualify the large number of notified agreements and to continue the discussion regarding systemic issues.[1] The reports of the minutes of the CRTA, just as they were from the GATT working groups, have great value and should be reviewed on several counts. First, many of the old arguments from the GATT years can be documented as yet unresolved. In addition, new complexities have been added in the context of globalisation where agreements can be more extensive in capturing a wider range of movements. The occurrence of overlapping regional agreements (and systems) has also increased.

---

[1]   To paraphrase the terms of reference for the CRTA : a) to carry out examination of agreements and to present its report for appropriate action; b) to consider how the required reporting on the operation of such agreements should be carried out and to make appropriate recommendations; c) to develop procedures to improve the examination process; d) to consider the system implications of such agreements for the multilateral trading system and the relationship between them, and to make appropriate recommendations to the General Council; and e) to carry out additional functions assigned by the General Council. WTO, Document WT/L/127, para. 1.

As we have completed the review of the WTO cases to date, what is perhaps most interesting is to survey the CRTA discussion, as related by the delegates from their own recorded statements, and to make the comparison to the Panel and Appellate Body rulings. Especially for the so-called intractable issues, one can find statements on record that accord well with the direction taken by the Appellate Body. For those remaining contra to the legal developments, perhaps the burden shifting aspect of the review process will also play a role in revising these positions in the future.

11.2 CRTA systemic issues

The status of the work program of the Committee on Regional Trade Agreements (CRTA) can be outlined by way of introduction. According to the Committee's Annual Report for the year 1999, as of the end of third quarter of the year, a total of 118 regional trade agreements had been notified to the WTO. 93 of these were notified under GATT Article XXIV.[2] As indicated by the Report, of the 72 Agreements under its current purview, draft reports had been distributed and were under consideration for about one-half. While headway had been made in the examination of a number of regional trade agreements, the Committee was unable to indicate that it had finalised reports on any of the examinations.[3]

Besides the technical and administrative difficulties of reporting and reviewing individual agreements, it is also the case that an absence of consensus in the Committee regarding a number of outstanding interpretive issues continued to delay the review process.[4] This leads one to suggest that WTO case developments, as discussed in the previous chapter, can lend some clarity to the settlement of some of the outstanding systemic issues. However in approaching the application of WTO law to the CRTA process, some differences between adjudication and review of regional agreements may also be kept in mind. First, the CRTA is ma ndated by its terms of reference to carry out evaluation of agreements and to make a report recommending appropriate action. While this implies a judicial action by way of taking a decision, the CRTA process is not a judicial one, but is suggested

---

[2] CRTA, *Report (1999) of the Committee on Regional Trade Agreements to the General Council*, WT/REG/8, 11 October 1999, para. 5, attached to this text as Appendix Three. The figure includes accessions and parallel notifications on services arrangements as separate agreements. Fourteen regional trade agreements were notified under the Enabling Clause (Decision of 28 November 1979), and eleven under GATS Article V.

[3] CRTA, Ibid., para. 15. The comparable number of notified agreements for 1996 was 32. CRTA, First Session, Note on the Meeting of 21-22 May, 1996, WT/REG/M/1, para. 14. This number would reflect the backlog inherited by the CRTA as notified prior to establishment of the Committee.

[4] For example, "Two aspects in particular, SAT and ORCs, had been the subjects of lengthy discussions, but without any sign of any consensus being reached, and without sign of much willingness on the part of some to engage in the exercise". Statement by Hong Kong, CRTA, WT/REG/M/18, 22 July 1998, para. 48.

to be rather political in nature.[5] It may be offered in this vein that the CRTA operates within an "executive" sphere akin to administrative action that makes factual determinations having possible legal effect in later judicial review. If this characterisation is correct, it can be said that the CRTA is bound by WTO panel and AB law which has lent interpretations that can be applied to the process. However, it is not so clear as to how bound the CRTA is in exercising its authority in this more consensual process. Particularly, whether its "decisions" or recommendations are also subject to "appeal" in the DSU. This is only to suggest that the DSU legal developments may not be comparable to the situation of "lower" court that is clearly bound to apply its higher court rulings for new cases arriving on point.

Thus, while some case interpretations may appear to have far-reaching consequences for the CRTA process, the CRTA itself may not be so impressed. However, this same consideration of judicial/executive division within the WTO may also give rise to certain positive extensions of WTO case-law development that would not occur even in the context of later cases in the DSU. For example, it is suggested below that the Appellate Body's test for invoking an Article XXIV exception may apply as well to the rules that govern intra-regional trade. In the DSU context this is an acknowledged abstraction, as it is difficult to identify a complainant for such a case. Not so in the CRTA however, where reviewing parties can determine to apply such criteria without the presence of a complainant. Overall, it is believed that comparing the cases to the positions of delegates expressed in the CRTA is a helpful exercise. Over time, it is more likely than not that the legal interpretations will take hold in the CRTA.

11.2.1 *Interaction between regional trade agreements and the multilateral rules – generally*

Two opposing views of the relation between regional trade agreements and the multilateral system have generally been identified. As reported by the Secretariat, one view has held that Article XXIV only derogates from GATT Article I MFN. The other has held that the Article operates as an exception from any and all of the provisions of the GATT, provided that the regional members do not abridge the rights of third parties to the wider agreement.[6] One proponent of this second view has also cited international law regarding the interpretation of treaties in support. Thus, from the EC,

---

5   F. Roessler, *The Institutional Balance Between the Judicial and the Political Organs of the WTO*, paper presented at Harvard University, Conference titled, Efficiency, Equity and Legitimacy: The Multilateral Trading system at the Millennium, June 1-2, 2000, p. 9.

6   As summarised in CRTA, *Synopsis of "Systemic" Issues Related to Regional Trade Agreements*, Note by the Secretariat, WT/REG/W/37, 15 February 2000, para. 27.

"(A)rticle XXIV:4 contained a balance between the legitimacy of forming an RTA and the responsibility as a 'citizen of the GATT' to do so in a way which did not raise barriers to third-party trade. In other words, where barriers were lowered legitimately and preferentially between the parties to an agreement, the net position of third parties should not be affected. This was not surprising in light of international law on multilateral treaties, which held that generally, parties to a multilateral agreement could form subsequent agreements between a subset of the membership of the wider agreement, varying their rights and obligations as between themselves, provided they did not abridge the rights of third countries to the wider, underlying agreement. Article XXIV:4 seemed to do no more than to translate into the language of trade policy that wider principle".[7]

It is made clear from the Turkey Textiles Appellate Body Report that the more restrictive view limiting the Article XXIV exception only to Article I MFN has not been sustained. Rather, the proviso of Article XXIV:5 permits the possibility that other GATT Articles might also be violated by regional members when the conditions of the Appellate Body's test have been met.[8] However, the EC view that regional members may, "(vary) their rights and obligations as between themselves, provided they did not abridge the rights of third countries", may also be an overstatement to the extent that such a legal test varies from that formed by the AB as to non-members.

The better approach is to consider that the test employed by the Turkey AB Report applies for members and non-members alike. This would provide a limitation on the rights of members to suspend the operation of GATT Articles as between them. Rather, they must also show: a) that the arrangement overall meets the conditions of paragraphs 5 and 8 of Article XXIV; and b) that the infringement between members is necessary in order to complete the arrangement. This application of the test would allow the CRTA to apply the same examination criteria for members (paragraph 8) as it would then apply for non-members (paragraph 5). It would also place the burden upon regional members to justify internally trade-restrictive measures as necessary in order to complete the requirements of paragraph 8. Such a result is argued here to be appropriate.[9] For CRTA practice, this also sug-

---

[7] EC Statement, WT/REG/M/14, 24 November 1997, para. 13. It seems clear the reference is being made to the VCLT, Article 41, as discussed also Infra, Chapter Twelve.

[8] As formulated, GATT Article derogations are permitted where regional members have met all the requirements of Article XXIV, paragraphs 8 and 5, and where the violation or infringement is necessary in order to implement the regional trade agreement. WT/DS34/AB/R, para. 58.

[9] Thus for example, where regional members included a sectoral arrangement imposing trade intra-regional restrictions. They would be required according to the Turkey AB test to demonstrate that the regional agreement nevertheless complied with paragraph 8 coverage requirements, and if so, that the violation was "necessary" in order to complete the larger arrangement.

gests that the act of "contracting out" by regional members would be more limited to the unusual circumstances of adjustment within the interim period, or where paragraph 5 considerations dictated residual internally restrictive measures.

11.2.2 *Relationship between article XXIV provisions*

Much of the CRTA discussion revolves around the relationship between paragraphs four, five and eight of Article as these paragraphs contain the core legal requirements, or are said to inform the legal requirements.

11.2.2.1 The legal effect of paragraph 4, the trade-creation test
The interplay between the paragraphs can be seen in the role that different delegations assign to the provisions of Article XXIV:4. Some parties make the point that while paragraph 4 may not actually impose specific legal criteria of its own, it nevertheless informs the provisions overall by imposing certain economic goals within which the legal provisions should be interpreted. Specifically, this question is whether qualified formations should be made to show evidence of external trade creation, or at least be able to indicate that trade diversion will not occur as a result of the elimination of trade barriers between members. Thus, there has been an ongoing question of whether Article XXIV should entertain certain economic tests in conjunction with its legal criteria, and if so, how such a requirement should relate to the legal provisions. From Korea,

> "(S)ince there was no agreement as to the meaning of the term "substantially all the trade", it seemed the examination of trade effects of RTAs was very important." And, "... the Committee should not limit too narrowly the legal reading of paragraph 4".[10]

The view taken here has been that introducing an economic criteria undermines the paragraph 8 requirements, and results in a reading that paragraph 5 requirements, in light of this view of paragraph 4, would supersede paragraph 8. Some CRTA members appear to share a similar conclusion. From the United States,

> "With respect to the focus on economic rationale, she stressed that in a legal organization, Members needed to focus on what they had committed themselves to legally ... A key word in that paragraph (4) was 'should' -- the language did not read '*is* to

---

[10] CRTA, WT/REG/M/15, 13 January 1998, para. 20. According to the CRTA, this view has been supported in varying degrees by Australia, India, HKC, Japan and Korea. CRTA, WT/REG/W/37, 15 February 2000, para. 34 and note 77. This position is similar to Dam's 1963 argument, that Article XXIV:4 should be creatively re-interpreted to provide for a trade-creation standard. See this text, Part Two Conclusion.

facilitate trade' and '*will not* raise barriers'; ... There was no test in Article XXIV:4, and it was never intended that there should be one in it".[11]

The European Community representative also took the view that legal obligations as expressed took priority over economic considerations:

> "... as the United States representative had said, Article XXIV was a set of rights and obligations and part of an Agreement constructed from rights and obligations ... The key point made by his delegation earlier was that Article XXIV could not be used to support the argument that there ought to be an economic test applied in addition to the other rights and obligations contained in the Article in clearer terms...The questions arising with respect to trade creation and trade diversion and general questions of economics might fall under the heading of 'what the rules or rights and obligations ought to be'... Article XXIV did not support economic arguments as a basis for evaluating actual preferential trade agreements...".[12]

The question of whether paragraph 4 recites a distinct legal obligation within the Article has long been at issue, but has been resolved in favour of a non-obligatory construction by the Turkey Appellate Body. Recalling from Chapter Ten, paragraph 4 expresses "purposive" and not "operable" language. Thus,

> "It does not set forth a separate obligation itself, but, rather, sets forth the overriding and pervasive purpose for Article XXIV which is manifested in operative language in the specific obligations that are found elsewhere in Article XXIV".[13]

Although WTO Members who have been less regionally active have supported a trade-creation criteria, this view of the Article has been rejected. Rather, the legal requirements as already expressed in paragraph 8 and 5 control and give effect to the purpose expressed in paragraph 4. As such, the case for restraining future regional agreements in the review mechanism should not be based upon the trade diversion argument. What can be given emphasis instead is that the paragraph 8 requirements should be examined on their own merits in order to determine the actual coverage obligations necessary for regional parties to meet.

This similar consideration is evident for paragraph 4's relation to paragraph 5. As the Community representative indicated in the same comment, the view taken of Article XXIV:4 directly informs the requirements of Article XXIV:5 as this

---

[11] U.S. Statement, CRTA, WT/REG/M/15, 13 January 1998, para. 24. Similarly, "(T)he representative of Brazil said his delegation was of the view that the question of trade diversion or trade creation was not part of the test of conformity with Article XXIV ..." Ibid, at para. 21.

[12] EC Statement, CRTA, WT/REG/M/15, Ibid., para 25.

[13] WT/DS34/AB/R, para. 57.

paragraph describes the 'outward looking' or external requirements of a formation. Where Article XXIV:4 is not given the gloss of an additional economic-effects examination, then it follows that paragraph 5 would be interpreted as essentially a standstill provision not to raise new barriers to the trade of non-members by increasing duties or by other regulations of commerce (ORCs). As to paragraph 8, paragraph 5 would also then not be viewed as imposing a separate condition upon regional parties to avoid liberalising measures solely because they may generate externally diverting effects.

As the Appellate Body appears to have cleared away the issue of paragraph 4 and its trade creation overtones, it has also opened the avenue for a more constructive discussion regarding the content of the other paragraphs' obligations and the relationship between these remaining requirements, particularly for paragraphs 5 and 8.

11.2.2.2 Paragraph 5 and 8, the sequence of findings in examination

If it is understood that Article XXIV:4 can not expand the meaning of paragraph 5, then the important relationship between paragraphs 5 and 8 may also be illuminated. This text has argued that XXIV:8 requirements are inherently definitional to qualifying as either a free-trade area or customs union, and should derive an affirmative recommendation on that basis prior to any assessment of external effects which might fall under the tests required of paragraph 5. This view has also been taken up in part by the European Community in the CRTA minutes:

> "Paragraph 8 contained the internal definitions or tests which parties forming a customs union or an FTA had to meet in order to benefit form the general derogation contained in the opening sentence of Article XXIV:5, whereas separately paragraph 5(a) and (b) dealt with the relations between the partners to a preferential agreement and third parties".[14]

The Turkey Appellate Body has also appeared to take a position on this point. The two-part test provided by the AB required first that both paragraph 8 and 5 must be met; and second, that the measure must be necessary in order for the formation to be completed. However, as also indicated by the AB, it may not always be possible to make a determination on whether a measure would *prevent* the formation of a customs union, "without first determining whether there *is* a customs union."[15] This determination could not possibly be made in the course of an examination of paragraph 5, as this proviso pre-supposes that a customs union or free-trade area is

---

[14]   CRTA, WT/REG/M/16, para. 58, p. 14. From the U.S., "With regard to the question of whether Article XXIV:8 was internal or external, ... she would argue it was the piece which governed the internal regulations of the RTA, containing the definition of a customs union and an FTA."
[15]   WT/DS34/AB/R, para. 59.

being formed.[16] This should suggest that whether a plan and schedule constitutes a free-trade area or customs union can be determined prior to its implementation in the course of surveying the intent of the members as to their legal commitment to form such an arrangement. These matters would fall exclusively under paragraph 8.[17]

Therefore, if there is any argument for bifurcating an examination process in order to avoid an external-effects examination for otherwise non-qualified agreements, this point should be drawn at the juncture between paragraphs 8 and 5 so as to make a paragraph 8 finding prior to a paragraph 5 examination. If defects are presented in the qualification of an arrangement according to that considered first, the process would be essentially finished, or plans amended accordingly, as no affirmative recommendation would be obtained determining that a free-trade area or customs union was being formed. What is suggested is a bifurcated procedure whereby the first step must be passed prior to a consideration of the second.

Clarifying the examination in this manner would also contribute to a determination of what matters should be handled at which juncture. For example, the question of whether a trade liberalising measure undertaken according to paragraph 8 also presents certain negative external effects would be divisible, the external aspect considered in a second step of the procedure as relating to paragraph 5. In short, paragraph 8 would be viewed as listing requirements and criteria that are expected to be undertaken by regional parties, and not as a list of requirements that may be undertaken by regional parties as long as they do not hurt non-members.[18]

11.3   Individual Article provisions

11.3.1 *Article XXIV:8 (a) and (b), "substantially all trade"*

As reported by the Secretariat, a lack of consensus on the meaning of substantially all trade (SAT) has repeatedly led to impasse in the examination of regional trade agreements. As described, two approaches, not necessarily mutually exclusive, have been advanced since the GATT-1947 years. One is quantitative, using a type of statistical benchmark to designate a percentage of trade. The other is qualitative,

---

[16] Article XXIV:5 reads in part: "Accordingly, the provisions of this Agreement shall not prevent ... the formation of a customs union or of a free-trade area ... provided that ...".

[17] This interpretation was advanced in this text, Supra, Chapter Three Conclusion.

[18] An example of this second view is reflected in a number of comments that continue to assert that regional members may not prohibit the use of safeguards upon their internal trade. Here is a clear case where the settling of internal requirements according to Article XXIV:8 would inform the parameters of Article XXIV:5 considerations. For example, Japan comment on the elimination of emergency measures and anti-dumping actions in the Canada-Chile Free-trade Area. CRTA, WT/REG/38/M/2, paras. 9 and 10. The issue is discussed in greater detail below.

which refers to the notion that no sector (or major sector) could be excluded.[19] The Turkey Panel and the Appellate Body did not address the meaning of "substantially" on point as to the internal trade requirements of either customs unions or free-trade areas respectively according to sub-paragraphs 8 (a)(i) and (b). Rather, the discussion concerned its qualification as found in sub-paragraph 8(a)(ii), providing for the common external tariff requirement of a customs union. Thus, the term "substantially" was raised as to the phrase "substantially the same" duties and other regulations of commerce. With this distinction in mind, the Appellate body affirmed the Panel's view that the term "substantially" in this provided both quantitative and qualitative elements. If applicable to the internal trade context, this would suggest that the CRTA should disband the arguments for an exclusive approach either way, in favour of a combined treatment. While this does not provide a test by itself, it does eliminate the suggestions that one approach should be used exclusively.[20]

Along the same analogy between "substantially the same" and "substantially all" is also the difference in emphasis between a more flexible interpretation advanced by the Turkey Panel as compared to the Appellate Body. Although the AB commenced its analysis by repeating Dam's quip that "substantially" must refer to something less than "all", but something considerably more than "some", it went on to refute the Panel's notion that "comparable" duties and regulations could qualify for the requirement. In this, flexibility is available for regional members, but this flexibility is also limited. "Therefore, in our view something closely approximating 'sameness' is required ...".[21] Thus, "comparable" duties and regulations are not sufficient, and in rejecting this lower threshold, the AB also qualified the term "substantially". For Article XXIV:8(a)(ii), the phrase "substantially the same" trade regulations required a higher degree of "sameness", since the term "substantially" was understood by the Appellate Body to qualify the word "same".

While it was not necessary in this case for the Appellate Body to direct the same emphasis as to the internal trade requirement under sub-paragraphs 8 (a)(i) or (b), one can fairly determine that the same interpretation would control. Thus, the word "substantially" would be understood to qualify the word "all" for the purposes of the SAT requirement as well. Although one would not say that this offering would be sufficient to settle the longstanding issue over the meaning of the phrase, it does at least generate some guidance in support of a stronger as opposed to a weaker

---

[19] CRTA, WT/REG/W/37, 15 February 2000, para. 54. For qualitative, it is claimed that listing all sectors does not necessarily result in free trade. Ibid., para. 54 (a) and (b). There are arguments against using each approach exclusively. For quantitative, regional parties would then have license to exclude a set amount of trade. The U.S., Canada and the EC found certain objections to an Australian proposal to cover 95% of the Harmonized System (HS) tariff lines. See CRTA Note on the Meetings of 4-5 and 7-8 May, 1998, WT/REG/M/17, paras. 12-29.

[20] There are a number of combined approaches that have been advanced in the CRTA discussion on systemic issues. For one example, see Australia, WT/REG/W/22/add.1, paras. 9-10.

[21] WT/DS34/AB/R, paras. 48-50.

requirement. It will remain to be seen whether CRTA parties can derive from this expression some concrete basis for making examination under criteria with this emphasis.

11.3.2 *Partial preferences*

One aspect that could be challenged even while a defined standard does not emerge is the situation where trade in some sector is only partially liberalised between members by a positive preference, the remainder being left "uncovered" (assumedly) at MFN level. This should be accommodated in the interim period prior to a resolution of the trade to zero duty preference. However, delegate opinions clearly do not agree with this view. In the Examination of the Interim Agreement between Slovenia and the European Communities in March of 1998, the United States representative commented that it was difficult to discern whether substantially all the trade was being covered. Additionally, "(S)he saw no evidence in Article XXIV that allowed for preferences short of going to zero, and she invited the Parties to the Agreement to react to this. The representative of Hungary responded,

> "... since no sector was left out, it was irrelevant whether some sectors were treated in the Agreement itself, or in Protocols, Annexes or separate agreements. It was his delegation's firm view that nowhere in Article XXIV:8(b) was it in any way forbidden to grant preferential treatment to certain products at a level less than the m.f.n. rate but more than zero".[22]

The EC representative's response concurred with the view of Hungary.

> "His delegation had consistently argued for decades that it was perfectly possible to form a free trade agreement consistent with Article XXIV:8(b) with preferences contained within the agreement short of elimination. He would go so far as to suggest that that amounted to a sort of consistent subsequent practice within the broader rules of interpretation on international law".[23]

---

[22]   WTO, Committee on Regional Trade Agreements, Examination of the Interim Agreement between Slovenia and the European Communities, WT/REG32/M/1, 12 March 1998, paras. 13-17, pp. 3-4. Continuing from the Hungary representative: "Article XXIV:8(b) talked about elimination of duties on substantially all the trade, and if there were some duties which were decreased but not to zero, it did not mean that that was not in compliance with Article XXIV:8(b)." Ibid at para. 15.

[23]   Ibid., at para. 16. From the EC representative, "... so far as the provision of preference within a free trade agreement short of full elimination was concerned, there was a body of consistent subsequent practice within the WTO embracing Members well beyond the EC and its partners, which suggested that their interpretation was a reasonable one shared by at least a broad, if not a general, community of opinion." Ibid., para. 19. the U.S. representative replied, "While she found interesting the comment on the accepted body of opinion, she noted that in the WTO for tariff preferences they were either given through a waiver or through certain provisions of the Enabling Clause."

If subsequent practice developed on this point, it has done so in the absence of acquiescence of a significant number of other GATT parties. From the earlier working group practice, it cannot be documented that a resulting partial preference has ever been determined to qualify under the term "elimination". It may more likely be the case that resulting partial-preference sectors cannot be included under the concept of "elimination of duties" and be counted as a portion of the trade that has been dedicated to meet the SAT test. While it is apparent that the EC position on this question has not meaningfully advanced since the 1958 Overseas Association, it may also be the case that within the current legal setting of the WTO, that this position has become tenuous at best. Consider that a challenge would arise under MFN to extend the partial preference for a particular product to a non-member. This would raise the Article XXIV defence and the panel would be required to rule that, assuming that other trade was covered to sufficiently meet the SAT test, that it was "necessary" for the parties to engage this partial preference for this product in order to complete the regional formation. Given that parties have ten years under the Article to resolve transitional measures, it is difficult to imagine a panel ruling this test in favour of the regional members. It also seems plausible that in determining coverage for SAT, that the panel would be inclined to simply subtract the partial preference sectors from the total, since duties and/or other restrictive regulations of commerce had not been "eliminated". As in Bananas I and II, the panel could also recite the availability of the enabling clause and/or the general waiver provisions of Article XXV as the appropriate alternative means for Members to proceed with reductions less than to zero.

What comes forward from this example is the recognition that Article XXIV is a conditional exception and that the burden has been shifted to regional members who seek to invoke it. This allocation of burden affects the demonstration necessary to validate a particular GATT violation, but it also has impact upon the process of determining an SAT standard in the CRTA. If it is plausible or possible that a panel would proceed as above in regard to partial preferences, then the CRTA should likewise adopt a similar approach in examinations. We will discuss this point further below in the section on institutional considerations, but for now, a single point is offered. The absence of a consensus on the meaning of SAT has benefited regional proponents in the past. However, barring an amendment to the Article, it does not appear that this will be the case in the future.

11.3.3 *Relationship of listed-article exceptions as to the scope of SAT*

One area where more juridical guidance could contribute to defining the SAT requirement is in the relationship of the excepted Articles of XI-XV and XX as to the term "substantially." Here the interpretation made by both the Turkey reports is not clear as the discussion of the permitted internal measures was only ancillary to the question of externally-applied quantitative restrictions. For the Panel, the exception listing did appear as some evidence of the flexibility intended by the use of the term "substantially".[24] The Appellate Body agreed that "some flexibility" was offered, but cautioned that the degree of flexibility was, "limited by the requirement that 'duties and other restrictive regulations of commerce' be 'eliminated with respect to substantially all' internal trade."[25]

There may be two views possible for these listed Articles that address a common point as to the meaning of substantially-all trade. One is whether the requirement should be calculated so as to deduct from SAT all of the trade that is affected by measures taken according to the listed exceptions. This would suggest that the SAT requirement would not constitute a "once-made" determination. Since regional members could invoke the listed exceptions before, during and after their formation, the amount of trade covered for SAT would necessarily vary over time. In this regard, one may recall an earlier working group review on the Yaoundé II Convention wherein the EEC took this position. There, the EEC indicated that it would notify the GATT parties at the time when internally restrictive measures exceeded a level necessary to retain coverage for substantially all trade. By this view, regional agreements are conceded as necessarily dynamic and may, at any given point in time, be either within or without the SAT requirement. This would have implications for challenges in the DSU, since the Panel might necessarily determine that compliance with paragraph 8 was being made for a post-interim regional agreement at the moment in time that the defence was being raised. There is also an implication for the CRTA review, which is accorded the authority to engage in biennial reviews, since it also suggests that CRTA members have a continuing capacity to alter or withdraw a previous recommendations as affected by the circumstances found upon later periodic reviews.

An alternative view would consider that the listed exceptions in Article XXIV do not relate to the meeting of the SAT requirement at all. Here, the text of paragraph 8 would be read to mean that members must cover SAT, *except* where necessary for those restrictions permitted in the listed Articles. This interpretation would permit regional members to adopt measures affecting internal trade in the context of the listed GATT Articles, and according to requirements imposed by those provisions for those exceptions, few of which allow permanent deviations in any case. Measures undertaken by members that fell outside the listed Articles would remain a continuing factor in determining the availability of the exception, as outlined above. It would seem that an advantage to this characterisation is that the legal security of a recommendation in the CRTA would be promoted, and the defence of Article XXIV for a qualified agreement would be more secure in a dispute proceeding.

---

[24] "We note ... the possibility for parties to a customs union to maintain certain restrictions of commerce on their trade with each other, including quantitative restrictions (... where necessary, those permitted under Articles ...)". This implies that even for "substantially-all trade ... ", certain WTO compatible restrictions can be maintained. "WT/DS34/R, paras. 9.146-9.151,at para. 9.150.

[25] WT/DS34/AB/R, para. 48.

It does not appear from the cases that a clue to the interpretation either way has been forwarded on this point. The argument here, and as developed below, is that the second view is most appropriate to the realisation of an operable system to qualify agreements. This would mean that the CRTA undertakes an examination of an agreement prospectively as regarding the final outcome outlined to be achieved by regional members. This is based upon details of the plan and schedule forwarded by the members. Measures sought to be retained (or not stated to be subject to elimination) would be a factor in assessing the SAT requirement. There would be no examination of measures falling under the listed Articles exceptions, except perhaps following the interim period and in regard to the requirement of "necessity".

The possibility of this simplified approach would also however be conditioned upon a conclusion to the issue of the exhaustive listing. The resulting interpretation would either have to affirm for final agreements that the listing of Articles was exhaustive, or alternatively, that any non-listed exceptions undertaken by members would be subject to ongoing examination in the context of the SAT requirement. Both for the CRTA and for DSU proceedings, this would infer that the application of restrictive measures between regional members not falling under the provisions of either Articles XI-XV and XX, would be undertaken at the risk of the members in regard to their compliance with SAT.

This second option appears to have been endorsed also by the Argentina Footwear Panel, but in its permissive view of regional safeguards, other problems arise. In order to validate or reject the approach, a more detailed discussion on the issue of the exhaustive listing which incorporates the reports from the Turkey textiles and Argentina Footwear cases is required.

11.4   Paragraph 8 and the exhaustive listing

The debate definitely continues in the CRTA over the Article XXIV:8 listing of exception articles (XI-XV and XX), as they may either constitute an exhaustive or non-exhaustive listing. For an example from Japan,

> "With regard to the list of exception in Article XXIV:8, his delegation's position...was that the fact that Article XXI (security exceptions) had not been included indicated that the list was not exhaustive; thus this paragraph should be considered in the context of other provisions and the spirit of the WTO as a whole. Regarding the application of safeguards, it seemed there was discrimination when RTA parties did not apply safeguards to each other".[26]

---

[26]   CRTA, WT/REG/M/15, para. 18, p. 6. The U.S. position is apparently the same, but not elaborating. Ibid., para. 57, at p. 20.

The opposing view has been expressed by Australia, that a completed formation should not permit the use of safeguard measures between its members. This view and the middle "permissive" view is summarised in an EC delegate comment.

> "The Australian paper seemed to argue that Article XIX measures must not be applied between the members of an RTA ... His own delegation saw this as permitted but not mandatory".[27]

However, the EC has also suggested that this conclusion should not be the same for customs unions. Thus,

> "(I)t seemed that within the customs union the definition only made sense if Article XIX were not included in the list of exceptions in Article XXIV:8(a)(i). There could only be the continuation of safeguard measures in the long run, at the end of the transition period, in circumstances where it was not a proper customs union, as it did not make sense to maintain such a restriction within a customs union".[28]

The argument in favour of an exhaustive listing was set out in Chapter 3.3.1. To briefly recall, that analysis referred to the placement of Article XXI in the Havana Charter for the ITO as a general provision, and not within the Commercial Policy chapter where the other exceptions were then located, together with the regional exception itself. Although the text here has also acknowledged that there are can be differences between customs unions and free-trade areas in regard to their respective capacity to eliminate internal trade restrictions, it has also cautioned that generalisations on this point are difficult. Examples of incomplete customs union can be raised, as well as more complete free-trade areas.[29] However, whatever validity is offered by the EC comment regarding the differences between the two forms, this distinction is certainly not reflected by Article XXIV:8 (a) and (b), as both sup paragraphs contain an identical listing of exception Articles. Further, drafting history, if anything, suggests more of the intent to convey or "extend" the customs union internal requirements to the free-trade area exception, and not to provide for a separate legal regime for the qualification of free-trade areas. Thus, one sees in the stated internal requirements an alignment of the provisions overall for free-trade areas and customs unions on the point of permitted exceptions.

The issue can be stated as whether the listing of Articles is exhaustive as describing *only* the measures that can be permitted between regional members. Here, the Turkey Appellate Body only noted that the terms of the sub-paragraph provide,

---

27 CRTA, WT/REG/M/14, para. 9, p. 4.
28 CRTA, REG/M/15, para. 44, p. 17.
29 See for discussion,Supra, Chapter 8.1.

"... that members of a customs union may maintain, where necessary, in their internal trade, certain restrictive regulations of commerce that are otherwise permitted under Article XI through XV and under Article XX of the GATT 1994".[30]

11.4.1 *Regional exclusion as a violation of the Safeguards Agreement*

This comment does not say that parties may *only* maintain such measures, but a determination on this point was also not at issue. As also related previously, the Argentina Appellate Body found that a customs union (or one of its members) violates Article 2.2 of the WTO Agreement on Safeguards (Safeguards Agreement) any time a safeguard is imposed that excludes another member from the application. This follows from the Appellate Body's recognition that Article 2.2 of the Agreement is unequivocal (and pre-eminent) in requiring that safeguard measures shall be applied to a product imported irrespective of its source. This infringement occurs, according to the Agreement on Safeguards, whether or not the application of the measure was made in a manner parallel to the sources of imports investigated. Thus, Article XIX as elaborated by the Agreement has been interpreted to require that all WTO Members fashion non-discriminatory application of their safeguards, subject of course to the detailed provisions of the Safeguards Agreement. Therefore, in order to validate any selective application (excusing other members) by a member of a customs union, or by the customs union on a member's behalf the following point emerges. No matter how parallel the investigation and application was structured, it seems that it would be necessary for the regional member or the customs union to successfully invoke an Article XXIV defence.

As also recited previously, two conditions must be fulfilled to overcome a finding of GATT inconsistency. First, the customs union must meet all the requirements of the Article XXIV sub-paragraphs 8(a) and 5(a); and second, the formation of the customs union would be prevented if it were not allowed to introduce the measure. As a part of sub-paragraph 8(a), regional members must meet the SAT test and eliminate duties and other restrictive regulations of commerce, except where necessary measures undertaken according to Articles XI-XV and XX (the listed Articles exceptions). Given this, it appears from the nature of the MFN violation as established by Article 2.2 of the Safeguards Agreement, and together with the defence necessary to validate a selective safeguard application, that the status of Article XIX as it is omitted from the list of exception Articles is going to be

---

[30] WT/DS34/AB/R, para. 48.

[31] It would argue that members are not permitted (or required) to apply intra-regional safeguards as a condition to meeting the paragraph 8 requirements. In conjunction with footnote one of the Safeguards Agreement, as long as member sources of injury are subtracted, the conditions of Article XXIV require that this deviation from the Article 2.2 of the Safeguards agreement is necessary to meet the Article XXIV requirements.

raised directly by the respondent party.[31] A resolution of the legal status of sub-paragraph 8(a)'s listed exception of Articles (XI-XV and XX) would be a pre-condition to the resolution of such a case.

Since Article XIX is not on the exceptions list, there is an argument to make that customs union members *and* free-trade area members *may not* have authority according to the requirements to make a non-selective non-discriminatory application of a safeguard. Thus, the issue could be stated as follows. Whether it is necessary for a customs union (or free-trade area) to make a selective investigation and application of its safeguard (so that other members are excluded from the measure) in order to meet the requirements as imposed by sub-paragraph 8(a)(i) or 8 (b) of Article XXIV?[32]

11.4.2 *Argentina Panel's permissive finding*

The Argentina Panel addressed this question as Argentina argued that it was compelled by Article XXIV:8 to apply its safeguards selectively and to omit other members. The EC's position was contrary, that Article XXIV:8 requirements on this point were not prohibitive but permissive. The Panel's summary of the EC position states that,

> "(A)rticle XXIV of the GATT *permits* the members of a customs union or free-trade area to decide whether, when applying a safeguard measure pursuant to Article XIX of GATT 1994 and the Agreement on Safeguards, to exempt other members of the customs union or free-trade area from the measure".[33]

This view could suggest that the customs union would determine in any particular case that a safeguard would be applied selectively or not. By inclusion, it also would encompass the view that a customs union could decide to make *all* of its safeguards selective or make *all* of its safeguards non-selective. This could occur by a treaty provision or by an authorised institutional enactment. In short, the permissive approach indicates that a regional grouping can treat the selectivity issue as a matter of choice, without the result having any legal implications on the paragraph 8 requirements.

The Panel appeared to identify this question as that left open by footnote 1 of Article 2.1 of the Safeguards Agreement, as the note states that the primary provision is not intended to pre-judge the relationship between Article XIX and paragraph 8 of Article XXIV. The Panel went on to recognise that a larger number of

---

[32] This does not mean however that the customs union would necessarily have to include the sources of injury caused by other customs union members in its investigation.

[33] Argentina Panel Report, para. 8.94, italics added.

regional trade agreements do impose safeguards upon intra-regional trade, while a few have chosen to prohibit such measures.[34] The Panel then ruled outright that Article XXIV:8 did not prohibit the use of intra-regional safeguards:

"(A)lthough the list of exceptions in Article XXIV:8 of GATT clearly does not include Article XIX, in our view, that paragraph does not necessarily prohibit the imposition of safeguard measures between the constituent territories of a customs union or free-trade area during their formation or after their completion".[35]

This would be seem to be an explicit adoption of the position for a non-exhaustive listing, and as this was advanced by the EEC also in the original Overseas Association report of 1958. This conclusion flowed from the Panel's analysis of the Article, wherein the adoption of a safeguard measure in any particular case may not overall undermine the substantially-all trade requirement. The Panel did leave open the possibility that an infringement of the SAT requirement could occur by the excessive use of safeguards between members.

"Thus we do not exclude the possibility that extensive use of safeguard measures within regional integration areas for prolonged periods could run counter to the requirement to liberalise 'substantially all trade' within a regional integration area. In our view the express omission of Article XIX of GATT from the lists of exceptions in Article XXIV:8 of GATT read in combination with the requirement to eliminate all duties or other restrictions of commerce on 'substantially all trade' within a customs union, leaves both options open, i.e., abolition of the possibility to impose safeguard measures between the member States of a customs union as well as the maintenance thereof".[36]

Support for this conclusion by the Panel was found in the difficulty of reconciling the Article's provisions for interim agreements with any interpretation permitting a selective prohibition. Thus, for transitional arrangements such as MERCOSUR,

"… the temporary lack of full integration of 'substantially all trade' due to the maintenance of intra-regional safeguards clauses would still be justifiable within this transitional status of the customs union. Accordingly, pending the completion of integration within MERCOSUR, the requirements of Article XXIV would not force Argentina to apply safeguard measures exclusively against third countries".[37]

---

[34] Argentina Panel Report, para. 8.96.
[35] Argentina Panel Report, para. 8.97.
[36] Ibid.
[37] Argentina Panel Report, para. 8.98.

It is not clear from this why the circumstances of interim arrangements should have any bearing on the issue of the exhaustive listing. A customs union or a free-trade area plan could be required to demonstrate, at the time of CRTA review, that *after* the interim period, that all selective safeguards will be eliminated between the members. Since interim agreements are limited by the GATT-1994 Understanding on the Interpretation of Article XXIV to a ten-year period, except for unusual circumstances, transitional selective measures would normally have ten years to be eliminated as applied to the trade between the members in any case. The factual issue on assessment should be whether the customs union or free-trade area plan is demonstrating evidence of a commitment undertaken by the members to eliminate intra-regional safeguards. Following the interim period, the arrangement could be assessed anew on the question of whether this condition had been fulfilled in fact. Thus, the point that such measures might be maintained during the interim period would seem to be irrelevant to the primary legal question, that being the legal status of the listing of Article exceptions as exhaustive or not. After all, the interim period contemplated by the Panel as above is only that: interim. Assuming that a CRTA review was timely prior to implementation, there is no reason to conclude that the maintenance of interim safeguards between members should violate the paragraph 8 prohibition, if the exclusion of Article XIX from the listed exceptions is a prohibition, or have any bearing on whether the arrangement would ultimately comply with the SAT requirement.

The Panel however ruled that the omission was not a prohibition, but rather an option for regional members, by its statement that,

> "That there is no doubt in our minds that the letter and spirit of Article XXIV:8 of GATT *permit* member States of a customs union to agree on the elimination of the possibility to impose safeguard measures between the constituent parties".[38]

The Panel adopted the argument made for permissive selectivity that was offered by the EC. Although it was not expanded upon, this EC position, as reported, highlighted the exceptional and temporary nature of safeguards, and the limitation of their application to only single products. These characteristics could also therefore be examined for possibly providing some reason for the omission of Article XIX from the paragraph 8 exceptions, while yet remaining a lawfully permissive option as between members, as according to the Panel. These considerations are discussed further below.

First however, the permissive possibility does appear to deviate from the requirement of Article 2.2 of the Agreement on Safeguards as the Appellate Body

---

[38] Argentina Panel Report, para. 8.99 (italics added). But, it then went on to apparently indicate that while Argentina and MERCOSUR may have provided as much, that they nevertheless retained the option of imposing selective safeguards when the customs union acts in its entirety. It is not clear how this second point goes to the issue.

found this to be an unqualified obligation, which establishes the point of GATT violation in the first instance. Whether or not safeguards are permissive between members would seem to then require a ruling by a panel that either a) the definition of a qualified agreement did not require a reference to the listing of Articles exceptions or b) that the maintenance of any permissive safeguards between regional members was necessary in order to complete the formation. As to post-interim formations retaining safeguards, the second point could be difficult to establish.

As to the definitional aspect, the Panel might have located the ambiguity in paragraph 8 that would have permitted a finding that the elimination of intra-regional safeguards was only optional as between members, or considered the inconsistency resulting from a permissive construction. Recalling the relevant text here,

"8.(a) A customs union shall be understood to mean the substitution of a single customs territory for two or more customs territories, so that

(i) duties and other restrictive regulations of commerce (except where necessary, those permitted under Article XI, XII, XIII, XIV, XV and XX) are eliminated with respect to substantially all the trade between constituent territories of the union or at least with respect to substantially all the trade in products originating in such territories ...".

Other restrictive regulations of commerce (ORRCs) are not duties, suggesting that the listed Articles are qualifying the term "other restrictive regulations of commerce". Assuming that a safeguard is also an ORRC, the paragraph calls for the elimination of such regulations of commerce *except where necessary* for those listed Articles themselves. As such, there seems to be little ambiguity in this text as it appears on its face to only permit the use of measures encompassed by the listed Articles. Rather, by referring the obligation to eliminate ORRCs and duties together to the SAT requirement, one could also conclude, at least following the Panel's reasoning, that it was wholly redundant to provide any of the listed Articles. Obviously, something more is at work in this construction.

One might identify that an ambiguity arises when considering the meaning of *necessity,* as to which events would raise the circumstances of permitting the use of the measures. *Necessity* could be viewed as a wholly internal phenomenon derived from the trade problems caused by the process of regional integration between the members. The listed articles would be then be those (only) permitted to address these adjustments, and also within the context of a final customs union or free-trade area. Article XIX measures are not one of the remedies permitted. In the alternative, the circumstances of necessity may arise from members taking actions in response to global or external conditions, which then must also necessarily be applied intra-regionally in order to either be effective, or possibly, to avoid undue harm to non-members in the application of such measures. In this construction all other types of restrictions, including those found for Article XIX or Article

VI, would always be permitted between members as they *may* be applied to address intra-regional trade problems, unlike the listed exceptions which *must* be applied internally when applied at all. This would support the Panel's interpretation.

11.4.3 *The permissive v. obligatory construction*

Hudec and Southwick carefully framed this *may or must* question and resolved it in favour of the latter view.[39] This was based upon their examination of the types of measures contained in the Articles listing. These would tend to be globally applied to all parties, would tend to apply across a range of products rather than as to particular products, and would also result from the types of problems caused by imports from whatever source. In all cases, great damage to non-members would result in selective applications wherein regional members would unfairly fill the demand caused by the application of the external measures upon non-member sources. Thus, their view of the exception listing is that it only acts to designate the types of exceptions that *must* be applied upon intra-regional trade when undertaken at all. One difficulty with this position, as acknowledged by the authors, is that in any particular case, an Article XIX action may also fall within this same rubric, considering the damage that can be done to non-members where both members and non-members are sources of the injury.

Their view does however fit well with the Panel's finding and the EC's position on the permissiveness of intra-regional safeguards. This is confirmed by Hudec and Southwick's contemplation that, as regional integration may evolve to an integrated market, that members then may then cease to apply the listed measures between them. However, this possibility also suggests an alternative view of the exceptions that would affirm support for the exhaustive listing. According to the customs union requirement in paragraph 8,

> "(A) customs union shall be understood to mean the substitution of a single customs territory for two or more customs territories, so that …".

Perhaps contrary to Hudec and Southwick, this provision suggests that the exceptions listed in paragraph 8(a) refer to a description of a finally completed customs union. In this completed edifice, the union as a whole and its individual members could certainly continue to encounter the various global problems described by Hudec and Southwick. However, to the extent that the listed articles permit GATT parties (generally) to address such global problems by the institution of measures which affect trade, as they are stated exceptions to GATT obligations, this does not mean that the listed measures themselves are equivalent to commercial policy

---

[39] R. Hudec and J. Southwick, *Regionalism and WTO Rules*, in M. Rodríguez, P. Low, B. Kotschwar (Eds.), **Trade Rules in the Making**, Organization of American States and the Brookings Institution, Washington D.C., 1999, pp. 47-80.

measures. Thus, a completed customs union could yet *even then* permit the exceptional measures to be applied as between its members and, as dictated by the listed Articles' own non-discrimination requirements, also upon non-members.

This point flows from the limitations inherent in the concept of the substitution of a single customs territory, as this substitution of territory does not infer the transfer of all national economic sovereign power. Thus, member states to a customs union could reasonably be understood to retain certain powers to intervene for domestic agriculture supply purposes, (Article XI:2, (a)-(c)), responsibility over their own currencies and external financial positions (Article XII), and responsibility for their individual IMF obligations (Article XV). As important, individual members could be understood to retain national (police power) authority for their own health and safety measures and the other legitimate objectives all encompassed by GATT Article XX. Even a cursory view of EC developments through the years would validate the position that these matters extend well beyond the legal parameters of the customs union, and even beyond the common and then internal market.[40]

What does fall within the concept of *substitution* of a customs territory are those matters dealing with commercial policy. These are the measures intended to provide a domestic protection benefit to domestic producers. Included here would be the use of tariff duties (to be eliminated), and other restrictive regulations of commerce, i.e., measures other than duties, such as quantitative restrictions (to be eliminated). Measures undertaken to address injury for either dumping or for emergency action on imports also fall within the gambit of commercial policy measures as they are also addressed to the domestic protection of producers.

Thus, while one can agree with Hudec and Southwick's characterisation of the listed measures as those addressing global concerns, the listed exceptions also appear to share a broader framework in that they do not describe measures intended to address commercial policy concerns at all. Rather, they are measures enacted for purposes that remain well within the sovereign domain of members that would not likely ever be accorded to a customs union by operation of Article XXIV and its requirement of substitution of customs territories. Since the Article employs the term *substitution* in defining a customs union, it would seem more reasonable to conclude that the measures attributable to individual territory commercial policy are to be substituted by the customs territory as a whole for the purpose of making consistent external applications. Otherwise, there would not be a true *substitution* of territories, or rather, such a substitution would only be effective for some commercial policy purposes, but not for others.

If this reading is correct, then the "permissive" construction argued by the EC, and as adopted by the Argentina Panel is inconsistent and should be rejected outright. In the permissive view, a customs union would be required to establish a

---

[40] GATT Article XXI also refers to matters that do not fall under the category of policy measures, but which affect trade.

common external regime by applying substantially the same duties and other regulations of commerce to the trade of territories not within the union (Article XXIV:8(a)(ii)). It would not, however, be likewise obliged to assume any authority for other commercial instruments that could have the effect of undermining this harmonisation entirely. Individual member-states could continue to operate their anti-dumping and safeguard regimes in respect to other members, therefore necessarily retaining the power to conduct individual commercial policy as to the trade of non-members. The resulting territory would not be given the capacity to harmonise these individual measures externally. Alternatively, if the customs union did have the power to harmonise the application of such measures externally, then one would query, by what legal basis would its members have to continue to derive an authority to apply such measures as to the other members?[41]

The final argument for the "permissive" construction is found in the provisions of paragraph 8(b) for free-trade areas. For them, there is no compelled substitution of a single customs territory for constituent territories, but rather only a "group of two or more customs territories…" Since no new territory is created, these members may retain national commercial power as a matter of GATT law. However, it should be recalled from Chapter Two that the free-trade area provisions of Article XXIV do not inform the customs union provisions. Rather, the drafting history is clear that the opposite transaction occurred whereby the United States proposals for customs unions were forwarded at Geneva and settled there. As indicated, the free-trade area notion was not advanced until the Havana sessions. At this time, the listed exceptions were also included and the term "substantially" was moved to its present position as qualifying the term "trade", rather than the term "elimination".[42]

Hudec and Southwick have suggested that this relocation reflected the new flexibility required in the Article by the insertion of the listing of Articles permitted as exceptions. One could also suggest that the term could have been relocated to accommodate the free-trade area exception. As they also indicate, this is a speculative matter. However, what is not so speculative is that the final result established an identical set of internal requirements for both customs unions and free-trade areas. Thus, while the possibility must have been evident that a different list of Article exceptions could have been entertained to vary the requirements between customs unions and free-trade areas, this was not done. Thus, if there is any paral-

---

41   However, as suggested by Hudec and Southwick, there remains the possibility of severe hardship for non-members which flows from any construction mandating that a safeguard taken by a union must be applied selectively so as to exempt all customs union members from its application. This problem appears to be resolved by footnote 1 to Article 2.1 of the Safeguards Agreement. There it is provided that a customs union may act on behalf of a single member. Third-party trade to the rest of the union need not be detrimentally affected where this trade is not injuring the other union members.

42   The earlier draft stated, "all tariffs and other restrictive regulations of commerce are substantially eliminated".

lel interpretation to be made between sub-paragraphs 8(a) and 8(b), the customs union provisions should be seen as informing those for free-trade areas, and not the other way around.

In this respect, one can always argue that in order to avoid conflicting interpretations between the provisions, that the customs union requirements should be "read down" to reflect what is only possible for a free-trade area. Essentially, this is the permissive argument. More convincingly, one can argue by the same logic that the free-trade area provisions should be "read up" to those of the customs union. Since free-trade areas need not form a substitution of customs territories, differing commercial policy measures as directed to non-members would occur as a matter of course. This does not however mandate that those same commercial policy measures need to be applied to the trade of other members, nor that they are necessarily permitted to be so applied by Article XXIV.

11.4.4 *Safeguards Conclusion: parallelism and the exhaustive list*

A remaining point to clarify is whether the Argentina Appellate Body has foreclosed any later interpretation in favour of an exhaustive listing. The AB did conclude that a customs union member committed an initial violation in excluding other members from the application of a safeguard, whether this application was made in parallel with the sources of investigation or not. As stated,

> "... we wish to underscore that, as the issue is not raised in this appeal, we make no ruling on whether, as a general principle, a member of a customs union *can exclude* other members of that customs union from the application of a safeguard measure".[43]

That the possibility remains for a customs union to so exclude one of its own members from a safeguard is also exhibited by the Findings and Conclusions wherein the Appellate Body,

> "(d) reverses the Panel's findings and conclusions relating to footnote 1 to Article 2.1 of the Agreement on Safeguards and Article XXIV of the GATT 1994, and concludes that Argentina, on the facts of this case, cannot justify the imposition of its safeguard measures only on non-MERCOSUR third country sources of supply on the *basis of an investigation* that found serious injury or threat thereof *caused by imports from all sources*, including imports from other MERCOSUR member States".[44]

If it is the case that a fully fledged customs union can meet the requirements of the GATT and its Safeguard Agreement by making selective investigations and appli-

---

[43] Argentina AB Report, para. 114, italics added.
[44] Argentina AB Report, para. 151. Italics added.

cations of safeguards in parallel, then a point of clarity has been added to the legal practice under Article XXIV. The introduction of "parallelism", which seems to be installed by footnote 1 to the Safeguards Agreement, calls for equity in the application of safeguards which matches the sources of imports investigated to support the action. If a single member, rather than the union as a whole is being injured, it appears more than reasonable that the trade of third parties to the union should not be disrupted disproportionately. Likewise if the union is injured as a whole, then territory treatment would suggest that its measures be applied to the territory as a unit. What parallelism requires in this case is that injury caused by fellow union members be not attributed to third parties.

The possibility of a permissive choice between these avenues for customs unions and free-trade areas does however remain problematic in regard to intra-regional trade. Following the EC position expressed in the Argentina Panel, the union has an option to either exempt or include other members in the investigation and application of safeguards. This discretion can be employed on a case by case basis. However, parallelism itself does not seem to require this step. In the case where other members were required to be exempt from the application of a measure, their contribution to injury should also be disregarded in any case. While this may be a burden for transitional unions, for a completed union this would not be unreasonable in light of the concept of the substitution of territories. The introduction of the parallelism requirement appears to leave open the possibility that if regional members were required to exempt their partners from safeguard actions in respect of the exhaustive list, that this step can be taken without causing any undue injury to third parties.

It is clear that the EC favours this view of "permissive selective parallelism", as it raised the complaint in the Argentina case and advanced the permissive argument. However, where a customs union has retained a permissive option, there may be an additional difficulty where a complainant can argue that the respondent customs union was "picking and choosing" which safeguards would be applied globally and which would be applied selectively. Such discretion, whether or not consistent with the requirements of sub-paragraph 8(a), would be at least inconsistent with any respondent argument that it was compelled to make selective applications according to the listing of Articles exceptions. One should not have it both ways, arguing on one hand that parallel selectivity is necessary according to the Article, but then permissive on a case by case basis in practice.

11.5   ORCs and ORRCs

An extensive discussion in the CRTA is also engaged over the term "other regulations of commerce"(ORCs) as it is employed in paragraph 5 and paragraph 8(a)(ii), and the term "other restrictive regulations of commerce" (ORRCs) as it is found in paragraphs 8(a)(i) and (b). Issues raised include whether the two terms are synonymous, and whether they are or not, what types of regulatory and internal measures can be captured by either. This last question includes the issue of whether rules of origin can be considered an ORC or an ORRC. Again there is a tension between regional members and non-members on these questions, as internal liberalisation across a whole range of so-called regulatory activities would necessarily have the effect of reducing internal barriers at the expense to external trade.

The Turkey Panel offered an ambitious definition for ORCs, which was not rebutted by the Turkey Appellate Body. At least for the context of paragraph 5,

> "(M)ore broadly, the ordinary meaning of the terms 'other regulations of commerce' could be understood to include any regulation having an impact on trade (such as measures in the fields covered by WTO rules, e.g., sanitary and phytosanitary, customs valuation, anti-dumping, technical barriers to trade; as well as any other trade-related domestic regulation, e.g., environmental standards, export credit schemes). Given the dynamic nature of regional trade agreements, we consider that this is an evolving concept".[45]

The above definition appears to contemplate the entire range of government actions that can affect external trade, many internal and regulatory by nature, and certainly broader than the category of "measures other than duties" upon importation in the sense of Article XI.[46] While broad, since the analysis of paragraph 5 relates to the impact of undertaken measures upon non-members, there is every reason to believe that the above definition of ORCs would be sustained. This, at least to the extent that new restrictive regulatory measures undertaken in the course of a customs union or free-trade area formation had the effect of raising new barriers to trade of non-members.

However, the definition provided above may not find a ready application for the paragraph 8(a)(ii) use of the term ORC, as relating to a customs union formation. If the same test were applied, then the adoption of the substantially the same duties and ORCs must be undertaken by customs union members in regard to those factors provided above. This also seems to be an impossible construction, since it would require customs union members to externally harmonise all of the regulatory measures that can possibly affect trade. This is far in excess of what a customs union could reasonably be understood to require.[47]

Thus, one is left with an overwhelming sense that the Panel's definition must either be limited to paragraph 5 considerations, or since the identical term is used

---

[45] Turkey Panel Report, para. 9.120.

[46] GATT distinguishes between measures applied upon importation (Article XI) and those applied to imported goods (Article III) See, *Canada – Administration of the Foreign Investment Review Act*, Report of the Panel, 7 February, 1984, L/5504, 30S/140, paragraph 5.14.

[47] In point, only since the ECJ Opinion of 1/94 has it been explicitly ruled that the EC customs union has external exclusive competence in regard to technical barriers to trade.

in both paragraph 5 and 8, that the definition is simply overstated as it would define ORCs generally. One other possibility is that the definition may only be applicable to measures undertaken by regional members that are distinct and discriminatory as to non-members. Much of the traditional authority held to the view that Article XXIV provides for derogation only from Article I MFN. Even while the Turkey AB has opened the possibility for violation of other GATT Articles, Article I in any case acts to subject matters falling under paragraph four of GATT Article III to the MFN obligation. Thus, where one regional party accords internal treatment more favourably to another regional partner, for example by an act of recognition, this is also an MFN issue as to the non-member, by operation of Article I. Thus, regional parties can only advance selectively under these conditions if the agreement is qualified according to Article XXIV, and assumedly meeting the Turkey AB test for excusing a violation, or falls under other provisions for recognition that accord certain opportunities without reference to regional formations.[48]

However, this is not to say that Article XXIV requires parties to engage in non-tariff barrier liberalisation within the region via external harmonisation of these regulatory aspects, a conclusion that would be forced if the Panel definition applied also to ORCs as it is found in paragraph 8(a)(ii). Rather, one would take the view that where regional parties advance liberalisation in the field of non-tariff barriers, this action would not be "necessary" for the completion of the formation according to the requirements of paragraph 8. Further, any measures undertaken in eliminating non-tariff barriers should remain actionable according to paragraph 5 where such actions had the effect of raising new barriers to trade to non-members.

A caveat to this view is that ORCs as defined by the Panel also cannot possibly be equivalent to ORRCs as contained in paragraph 8. Unlike the imposition of a quantitative restriction, the regulatory aspects considered by the Panel are not easily encompassed in a reasonable definition of "other restrictive regulations of commerce". This limitation is raised outright if one considers that if the definition were to be the same for ORRCs, then any regulatory matter affecting trade between the parties would be subject to elimination as between them. The drafters certainly had no point of reference to contemplate this deeper level of regional integration. This consideration suggests that ORRCs and ORCs are not synonymous, assuming that the Panel definition is now GATT law. If a regulatory matter that is liberalised in the course of a regional formation affects third parties, then the consideration is brought under paragraph 5. If it constitutes a GATT violation (Article I), the regional members would not be in the position to argue its necessity, as in the case of the elimination of a tariff duty, since these matters are not, as argued here,

---

[48] For an author's analysis of mutual recognition for conformity assessment procedure for goods and services, see James Mathis, *Mutual Recognition Agreements – Transatlantic Parties and the Limits of Non-tariff Barrier Regionalism in the WTO*, Journal of World Trade, v. 32, No. 6, December 1998, pp. 5-31.

ORRCs, and are therefore not required to be eliminated. The effect of this interpretation would be to render discriminatory regulatory harmonisation actionable under GATT law.

Another ORC consideration would relate to the external effects of preferential rules of origin. This has also been raised by working group members through the years and continues as a source of commentary in the CRTA. One notes that origin rules were not listed in the Panel's definition provided above. A difficulty with forcing the expansive ORC definition to accommodate the external effects of rules of origin is found in the paragraph 5 text. In both paragraphs (a) and (b), there is a clear reference to comparing ORCs at the time of institution to the situation prior to the formation. Since the preferential rules of origin at issue would not have existed prior to the formation at all, there really is nothing to compare, unless one sought to compare the new preferential rules to the non-preferential pre-existing rules granting MFN treatment. That this has been a fairly intractable consideration might explain the obvious omission from the Panels own definition. However, the radical proposition to consider is, in the event new rules are more restrictive than the previous non-preferential rules, whether the burden should be on regional members to indicate why the additional restrictions are actually necessary in order to complete the regional formation.

This raises the question of preferential rules in conjunction with ORRCs. Since it seems that ORCs cannot be the same as ORRCs, one might also contemplate that rules of origin are to be considered in the second term for the purpose of qualifying substantially-all trade. Here there is no obvious requirement of a "pre-formation" comparison other than the expressed duty to eliminate ORRCs. But, this requirement can also be seen to raise a commensurate duty to "not create" new ORRCs. Since origin-basing is essential for the definition of the territory for which elimination of duties and ORRCs is to occur, both for customs unions and free-trade areas, whether such rules as applied comply with the SAT requirement would seem to fall under the scope of inquiry governed by ORRCs.[49] For an example, consider where a free-trade area contained a declaration liberalising all trade in industrial and agriculture products, but then only recognised as originating products those wholly-obtained from the soil of a member territory. The use of the origin rules in this case would clearly be acting to limit the scope of the free-trade commitment, and as it would necessarily be offered to be in compliance with the SAT requirement.

---

[49] For free-trade areas, the removal of barriers is to be accommodated for substantially all the trade between the parties as to products "originating in such territories." For customs unions, the same removal of barriers is to be accommodated for all the trade between the territories of the union, "or at least with respect to substantially all the trade in products originating in such territories." Article XXIV, paragraphs 8 (a) (i) and (b).

11.5.1 *Overlapping regional systems*

It was indicated above that the internal trade requirements for free-trade areas and customs unions are not distinguishable according to the provisions. Nevertheless, the functional distinction imposed by rules of origin is persistent in the choice of formations as these rules are a required aspect in any formation in the absence of a harmonised tariff. While origin rules have been long criticised for the ability to provide a protective effect as to trade with non-members, there is also an aspect of the rules that can serve internally protective purposes, as discussed in Chapter Eight. One recalls the following comment:

> "(T)he solution to these problems will not only condition the functioning of a free trade area; it will also, to some extent, govern its actual scope. The volume of goods which can circulate free of duty within the area will depend on whether these 'mixed' products are given exemption from duty in a more or less liberal manner".[50]

As suggested by Faber in the context of the EC-CEEC relationships, the development of full cumulation among pre-existing free-trade partners is a difficult task. This is subject not only to internal protective pressures opposing mixing of inputs in the larger destination market, but also within the partner markets where even a lesser diagonal treatment can conflict with certain industrial promotion and investment policy goals.[51]

The possibility for reviewing the quality of cumulation intended within a proposed formation may not be so far beyond the purview of CRTA review as to be disregarded as only a longer term prospect. This follows if one acknowledges that the design of the rules determines whether a declared free-trade area is in fact an "area", as this term is also entitled to be defined as a requirement, within which duties and other restrictive regulations of commerce have been eliminated. Thus for example, if an agreement between more than two members were proposed without provisions for diagonal cumulation, this might also suggest that a free-trade "area" is not being intended. If this result were a possibility, then the reverse scenario should also be considered. Thus, where a party establishes distinct free-trade areas with multiple parties but providing only for diagonal cumulation, then the later establishment of a regional cumulation system as between all of the members

---

[50] "This is a special problem, therefore, which does not arise in the customs union when the common external tariff has come into force." OEEC, (1957), Supra, Chapter 8, note 7, at p. 11.

[51] Pitou van Dijck, and Gerrit Faber, (Eds), **The External Economic Dimension of the European Union**, Kluwer Law International, Dordrecht, 1999. "Diagonal" referring here to where the use of materials which is designated as already originating in any of the partner countries is permitted. "Full" cumulation referring here to where processing is permitted to be cumulated between the free trade parties. Both terms can apply to one agreement with more than two parties, or where separate agreements are linked.

might also infer that a new free-trade area was being formed and should then be notified and reviewed accordingly.

It is more difficult to imagine that the capacity for review could be extended to require a full cumulation among members to a single agreement, even though true "area" treatment does more closely resemble the quality of movement by free circulation possible to achieve in a completed customs union. However, that free circulation is possible for a customs union does not mean that it is likewise mandated by the legal requirements. One can admit the possibility that between multiple parties to a single agreement, that a type of objection could be raised if the arrangement was internally bilateral, i.e., if only one territory retained cumulation with the others but the others did not provide for cumulation as between them. This formation could be treated *defacto* as creating not a single free-trade area, but rather two free-trade areas whereby one member was common to both.

This raises the most difficult scenario to contemplate upon review, but also pressing as a systemic issue. This is the resulting "area" which may fail to result from multiple (bilateral) free-trade areas with members common to more than one arrangement. The power to examine the overall structure of resulting arrangements, including previously examined formations, would be resisted by proponents, since each review is likely to be understood as limited to an analysis of the single agreement under notification. However, when one country is a party to more than one free trade area, the resulting structure of overlapping free trade areas has also been cited for its potential to provide for protective effects on the trade "between the members".

As some of these questions move to contemplate complex regional structures, it does appear that certain limitations to the text provisions of Article XXIV become more apparent. As the term "rule of origin" is not even stated in Article XXIV, one acknowledges that there is a stretch engaged by any argument that the Article has been given the instruments to address these aspects. As one notes the continuing work engaged to harmonise non-preferential rules as a result of Uruguay Round undertakings, it can only be hoped that Article XXIV considerations will eventually be brought into this process. An alternative would be to permit the subject of such rules to be expressly undertaken in negotiations regarding Articles XXIV in any later Round.

11.6   Institutional considerations

The test for excusing a GATT violation posed by the Turkey Appellate Body has raised the distinct possibility for a Panel to examine the compatibility of a regional agreement according to Article XXIV. Only a handful of regional agreements over the history of GATT and WTO have been able to derive affirmative compatibility recommendations regarding the requirements of Article XXIV. In the Turkey case, the Turkey-EC customs union was also without a recommendation from the

CRTA. The Panel found it unnecessary to undertake such an assessment, instead going forward from the position that the Turkey-EC arrangement was *arguendo* compatible. This coincided with the Panel's opinion that compatibility assessments were in any case within the province of the CRTA. This reflected the Panel's assessment that a division of authority was present between panels and the special procedures of the CRTA. Thus, in a case where the CRTA recommended that a regional formation was compatible with the requirements of Article XXIV, any particular measures could nonetheless be examined, according to the panel's authority to evaluate particular measures presented by a claimant. Likewise, the absence of an affirmative recommendation would also be irrelevant, at least for the Article XI measures contemplated in that case, since Article XXIV was determined by the Panel to not provide an exception for them in any case.

Since the Turkey Appellate Body reversed the panel's findings as to which measures can be excepted by Article XXIV, one can see how the AB then moved to the question of the scope of competence for panels to make compatibility assessments. However, there was, arguably, a shorthand prescription available not undertaken by the Appellate Body. Since Turkey had not obtained an affirmative recommendation from the CRTA in regard to the compatibility of its customs union, the defence could have been dismissed outright in the absence of Turkey's ability to invoke the exception as based upon such an affirmative compatibility recommendation. This would have recognised the jurisdictional demarcation suggested by the Panel. It would have presented two difficulties however. First, the question of the compatibility of this particular arrangement was actually not at issue on appeal before the Appellate Body. Thus, the Appellate Body was also limited by the argument that the Turkey-EC customs union was *arguendo* compatible. This particular twist may not likely occur again, since there is guidance now that the appropriate claimant response to a regional member invoking an Article XXIV exception in the future will be that the formation in question is *arguendo* in compatible. The second consideration is more persistent. If, as the Appellate Body argued, Article XXII and XXIII, as exhibited in the DSU provisions and together with Article XXIV:12, compel the panel to assess *any matter* arising from the application of Article XXIV, then complaints against measures as well as defences of compatibility must all be taken on board to give effect to the rights of WTO Members to invoke the DSU.

This aspect of the ruling is controversial. Not only from an institutional standpoint regarding the balance of powers between the judicial and rulemaking functions within the WTO, but also as a practical matter in that a complex analysis required by the Article XXIV provisions may now be required to be undertaken by future panels. However, as to the second point, having determined that panels have this power, one can also see the practical necessity rising for regional members to make their best efforts to obtain an affirmative clearance from the CRTA.[52] The

---

[52] One aspect that could be helpful for the CRTA is the Panel's affirmation that CRTA reviews need not be concerned with the legality of individual measures, since these are reserved by operation

alternative course would be to assume the legal risk incumbent by the process of panels making compatibility determinations according to paragraphs 8 and 5 on a case by case basis. In point, this appears to be the situation as it stands, but with one clear difference from past practice. The Appellate Body has made it plain, in its description of the two-part test, upon whom the burden of proving compatibility shall reside. Since a regional member invokes the defence, it is this member which must act affirmatively to establish the point. While this ruling was foreseen in the earlier GATT panel cases, now it is explicit.

The panel and AB developments have begun the process of shifting the burden to the proponents in an institutional sense as well. This may result in the eventual "judicialisation" of the CRTA special procedure. If one can now say that the legal status of trade agreements remains an open question in the absence of a recommendation or decision from the CRTA, then regional members should be able to calculate the value in seeking affirmative recommendations for their agreements in order to secure some legal security in a later challenge. Thus, although the weakness of a consensus-based process has worked against stricter interpretations in the past, perhaps this same consensus approach will reverse the burden to proponents in the future. If a recommendation or decision is necessary to secure an agreement from legal challenge, then every party with a vote can demand satisfaction on the agreement's compatibility. Instead of the lowest common denominator being tacitly accepted as the coverage requirement to be met, a higher threshold could emerge to satisfy review parties, who otherwise refuse to provide their acceptance of the plan. This would suggest that proponents might need to be far more flexible in amending provisions of trade agreements in the future then they have been in the past and that implementation should be delayed until the Committee has performed its tasks. A final effect on the process may be that the major regional proponents could support the development of more clear compatibility guidelines within which they can make their arguments for recommendations, since this would permit the processing of notified agreements which would result in recommendations.

It is also possible to consider that the review procedure be either bifurcated or even trifurcated. A positive recommendation according to consensus would have to be made at each step before passing to the next. The first step would entail compliance with Article XXIV:7 regarding the sufficiency and timeliness of information provided for the examination. If the reviewing delegates were not convinced that the material provided was adequate in meeting the disclosure guidelines, then no substantive review would commence. A second step would entail an affirmative

---

of GATT law for challenge in a later proceeding. See Panel Report, note 338: "(T)he purpose of examination (under) 5(a)…would not be to determine whether each individual duty or regulation existing or introduced …is consistent with all the provisions of the WTO Agreement …" Citing therein, Understanding read out by the Chairman of the Council for Trade in Goods, 20, Feb., 1995, (WT/REG3/1).

recommendation regarding paragraph 8, that the plan and schedule as submitted indicated that a free-trade area or customs union would result at the conclusion of the interim period. As argued throughout, the failure to obtain a recommendation on this paragraph would terminate the review, since there is little reason to raise paragraph 5 matters if a qualified agreement cannot be formed according to the plan of the members.

Part Five:
RESTRAINING REGIONALISM IN THE NEW MILLENNIUM

Introduction: WTO rules in a multipolar system

The WTO has come into full force and effect and the use of regional trade agreements by major parties has also been on the increase. As Martin Wolf recently noted, The European Union was the first of the economic powers to make a preferential trading system a central element in its commercial diplomacy. The United States followed in the 1980s, and continues to develop its strategy in the Free Trade for the Americas (FTAA) arrangements.

> "Now it is the turn of Asia. Soon every significant trading power will be scrambling for preferential access. Once it began, this spread of preferential trade was inevitable, since no country will willingly tolerate a permanent disadvantage in important markets".[1]

One view from U.S. business is that Europe has outpaced the Americans in exploiting the regional opportunities. The call from the Business Roundtable is to commence the "catching up" process, and not necessarily as an adjunct to multilateral trade liberalisation. Shortly after President G.W. Bush took office, the Roundtable issued a new report documenting the concerns of U.S. business in being excluded by the preferential agreements of other countries, notably the European Union.

> "But what emerges from the data is a picture of a United States that is active on disputes, WTO accessions and other important trade matters but is on the sidelines as regards major agreements, compared to our most important trading partners...(I)n conclusion, U.S. companies, workers and farmers are being surrounded by preferential trade agreements negotiated by their foreign competitors' governments. Time is running out for the United States to get back into the game."[2]

Cited by way of index in this report was use of discriminatory tariffs, services provisions, product standards and regulations, and investment protection and liberalisation. Thus, the field of play for the U.S. foreign government competitors would necessarily include, bilateral regional integration agreements, customs unions and

---

[1]   Martin Wolf, *Bush's Free Trade Responsibility*, Financial Times, April 25, 2001, p. 17.
[2]   U.S. Business Roundtable, *The Case for U.S. Trade Leadership: The United States Is Falling Behind*, Washington, D.C., 2001, pp. i and ii.

free-trade agreements, bilateral investment agreements, bilateral mutual recognition agreements, and even (perhaps) bilateral competition policy co-operation agreements.

A difference between Asia and its European and American counterparts is that the question of who is the leader is not yet settled and the battle may be just commencing. The emergence of China as a market player acceded to the WTO introduces a large economy factor and the likelihood of competition between major Asian economies on the regional markets. Perhaps Japan has already initiated its defensive response in outlining the prospects for regional integration with Singapore and South Korea. While China is not yet a WTO Member, its hands remain tied for regional endeavours by Article XXIV:10, as a voting waiver remains required for formations with non-Members. It has however already issued press statements suggesting that a preferential relationship with ASEAN or its members might be desirable. If large players in the neighbourhood determine that regionalism is the preferred response to EU and U.S. initiatives, then many territories may be too small to stand independent within the GATT MFN framework. They may either have to join together (higher levels of integration for ASEAN, or expansion of ANCZERTA for examples) or eventually join with one of the competing leaders in some possibly "ever-closer" arrangement.

The term "multipolar" is appearing more frequently to describe the presence of several trading systems each attached to a leading economy that serves as the fountain for trade, investment and technology transfer. Assumedly these systems would have to be nearly autonomous for the term to meaningfully apply in contrast with what is multilateral. However, before taking multipolarism for granted, the likelihood of such edifices of independent systems *not* emerging should also be considered. For now, this appears to hinge on two developments. The first would be the inability of the EC and the ACP territories to resolve a GATT-permissive vehicle for re-establishing the preferential system post-Lomé. This is a WTO question and commentators are already on record calling for revisions of GATT Article XXIV, as necessary, to permit the flexibility required to accommodate free-trade areas among greatly divergent development levels.[3] The old Overseas Association issue of applying the GATT development articles to Article XXIV:8 appears to be nearly ready for a replay.

The other factor is the U.S. and whether it will finalise its participation in the FTAA for North, Central, and South America. While this problem seems inextricably linked to the fast-track authority debate in Congress, recent comment suggests that the commercial interests, having long opposed the conditionality of human and

---

[3]   See for example, F. Matambalya and S. Wolf, *The Cotonou Agreement and the Challenges of Making the new EU-ACP Trade Regime WTO Compatible*, Journal of World Trade, V. 35, No. 1, 2001, pp. 123-144. From page 140, "(L)ikewise, it might be necessary to amend Article XXIV of the WTO, so that it caters for asymmetrical liberalisation."

labour rights or the environment, may well be on the point of compromising.[4] In any case, FTAA negotiations continue.

To attempt a balanced view, it is not clear at all that a multipolar paradigm can emerge with autonomous trading regimes intact. There are many "out of market" initiatives also taking place. Examples include the EC-Mexico free trade area (already signed), a Korea-Chile free-trade area (discussed), various Canadian proposals both east and west, the U.S. Opportunity preferences for Africa (enacting), etc. Only a customs union framework can effectively prevent individual members from reaching across to another hub and spoke framework. Such advanced integration is not likely to be in the offering for any of the large "North-South" systems being discussed here.[5]

There is also no uniform opinion that any of these developments are harmful for the interests of the multilateral trading system in the WTO or for the various agreements with which it is entrusted. As in the past however, economists and lawyers are looking into different aspects and asking different questions. For economists such as William Ethier, it is important to move beyond a Vinerian analysis of trade creation and diversion. Adding the factor of investment, multilateralism and North-South preferential arrangements, all are reinforcing each other where the multilateral system has led the need to open markets, and whereby later developed/developing country arrangements can deliver the meaningful development values of investment and trade. Thus,

"(6) The regional arrangements, by in effect internalizing a critical externality, help spread the benefits of the multilateral trading system around the globe and enhance its value to all participants, thereby reinforcing, rather than undermining, support for multilateralism".[6]

Whether the institutional fabric of the WTO is strong enough to bind the major actors as to each other does not seem to be at the heart of the issue. Certainly there is a constant hand wringing about the various EU-U.S. trade disputes. However,

---

4   See for example, J. Bhagwati, *How Not to Get Trade Going*, online article, his web site, 2001. He criticises the USTR for any emerging compromise on these issues in the fast-track authority debate.

5   For one critique of EU out-of-market agreements, See A. Sapir, *EC Regionalism at the Turn of the Millennium: Towards a New Paradigm*? CEPR, Discussion Paper Series, #2629, November 2000. From p. 10, "(T)he two emerging trade blocs need not, but could, become closed, or even antagonists."

6   W. Ethier, *Regionalism in a Multilateral World*, The Journal of Political Economy, V. 106, No. 6, Dec. 1998, pp. 1214-1245, at p. 1242. However, Ethier's point that the developing country derives a marginal edge over its non-regional counterparts also presents issues for the multilateral system, albeit not necessarily economic ones. Ibid., at point (5). See also, World Bank, **Trade Blocks**, World Bank Research Report, Washington D.C., 2000. From p. 90, "(O)ne reasonably firm conclusion is that for most developing countries, and especially for the poorer ones, a North-South RIA with a large industrial country is likely to be superior to a South-South RIA with a developing country".

panels and the Appellate Body have demonstrated that cases can be ruled in order, and the backlog from the GATT-47 era is nearly cleared. Implementation and retaliation remain issues, but these aspects were also problematic back when cases were being blocked. It is even possible that the strong legal fabric of the WTO itself is partly a cause of the trend to a multipolar trading system. As long as the leaders are "locked-in" then perhaps the system can tolerate a bit more sphere-of-influence building than it would or could otherwise.

This book throughout has taken a bit less *real politik* perspective than the above. Rather, the emphasis has been on considering the quality of the relationship between the members to regional systems. What level of free movement are members entitled to receive or compelled to grant within their agreements; and what duty of oversight (if any) does the WTO have to insure it? Perhaps the most cynical component of this study has been the recalling suggestion that a large country operating within a regional environment can do better to open and close the sectors of its interest than can its smaller partner. While this is not really a matter for legal proof, the problem of large-small has been prevalent in commercial diplomacy from the earliest times. In point, GATT MFN appears in significant part to have served as a remedial measure. Likewise, no one has either demonstrated, at least not to the author's satisfaction, that the process of globalisation has rendered the concept of dominance and dependency entirely irrelevant. That north-south regional integration is being favourably observed for certain economic aspects, as Ethier argues above, does not settle the question from a legal-system view. It may well be that individual developing countries do better in regional agreements with rich neighbours. That assumes among other things, that there is a meaningful prohibition against negative preferences within such systems, that preference for investment and trade does not result in price-raising dominant positions, that sensitive sectors on the developed economy's part are also opened, et cetera. It also doesn't say very much about whether the remaining commercial policy apparatus of the members retain any interest in participating in the residual multilateral system.

Thus, the law question, as it relates to multilateral/multipolar, has been approached here from the viewpoint of an existing rules-based system (the WTO and its Agreements). It asks two questions. Whether the principle rules of the system would have remaining force for members within regional systems as to the other regional members (internal)? Second, whether non-members also retain the right to apply the WTO rules to each of the regional members (external)? The second question is well on the way to having been answered in full by the WTO Dispute Settlement Body. The first question is overdue for an answer. To this author, the interests are identified first. To the extent that regional members can be either persuaded or compelled to continue applying GATT rules and regimes internally, then the risks incumbent to multipolarity, for whatever threat it may pose, should also be duly minimised.

This Part concludes the book with two chapters. Chapter Twelve raises the treaty law framework as found in the Vienna Convention on the Law of Treaties

(VCLT) as a context for analysing the question of applying GATT regimes within regional systems. This considers first the practice of modifications in GATT-1947 and then the VCLT provisions as they might apply to the WTO. This attempts to answer the first question posed above in the affirmative. The argument constructed is that there is no right of general waiver in the GATT other than by permissive joint action of the Members (GATT Article XXV), and for notification for suspension in other exception Articles, including GATT Article XXIV itself. This Article fulfils the VCLT requirement of an express permissive right of modification, subject of course to its own terms. For intra-regional contingent measures, the determination of whether they are permitted within this right of modification calls again the question of the exhaustive listing of Articles as contained in Article XXIV:8. If the listing is exahustive, then WTO does not extend to members the use of these measures. If the listing is not exhaustive, then members who apply internal measures remain subject to the other GATT rules.

The final chapter closes the book by providing an outlook on the EC--ACP arrangements being proposed for the resurrection of their free-trade area qualification. These new agreements outlined within the Cotonou Agreement framework will either accommodate themselves to the WTO rules, or as before, the rules will be stretched to accommodate them. Since the history of regionalism in the GATT was framed by so many of the issues presented in the original EEC Overseas Association, a return to the proposed successor will hopefully grant the reader a sense of completing the circle.

Chapter 12
A TREATY LAW FRAMEWORK FOR THE INTERNAL
TRADE REQUIREMENT

"(T)he Working Party is of the view that the text of paragraph 5(a) of Article XXV is general in character; ... (and) stating in respect to the analogous provision of the (ITO) charter that, 'it was finally agreed that all the obligations undertaken by members ... should come within the purview of this general provision'." *GATT BISD (1953).*

12.1 Introduction

This chapter turns to the treaty law context to resolve the question of whether GATT rules continue to apply in force between regional members as to their internally trade-restrictive measures. The factual question arises, whether hypothetical or not, where a regional member applies some MFN deviation or restrictive measure to the trade of another member, but then does not likewise apply the restriction to the trade of non-members, either on the same basis or to the same degree. Such practices could include deviations from Article I MFN, Article XI measures taken without Article XIII MFN application, and the use of selective safeguards without reference to GATT Article XIX and the WTO Agreement on Safeguards.

The sequence for discussion will be first to treat the concept of bilateral modification to GATT rules in a positivist manner as according to the context of GATT-1947 provisions themselves. However, since the WTO and its annexed Agreements constitutes a multilateral treaty, the relationship of relevant Articles of the Vienna Convention on the Law of Treaties (VCLT) is the primary topic considered in the chapter. The final section will analyse the manner in which GATT Article XXIV acts as a permissive provision for modification in the GATT as according to the VCLT analytical framework.

12.2 Modifications and Suspensions in GATT-47 practice

A violation of a GATT Article constitutes a nullification and impairment of an obligation as provided by GATT Article XXIII. This is actionable to the extent that a panel procedure may be commenced and a finding made that the practice violates the Article and should be modified to bring the conduct into conformity. That the offending measure flowed from the provisions of a later agreement made by two or more GATT parties would not affect this outcome as to a third party's GATT rights, except perhaps to the extent that the purpose of that agreement invoked some listed exception as a defence.[7]

As for two or more GATT parties agreeing to suspend GATT obligations only as between them, the picture of how GATT law should treat such modifications is not so historically clear. While in principle it appears that such modifications may well have constituted GATT violations, in practice, GATT's institutional capacity to exercise meaningful control over such suspensions appears to have been limited. Many of these agreed-upon deviations fell under the category of what came to be known in the GATT-47 era as "grey-area" measures, meaning either that their legality was not clearly established, or that it was uncertain whether GATT law was actually governing.

Most of the issues in this category relate to the interface between GATT Articles XI, XIX and XXV. GATT Article XXV constitutes the Agreement's provisions for approval of suspension of GATT Articles and obligations. This Article is a "catch all" requiring notification of the measure to be given validation only by the joint action of the Contracting Parties. The Article has been interpreted to govern all of the GATT obligations in the cases where some other stated exception cannot be applied. The practice for Article XXV shows that its scope extends not only to unilateral actions but to agreements enacted by subsets of GATT parties as well. Of the agreements located for examination however, all appear to relate to seeking a waiver from an obligation as to the GATT rights of third parties. As giving meaning to the notion of "grey area" measures, it has not been so clear that the Article XXV waiver is also applicable as a matter of law for subset agreements where the suspension is only effected as between those parties.

The practice in the area of voluntary export restraints is on point. Where parties avoided the Article XIX procedures either by non-notification or in failing to apply safeguards by MFN, it would seem that this "violation" could only be lawfully waived making an application of Article XXV. In point, a significant number of GATT parties believed these "agreements" to be in violation of GATT rules. Since they were not brought under Article XIX or Article XXV, they have been characterised as measures other than duties (Article XI), but also failing the Article XIII requirement of application by MFN. Thus, where these parties did not invoke Article XXV, the measure itself may well have been "out of GATT", but not necessarily suggesting that GATT rules had not been violated by the suspending agreement.

A meaningful number of GATT parties have not taken this legalistic a view of their own modification agreements where these were not seen to directly infringe the GATT rights of other parties. This suggests that parties have viewed their market restrictive agreements (negative preferences) as not subject to GATT rules even while acknowledging that their market liberalising agreements (positive preferen-

---

[7]   The justifications for redeeming a violating measure as found in Article XX and other listed exceptions.

ces) were subject to the rules. A notice and waiver would be required for the second but not for the first.

The legal basis for this distinction is also not clear, but it could flow from the viewpoint of the customary rules of interpretation acknowledging that States have the power to make later treaties and that those later in time override earlier inconsistent agreements. Parties may also differ on the question of whether a GATT rule is ever violated in the absence of a complainant. Functionally, since invoking the MFN obligations as contained in Article XIX or XIII could surely raise third-party complaints, a practice of engaging bilateral suspensions to avoid an examination of the particular measure might also have been expedient. However, within GATT commentary, there is a long line of argument indicating that GATT violation does occur in the case of bilateral suspension of the rules. For this context, a brief survey of some of this relevant comment on Articles XIX, XI, and XXV can be provided.

12.2.1 *Bilateral Safeguards*

A party invoking Article XIX appears to have an MFN obligation in regard to the undertaking of a safeguard. Dam advocated the view that MFN applied absolutely to the invocation of a safeguard measure irrespective of the particular source of injury.[8] His analysis compared Article XIX with that of Article XXVIII (for Modification of Schedules). He reasoned that although there was no necessity for the applicant party under Article XIX to offer compensatory readjustment of the tariff schedule,[9] MFN must be nevertheless be applied upon the initial act of suspension even to those parties who were not contributing to the injury. This was based upon his view that, "the general arguments against discriminatory tariffs apply as fully to Article XIX increases as to any other increases."[10] Thus, to consider how MFN applied to Article XIX, it was first necessary to observe the original suspension made by the applicant (MFN is required) and then, the retaliatory suspension made by the affected party. This second action was distinguishable and not, in his view, subject to MFN control since the only party that would be injured if MFN was not applied was the party invoking the safeguard in the first place.[11]

---

[8] Kenneth W. Dam, **The GATT: Law and International Economic Organization**, The University of Chicago Press, 1970, (Midway Reprint, 1977) at p. 100.

[9] An underlying assumption applied that a balancing of concessions would be effected by the retaliatory suspension of substantially equivalent concessions or other obligations. K. Dam, Ibid., at p. 100.

[10] K. Dam, Ibid., at p. 104.

[11] Dam found this distinction supported in the drafting of the text, where paragraph 3(a) of the Article dealing with retaliation refers to suspension of, "the application (of concessions) to the trade of contracting party taking such action." This reference is absent in paragraphs 1 and 2 dealing with original suspensions. It is also absent for emergency retaliation. Dam explains this difference as relating to the fact that only in non-emergency (ordinary) retaliation would the contracting parties have the opportunity to review and determine that the retaliatory action was appropriate in not applying MFN.

Dam's view could be cited to support the proposition that Article I MFN treatment is required when a party seeks to revoke a concession on a selective basis, whether this selective treatment is made upon the consent of the other GATT party or not.[12] Later reported discussions by the contracting parties tends to confirm his position as it was raised on occasion that Article XIX could be modified to accommodate selectivity. This was resolved in the WTO Agreement on Safeguards permitting certain selective applications as exceptions to the stated MFN rule. However, consistent with prior Secretariat opinion, there remained no acknowledgement that a non-notified selective restraint taken in whatever form would be in GATT conformity.[13]

12.2.2 *Measures other than duties*

If parties have not invoked a notification to establish a quantitative safeguard, then the measure undertaken would appear to come under Article XI. The issue of whether these suspensions are lawful as between two parties according to this Article can be taken up by the treatment of a hypothetical modifying the facts of an existing GATT Panel Report, the EC's 1987 challenge to the US-Japan Semiconductor Agreement.[14] The panel found that Article XI's prohibition against measures other than duties applied to a system of export monitoring as this was conducted by Japan as to the EC market. The issue of bilateral modification would have been raised if the EC had also framed a complaint alleging an Article XI violation as between Japan and the U.S. Assuming for hypothetical that the Japan restraint policy was also directed to the United States market as an aspect of that bilateral agreement, such a complaint would have raised the legal question of whether GATT permits an agreement between only two parties to suspend the application of Article XI. That Article XI measures were viewed as also subject to

---

An interpretive note to the Havana Charter is cited by him to support the construction whereby any suspension according to paragraphs 1(a), 1(b) and 3(b), "must not discriminate against imports from any Member country ...". However, the note was not provided in the final GATT provisions. Citing, Havana Charter, interpretive note, Ad Article 40, in K. Dam, 1970, Ibid., at p. 105, his note 57.

[12] The MFN obligation is stated as a requirement to accord it. it. Sir Gerald Fitzmourice in his third International Law Commission Report (U.N. Doc. A/CN.4/115), adopted an approach for "Legality of Object". Certain multilateral treaties were not of the mutually reciprocating type, but either *interdependent* by nature (a fundamental breach by one party would justify non performance by all others and not merely just as to the defaulting party) or *integral*, where the force of obligation was self-existent, absolute and inherent for each party, "and not dependent upon a corresponding performance by the others." S. Rosenne, **Breach of Treaty**, Grotius Publications, Cambridge, 1985, at p. 87.

[13] See generally on this point, GATT, **Analytical Index, Guide to GATT Law and Practice**, 6th Edition, 1994, pp. 493-495, citing Council discussions in 1978, and a 1984 Note by the Director-General recited from BISD 31S/136. "In fact, 'voluntary' export restraints are clearly contrary to the present rules of the General Agreement and are only 'outside the General Agreement' in the sense that governments have not brought them formally to the GATT for examination." Ibid.

[14] *Japan – Trade in Semi-Conductors*, Report of the Panel, GATT, 35 BISD 116, 4 May, 1988.

MFN requirements by Article XIII was well established from the GATT-47 Practice.[15] Thus, even without a reference to a treaty law interpretation, it could appear that the unequivocal nature of GATT Article XI's stated obligation would have led the panel to rule that the export restraint was also unlawful as to the consenting party.

12.2.3 *Practice as to Article XXV waivers*

If parties have not invoked Article XIX and have introduced a measure violating Article XI, but without MFN as required by Article XIII, then the measure would stand in violation of the GATT unless it received a waiver according to the Article XXV procedures. Article XXV, titled *Joint action,* grants to the contracting parties a right to waive GATT obligations as between the parties. Paragraph 5 of this Article provides that,

> "(I)n exceptional circumstances not elsewhere provided for in the Agreement, the CONTRACTING PARTIES may waive an obligation imposed upon a contracting party by this Agreement ...".

This provides the oversight function on behalf of the contracting parties in regard to subsets of parties seeking to suspend GATT obligations. It is applicable to all unilateral acts of a single party where that party is seeking to obtain a suspension of an obligation. It is exclusive as it grants the power of waiver to the Contracting Parties jointly rather than to any subset of them. The object of the waiver is also broad enough to encompass modifications entered by two or more parties to the Agreement, at least where they are suspending an obligation as to another GATT party, as has been asserted through the practice, and irrespective of whether the suspension was incorporated in some later agreement. As expressed by an early working group,

---

[15]   Again from the Director-General's 1984 Note, "Measures limiting exports to certain contracting parties only are, in any case, contrary to the provisions of Article XIII (except in the exceptional situations laid down in Article XIV) which provides for the non-discriminatory application of such restrictions." Supra, note 13. A contemporary view of legal interest would support such a claim by a member extending beyond just those parties who can show an infraction of their direct legal interest in the matter. *European Communities – Regime for the Importation, Sale and Distribution of Bananas,* WT/DS27/AB/R, 22 August 1997, paras. 132-138; at para. 136, and concurring with the panel that, "... with the increased interdependence of the global economy, ... Members have a greater stake in enforcing WTO rules than in the past since any deviation from the negotiated balance of rights and obligations is more likely than ever to affect them, directly or indirectly."

"(T)he Working Party is of the view that the text of paragraph 5(a) of Article XXV is general in character; ... (and) stating in respect to the analogous provision of the (ITO) charter that, 'it was finally agreed that all the obligations undertaken by members ... should come within the purview of this general provision'."[16]

One possible inference to draw is that under GATT practice, no single party had the legal authority under the Agreement to consent to the suspension of a GATT obligation owed to another without recourse to a specialised exception, and failing that, the joint action of all the Contracting Parties. This, since it is they who have been granted the power to, "waive an obligation imposed upon a contracting party by this Agreement."

However, the practice for Article XXV waivers appears to be confined to those cases where the waiver sought affected the rights of GATT parties non-signatories to the modification. Only a few possible examples from the earliest GATT practice can be cited where parties may have invoked the Article XXV procedure to suspend GATT rules as between only them.[17]

For affected third parties, the power of contracting parties to engage in the oversight of modifications as contained within subset agreements has definitely been asserted on a number of occasions. For only one example, the Decision of the Contracting Parties regarding the Agreements on Trade in Bovine Meat and Dairy Products (1980), made its determination that those "code" signatories could not only not act to amend the General Agreement, which would require unanimity, but further,

"3. The Contracting Parties also note that the existing rights and benefits under the GATT of contracting parties not being parties to these Agreements, including those derived from Article I, are not affected by these Agreements."[18]

Although not within the context of Article XXV, GATT Decisions have also held that GATT dispute resolution would not be competent to adjudicate the rights and obligations arising from the provisions of agreements made between two GATT parties. However, the question of whether such agreements may or may not be in

---

[16] "GATT, 1953 BISD, 86, recited in J. Jackson, **World Trade Law and the Law of GATT**, the Mitchie Company, Charlottesville, Virginia, 1969, at p. 544. See also, the Working Party for the European Coal and Steel Community (1952), GATT Analytical Index, Supra note 13 at p. 818, citing BISD 1S/85, p. 86, paras. 2-3

[17] John H. Jackson, *The Puzzle of GATT*, Journal of World Trade Law, Vol. 1, No. 2, 1967, p. 154. As Jackson characterised the early practice, one category of use for Article XXV was for, "waivers granted for import quotas on agriculture goods (primarily to 'legitimize' prior action otherwise in violation of GATT)." Also for MFN, "an action in 1951 that may have been a waiver, which 'took note' of US suspension of GATT treatment towards Czechoslovakia." Ibid., citing GATT, 1952 BISD, Vol. II, p. 36.

[18] L/4905, BISD 26S/201, para. 3. Quoted in GATT, Analytical Index, Supra note 13 at p. 935.

conformity with the GATT law has not been foreclosed. Thus, in the 1949 Margin of Preference Decision the Contracting Parties denied the availability of the dispute procedure to such an agreement, but added the following caveat:

> "(T)his Decision by its terms clearly refers only to the determination of the rights and obligations as between the parties to the bilateral agreement and arising from the agreement. It is, however, within the competence of the Contracting Parties to deter-mine whether action under such a bilateral agreement would or would not conflict with the provisions of the General Agreement."[19]

Here there appears to be a right preserved for non signatories to challenge not only the effects caused by the specialised agreement, but also the legality of the agree-ment itself as it may either conform or not conform with GATT obligations. Where the subset agreement has not been taken in accord with Article XIX or XXV, those enacting parties may not have a recourse to GATT dispute settlement regarding a breach of their own bilateral arrangement. Nevertheless, the inapplicability of dis-pute procedures does not equate to a conclusion that the agreement itself is GATT consistent.

Although the legal status of such agreements remained at issue in the GATT-47, it would also seem that notification would be required by parties making a modi-fication. Without notification, the other GATT parties have no basis or opportuni-ty to determine whether or not their rights have been affected. Where such a waiv-er was not sought, then one may conclude that the suspension of GATT obligations contained within may, at least, have been *voidable* by any later determination of the Contracting Parties acting jointly.[20]

12.3   The Vienna Convention (VCLT) and the WTO

For GATT-1947 practice, the question of modifications between two members has been examined solely within the context of the GATT Articles themselves. With the entry of the WTO and its explicit establishment as a treaty, a larger framework for interpreting the WTO Agreement has also been raised, as the customary rules of interpretation of public international law are now explicitly made applicable to the interpretation of provisions. The basis for this change derives from the WTO's es-tablishment as an international organisation (WTO Agreement, Article I and XIII),

---

[19]   Decision on Margin of Preference, adopted 9 August 1949, reported in Gatt, Analytical Index, Ibid, at p. 671. Some later GATT practice did take up the substantive terms of parties' bilateral agree-ments. See for example, *Canada - EC, (Wheat Exports) Article XXVIII Rights*, Award by the Arbitrator, (1991) BISD 37, p. 80.

[20]   As contrasted with *void*. As from the Blacks, "That may be avoided, or declared void; not abso-lutely void, or void in itself." **Blacks Law Dictionary**, rev. 4th ed., West Publishing, St. Paul, 1968.

and from the recognition that the Agreement is a treaty, its provisions subject also to the rules of interpretation as derived from customary international law.[21] As it is provided within the WTO dispute settlement context, Article 3.2 of the Dispute Settlement Understanding provides that this dispute system shall function within the WTO to clarify the existing provisions in accordance with the customary rules of interpretation of public international law. From this, the Appellate Body commenced applying Article 31 of the Vienna Convention on the Law of Treaties (VCLT, 1969)[22] for the purpose of designating the framework for interpreting disputed WTO provisions.[23] This VCLT provision serves itself as a codification of the customary legal rules regarding treaty interpretation.[24]

The question of applying other VCLT Articles to WTO provisions, or to the WTO as a whole in relation to other treaties, is not settled. If limited solely to the portion of the VCLT only designated for interpretation, and only to determine the meaning of a WTO Agreement provision, then this narrower view would suggest that only Part III of the VCLT (Articles 26-38, titled "Observance, application and interpretation of treaties") would be applicable.[25] On the other hand, public international law applies to treaties and necessarily to the relation of treaties to each other. Commentators have indicated that the WTO Appellate Body has itself taken the DSU Article 3 point of reference to include not only the principles of international law relating to interpretation, but to principles of international law generally.[26] McRae has indicated that VCLT Article 30 would be the reference point for

---

[21] From *Japan – Taxes on Alcoholic Beverages*, 4 October 1996, (AB-1996-2), at 15. Quoting, "The WTO is a treaty ...".

[22] Vienna Convention on the Law of Treaties, (VCLT), concluded at Vienna 23 May 1969, entry into force, 27 January 1980, UN Doc A/Conf 39/28, UKTS 58 (1980), 8 ILM 679.

[23] Thus, WTO Agreements are to be interpreted in good faith in accordance with the ordinary meaning of the terms in the context and in the light of the object and purpose of the treaty. VCLT, Article 31, Applied first in *United States – Standards for Reformulated and Conventional Gasoline*, 29 April 1996 (AB-1996-1), at p. 17.

[24] VCLT Preamble, "Believing that the codification and progressive development of the law of treaties achieved in the present Convention ..."; and, "Affirming that the rules of customary international law will continue to govern questions not regulated by the provisions of the present Convention, ...". See also, *Report of the International Law Commission on the Work of the Second Part of Seventeenth Session*, Monaco, 1966, Commentary to Article 37, UN General Assembly, 21st Session, Official Records, Supp. No. 9 (A/6309/Rev.1), reprinted in, American Journal of International Law, V. 61, (1967), at p. 350. "(5) ... Accordingly, the Commission confined itself to trying to isolate and codify the comparatively few general principles which appear to constitute general rules for the interpretation of treaties."

[25] This view would recognise that not all WTO Members are signatories to the VCLT, and that the explicit reference to the customary rules of public international law made in the WTO Dispute Settlement Understanding was restricted by its terms only to interpretations of provisions within disputes.

[26] "The practice of the Appellate Body suggests that the WTO agreements are interpreted and applied in the light of 'relevant rules of international law'. D.M. McRae, *The WTO in International Law: Tradition Continued or New Frontier?*, Journal of International Economic Law, V. 3, No. 1, 2000, pp. 27-41, at p. 37, citing *EC Measures Concerning Meat and Meat Products (Hormones)*, 16 January 1998, (WT/DS26/R), at case para. 124. But see contrary, D. Palmeter and P.C. Mavroidis, *The WTO*

dealing with successive treaties dealing with the same subject matter as, "(T)his provision is clearly relevant as well when looking at prior subsequent international agreements that may be inconsistent with the WTO agreements."[27]

As for the VCLT itself, its terms allow application to the WTO, as Article 5 states that the Convention shall apply for treaties constituting the constituent instrument of an international organisation, and for those adopted by an international organisation. The international law scholars, and the Appellate Body, will continue the debate regarding the interpretation of Article 3 of the DSU and the application of the VCLT to the WTO over time. For the purposes here, one will be asked to assume that the VCLT should be examined to shed light on the relationship between the WTO and later modification agreements made between a subset of Members. At least in this way one can consider a scenario that includes a treaty law framework for modifications.

12.3.1 VCLT Articles 30 and 41

Degan is of the opinion that perhaps the greatest contribution to the law of treaties made by the International Law Commission, and its Special Rapporteur Sir Humphrey Waldock, was to provide a sequence of rules to embrace the situations caused by later (successive) treaties.[28] Elaborating on the scheme as it extends across VCLT Articles 30, 41, 53, 59, 60, and 64, Degan relies upon the hierarchy as organised by Nguyen Quoc Dinh, as described in 1975.[29] Accordingly, where two or more parties to an earlier multilateral treaty conclude a new agreement in order to modify it *inter se,* VCLT Articles 30(5) and 41 apply.[30]

12.3.1.1 Successive treaties according to VCLT Article 30
VCLT Article 30 titled, *Application of successive treaties relating to the same subject-matter* establishes its pertinent rule in paragraphs 4 and 3, that where the parties to the later treaty do not include all the parties to the earlier one, that the earlier treaty applies, "only to the extent that its provisions are compatible with those

---

Legal System: Sources of Law, American Journal of International Law, Vol. 92, 1998, pp. 398-413, at p. 406. "The customary rules of interpretation are, so far, the only portions of customary international law to have found their way meaningfully into WTO dispute settlement.", and taking into account the Hormones AB report.

[27] D. McRae, Ibid., at p. 38, but noting, "… whether the formal rules of Article 30 will be an adequate response to the problem of overlap between agreements remains to be seen." Also, his note 52 and cite to Sinclair on treaties therein.

[28] V.D. Degan, **Sources of International Law**, Martinus Nijhoff Publishers, The Hague, 1997, p. 425.

[29] Ibid., citing Nguyen Quoc Dinh, *Droit international public*, Paris 1975, pp. 255-264, Degan's note 115.

[30] The example provided as: "Earlier treaty between States: A,B,C,D,E,F…. Later treaty between States: B and C; or B,C, and D." i.e., a subset consisting wholly of members to the earlier multilateral treaty. Degan, Ibid., at p. 426.

of the later treaty."[31] This general "last in time" rule (*lex posterior derogat legi priori*) is however stated to be conditional by Article 30 itself in paragraph 5. This states that paragraph 4, "is without prejudice to article 41."[32]

12.3.1.2 Modification to treaties according to VCLT Article 41

Thus, according to the VCLT scheme, a later treaty between a subset of members cannot be presumptively understood to negate the relevant provisions of the earlier treaty. Rather, Article 41 of the VCLT must be considered first for its requirements in order to determine whether or not the obligations of the first have become modified or suspended in light of the second.[33] VCLT Article 41, titled, *Agreements to modify multilateral treaties between certain of the parties only,* provides in part that,

> "1. (T)wo or more of the parties to a multilateral treaty may conclude an agreement to modify the treaty as between themselves alone if:
> (a)   the possibility of such a modification *is provided for* by the treaty; *or*
> (b)   the modification in question *is not prohibited* by the treaty *and*:
>   (i) does not affect the enjoyment by the other parties of their rights under the treaty or the performance of their obligations;
>   (ii) does not relate to a provision, derogation from which is incompatible with the effective execution of the object and purpose of the treaty as a whole ....".[34]

An *inter se* agreement was understood by the drafters to the Vienna Convention to be more likely to disrupt the object and purpose of a multilateral treaty than a treaty amendment that required the participation of all parties.[35] Thus, the condition by

---

[31]   VCLT, Article 30, para. 3.

[32]   In addition, VCLT Article 30, para. 5 also provides that para. 4 is without prejudice to, "any question of responsibility which may arise for a State from the conclusion or application of a treaty the provisions of which are incompatible with its obligations towards another State under another treaty."

[33]   Suspension by a subset of parties to a multilateral treaty is covered by VCLT Article 58, the provisions of which are identical to those of Article 41 in its entirety. Thus, whether later parties 'modify' or 'suspend' is not material in this context. That there is no "later in time" presumption for modifications in this context may be at significant variation from the view of a number of GATT-47 parties. See the discussion above concerning GATT Articles XIX and XXV.

[34]   VCLT, Article 41, italics added. The remaining text of the Article states, "2. Unless in a case falling under paragraph 1(a) the treaty otherwise provides, the parties in question shall notify the other parties of their intention to conclude the agreement and of the modification to the treaty for which it provides."

[35]   The term *inter se* was employed by the International Law Commission. The concept of 'modification' is clearly distinguished from other VCLT Articles dealing with treaty amendments. *Inter se* being, "... an agreement entered into by some only of the parties to a multilateral treaty and intended to modify it between themselves alone." Report of the International Law Commission, supra, note 24 at p. 384. See also, P. Reuter, **Introduction to the Law of Treaties**, Pinter, London, 1989, at p. 104, para. 207: "(I)f on the contrary, the new text were from the outset directed only at some of the contracting parties, this would amount to a 'modification', and this change in terminology involves the application of stricter rules as laid down in article 41."

which such modifications are permissible under the Convention are more narrow-ly prescribed.[36] This close control over the grant of a right of modify is expressed by the leading paragraph of Article 41 where "Two or more parties ... may con-clude an agreement to modify ... *if,*". This suggests that whatever inherent power States may have to form treaties has been circumscribed in the circumstances of later modification in relation to their prior multilateral obligations. This aligns with the comment of the Commission as it stressed that, "... the application, and even the conclusion of an inter se agreement incompatible with the object and purpose of the treaty may raise a question of State responsibility".[37]

As indicated by the sub-paragraphs recited above, there are two possibilities provided which may grant the right of modification.[38] The first is where the mul-tilateral treaty permits a "contracting out" by its members, as the possibility of pro-viding for such a modification would be expressly stated by the treaty.[39]

The second possibility, which is an alternative to the first, is where such modi-fications are not prohibited by the multilateral treaty. This separate possibility is contemplated by the Vienna Convention in Article 41 in sub-paragraph 1(b), with the additional requirements that the enjoyment of the rights of other members are not affected and that the modification does not cause a derogation from a provision which is incompatible with the object and purpose of the treaty as a whole.

That the VCLT Article expressly considers both possibilities of *permitted* (or) *not prohibited* establishes a hierarchy of consideration within Article 41 itself. If a treaty provides an express permissive right to modification, (parties are entitled to modify) the conditions stated in 1(b) (i) and (ii) would not be considered as having any bearing on the right to modify. In this case the terms of the granting treaty, the first treaty, would dictate and control the circumstances by which modification may be entertained. At the other extreme, if the first treaty expressly prohibits modifications (parties shall not modify), then certainly 1(a) is not applicable. Likewise, the conditions provided in 1(b) (i) and (ii) could not be raised to justify a modification, since the treaty is prohibiting them.

---

[36] "Under the present article, therefore the main issue is the conditions under which *inter se* agreements may be regarded as permissible." ILC Reports, Supra note 24 at p. 384.

[37] Degan, supra note 28 at p. 432, citing AJIL 1966, p. 384, para. (1), his note 118.

[38] The conference deleted the International Law Commission's proposal for an article permitting modification by subsequent practice. R.D. Kearney and R.E. Dalton, *The Treaty on Treaties*, American Journal of International Law, V. 64, 1970, at p. 525.

[39] "Paragraph 1(a) necessarily recognizes that an inter se agreement is permissible if the possi-bility of such an agreement was provided for in the treaty: in other words, if 'contracting out' was con-templated in the treaty." ILC Reports, Supra note 24. For example, the United Nations Convention on the Law of the Sea, 10 December, 1982, Article 311, paragraph 3, whereby *inter se* agreements are sta-ted as permitted according to certain conditions. U.N. Doc. A/CONF.62/122, cited in S. Rosenne, Supra note 12 at p. 85. The vast majority of *inter se* agreements are unexceptionable. R.D. Kearney and R.E. Dalton, Ibid., at p. 524. Degan cites for example the 1963 Vienna Convention on Consular Relations, providing, "(N)othing in the present Convention shall preclude States from concluding international agreements confirming or supplementing or extending or amplifying the provisions thereof." Degan Supra note 28 at p. 431.

If a treaty is silent on the question of modifications, containing no articles that explicitly refer to the possibility of modification as permitted or prohibited, then it would appear that the conditions of 1(b) are able to applied. Otherwise there would have been little point for the drafters to include the possibly of *not prohibited* modifications for those cases where the treaty was not expressly permissive. This appears to be the interpretation also posed by Sinclair, as, "(A)ccordingly, Article 41 imposes three conditions on the conclusion of *inter se* agreements, where such agreements *are not contemplated* in the original treaty."[40] In these cases, the assumption is made that the treaty, since it does not expressly permit modifications, is rather silent on the questions of what modifications should be permitted. Therefore, sub-paragraph 1(b) goes on to provide its own criteria as listed in (i) and (ii).[41]

12.4   GATT/WTO provisions for permissive modifications

The Agreement Establishing the World Trade Organization (The WTO Agreement) does not provide an Article expressly granting the right of two or more parties to enter into a modifying bilateral agreement. Article X of the WTO Agreement only provides for amendments according to the submission of proposals to the Ministerial Conference, and then acceptance of such amendments only by action of the Members. As for the GATT, Article XXX also provides for amendments, but only by action of the Contracting Parties. WTO Article XIII does make provision for non-application of the Agreements, but only by reservation at the time of accession of a new Member. GATT Article XXXV referring to non-application imposes the same requirement that such an act of non-application be implemented only upon the act of accession.

---

[40]   (Emphasis added) to indicate that the three conditions apply only to those cases where the treaty does not already expressly permit modifications. Sinclair, **The Vienna Convention on the Law of Treaties**, 2d ed., Manchester University Press, 1984, pp.108-109. As for the first provision of Article 41 I(b), requiring that the treaty not prohibit modification, Sinclair stated that, "(t)he first of these conditions is self-evident and unexceptionable." Ibid., at p. 109. One may gather from this comment that the prohibition contemplated must be expressly stated.

[41]   The final Article 41 expressed a reordering of these conditions. In the 1966 ILC Report, the requirement that the treaty *not prohibit* modifications was listed as the final requirement. Then titled Article 37 and providing for three *cumulative* conditions for sub-paragraph (b). To paraphrase, that the modification in question did not (I) affect the enjoyment of the other parties of their rights or obligations; (ii) was not incompatible with the object and purpose of the treaty as a whole; and (iii) "is not prohibited by the treaty." In the final accepted Article, (iii) was promoted to the first stated condition of sub-paragraph (b), as quoted in the primary text above. The change clarifies, that if modifications are not prohibited, only then would one proceed to investigate the other stated requirements (i) and (ii). See ILC Report , Supra note 24, at pp. 383-384. The final version also seems to make it more clear that Article 41 I(b) considerations apply only to those circumstances where the multilateral treaty is not expressly permissive.

GATT-94 does appear to provide avenues for permissive modification, including Article XIX for effecting emergency measures together with the WTO Agreement on Safeguards, Article XXV for granting of waivers, and Article XXIV itself together with the 1994 Understanding regarding the interpretation of that article. All of these Articles expressly provide certain avenues for parties to engage in later modifications of their obligations, but of course with certain oversight by the Members and in accord with the provisions of the Articles themselves. If it is correct that these GATT provisions can be characterised as providing a permissive opportunity for modifications, then one should conclude that VCLT Article 41 1(a) is effective, rather than 1(b). As above, this follows from the fact that the VCLT Article 41 states these two possibilities in the alternative.

Thus, there appears to be a threshold question of whether GATT Articles XIX, XXV and/or XXIV fulfil the conditions of VCLT Article 41 1(a). If so, and this is the point, then any alternative means of modification undertaken by WTO Members would not be permitted modifications under the GATT in accord with the VCLT. Parties would not have a basis to invoke any of the considerations or possibilities provided for by sub-paragraph 1(b) in order to validate their other modifications.

There is the possibility of a supplemental construction which comes to the same conclusion. If the GATT provisions as mentioned provide certain permissive avenues for modifications, then depending upon how one characterises the exclusiveness of these avenues, it may also follow that other, non-prescribed, alternative forms of modifications are also being sought, according to the object and purpose of the Agreement, to be effectively foreclosed. In this case, one may say that while the GATT does not expressly prohibit modifications, the overall structure of the treaty may be acting to prohibit modifications by implication.[42]

12.4.1 *GATT Article XXIV as a modification provision*

As indicated, The VCLT Article 41 1(a) provides a right for two or more parties to modify the treaty as between themselves where the treaty permits such modification. GATT Article XXIV:5 states that,

"… the provisions of this Agreement shall not prevent, as between the territories of contracting parties, the formation of a customs union or of a free-trade area…provided that …".

---

[42] In the 1966 ILC Report, the commentary admits that there is an overlap between the prohibition condition and that one requiring compatibility with the object and purpose of the treaty, since an agreement incompatible with the object and purpose, "may be said to be impliedly prohibited by the treaty." This could suggest that the absence of an express prohibition in the treaty may not absolutely foreclose a finding of prohibition. Article 41 1(b). ILC Reports, 1966, Supra note 24 at p. 384. This comment however was also framed in the context of the earlier draft of the Article.

This phrase in Article XXIV appears on its face to grant a permissive, albeit conditional, right for members to make modifications by forming free-trade areas and customs unions. As this paragraph has been interpreted by the Appellate Body in the Turkey Textiles Report, the conditional right to modify is granted to the parties upon a showing that paragraphs 8 and 5 have also been fulfilled. As is also known, in order to assess whether these conditions are met, parties seeking this avenue of modification must also, as in the case of Article XIX and Article XXV, provide notification. For regional agreements, this is accomplished according to Article XXIV:7 which requires the submission of a plan and schedule. What is evident, in the context of the VCLT framework, is that GATT has generated its own scheme for permissive modifications. The scope of these modifications for Article XXIV, as has also been ruled by the Appellate Body, extends to the possible violation (suspension) of all GATT rules as to non-members, depending upon whether such suspensions can be deemed necessary in order to meet the paragraph 5 and 8 requirements.

GATT Articles XIX and XXV should clearly be seen to have the capacity to grant permissive modifications which suspend the application of GATT rules as between the modifying parties. For Article XIX, that constitutes the core of its rationale, albeit with MFN considerations attached. Article XXIV permits the formation of regional trade agreements also as modifications, which necessarily directly affect the rights of other WTO Members, primarily to receive MFN treatment. However, it appears that this grant of a modification is also limited by the types of suspensions as to GATT articles and considerations of internal trade coverage that are provided by paragraph 8. Thus, Article XXIV *requires* that duties be eliminated, an action not otherwise required by GATT law. To the extent that ORRCs may extend beyond the notion of quantitative restrictions as prohibited by GATT Article XI, this requirement to eliminate may also exceed the generally applicable GATT requirements. Where necessary, members may yet impose restrictions in the form permitted by Article XI-XV and XX. Thus, the suspension of the application of these exception Articles is not a requirement for regional members to meet. Other restrictive regulations that may be imposed between Members generally are not listed. What is further absent in the paragraph is either a permission or a requirement for members to suspend the application of other GATT Articles.

12.4.2 *What internal suspensions are permitted?*

The question of what GATT obligations may be suspended as between regional members remains the core consideration in this discussion. As from the introduction, a divergence of GATT obligations as applying to trade between regional members could be raised whenever treatment between them is different than MFN treatment (better or worse) but in any case not conducted according to free trade (zero duty, no quantitative restrictions). The question may occur both in the case where the treatment provided is more favourable than MFN (positive preference) as well as less favourable than MFN (negative preference), although the focus here has been upon the latter.[43] At the outset, if Article XXIV were interpreted to require completely free trade for all of the trade of the parties excepting only those Articles as listed in paragraph 8 of Article XXIV, then a resolution of the question would also be made differently. There, regional members would not have any legal basis under the Article to take measures (in a completed formation) which would come under Articles VI or XIX, since they are not listed exceptions. Article XI and Article XX measures could continue to be applied, but only as according to the non-discrimination requirements imposed for the use of these exception by GATT Article XIII and the preamble of Article XX.[44]

If it is determined that trade coverage within a completed regional agreement need not be absolute (substantially-all trade and a non-exhaustive listing), then the question of what restrictive measures to this trade are permitted is again raised. It has been noted already, that this can be an issue in regard to so-called partial preferences (reductions in tariffs not to zero, or the use of tariff-quotas) and also in the retention of certain quantitative restrictions. Schoneveld treated these restrictive measures in the context of sector annexes attached to trade agreements.[45] He stated that the arrangements in question commonly have provisions for quantitative limits upon certain exports coupled with an agreement to manage exports to insure that trade does not exceed designated quantities. This is accompanied by an additional agreement for the parties to avoid situations that would call for express protective measures and finally, a provision for protective measures to be installed when they are deemed necessary.[46] Whether or not one adopts his characterisation as to the trade-restrictive intent underlying these agreements, a means of assessing the relationship of the GATT generally to them can be suggested.

This would consider whether such special bilateral agreements would be GATT lawful in the absence of any reference to Article XXIV. If not, then a second examination would be undertaken to identify what aspect of Article XXIV has acted to validate such a restriction. If this cannot be identified, then a conclusion could be

---

[43] The positive-preference aspect asks whether tariff preferences between members short of zero are exempt from MFN, and/or whether they can be included as coverage for Art. XXIV:8 internal requirements.

[44] However, even in this strictest of interpretations, there still would be the question of the application of these GATT Articles as to interim agreements. Then, the issue would be whether or not transitional restrictive measures employed between regional members must comply with GATT Articles.

[45] F. Schoneveld, *The EEC and Free Trade Agreements, Stretching the Limits of GATT Exceptions to Non-Discriminatory Trade?*, Journal of World Trade, V. 26, No. 5, pp. 59-78 at p. 68, citing EEC OJ 1981 L 137/21.

[46] F. Schoneveld, Ibid., at p. 69. He uses EC-Thailand, Manioc as his example to draw out the provisions, citing OJ 1982 L 219/53. As he concluded, "In almost all the sectoral trade agreements concluded by the Community, particularly when the products concerned are agricultural products, these orderly trade provisions are the real purpose of the agreements." Here, attention is directed to the possible (hypothetical) inclusion of sector agreements within free-trade areas.

made that that the regional members have made a violation of a GATT Article, and it must be validated by some other Article exception or the general waiver.

As recalled from the previous chapter, a divergence of opinion on this question has been recorded in the CRTA in the Examination of the Interim Agreement between Slovenia and the European Communities in March of 1998.[47] The EC representative indicated that

> "His delegation had consistently argued for decades that it was perfectly possible to form a free trade agreement consistent with Article XXIV:8(b) with preferences contained within the agreement short of elimination. He would go so far as to suggest that that amounted to a sort of consistent subsequent practice within the broader rules of interpretation on international law".[48]

However, the U.S. representative replied,

> "While she found interesting the comment on the accepted body of opinion, she noted that in the WTO for tariff preferences they were either given through a waiver or through certain provisions of the Enabling Clause".

What is clarified by the VCLT context regarding Article 41 1(a), is that there is certainly no general right of modification to be accorded to parties of a multilateral agreement by subsequent practice, at least to the extent that no such provision was adopted by the VCLT Convention, and further, that no reference to subsequesnt practice is found either in either Article 41 1(a) or 1(b). In addition, the possibility of deriving a flexible grant of modification within Article XXIV arrangements under the conditions prescribed by Article 41 1(b) also appears innaplicable. Recalling a separate EC statement from the earlier CRTA discussion,

> "...where barriers were lowered legitimately and preferentially between the parties to an agreement, the net position of third parties should not be affected. This was not surprising in light of international law on multilateral treaties, which held that generally, parties to a multilateral agreement could form subsequent agreements between a subset of the membership of the wider agreement, *varying their rights and obligations as between themselves, provided they did not abridge the rights of third countries to the wider, underlying agreement.* Article XXIV:4 seemed to do no more than to translate into the language of trade policy that wider principle".[49]

---

[47] WTO, Committee on Regional Trade Agreements, Examination of the Interim Agreement between Slovenia and the European Communities, WT/REG32/M/1, 12 March 1998, paras. 13-17, pp. 3-4.

[48] Ibid., at para. 16.

[49] EC Statement, WT/REG/M/14, 24 November 1997, para. 13, emphasis added. It seems clear the reference is being made to VCLT, Article 41 1(b).

If Article XXIV is a permissive grant of modification according to VCLT 41 1(a), then the statement above is also incorrect, as there is no additional test to be applied to Article XXIV that would contemplate the rights of enjoyment of non members or reference to the object and purpose of the treaty. Likewise, if the terms of Article XXIV is permissive, then only the terms of Article XXIV control the intended modification, and the question again turns upon whether that Article itself prescribes such partially restrictive measures as between the regional members.

12.4.3 *Resolving the diametric views of the Article XXIV exception*

What one sees finally is that two distinct views of the regional exception also turn upon one's interpretation of VCLT Article 41 and its two subparagraphs. One view, initially raised by the regional proponents to the Overseas Association, was that uncovered trade in an otherwise qualified regional agreement is beyond the scope of application of the GATT Agreement. Once invoked, there is no binding relationship between GATT rules and the nature of the relationship determined between regional members. One might recall that as to the external aspects, this autonomous view of the Article was raised by respondents in both of the GATT panels (Bananas I and II) and in the WTO Turkey Textiles Panel and AB Reports. These bodies have consistently ruled to the contrary on this point as to the rights of third parties. The VCLT provisions analysed do not seem to lead to any conclusion that GATT rules provide for any greater flexibility in compliance for internal parties.

This opposing view suggests that regional members remain WTO Members and that GATT law has continuing application to their trade. Thus, where a GATT Article states that "Members shall", then regional members are also bound by that obligation. To suspend it, they should be able to identify how the action is necessary in order to comply with the requirements of Article XXIV, or should identify some other exception, or obtain a waiver as according to the same procedures that govern WTO Members generally. This view would characterise Article XXIV as providing no exception for the deviation from GATT Articles other than those that members must necessarily undertake in order to complete regional trade requirements. This would be a comparable test as determined by the Appellate Body in the Turkey Textiles case, but as directed to regional members themselves. From the VCLT context, at least if Article 41 1(a) is the appropriate provision, there would appear to be every reason to conclude that the Convention would give this principle test the same effect in regard to the legality of internally restrictive measures contained within a regional agreement.

In the case of the specialised safeguard regimes, this would have an impact in two ways. If the listing of Articles in paragraph 8 of Article XXIV was determined to be exhaustive, then as above, regional members would have to determine their commitment to eliminate safeguards from their trade upon the completion of the interim period. If the listing was determined to not be exhaustive, then regional members could entertain safeguards in a completed customs union or free trade area. However, those safeguards, and the regional regime regulating them would necessarily require ongoing compliance with GATT Article XIX and the WTO Agreement on Safeguards. While VCLT 41 1(b) might provide an argument for a *lex specialis* regional regime, 41 (a) does not, at least to the extent that Article XXIV, even if a permissive construction for Article XIX was determined, does not in any case provide for any deviation from GATT Article XIX.

The autonomous regime theory for Article XXIV would suggest that the Article provides for a complete permission to suspend the GATT's other Articles as to all of the uncovered trade between regional members. If valid, this view would have a bearing on the relationship between GATT and regional parties, particularly for Articles I, VI, XI, and XIX, as they would no longer be seen to apply to regional members who have qualified to take the exception accorded by Article XXIV. For an example, if Article XIX is suspended by the operation of Article XXIV, then it would follow that any sectoral arrangement seeking to manage the trade of the members, as described above by Schoneveld, would then be rendered lawful by the act of merely incorporating it within the framework of a free-trade area agreement. This interpretation would grant the widest possible latitude for regional members to compose and implement trade-restrictive measures between them. Thus, any case to be made for applying GATT rules to the trade of regional parties must first dispel the possibility that Article XXIV functions within GATT as a general right to conduct modification, other than by operation of the Article's own specialised waiver provisions as found in its paragraph 10.[50]

Such an interpretation would be also be a convoluted result for Article XXIV in direct conflict with the stated objective of the Article's exception. Paragraph 4 of the Article recognises that it is desirable to increase the freedom of trade by certain of these agreements, and views the purpose of such agreements to *facilitate* trade between their members. This suggests that regional trade flows should be enhanced as a result of the modification. This purpose would justify the granting of an exception for the positive preferences to be exchanged, since the whole purpose of these preferences would be to liberalise the conditions for intra-regional trade. However, this stated purpose of the article does not appear synonymous with the concept of *restricting* trade between constituent members. It would seem rather that the right of engaging a modification according to the Article is limited to the purposes expressed by the Article itself.

---

[50] This allows the contracting parties to waive certain defects in a free-trade area or customs union plan. However, a customs union or free-trade area must yet result.

12.5   Chapter Conclusion

This chapter has taken the position that GATT Articles XIX, XXIV and XXV regarding the suspension or modification of GATT rules between two or more parties are permissive modification provisions as according to VCLT Article 41 1(a). If it is correct that such modifications are permitted by the GATT according to the VCLT, then the possibility of invoking the criteria of VCLT 41 1(b), for multilateral treaties which are not permissive but not expressly prohibitive, would not seem to be provided. This is according to the construction of the VCLT Article made above that would only permits the consideration of non-prohibited modifications according to subparagraph 1(b) in the event that subparagraph 1(a) does not apply to the circumstances presented in the treaty.

An objection to this reasoning would be made that, as between two parties, as long as their suspension of GATT obligations does not harm other Members, or other Members choose not to complain, then modifications should be permitted. This argument essentially invokes again the considerations of VCLT 41 1(b) at the outset (no interference with rights, no diminishing of object and purpose). The difficulty with this position is that the considerations of VCLT 41 1(b) should not be raised in the case where the treaty is otherwise permitting modifications according to its own terms. As above, this is made clear by the construction of the Article as "either/or" between *permitting or not prohibiting.*

At the same time, a disregard for the construction of the VCLT Article in this manner also discloses a view of the multilateral treaty in question, suggested as being merely a platform upon which to engage in later bilateral arrangements. If this were so, then one could ask why the GATT would provide for any conditions regarding the oversight of bilateral arrangements, as according to the notification provisions found in all of the three Articles mentioned. Rather, that these provisions require notification implies that the designated avenues for modifications are intended to foreclose other less transparent possibilities.

Assuming that one would choose to press the interpretation that GATT permits modifications according to VCLT 41 1(b), some reference to the object and purpose of the GATT agreement would also then be appropriate. For this, we know that the GATT preamble dedicates the Agreement to the expansion of world trade and to the elimination of discrimination in international commerce. In order to achieve these goals, a number of core obligations are stated throughout the agreement. The manner in which these requirements are stated suggests also that the object and purpose of the GATT is intended to be realised by the imposition of a set of unconditional rules of conduct upon all of its contracting parties. This is to contrast with a framework established for merely conducting future bilateral relations directed to the expansion of trade.[51]

Thus, GATT Article I:1 declares that any favour granted by *any contracting party ... shall be accorded.* Article XI states that no prohibitions or restrictions other than duties *shall be instituted or maintained by any contracting party.* Article XIII specifies the conditions for certain permissible quantitative restrictions, but requires that *no restriction shall be applied by any contracting party ... unless the importation ... or the exportation of the like product to all third countries is similarly prohibited.* Likewise, for Article XIX and the WTO Safeguards Agreement, Article 2.2 of the Agreement provides that safeguard measures *shall be applied* to a product being imported *irrespective of its source.* Article 11 of the Agreement prohibits certain measures by stating that a *Member shall not seek, take, or maintain* a voluntary export restraint on either the import or export side.

What is seen from these provisions is a pattern of unconditional obligations addressed to each and every WTO Member. The obligations, on their face, do not entertain possibilities for selective application of the rules as to some and not others.[52] Likewise the rules do not raise avenues for bilateral suspensions between Members. They further do not appear to be optional only to the extent that parties agree to be bound by them. Although one may always suggest that all obligations are only enforceable to the extent that an injured party chooses to take redress, this appears to deny the unconditional nature of the obligations at the outset, as they make no such limitation to their own applicability.

Where the GATT rules are fashioned as above, it seems difficult to draw an interpretation that the customary rules of international law would endorse the practice of Members to develop modifications by means other than those set out in the General Agreement. If so, bilateral parties may not argue that all modifications are permitted as long as the rights of other parties are not affected, or that the modification is not incompatible with the object and purpose of the treaty. This may well serve as a criteria for the joint action of the contracting parties in applying GATT Article XXV, but these considerations do not otherwise operate as an independent criteria which serves to endorse a bilateral modification.

Although Article XXIV provides the basis for establishing certain bilateral preferential agreements in the form of free-trade areas and customs unions, these agreements remain, just as Article XXIV remains, within the multilateral framework of the General Agreement and the WTO. It does not follow as plausible that a region-

---

[51] This point is drawn from Reuter, Supra note 35 at p. 103. Asking the question, whether or not a multilateral treaty, "can be divided into a series of independent bilateral agreements without losing (its) raison d' être ... Some multilateral treaties go beyond the framework of simple reciprocity and cannot be broken down into a collection of bilateral undertakings."

[52] The WTO Safeguards Agreement does provide for selectivity, but also according to its own rules regarding notification and monitoring by the WTO Safeguards Committee.

al party can derive an exception from Article I or XI by incorporating a trade restriction into an Article XXIV arrangement. One qualification to this conclusion, however, is that Article XXIV:8 also provides its own listing of permitted quantitative restrictions that may be applied between regional partners, where necessary.

Chapter 13
BOOK CONCLUSION: RECENT DEVELOPMENTS

13.1 Introduction

The gradual appearance of a judicial character to the qualification and maintenance of regional trade agreements has begun its have impact on the future plans of regional actors. This is most evident in the developments concerning the European Union relationship with seventy African, Caribbean and Pacific (ACP) territories in the Lomé IV Convention. The trade component of the first Convention was configured by its own declaration to provide for non-reciprocal preferences in favour of the ACP countries. This facial declaration to the Agreement also successfully condemned its possibilities to shelter preferences granted under Article XXIV, as ruled in 1993 and 1994 in the unreported GATT panel cases of Bananas I and II. Lomé IV was also the subject of a GATT Working Group Review in 1993. As in the original Overseas Association review from 1958, the parties to the process again disagreed over the relationship between Part IV of the GATT (Trade and Development) and Article XXIV:8 requirements.[1]

Following that report the EC and those ACP members who were also GATT parties requested a waiver according to GATT Article XXV:5, and as documented, without prejudice to their position that Lomé IV remained compatible with Article XXIV in light of Part IV. This waiver was granted by a Decision of the Contracting Parties in December of 1994 and remained effective until the expiry of the Convention on 29 February, 2000. The terms of the waiver were later contested through additional dispute resolution cases in the WTO Bananas cases. At this writing, an application to extend the waiver has been made by the EC-ACP parties but a decision has not yet been taken in the WTO.

This brief outline demonstrates the effect of even the non-binding GATT dispute settlement process on the actions taken by regional members. Although the working group as according to pattern, did not make a recommendation either negative or affirmative, the Lomé IV parties on this first occasion sought the coverage of a waiver under another GATT Article exception. Although the request was made without prejudice to the traditional position that Part IV of the GATT applied within the listing of paragraph 8 of Article XXIV, the traditional practice, as indicated by the Bananas I and II arguments, would have been conducted differently. This would assert that the Agreement had been duly notified and examined and that the Article XXIV exception was therefore operative and not even subject to a

---

[1] Report of the Working Party adopted 4 October 1994, BISD 41, p. 125.

review when invoked in an Article XXIII proceeding. Thus, although unreported, the reasoning of the cases apparently informed the process sufficiently to draw the ACP parties to Article XXV, a first-time occurrence in the history of the Community's relationship with the ACP countries, from the Overseas Association, through the Yaounde Conventions, and then from Lomé I through IV.

The tentative nature of waiver under the new WTO rules has also returned the EC-ACP relationship full circle to the Overseas Association considerations as it is now agreed to qualify most of it in the form of free-trade areas according to Article XXIV. This would allow the dissolution of the waiver and establish the legal certainty necessary to engage the preferential relationship over a stable longer term. One may recall from Chapter 4.3 that the guise of reciprocity for preferences was dropped by the EC and ACP for the Lomé I Convention, a change that was only opposed by a single member of the GATT working group at that time.

13.2   The Cotonou framework

The framework agreement for establishing new free-trade areas is found in the EC-ACP Partnership Agreement signed in February 2000 in Cotonou.[2] Title II of Part 3 of the Agreement (Economic and trade Cooperation) contains the agreed-upon outline for establishing future trade preference relations between the members. This Title extends from PA Article 34 through Article 52 and is divided into Chapters 1: Objectives and principles; 2: New trading arrangements; 3: Cooperation in the international fora; 4: Trade in services; 5: Trade-related areas; and, 6:Cooperation in other areas.

PA Article 35 (Principles) provides at para. 3 that this cooperation shall take account of the different needs and levels of development of the ACP countries and regions, and that the Parties reaffirm their attachment to ensuring special and differential treatment for all ACP countries and to maintaining special treatment for ACP LDC's. PA Article 34 (Objectives) states at para. 4 that the economic and trade cooperation,

"shall be implemented in full conformity with the provisions of the WTO, including special and differential treatment, taking account of the Parties' mutual interests and their respective levels of development".

---

[2]   At this writing the Agreement is only located on the EC Commission and other web sites. See, http://www.europa.eu.int/comm/development/cotonou/index_en.htm(.) It is titled, "Partnership Agreement Between the Members of the African, Caribbean and Pacific Group of States of the One Part, and the European Community and its Member States, of the Other Part". It is commonly referred to as the Cotonou Agreement or the EC-ACP Partnership Agreement, or simply, the PA.

The PA provides for a preparatory period, ending on December 31, 2007 at the latest, during which a series of Economic Partnership Agreements (EPAs) will be negotiated between the EC and regional groupings of ACP countries, or in some cases, between the EC and individual ACP countries (PA Article 37). By all accounts these EPA's would be intended to qualify according to Article XXIV as free-trade areas and with the interim-agreement period to run from 2008. Thus, the earliest completed arrangements would be finally implemented in 2018, as Article XXIV:5 provides for a ten year interim period. For the transitional period until 2008, while negotiations and capacity building continue, the parties would continue to rely upon an Article XXV waiver.

A possibility for ACP countries that do not wish to enter formal EPAs with the Community is provided. According to PA Article 37(6), A review will be made in 2004 for those "non-LDC" ACP countries who decide that they are not in a position to enter such agreements, and that alternative possibilities will then be assessed. The conditions for these preferences are that they will conform with WTO rules, but also be, "equivalent to their existing situation…". This has been taken to mean that the existing level of preferences granted according to Lomé IV will not be diminished for the ACP countries opting out of the EPA process. This, even while the free-trade vehicle will assumedly not be employed as between them and the Community. For those ACP countries remaining in the EPA process, PA Article 37(5) also indicates that the negotiations shall take account of the regional integration process within the ACP. This would suggest that where distinct regional groupings have been formed in the ACP, either as free-trade areas or customs unions, that these entities will also be respected in the formation of the EPAs. A third status category is also identified in PA Article 37(9) for those least-developed LDCs (LLDCs) that will not be parties to EPAs but will rather receive duty free access for essentially all products to the EC market and without any requirement of reciprocity.

Overall, the PA framework obviously sets a number of possibilities for ACP countries. Aside from the LLDC unilateral provisions for tariff-free access, "(I)t is likely to result in a combination of situations with some ACP countries keeping Lomé, some negotiating EPA's as regions, some negotiating individual EPA's and others negotiating with the EU to obtain another type of agreement."[3] Since none of the actual governing agreements are scheduled to commence negotiations until September of 2002, only conjecture can be accommodated in characterising the resulting agreements. This is particularly the case for the non EPA parties who also are not LLDCs. Since the intent of the PA overall is to remove the ACP regime from the Article XXV waiver, it would appear that the primary point of reference for the ACP countries falling into this category, if any choose to do so, must be the Generalised System of Preferences (GSP). However, the PA states that the quality

---

3   ECDPM, *Economic Partnership Agreements*, Lomé 2000, No. 14, June 2000, p. 2.

of preferences already provided in Lomé would be retained. Thus, to any extent that the existing preferences exceed those granted to like developing countries in the GSP, there would not seem to be a legal avenue in the WTO to frame any non-reciprocal preference agreement with these non EPA ACP countries. The alternative would be that GSP preferences are upgraded to the Lomé IV levels, thereby effectively extending Lomé IV preferences to all non-ACP WTO Members similarly situated as to their development levels.

This potential for discrimination as between developing countries at comparative levels has been apparently recognised for the treatment of the LLDC's as well, but has also been diffused from the outset. The PA grants to these poorest ACP countries a non-reciprocal grant of free market access to the Community. In conjunction with this PA provision, the Community has also proposed extending duty free treatment on a similar, if not an identical basis, to the LLDCs who are also not ACP members. This proposal has now been formulated in the spring of 2001 as the "Everything but Arms" (EA) initiative. As this becomes effective Community policy, the legal problem of discriminating within the GATT's enabling clause as between the LLDCs will not emerge.

This also recognises the simple legal reality that the Community, nor any other territory granting GSP, can make distinctions for the purposes of these preferences as between like developing countries without violating Article XXXVII of the GATT and/or the 1979 enabling clause decision adopted by the GATT Contracting Parties.[4] Thus, if there is a distinction for granting non-reciprocal preferences to be made between LLDCs and LDCs, this should be accommodated within the structure of the enabling clause decision. What can not be accommodated is a distinction for the same purposes between ACP LLDCs and non-ACP LLDCs, and between ACP LDCs and non-ACP LDCs. The only possible accommodation that permits that discriminatory distinction is found in the terms of Article XXIV, but as we well know, paragraph 8 requirements for that Article also require reciprocity. Thus, for those ACP LDCs that choose not to travel the Article XXIV free-trade area route with the Community, it appears that their preferences will inevitably be demoted to GSP levels.

---

[4]   The Enabling Clause Decision of 28 November 1979, BISD 26S/203. This permits developed countries to accord differential and more favourable treatment to developing countries, and applies to, "2(a) Preferential tariff treatment accorded by developed contracting parties to products originating in developing countries in accordance with the Generalized System of Preferences ...". Note 3 to this sub-paragraph refers to the, "Decision of the Contracting Parties of 25 June 1971 relating to the establishment of 'generalized non-reciprocal and non-discriminatory preferences beneficial to the development countries' (BISD 18S/24)." Thus, the Enabling Clause suspends Article I MFN for preferences extended to developing countries, but not suspending non-discriminatory treatment as between them regarding their designation within categories. See Infra note 6.

13.3   The EPAs and Article XXIV

The primary challenge in implementing a far more graduated and complex ACP preferential system will likely fall within the domain of the EPAs themselves. As above, none of these agreements have commenced negotiations. However, commentary has already noted the potential conflicts arising in the prospective efforts to qualify the EPAs according to Article XXIV. This flows, as did the Overseas Association, from the desire of the parties to the agreements to continue to receive "asymmetrical" treatment. This apparently is raised both as to the time of implementing trade coverage as to the ACP members in respect of the Community's obligations and, more germane, to the resulting coverage of trade maintained between the Community and the ACP country or region concerned. For the first, Article XXIV:5 as elaborated by the GATT 1994 Understanding establishes that ten years shall be the interim period, but for exceptional circumstances which will have to be justified. While it would seem not unlikely that WTO delegates to the CRTA may tolerate a North-South interim arrangement for something more than the prescribed ten years, the Understanding makes it clear that exceptional circumstances must apply for an extension. Certainly an open-ended interim period is no longer possible, just as interim arrangements leading to interim agreements is also no longer possible for tacking. During whatever interim period is settled, during that time there is no requirement that symmetry must occur in the tariff cuts and the Community can certainly proceed at a faster pace of cutting, as long as the net result at the ending date is the final establishment of a free-trade area.

However, once this interim period is over, there is no basis under Article XXIV to allow continuing asymmetry in the coverage of trade as between the Community and ACP. Whether the CRTA in the year 2008 (or 2018) is applying a quantitative or qualitative indicator (or both) for the substantially-all trade (SAT) requirement, the elimination of duties and ORRCs will be required to be effected as "between" the constituent parties.

While no one knows what criteria will eventually emerge for SAT, this text has argued that it is more likely than not that a criteria will in fact emerge, due in no small part to the burden shifting resulting from the Turkey Textiles AB report. Huber suggests that the high coverage required will be both quantitative and qualitative. For the first, this could encompass 90 percent of current trade and 90 percent of the tariff lines listed in the Harmonized System.[5] For qualitative, no major sector may be excluded. If this or similar criteria is eventually adopted, one can begin to recognise the daunting task facing the EPA ACP partners in realising such

---

5   J. Huber, *The Past, Present and Future ACP-EC Trade Regime and the WTO*, European Journal of International Law, Vol. 11, No. 2, 2000, pp. 427-438, at p. 434. One World Bank Report recommends 95% of trade after ten years and 98% after 15 (and the abolition of contingent measures -- safeguards and anti-dumping). World Bank, **Trade Blocks**, World Bank Research Report, Washington D.C., 2000, at pp. 117-118.

high exchanges with the Community. The Community will be receiving a broad range of preferential access to these ACP territories. Non-competitive enterprises operating in previously closed and thin markets will be challenged to extinction. However, the difficulty of opening the Community market so broadly to such a large group of developing countries should also not be taken for granted. As the negotiations progress, the question not only of symmetry but of total coverage itself should be subject to close observation on both sides of the EC-ACP relationship.

In this respect an additional consideration for the problem of symmetry should also be considered. It appears likely that the EPA regional agreements and individual country agreements may require variations as between them in regard to coverage. This appears to follow from several references in the PA, including Article 35(3) where,

> "Economic and trade cooperation shall take account of the different needs and levels of development of the ACP countries and regions. In this context, the Parties reaffirm their attachment to ensuring special and differential treatment for all ACP countries and to maintaining special treatment for ACP LDCs and to taking due account of the vulnerability of small, landlocked and island countries".

What is open to consider by this provision is that there would be some certain likelihood that EPA provisions would vary as between the different agreements. While this will respect a tailored development approach, it would be of concern to developing and developed WTO Members where the coverage criteria being used to make an examination would necessarily dictate the degree of flexibility accorded to each EPA member, and to the EC overall. If, as suggested by Huber, ten percent of existing trade and 10 percent of all tariff lines were to be dropped from coverage, this would be the margin of flexibility permitted to vary one agreement from another to deal with the particular problems confronted by each arrangement. If CRTA delegates believe that the EC is likewise entitled to have this flexibility in regulating the sensitive sectors on its own behalf, then so be it, as long as the criteria is imposed impartially for all agreements. In point, this would be far preferable then the current situation where there remains an absence of any quantitative criteria.

13.4   Installing a fixed criteria for SAT

As noted from the CRTA minutes cited in Chapter 11.3, major regional parties including the U.S. and EC continue to express reservations about a fixed indicator for the quantitative criteria, partly on the basis the territories will only meet the minimum requirement without seeking to generate higher levels of coverage. In light of the difficulties imposed by North-South agreements, of which the EPAs are only the most recent examples, this view of the quantitative criteria begs the question. One could see far broader variations between the EPA agreements emerging to balance the issue of qualification as against sensitive sectors then the levels imposed by a 90 percent rule. Given that the EPAs could ultimately generate significant diversion for the preferences that are selected, the degree of flexibility allowed for SAT is going to have a direct bearing on how many agreements go through and how much trade is made free within them.

What could be hoped for is that a repeat of the early GATT-47 reviews does not occur. This would occur if no criteria were determined and non-members would gradually acquiesce for lower coverage as less trade diversionary to them. The EPAs would go through the CRTA process without affirmative recommendations or recommendation regarding amendments. This result would revert the post-Lomé agreements to the legally hazy status of the pre-Article XXV waiver, but with some added capacity to tailor institutional and trade arrangements per region and individual country. Given that different ACP territories produce different products, this flexibility would also inure to the EC.

WTO Members should attempt to avoid this outcome in favour of a set criteria, even if mechanically applied, which would then provide the EPA members a clear target to hit and granting flexibility only within the designated margin to adapt agreements to particular circumstances. Although this may divert some additional trade from non-members, there may also result a fewer number of EPA's generating preferences. Even if no fewer arrangements result, the longer-term systemic aspects for the WTO will be benefited where there will be recognised a legal distinction between the commitments necessary to be granted greater preferential treatment then what is accorded in the GSP. Otherwise, discrimination against like-situated GSP parties will be a result where the EPA members receive better preferences but are only making reciprocal commitments according to an opaque standard. If the EC itself is not prepared to settle upon a quantitative indicator, as it has remained resistant on this concept to now, then the CRTA delegates and other WTO Members who are not EPA beneficiaries should signal the difficulties for the process early. This would let the EPA parties know that while the EC is a withholding party on the settlement of SAT criteria, then their next round of regional trade agreements may not receive a warm welcome upon review.

Although this seems harsh, the risk of a large number of developing countries finalising free-trade areas with the Community without such a prescribed standard is also haunting, as it fully recalls the intractable problems of developed-developing country agreements that were raised in the original Overseas Association review. Without criteria, there is little reason to think that the next set of reviews will turn out more favourably. The higher risk now posed in the WTO is to also lose the judicial progress that has been made in giving some legal effect to the Article XXIV requirements.

13.5   Proposals to amend Article XXIV to accommodate the EPAs

Any major North-South agreement poses this problem and the EPAs are no exception in raising the prospects of modifying Article XXIV in respect of Part IV of the GATT. Because it is so difficult to establish a free-trade area between developed and developing, some special criteria will always argue for placement within paragraph 8 requirements to accommodate these special parties. This would facilitate the formation of something less than a free-trade area, but which would still have the same name and be able to derive the legal benefits of the exception to the same degree. Although it is early in the process, these calls are already going up. For one example,

> "(L)ikewise, it might be necessary to amend Article XXIV of the WTO, so that it caters for asymmetrical liberalisation, involving developed and developing economies. In this regard, the essence of provisions to give an unambiguous guiding framework for implementing North-South integration is evident. Notably, the pertinent issues are not appropriately addressed by Article XXIV either separately, or in conjunction with any of the other WTO provisions."[6]

This is a remarkable position given the historical context of the EC-ACP preferences and their relationship to Article XXIV. After fifty years of not seeking any formal amendment to the Article to facilitate looser asymmetrical North-South agreements, now there are calls to amend Article XXIV. As indicated by Matambalya and Wolf, this development should also now occur result of the panel cases both relating to the problems of the ACP waiver and to the rulings in the Turkey textiles case. Thus, "(T)he conclusions of the Turkey Panel show in particular, how devious it might be for the EU and ACP States to loosely build the EPA trades (sic) regime on Article XXIV of the GATT."[7]

However, for what possible reason should the EC and the ACP, or any other North-South arrangement, be permitted to loosely build free-trade areas under the guise of Article XXIV? Just as the Article begins to receive the benefit of legal interpretation that is so long overdue, it now only becomes apparent that the rules do not serve looser free-trade area formations. Non-members have been making

---

[6]   F. Matambalya and S. Wolf, *The Cotonou Agreement and the Challenges of Making the New EU-ACP Trade Regime WTO Compatible*, Journal of World Trade, Vol. 35, No. 1, 2001, pp. 123-144, at p. 140. The reference to "other WTO provisions" refers at least in part to the enabling clause decision as, "… the developing countries are a heterogeneous group, something not appropriately addressed by the Enabling Clause or any other WTO provisions." Ibid. Huber (and this author) appear to disagree as, "(P)articipation in the system may therefore be made subject to graduation or differentiation according to the level of development of the different beneficiaries of the system …" Huber, Ibid., at p. 436.

[7]   The article was apparently submitted prior to the AB Turkey Report as only the panel case was discussed. Ibid., at p. 137.

this point to little avail throughout working group history, but just as this point starts to bite, advocates of particular North-South arrangements commence a call for the Article's amendment. This amendment would once and for all take care of the troublesome problem of how to grant preferences better than GSP without subjecting parties to the problem of reverse preferences.

Even the EC should resist this approach. If the United States is also entering free-trade areas with all of the developing countries in Central and South America, then certainly an amended and looser approach will facilitate that process as well. Just as the EC and EPA parties will not be members to the FTAA, so also will the United States and its FTAA partners not be members of the EPAs. More important, as is clear from the relative preferences contemplated for both of the regional systems in excess of GSP, there will be a number of developing countries that will not be parties to either. Thus the logic of facilitating North-South free-trade areas by a new construction for Article XXIV, essentially reading in Part IV as did the Overseas Association members in 1958, seems to lead to a rather harsh result. As to the EC, developing territories who by historical accident were not within a special European colonial relationship are left out. As to the United States, developing countries that happen to be located on the wrong continent are also left out.

One recalls this portion of the Panel ruling from Bananas II for the purposes of clarification.

> "Had non-reciprocal agreements between developed and developing parties been considered justifiable under Article XXIV and Part IV, the decisions of the CP (contracting parties) on the GSP and the Enabling Clause would have been largely unnecessary. Developed countries could simply have formed a 'free-trade area' with selected developing countries by reducing barriers unilaterally on imports from those countries".[8]

13.6 Book Conclusion

Any WTO developments that exact more precise standards for regional trade agreements are bound to influence the design of later agreements and the manner in which proponents declare them in the WTO. This process has commenced as a function of both judicial action and the CRTA systemic discussions which are placing the positions of the parties on record. There is a growing support for the notion that paragraph 8 criteria can be stated and applied both to new and existing agreements. However, the interaction between proponents and the review process also necessarily continues and the reverse interaction must also be acknowledged.

---

8   DS38/R, para 162.

In spite of developments that have lent support for more rigorous examination criteria, the quality of agreements actually submitted for review can also undermine the prospects for these more advanced interpretations to emerge. In no area is this more evident than in the declarations for free-trade areas between developed and developing territories.

Since both the United States and European Union are embarked upon ambitious regional systems concerning developing countries, it is reasonable to inquire whether these new regional formations will see a replay of the old intractable points of interpretation of the GATT's rules for qualifying free-trade areas. These points of conflict can be avoided by respecting the demarcation established between multilateral and generalised preferential systems as entertained by the enabling clause decision, and the qualifying rules for more complete formations under Article XXIV. The alternative is to insist again that reviewing parties will necessarily deadlock over whether partial agreements between parties of vastly unequal development levels should be forced within the confines of GATT's regional trade exception.

Perhaps better to consider the larger development dimension in the context of what might be accomplished by MFN with more open borders for the trade of sensitive products from the developing world at large. While this has been written, a great scepticism has emerged in regard to the value and legitimacy of the WTO and its multilateral trading system. While the political and economic benefits accruing to the leaders to only engage a limited subset of the developing countries is well understood, the systemic impact of these resulting spheres should not be discounted. Those left out of the preferential process will see little value in MFN, as it will ultimately accord so little in contrast to what is promised in the larger preferential universe.

APPENDICES

Appendix One
GATT ARTICLE XXIV

PART III

Article XXIV

Territorial Application _ Frontier Traffic _ Customs Unions and Free-trade Areas

1. The provisions of this Agreement shall apply to the metropolitan customs territories of the contracting parties and to any other customs territories in respect of which this Agreement has been accepted under Article XXVI or is being applied under Article XXXIII or pursuant to the Protocol of Provisional Application. Each such customs territory shall, exclusively for the purposes of the territorial application of this Agreement, be treated as though it were a contracting party; *Provided* that the provisions of this paragraph shall not be construed to create any rights or obligations as between two or more customs territories in respect of which this Agreement has been accepted under Article XXVI or is being applied under Article XXXIII or pursuant to the Protocol of Provisional Application by a single contracting party.

2. For the purposes of this Agreement a customs territory shall be understood to mean any territory with respect to which separate tariffs or other regulations of commerce are maintained for a substantial part of the trade of such territory with other territories.

3. The provisions of this Agreement shall not be construed to prevent:

(*a*) Advantages accorded by any contracting party to adjacent countries in order to facilitate frontier traffic;

(*b*) Advantages accorded to the trade with the Free Territory of Trieste by countries contiguous to that territory, provided that such advantages are not in conflict with the Treaties of Peace arising out of the Second World War.

4. The contracting parties recognize the desirability of increasing freedom of trade by the development, through voluntary agreements, of closer integration between the economies of the countries parties to such agreements. They also recognize that the purpose of a customs union or of a free-trade area should be to facilitate trade between the constituent territories and not to raise barriers to the trade of other contracting parties with such territories.

5. Accordingly, the provisions of this Agreement shall not prevent, as between the territories of contracting parties, the formation of a customs union or of a free-trade area or

the adoption of an interim agreement necessary for the formation of a customs union or of a free-trade area; *Provided* that:

(*a*) with respect to a customs union, or an interim agreement leading to a formation of a customs union, the duties and other regulations of commerce imposed at the institution of any such union or interim agreement in respect of trade with contracting parties not parties to such union or agreement shall not on the whole be higher or more restrictive than the general incidence of the duties and regulations of commerce applicable in the constituent territories prior to the formation of such union or the adoption of such interim agreement, as the case may be;

(*b*) with respect to a free-trade area, or an interim agreement leading to the formation of a free-trade area, the duties and other regulations of commerce maintained in each if the constituent territories and applicable at the formation of such free-trade area or the adoption of such interim agreement to the trade of contracting parties not included in such area or not parties to such agreement shall not be higher or more restrictive than the corresponding duties and other regulations of commerce existing in the same constituent territories prior to the formation of the free-trade area, or interim agreement as the case may be; and

(*c*) any interim agreement referred to in sub-paragraphs (*a*) and (*b*) shall include a plan and schedule for the formation of such a customs union or of such a free-trade area within a reasonable length of time.

6. If, in fulfilling the requirements of sub-paragraph 5 (*a*), a contracting party proposes to increase any rate of duty inconsistently with the provisions of Article II, the procedure set forth in Article XXVIII shall apply. In providing for compensatory adjustment, due account shall be taken of the compensation already afforded by the reduction brought about in the corresponding duty of the other constituents of the union.

7. (*a*) Any contracting party deciding to enter into a customs union or free-trade area, or an interim agreement leading to the formation of such a union or area, shall promptly notify the CONTRACTING PARTIES and shall make available to them such information regarding the proposed union or area as will enable them to make such reports and recommendations to contracting parties as they may deem appropriate.

(*b*) If, after having studied the plan and schedule included in an interim agreement referred to in paragraph 5 in consultation with the parties to that agreement and taking due account of the information made available in accordance with the provisions of sub-paragraph (*a*), the CONTRACTING PARTIES find that such agreement is not likely to result in the formation of a customs union or of a free-trade area within the period contemplated by the parties to the agreement or that such period is not a reasonable one, the CONTRACTING PARTIES shall make recommendations to the parties to the agreement. The parties shall not maintain or put into force, as the case may be, such agreement if they are not prepared to modify it in accordance with these recommendations.

(*c*) Any substantial change in the plan or schedule referred to in paragraph 5 (*c*) shall be communicated to the CONTRACTING PARTIES, which may request the contracting parties concerned to consult with them if the change seems likely to jeopardize or delay unduly the formation of the customs union or of the free-trade area.

8. For the purposes of this Agreement:
(*a*) A customs union shall be understood to mean the substitution of a single customs territory for two or more customs territories, so that

(i) duties and other restrictive regulations of commerce (except, where necessary, those permitted under Articles XI, XII, XIII, XIV, XV and XX) are eliminated with respect to substantially all the trade between the constituent territories of the union or at least with respect to substantially all the trade in products originating in such territories, and,

(ii) subject to the provisions of paragraph 9, substantially the same duties and other regulations of commerce are applied by each of the members of the union to the trade of territories not included in the union;
(*b*) A free-trade area shall be understood to mean a group of two or more customs territories in which the duties and other restrictive regulations of commerce (except, where necessary, those permitted under Articles XI, XII, XIII, XIV, XV and XX) are eliminated on substantially all the trade between the constituent territories in products originating in such territories.

9. The preferences referred to in paragraph 2 of Article I shall not be affected by the formation of a customs union or of a free-trade area but may be eliminated or adjusted by means of negotiations with contracting parties affected.* This procedure of negotiations with affected contracting parties shall, in particular, apply to the elimination of preferences required to conform with the provisions of paragraph 8 (*a*)(i) and paragraph 8 (*b*).

10. The CONTRACTING PARTIES may by a two-thirds majority approve proposals which do not fully comply with the requirements of paragraphs 5 to 9 inclusive, provided that such proposals lead to the formation of a customs union or a free-trade area in the sense of this Article.

11. Taking into account the exceptional circumstances arising out of the establishment of India and Pakistan as independent States and recognizing the fact that they have long constituted an economic unit, the contracting parties agree that the provisions of this Agreement shall not prevent the two countries from entering into special arrangements with respect to the trade between them, pending the establishment of their mutual trade relations on a definitive basis.*

12. Each contracting party shall take such reasonable measures as may be available to it to ensure observance of the provisions of this Agreement by the regional and local governments and authorities within its territories.

Appendix Two
GATT-1994 UNDERSTANDING ON THE INTERPRETATION
OF ART. XXIV

Understanding on the Interpretation of Article XXIV
of the General Agreement on Tariffs and Trade 1994

Members,

Having regard to the provisions of Article XXIV of GATT 1994;

Recognizing that customs unions and free trade areas have greatly increased in number and importance since the establishment of GATT 1947 and today cover a significant proportion of world trade;

Recognizing the contribution to the expansion of world trade that may be made by closer integration between the economies of the parties to such agreements;

Recognizing also that such contribution is increased if the elimination between the constituent territories of duties and other restrictive regulations of commerce extends to all trade, and diminished if any major sector of trade is excluded;

Reaffirming that the purpose of such agreements should be to facilitate trade between the constituent territories and not to raise barriers to the trade of other Members with such territories; and that in their formation or enlargement the parties to them should to the greatest possible extent avoid creating adverse effects on the trade of other Members;

Convinced also of the need to reinforce the effectiveness of the role of the Council for Trade in Goods in reviewing agreements notified under Article XXIV, by clarifying the criteria and procedures for the assessment of new or enlarged agreements, and improving the transparency of all Article XXIV agreements;

Recognizing the need for a common understanding of the obligations of Members under paragraph 12 of Article XXIV;

Hereby *agree* as follows:

1. Customs unions, free-trade areas, and interim agreements leading to the formation of a customs union or free-trade area, to be consistent with Article XXIV, must satisfy, *inter alia*, the provisions of paragraphs 5, 6, 7 and 8 of that Article.

Article XXIV:5

2. The evaluation under paragraph 5(a) of Article XXIV of the general incidence of the duties and other regulations of commerce applicable before and after the formation of a customs union shall in respect of duties and charges be based upon an overall assessment of weighted average tariff rates and of customs duties collected. This assessment shall be based on import statistics for a previous representative period to be supplied by the customs union, on a tariff-line basis and in values and quantities, broken down by WTO country of origin. The Secretariat shall compute the weighted average tariff rates and customs duties collected in accordance with the methodology used in the assessment of tariff offers in the Uruguay Round of Multilateral Trade Negotiations. For this purpose, the duties and charges to be taken into consideration shall be the applied rates of duty. It is recognized that for the purpose of the overall assessment of the incidence of other regulations of commerce for which quantification and aggregation are difficult, the examination of individual measures, regulations, products covered and trade flows affected may be required.

3. The "reasonable length of time" referred to in paragraph 5(c) of Article XXIV should exceed 10 years only in exceptional cases. In cases where Members parties to an interim agreement believe that 10 years would be insufficient they shall provide a full explanation to the Council for Trade in Goods of the need for a longer period.

Article XXIV:6

4. Paragraph 6 of Article XXIV establishes the procedure to be followed when a Member forming a customs union proposes to increase a bound rate of duty. In this regard Members reaffirm that the procedure set forth in Article XXVIII, as elaborated in the guidelines adopted on 10 November 1980 (BISD 27S/26-28) and in the Understanding on the Interpretation of Article XXVIII of GATT 1994, must be commenced before tariff concessions are modified or withdrawn upon the formation of a customs union or an interim agreement leading to the formation of a customs union.

5. These negotiations will be entered into in good faith with a view to achieving mutually satisfactory compensatory adjustment. In such negotiations, as required by paragraph 6 of Article XXIV, due account shall be taken of reductions of duties on the same tariff line made by other constituents of the customs union upon its formation. Should such reductions not be sufficient to provide the necessary compensatory adjustment, the customs union would offer compensation, which may take the form of reductions of duties on other tariff lines. Such an offer shall be taken into consideration by the Members having negotiating rights in the binding being modified or withdrawn. Should the compensatory adjustment remain unacceptable, negotiations should be continued. Where, despite such efforts, agreement in negotiations on compensatory adjustment under Article XXVIII as elaborated by the Understanding on the Interpretation of Article

XXVIII of GATT 1994 cannot be reached within a reasonable period from the initiation of negotiations, the customs union shall, nevertheless, be free to modify or withdraw the concessions; affected Members shall then be free to withdraw substantially equivalent concessions in accordance with Article XXVIII.

6. GATT 1994 imposes no obligation on Members benefiting from a reduction of duties consequent upon the formation of a customs union, or an interim agreement leading to the formation of a customs union, to provide compensatory adjustment to its constituents.

Review of Customs Unions and Free-Trade Areas

7. All notifications made under paragraph 7(a) of Article XXIV shall be examined by a working party in the light of the relevant provisions of GATT 1994 and of paragraph 1 of this Understanding. The working party shall submit a report to the Council for Trade in Goods on its findings in this regard. The Council for Trade in Goods may make such recommendations to Members as it deems appropriate.

8. In regard to interim agreements, the working party may in its report make appropriate recommendations on the proposed time-frame and on measures required to complete the formation of the customs union or free-trade area. It may if necessary provide for further review of the agreement.

9. Members parties to an interim agreement shall notify substantial changes in the plan and schedule included in that agreement to the Council for Trade in Goods and, if so requested, the Council shall examine the changes.

10. Should an interim agreement notified under paragraph 7(a) of Article XXIV not include a plan and schedule, contrary to paragraph 5(c) of Article XXIV, the working party shall in its report recommend such a plan and schedule. The parties shall not maintain or put into force, as the case may be, such agreement if they are not prepared to modify it in accordance with these recommendations. Provision shall be made for subsequent review of the implementation of the recommendations.

11. Customs unions and constituents of free-trade areas shall report periodically to the Council for Trade in Goods, as envisaged by the CONTRACTING PARTIES to GATT 1947 in their instruction to the GATT 1947 Council concerning reports on regional agreements (BISD 18S/38), on the operation of the relevant agreement. Any significant changes and/or developments in the agreements should be reported as they occur.

Dispute Settlement

12. The provisions of Articles XXII and XXIII of GATT 1994 as elaborated and applied by the Dispute Settlement Understanding may be invoked with respect to any matters arising from the application of those provisions of Article XXIV relating to customs unions, free-trade areas or interim agreements leading to the formation of a customs union or free-trade area.

Article XXIV:12

13. Each Member is fully responsible under GATT 1994 for the observance of all provisions of GATT 1994, and shall take such reasonable measures as may be available to it to ensure such observance by regional and local governments and authorities within its territory.

14. The provisions of Articles XXII and XXIII of GATT 1994 as elaborated and applied by the Dispute Settlement Understanding may be invoked in respect of measures affecting its observance taken by regional or local governments or authorities within the territory of a Member. When the Dispute Settlement Body has ruled that a provision of GATT 1994 has not been observed, the responsible Member shall take such reasonable measures as may be available to it to ensure its observance. The provisions relating to compensation and suspension of concessions or other obligations apply in cases where it has not been possible to secure such observance.

Each Member undertakes to accord sympathetic consideration to and afford adequate opportunity for consultation regarding any representations made by another Member concerning measures affecting the operation of GATT 1994 taken within the territory of the former.

Appendix Three
COMMITTEE ON REGIONAL TRADE AGREEMENTS
ANNUAL REPORT TO THE GENERAL COUNCIL FOR 1999
AND FOR 2000 (EXTRACTED)

(**) indicates deletion for this extract)

WORLD TRADE
ORGANIZATION

WT/REG/8
11 October 1999

(99-4279)

REPORT (1999) OF THE
COMMITTEE ON REGIONAL TRADE AGREEMENTS
TO THE GENERAL COUNCIL

Chairman: Mr. Krirk-Krai Jirapaet (Thailand)

I. INTRODUCTION

1. The terms of reference of the Committee on Regional Trade Agreements (CRTA) are:
"(a) to carry out the examination of agreements in accordance with the procedures and terms of reference adopted by the Council for Trade in Goods, the Council for Trade in Services or the Committee on Trade and Development, as the case may be, and thereafter present its report to the relevant body for appropriate action;
(b) to consider how the required reporting on the operation of such agreements should be carried out and make appropriate recommendations to the relevant body;
(c) to develop, as appropriate, procedures to facilitate and improve the examination process;
(d) to consider the systemic implications of such agreements and regional initiatives for the multilateral trading system and the relationship between them, and make appropriate recommendations to the General Council; and
(e) to carry out any additional functions assigned to it by the General Council."

(**)

III. EXAMINATION OF REGIONAL TRADE AGREEMENTS

5. To date, 118 RTAs have been notified to the GATT/WTO: 93 under GATT Article XXIV; 14 under the Enabling Clause; and eleven under GATS Article V. The Committee has currently under review a total of 72 agreements. The examination of 64 of these agreements has been referred to the Committee by the Council for Trade in Goods (CTG), seven by the Council for Trade in Services (CTS) and one by the Committee on Trade and Development (CTD). Draft reports on the examination of 30 agreements are currently under consideration; for 31 other agreements, reports are being drafted or factual examinations are currently underway. There are eleven RTAs for which factual examination has not yet started (see Attachment 2).

6. In the context of the examination of 41 individual agreements, the Committee also considered the System of European Cumulation of Origin, which modified or replaced earlier rules of origin provisions in those agreements.

7. At the 23rd Session of the CRTA, held in July 1999, the Chairman stressed the urgency of completing the reports on the examination of 30 RTAs for which the drafting process was already engaged. The drafting of six of these reports made progress during 1999, but the Committee has so far been unable to finalize any of them.

(**)

VII. FINAL REMARKS

15. The Committee has made substantial headway in the factual examination of a number of RTAs, but has been unable to finalize reports on any of these examinations. Progress in this regard was slowed, inter alia, by disagreement among Members on the interpretation of certain elements of those rules relating to RTAs, as well as on procedural aspects. Similarly, the Committee is not in a position to make recommendations to the General Council under item 1(d) of its Terms of Reference.

** (balance of report is omitted)

WORLD TRADE
ORGANIZATION

WT/REG/9
22 November 2000

(00-4975)

REPORT (2000) OF THE
COMMITTEE ON REGIONAL TRADE AGREEMENTS
TO THE GENERAL COUNCIL

Chairman: Mr. Edsel T. Custodio (Philippines)

(**)

III. EXAMINATION OF REGIONAL TRADE AGREEMENTS

5. To date, 220 RTAs have been notified to the GATT/WTO.[1] Of these, 191 agreements were notified under GATT Article XXIV, of which 109 are still in force today; 18 agreements were notified under the Enabling Clause;[2] and 11 were under GATS Article V.

6. The Committee has currently under examination a total of 86 agreements.[3] The examination of 79 of these agreements has been referred to the Committee by the Council for Trade in Goods, and six by the Council for Trade in Services.

(**)

V. PROCEDURES TO FACILITATE AND IMPROVE THE EXAMINATION PROCESS

(**)

12. At its Twenty-Seventh Session, the Chairman stated that the rationalization of the examination exercise went beyond finalizing a few reports. It also included clearing the large backlog of examination reports in process, and efficiently dealing with a relatively greater number of agreements notified to the WTO, compared to the past. This pointed

---

[1]   This figure corresponds to notifications of new RTAs, as well as of accessions to existing RTAs.

[2]   *Differential and More Favourable Treatment, Reciprocity and Fuller Participation of Developing Countries*, Decision of 28 November 1979.

[3]   Two RTAs notified under GATT Article XXIV are yet to be transmitted to the Committee for examination.

to the need for breaking the impasse on examination reports, held up for one reason or another, by adopting a practical way of addressing the backlog and reorganizing the examination procedures, so as to ensure in particular that substantive debate takes place in each round of examination of individual RTAs.

(**)

VII. FINAL REMARKS

17. The Committee has pursued its examination work and succeeded in concluding the factual examination of a number of RTAs, but has been unable to finalize reports on any of the examinations before it. As noted in paragraph 8 above, the Committee has discussed the practical difficulties and broader issues preventing progress and will focus on these on a priority basis.

18. New direction has been given to the Committee's work on systemic issues on the basis of Chairman's proposals, and this will be carried forward in 2001.

(**)

ATTACHMENT 2

List of RTAs Under Examination

RTAs for which factual examinations have been completed and the draft examination reports are in various stages of consultation and finalization (62):

ANZCERTA (services)	EC-Romania	Norway-Faroe Islands
Bulgaria-FYROM	EC-Slovak Republic	Poland-Lithuania
Canada-Chile	(goods and services)	Romania-Moldova
Canada-Israel	EC-Slovenia	Slovak Republic-Estonia
CEFTA	EFTA-Bulgaria	Slovak Republic-Latvia
Czech Republic-Estonia	EFTA-Estonia	Slovak Republic-Lithuania
Czech Republic-Latvia	EFTA-Hungary	Slovak Republic-Turkey
Czech Republic-Lithuania	EFTA-Israel	Slovenia-Croatia
Czech Republic-Turkey	EFTA-Latvia	Slovenia-Estonia
EC-P. of Andorra	EFTA-Lithuania	Slovenia-FYROM
EC-Bulgaria	EFTA-Poland	Slovenia-Latvia
EC-Czech Republic	EFTA-Romania	Slovenia-Lithuania
EC-Enlargement (goods	EFTA-Slovenia	Switzerland-Faroe Islands

and services)   Estonia-Latvia-Lithuania   Turkey-Bulgaria
EC-Estonia   Iceland-Faroe Islands   Turkey-Estonia
EC-Hungary (goods   Israel-Czech Republic   Turkey-Hungary
  and services)   Israel-Hungary   Turkey-Israel
EC-Latvia   Israel-Poland   Turkey-Lithuania
EC- Lithuania   Israel-Slovak Republic   Turkey-Romania
EC-Poland (goods   Israel-Slovenia
  and services)   NAFTA (goods and services)

RTAs under factual examination (17):

EC-Faroe Islands   Kyrgyz Republic-Azerbaijan,   Kyrgyz Republic-
EC-Turkey   Armenia, Belarus, Georgia,   Russian Federation,
EFTA-Morocco   Moldova, Kazakhstan,   Belarus and
EU-Tunisia   Russian Federation, Ukraine,   Kazakhstan
European Union (services) Uzbekistan and Tajikistan   Kyrgyz Republic-
Faroe Islands-Estonia   Kyrgyz Republic-Kazakhstan   Ukraine
Hungary-Latvia   Kyrgyz Republic-Moldova   Kyrgyz Republic-
Hungary-Lithuania   Kyrgyz Republic-Russian   Uzbekistan
                            Federation   MERCOSUR
                                                          Poland-Latvia

RTAs for which factual examination has not yet commenced (7):

EC-Israel
EC-Mexico
EC-Morocco
EC-Palestinian Authority Poland-Faroe Islands
Estonia-Ukraine
Turkey-Poland

** (balance omitted)

REFERENCES

Books and Journals

Abbott, Frederick, M. (1990), *GATT and the EC, a Formula for Peaceful Co-existence*, Michigan Journal of International Law, V.12, No. 1.

Akman, M., and Darton, M. (1997), *The Political Economy of Regionalism in World Trade*, Marmara Journal of European Studies, V. 5, No. 1-2.

Anderson, Kym and Blackhurst, Richard (Eds) (1993), **Regional Integration and the Global Trading System**, Harvester Wheatsheaf, London.

Baldwin, Richard (1994), **Towards an Integrated Europe**, Centre for Economic Policy Research (CEPR), London.

Bhagwati, Jagdish (1987), *Directly Unproductive profit-Seeking (DUP) Activities,* in J. Eastwell (Ed.) **The New Palgrave Dictionary of Economics**, Stockton Press, pp. 845-847.

——, (1991), **The World Trading System at Risk**, Harvester Wheatsheaf, London.

——, (1996), *Preferential Trade Agreements: The Wrong Road*, Law and Policy in International Business, Vol. 27, No. 4, pp. 865-872.

Bhagwati, J., and Panagariya, A. (1996), *The Theory of Preferential Trade Agreements: Historical Evolution and Current Trends*, The American Economic Review, V.86, No. 2, May 1996, pp. 82-88.

Baldwin, Richard (1992), *Eastern Enlargement of EFTA*, Center for Economic Policy Research, (CEPR), Occasional Paper #10.

Bergsten, F. (1997), *Open Regionalism*, The World Economy, August 1997, pp. 545-566.

Black, Henry C. (1986, rev. 4th ed.), **Blacks Law Dictionary**, West Publishing, St. Paul.

Bliss, Christopher (1994), **Economic Theory and Policy for Trading Blocks**, Manchester University Press

Bossche, Van den, A.M. (1991), *GATT: The Indispensable Link Between the EEC and Hungary?*, Journal of World Trade, V. 23, No. 3, 1991, pp. 141-155.

——, (1996), *The Competition Provisions in the Europe Agreements*, paper presented at a conference on Eastern Europe at the University of Ghent, 7-8 March 1996.

Bronckers, Marco (1995), *Voluntary Export Restraints and the GATT 1994 Agreement on Safeguards*, in Bourgeois, H.J., Berrod, F., Fournier, E (Eds), **The Uruguay Round Results, College of Europe**, European InterUniversity Press, Brussels, pp. 273-279.

Camps, Miriam (1959), *EFTA, A Preliminary Appraisal*, Political and Economic Planning (PEP publications), Occasional Paper #4, London.

Cortney, Philip (1949), **The Economic Munich**, The Philosophical Library, New York.

Cottier, Thomas (1996), *The Challenge of Regionalization and Preferential Relations in World Trade Law and Policy*, European Foreign Affairs Review, V. 2, No. pp. 149-167.

Culbertson, William S. (1925), *International Economic Policies*, D. Appleton, New York, p. 303, reprinted in Kress, Andrew J., (Ed), (1949), **The Economics of Diplomacy**, School of Foreign Service, Georgetown University, Washington, D.C.

——, (1937), *Reciprocity*, McGraw-Hill Co., New York, reprinted in Kress, Andrew J., (Ed), (1949), **The Economics of Diplomacy**, School of Foreign Service, Georgetown University, Washington, D.C.

Dam, Kenneth W. (1963), *Regional Economic Arrangements and the GATT, the Legacy of a Misconception*, University of Chicago Law Review, V. 30, No. 4, pp. 615-665.

——, (1970), **The GATT: Law and International Economic Organization**, The University of Chicago Press (Midway Reprint), 1977.

Degan, V.D. (1997), **Sources of International Law**, Martinus Nijhoff Publishers, The Hague, 1997.

Demaret, P., Bellis, J.F., and Garcia, G., (Eds) (1997), **Regionalism and Multilateralism After the Uruguay Round**, European University Press, Brussels.

De Melo, Jaime, and Panagariya, Arvind, (Eds) (1993), **New Dimensions in Regional Integration**, Center for Economic Policy Research, Cambridge University Press.

Dijck, Pitou van, and Faber, G., (Eds) (1999), **The External Economic Dimension of the European Union**, Kluwer Law International, Dordrecht.

Dornbusch, Rudiger, W. (1993), *The Case for Bilateralism*, in Salvatore, D., (Ed.) **Protectionism and World Welfare**, Cambridge University Press, Cambridge, pp. 180-199.

——, (1992), *Multilateral and Bilateral Trade Policies, Historical Perspective*, paper #9, collected in, World Bank CEPR conference, Washington D.C.

Douglas, Irwin A. (1995), *The GATT in Historical Perspective*, AEA papers and Proceedings, Historical Perspectives on International Institutions, Vol. 85, No. 2, pp. 323-328.

Drestler, I.M. (1992) **American Trade Politics**, 2d edition, Institute for International Economics, Washington D.C.

Dunlap, James B., and King, Robert N. (1974), *Regional Economic Integration and GATT: the Effects of the EEC-EFTA Agreements on International Trade*, Law and Policy in International Business, V.6, pp. 207-235.

Eastwell, J., (Ed.) (1987), **The New Palgrave Dictionary of Economics**, Stockton Press, 1987.

Enders, Alice, and Wonnacott, Ronald J. (1995, preliminary), How Useful is the NAFTA Experience for East-West European Integration?

——, (1996), *Liberalization of East-West European Trade*, The World Economy, V.19, No. 3, p. 261.

Ethier, Wilfred J. (1998), *Regionalism in A Multilateral World*, The Journal of Political Economy, V. 106, No. 6, pp. 1214-1245.

Forrester, Ian S. (1980a), *EEC Customs Law: Rules of Origin and Preferential Duty Treatment--Part One*, European Law Review, V.5, pp. 167-197.

——, (1980b), *EEC Customs Law: Rules of Origin and Preferential Duty Treatment--Part Two*, European Law Review, V.5, pp. 257-286.

Franck, Thomas, M. (1995), **Fairness in International law and Institutions**, Clarendon Press, Oxford.

Gardner, Richard, N. (1980), **Sterling-Dollar Diplomacy in Current Perspective**, Columbia University Press, New York.

Greenaway, David (1989), **Economic Aspects of Regional Trading Arrangements**, Harvester Wheatsheaf.

Haight, F.A. (1941), **A History of French Commercial Policies**, Macmillan, New York.

——, (1972), *Customs Unions and Free Trade Areas Under GATT: A Reapraisal*, Journal of World Trade Law, V. 6, No. 4, pp. 391-404.

Heilperin, M.A. (1946) **The Trade of Nations**, Longmans, London and New York, 1946.

Hindley, Brian (1994), *Safeguards, VER's and Anti-dumping Actions*, in OECD Secretariat, **The New World Trading System**, 1994, pp. 91-102.

Hirschman, Albert O. (1945), **National Power and the Structure of Foreign Trade**, University of California Press, Berkely, Expanded edition, (1980), University of California Press, Berkely.

Holmes, Peter, and Mathis, James (1997) *Europe Agreement Competition Policy for the Long Term: an Accession Oriented Approach*, in Fritsch M., and Hansen H. (Eds.), **Rules of Competition and East-West Integration**, Kluwer Academic Publishers, Dordrecht.

Horovitz, Dan, (1990), *EC-Central/East European Relations: New Principles for a New Era*, Common Market Law Review, V. 27, pp. 259-284.

——, (1991), *The Impending 'Second Generation' Agreements Between the European Community and Eastern Europe--Some Practical Considerations*, Journal of World Trade, V. 25, No. 2, pp. 55-80.

Huber, J., (1981), *The Practice of Examining Regional Agreements Under Article XXIV*, Journal of Common Market Studies, Vol. 19, No. 3.

——, (2000), *The Past, Present and Future ACP-EC Trade Regime and the WTO*, European Journal of International Law, Vol. 11, No. 2, pp. 427-438.

Hudec, Robert (1990), **The GATT Legal system and World Trade Diplomacy** (2d. ed.), Butterworth Legal Publishers, Salem, N.H.

——, (1993), **Enforcing International Trade Law: The Evolution of the Modern GATT Legal System**, Butterworth Legal Publishers, Salem, N.H.

——, (1993), comment on M. Finger, *GATT's Influence on Regional Arrangements*, in de Melo, Jaime, and Panagariya, Arvind, (Eds), **New Dimensions in Regional Integration**, Center for Economic Policy Research, Cambridge University Press.

Hudec, R., and Southwick, J. (1999), *Regionalism and WTO Rules*, in M. Rodri'guez, P. Low, B. Kotschwar (Eds.), **Trade Rules in the Making**, Organization of American States and the Brookings Institution, Washington D.C., pp. 47-80.

Huis, Leah (1992), **Globalizing the GATT**, The Brookings Institution, Washington, D.C.

Hull, Cordell (1948), **The Memoirs of Cordell Hull**, Macmillan, New York, 1948.

Isaacs, Asher (1948), *More Recent Commercial Policies in Europe*, from **International Trade**, R.D. Irwin, Inc., Chicago, reprinted in Kress, Andrew J., (Ed), (1949), **The**

Economics of Diplomacy, School of Foreign Service, Georgetown University, Washington, D.C., pp. 360-407.

Jackson, John H. (1967), *The Puzzle of GATT*, Journal of World Trade Law, Vol. 1, No. 2.

——, (1969), **World Trade Law and the Law of GATT**, the Mitchie Company, Charlottesville, Virginia.

——, (1983), *Equality and Discrimination in International Economic Law*, The Year Book of World Affairs 1983, pp. 224-239.

——, (1996), *Perspectives on Regionalism in Trade Relations*, Law and Policy in International Business, V. 27, No. 4, 1996, p. 873-878.

Johnson, Harry Gordon (1968), **Harmonization of National Economic Policies Under Free Trade**, University of Toronto Press.

Kearney, R.D., and Dalton, R.E. (1970), *The Treaty on Treaties*, American Journal of International Law, V. 64, at p. 524.

Kelly, P., and Onkelinx, I. (1986), **EEC Customs Law**, ESC Publishing, Oxford.

Kemp, M. and Wan, H.Y. (1976), *An Elementary Proposition Concerning the Formation of Customs Unions*, Journal of International Economics, V.6, No 1, February, 1976, pp. 95-97.

Keynes, J. M. (1920), **The Economic Consequences of the Peace**, Harper and Row, New York, 1971 Edition.

Kock, Karin (1969), **International Trade Policy and the GATT, 1947-1967**, Almqvist & Wiksell, Stockholm.

Kreinin, M.E. (1975), *European Integration and the Developing Countries*, in B. Balassa (Ed.) **European Economic Integration,** North Holland, pp. 327-364.

Kress, Andrew J. (Ed), (1949), **The Economics of Diplomacy**, School of Foreign Service, Georgetown University, Washington, D.C.

Machlup, Fritz (1977), **History of Thought on Economic Integration**, Macmillan, London.

Marescou M., and Montaguti E. (1995), *The Relations Between the European Union and Central and Eastern Europe: A Legal Appraisal*, Common Market Law Review, V. 32, pp. 1327-1367.

Matambalya, R., and Wolf, S. (2001), *The Cotonou Agreement and the Challenges of Making the new EU-ACP Trade Regime WTO Compatible*, Journal of World Trade, V. 35, No. 1, pp. 123-144.

Mathis, J. (1998), *Mutual Recognition Agreements – Transatlantic Parties and the Limits of Non-tariff Barrier Regionalism in the WTO*, Journal of World Trade, V. 32, No. 6, pp. 5-31.

——, (1999) *The Community's External Regional Policy in the WTO*, in van Dijck, Pitou and Faber, G. (Eds), **The External Economic Dimension of the European Union**, Kluwer Law International, Dordrecht.

McMillan, John (1993), *Does Regional Integration Foster Open Trade*, in K. Anderson and R. Blackhurst, (Eds), (1993), **Regional Integration and the Global Trading System**, Harvester Wheatsheaf, pp. 292-310.

McQueen, Matthew (1982), *Lomé and the Protective Effect of Rules of Origin*, Journal of World Trade, V. 16, No. 2, pp. 119-131.

McRae, D. M. (2000), *The WTO in International Law: Tradition Continued or New Frontier?*, Journal of International Economic Law, V. 3 No. 1, pp. 27-41.

Meilke, Karl and Sarker, Rakhal (1996), *National Administered Protection Agencies: Their Role in the Post-Uruguay Round World*, International Agricultural Trade Research Consortium, Working paper #96-1, pp. 13-19.

Messerlin, P. (1994), *Central European Countries' Trade Laws in the Light of International Experience*, Discussion Paper No. 1044, Centre for Economic Policy Research (CEPR), London.

Nicolaides, Phedon and Mathis, James (1996), *European Community Competition Rules in the Associated Countries of Central and Eastern Europe: How to Ensure Effective Enforcement*, Aussenwirtschaft, V. 51:4, pp. 485-512.

Palmeter, David (1996), *Some Inherent Problems with Free Trade Arrangements*, Law and Policy in International Business, Vol. 27, No. 4, pp. 991-998.

——, (1996), *Rules of Origin in Regional Trade Agreements*, Leige Paper, collected in Demaret, P., Bellis, J.F., and Garcia, G. (Eds), (1997), **Regionalism and Multilateralism After the Uruguay Round**, European University Press, Brussels.

Palmeter, D., and Mavroidis, P.C. (1998), *The WTO Legal System: Sources of Law*, American Journal of International Law, Vol. 92, pp. 398-413.

Panagariya, Arvind, (2000), *Preferential Trade Liberalization: The Traditional Theory and New Developments*, Journal of Economic Literature 38, June 2000, pp. 287-331.

Patterson, Gardner (1966), **Discrimination in International Trade, The Policy Issues, 1945-1965**, Princeton University Press, Princeton.

Pomfret, Richard (1997), **The Economics of Regional Trading Arrangements**, Clarendon Press, Oxford.

Reuter, Paul (1989), **Introduction to the Law of Treaties**, Pinter, London.

Roessler, Frieder (1993), *The Relationship Between Regonal Integration Agreements and the Multilateral Trade Order*, in K. Anderson and R. Blackhurst, (Eds), (1993), **Regional Integration and the Global Trading System**, Harvester Wheatsheaf, pp. 311-325.

——, (2000), *The Institutional Balance Between the Judicial and the Political Organs of the WTO*, paper presented at Harvard University, Conference titled, Efficiency, Equity and Legitimacy: The Multilateral Trading System at the Millennium, June 1-2, 2000, 26 pp, at p. 9.

Rosenne, Shabtai (1985), **Breach of Treaty**, Grotius Publications, Cambridge.

Sampson, Gary (1994), *Regional Trading Blocks and World Economy*, Address for Queen's Unversity of Belfast, Mimeo, 2 June, 1994.

Sapir, A. (2000), *EC Regionalism at the Turn of the Millennium: Towards a New Paradigm?* CEPR, Discussion Paper Series, #2629.

Schoneveld, F. (1992), *The EEC and Free Trade Agreements, Stretching the Limits of GATT Exceptions to Non-Discriminatory Trade?*, Journal of World Trade, V. 26, No. 5, pp. 59-78.

Sinclair, I. (1984) **The Vienna Convention on the Law of Treaties**, 2d ed., Manchester University Press.

Snape, Richard H. (1993), *History and Economics of GATT's Article XXIV*, in K. Anderson and R. Blackhurst, (Eds), (1993), **Regional Integration and the Global Trading System**, Harvester Wheatsheaf. pp. 273-291.

Tasca, Henry J. (1939), **World Trading Systems**, International Institute of Intellectual Cooperation, League of Nations, Paris.

Torre, Augusto de la, *Regional Trade Arrangements*, International Monetary Fund, Occasional Paper #93.

Viner, Jacob (1950), **The Customs Union Issue**, Carnegie Endowment.

Völker, E.L.M. (1993), **Barriers to External and Internal Community Trade**, Kluwer, Deventer.

Weiss, F.W. (1986), *The European Free Trade Association after Twenty-five Years,* Yearbook of European Law, Vol. 5, pp. 287-323.

——, (1990), *The Functioning of the Free Trade Agreements*, in Jacot-Guillarmod, Oliver (ed**.), L' avenir du libre-échange en Europe: vers un Espace économique européen?** Schulthess Polygraphischer Verlag AG, Zurich, pp. 61-78.

——, (1995), *The General Agreement on Trade and Services 1994*, Common Market Law Review, V.32, pp. 1177-1225.

Whidden, Howard, P. (1945), *Preferences and Discriminations in International Trade*, Committee on International Policy, Carnegie Endowment for International Peace, New York, 1945, pp. 5-30, reprinted in Kress, Andrew J., (Ed), (1949), **The Economics of Diplomacy**, School of Foreign Service, Georgetown University, Washington, D.C..

Wilcox, C. (1949), **A Charter for World Trade**, MacMillan, New York.

Winters, L. Alan (1996), *Regionalism versus Multilateralism*, World Bank Policy Research Working Paper, #1687, Washington D.C.

Wonnacott, Ronald J. (1996), *Trade and Investment in a Hub-and Spoke system Versus a Free Trade Area*, The World Economy, Vol. 19, No. 3, pp. 237-252, at p. 237.

European Community Documents

European Commission, (1993), Directorate-General for Regional Policies, Trade and Foreign Investment in the Communities' Regions: the impact of economic reform in Central and Eastern Europe, ISBN 92-826-5583-0, Luxembourg.

European Commission, (1994), The Europe Agreements and Beyond..., COM (94) 320 final, 13.07.94, Brussels.

European Commission, (1994), Follow up to Commission Communication on 'The Europe Agreements and Beyond: A Strategy to Prepare the Countries of Central and Eastern Europe for Accession', COM (94) 361 FINAL, 27.07.94, Brussels.

European Commission, (1995), White Paper on the Preparation of the Associated Countries for Integration into the Internal Market of the Union, 10-5-1995, COM (95) 163 Final, Brussels.

European Commission, (1997), *"Brittan Memorandum" on European Union Preferential Agreements*, Europe Documents, No. 2025, 27 Feb. 1997.

GATT/WTO Documents and Publications

GATT (1994), **The Results of the Uruguay Round of Multilateral Trade Negotiations, The Legal Texts**, Geneva.

GATT (1994), **Analytical Index, Guide to GATT Law and Practice**, 6th Edition, Geneva.

WTO (1995), **Regionalism and the World Trading System**, Geneva.

WTO (1998), Committee on Regional Trade Agreements, *Inventory of Non-tariff Provisions in Regional Trade Agreements,* WT/REG/W/26, Geneva.

WTO (1998), Committee on Regional Trade Agreements, *Note on the Meeting of 6-7 and 10 July, 1998*, WT/REG/M/18, 26 July 1998, Geneva.

WTO, (1998), Committee on Regional Trade Agreements, *Statement by the Delegation of Hong Kong, China on Systemic Issues*, WT/REG/W/27, 8 July 1998, Geneva.

WTO, (1998), Committee on Regional Trade Agreements, *Joint Communication to the WTO on the System of European Cumulation of Origin*, WT/REG/GEN/N/1, 16 November 1998, Geneva.

WTO, (1999), Committee on Regional Trade Agreements, Report (1999) to the General Council, WT/REG/8, 11 October 1999, Geneva.

WTO, (2000), Committee on Regional Trade Agreements, Report (2000) to the General Council, WT/REG/9, 22 November, 2000, Geneva.

WTO, (2000), *Mapping of Regional Trade Agreements,* WT/REG/W/41, 11 October, 2000, Geneva.

WTO, (2000), Committee on Regional Trade Agreements, *Synopsis of "Systemic" Issues Related to Regional Trade Agreements*, Note by the Secretariat, WT/REG/W/37, 15 February 2000, Geneva.

GATT-47 Reviews of notified regional trade agreements: (listed by chronology)

Nicaragua and El Salvador, Decision of 25 October 1951, 1952 BISD.

South Africa and Southern Rhodesia, 1952 BISD.

Nicaragua and Central American Free-trade Area, Decision of 13 November, 1956, 1957 BISD.

The Overseas Association, The Treaties Establishing the European Economic Community and the European Atomic Energy Community, 1958 BISD, Sixth Supplement, Reports 29 November, 1957, L/778, p. 70.

EEC, Report of the Intersessional Committee, 1959 BISD, Seventh Supplement, p. 69.

European Free Trade Association Examination of Stockholm Convention, Report adopted 4 June 1960, 1961 BISD, Ninth Supplement, L/1235.

Yaounde' (first) Convention, 1966 BISD, L/2441.

EEC- Israel, 1972 BISD, L/3581.

EEC-Tanzania, 1973 BISD, L/3721.

EC-Austria report, 1974 BISD, L/3900 (and reports for Iceland (L/3902), Portugal, (L/3901); Sweden, (L/3899); Switzerland & Lichtenstein (L/3893).

EC-Norway Report, 1975 BISD, L/3996.

EEC-Cyprus, 1975 BISD, L/4009.

EEC-Egypt, 1975 BISD, L/4054.

EC-Israel, 1977 BISD, L/4365.

Yaounde' II, 1972 BISD, L/3465.

ACP-EEC First Convention of Lomé, 1977 BISD, L/4369.

Other Organisational Documents and Publications

ECDPM, (2000), *Economic Partnership Agreements*, Lomé 2000, No. 14, June 2000, p. 2.

OECD (1994), *Globalization and Regionalism, Challenge for Developing Countries*, by Charles Oman, Paris.

OEEC (1957), Special Working Party for the Council, *Report on the Possibility of Creating A Free Trade Area in Europe*, C(57)5, 67 pages, Paris.

International Law Commission, Report on the Work of the Second Part of Seventeenth Session, Monaco, 1966, Commentary to Article 37, UN General Assembly, 21st Session, Official Records, Supp. No. 9 (A/6309/Rev.1).

United Nations, (1990), *Regional Trade Blocks, Recommendations of the Committee for Development Planning*, New York.

U.S. Business Roundtable (2001), *The Case for U.S. Trade Leadership: The United States Is Falling Behind*, Washington, D.C.

Vienna Convention on the Law of Treaties, concluded at Vienna 23 May 1969, entry into force: 27 January 1980, UN Doc A/Conf 39/28, UKTS 58 (1980), 8 ILM 679.

World Bank (2000), **Trade Blocks**, World Bank Research Report, Washington D.C.

INDEX